AMERICAN ARCHITECTS

Facts On File
New York • Oxford

A Survey of Award-Winning
Contemporaries and their Notable Works

LES KRANTZ

**To the mountain man
and his enlightenment.**

Editor and Publisher: **Les Krantz**

Executive Editor: **Charley Custer**
Contributing Editor: **Michael Weinberg**
Contributing Writers: **David Cahill, Al Gabor, Barbara Koenen, Mark Mravic**
Office Manager: **Debra Swank**
Assistant Manager: **Jean Lyons**

Facts On File, Inc.
460 Park Avenue South
New York NY 10016
USA

Library of Congress Cataloging-in-Publication Data

Krantz, Les.
    American architects / Les Krantz
       p.   cm.
    ISBN 0-8160-1420-5
    1. Architects--United States--Biography.   I. Title.
NA736.K7 1989
720' .92' 273--dc20
[B]
                                      89-1466
                                         CIP

Facts On File books are available at special discounts when purchased in bulk quantities for businesses, associations, institutions or sales promotion. Please contact the Special Sales Department of our New York office at 212/683-2244 (dial 800/322-8755 except in NY, AK or HI).

Printed in USA

10 9 8 7 6 5 4 3 2 1

CONTENTS

FOREWORD

Architecture and architects are everywhere we are, yet many architects are hidden behind their buildings. Seventy-five professionals may contribute to a freeway-interchange office block, yet only one of them is its 'architect.' Some architects spend their careers erecting our present-day temples of high architecture—the street-darkening towers, the model and new cities, the complexes ever multiplying across acres and miles—in such rich and fruitful collaboration with others that we will never hear their names. Others devote their careers to enveloping activities and needs that don't directly touch our lives—old peoples' homes, or poor peoples' homes, or rich peoples' homes—and so we never encounter or imagine work that has brightened or darkened lives not very far from our own.

This is the miracle of the practice of architecture, that in buildings good or bad the architect expresses and furthers literally every conceivable human activity, from the moment they make weight in the world. Architecture is a faultless mirror, not of mankind's potential or dreams, but very precisely of our achievements. And the architect--at once visionary and drudge, tyrant and servant, form-asker and form-giver, and up to his neck in city inspectors, concerned citizens, yearnings, budgets, bricklayers, and technology trumpeted from the mouths of salesmen--the architect makes out of all this chaos and possibility the hives that surround us, define us and have power to delight us.

His work is stitched out of many little mysteries which are often described in our individual entries, and we needn't dwell on them here. But larger mysteries and themes tie our more than 400 individual entries together, in interesting and sometimes startling ways. The opinions, visions and compromises expressed by these architects are diverse and even contradictory—as these architects prove, words and ideas in individual minds are used as creatively as bricks in mortar. We haven't attempted to harmonize these many voices but rather to express each one clearly.

You'll read that the Modernist movement is a mission here, but a madness there, and just down the road it's a bore, and somewhere else it's irrelevant because folks never liked that stuff. As the authority of Modernism wanes we see a strong resurgence of regional architecture in these pages, and reflected in our architectural descriptions are fascinating local differences of culture and climate that result in a rising diversity of building types. Contextualism— which sympathetically takes neighboring structures and ambience into account in new building designs—both creates and continues a new sensitivity to the richness of our existing built environment, from coast to coast. In regions largely developed in the Modernist era we even find architects struggling to resuscitate local traditions in communities where they've scarcely or never existed. Some regions—the Los Angeles area is striking in this regard—seem idea-intoxicated, while other areas seem scarcely to notice them. In the course of our descriptive entries some of movement and style names may seem vague, others may be annoying. This is the state of American architecture which it's been our delight to survey.

A word about our survey: this book does not contain the 400 best architects in America. Such a claim would invite 4000 competing lists. Rather, it is a survey of America's most prominent practitioners of architecture, a sampler which goes broader and deeper than any survey yet attempted. In thinning our possibilities for inclusion we required that every listed architect have a prize-winning practice. We corresponded with the principals of more than 12,000 architectural firms, soliciting information and nominations. We read and argued and begged wise counsel, with the hope that the sources of much of contemporary architecture's light and fury would find their way onto our pages.

Our entries are unique in including practitioners of every size and stripe, who may have little more than a measure of recognition in common. So *AMERICAN ARCHITECTS* conveys a breadth of practice unique in architectural publishing, and aspires to what we honor in our listed architects: to sum up the inconstancies and necessities of our built environment, that human life be enriched. Our bias has been to treat buildings as the best expressions of each architect's ideas, and we concentrate on describing just a project or two in each entry, to convey something of its individual challenges, solutions and complexities. This survey of America's architecture gives a thought-provoking and original picture of the nation which is served and sheltered by these award-winning practitioners. For all there is to enjoy in these pages, there's at least as much more to learn.

Finally, we've abridged some award and affiliate names. FAIA stands for Fellow of the American Institute of Architects, which is an honor given to AIA members of at least ten years' standing who have significantly advanced the profession. State chapters are listed uniformly as, for example, Ohio AIA, although older chapters may have other official names, e.g. Ohio Society of Architects. AIA regional council and local affiliate names have been shortened in the same way.

Charley Custer
Executive Editor

ABRAMOVITZ, MAX
(Building Design)
Abramovitz/Harris/Kingsland (212) 889-0255
30 Fifth Avenue   New York NY 10020

Born: 1908 **Studied:** Columbia University; Ecole des Beaux-Arts, Paris **Awards:** FAIA; Columbia University President's Award **Notable Works:** Avery Fisher Hall, Lincoln Center, New York City; Corning Glass Building, New York City; Krannert Center for the Performing Arts, University of Illinois, Champaign-Urbana Il COMMERCIAL/RETAIL: 50% HOUSING: 20% EDUCATION: 20% PLANNING: 10%

He has collaborated with longtime partner Wallace K. Harrison on some of the most famous and monumental architectural projects of the twentieth century. Ceding 'first billing' on early efforts like the 1947 United Nations Headquarters, he came into his own with the 1953 Corning Glass Building, also in New York City, which used the first successful full-glass skyscraper wall. He believes that structures should be built around a single, clearly delineated architectural thought, whose 'cadences' reverberate through the space, making it more than shelter. He uses the full architectural palette of materials and technologies to develop this thought while meeting end-users' needs. Clients and end-users, in fact, take unusually active roles in his design process. In his design for Brandeis University's Inter-Faith Chapels in Waltham MA, he consulted with representatives of three campus religious groups to ensure that the facility reflected elements of each faith's aesthetic tradition. He is most comfortable working with large, lofty, open areas; in the last two decades he has become one of the world's foremost auditorium architects.

ABT, WHELDON A.
(Building Design, Renovation)
Wheldon A. Abt, Architect (914) 695-1444
90 Crystal Run Road Middletown NY 10940

Born: 1945 **Studied:** Rensselaer Polytechnic Institute; Harvard Graduate School of Design **Awards:** *Remodeling* merit award **Notable**

Works: Crystal Run Corporate Park, Middletown NY; Madfox Associates renovation, Goshen NY COMMERCIAL 75%, RESIDENTIAL 25%

His buildings are highly site responsive and typically feature strong, simple shapes and materials. His Crystal Run Corporate Park in Middletown NY was an early (1985) large back-office project built at a distance of 60 miles from New York City. Marketed to large metropolitan office-space users as well as mixed local businesses and commercial users, its developers aimed successfully to take advantage of lower housing, land and labor costs at the metropolitan fringe in relocating labor-intensive office functions. Their success has brought similar development into surrounding Orange County sites.

The project went up in stages over half a dozen years, becoming a loose campus of 5 buildings sized from 25,000 to 170,000 square feet, a half-million square feet in all. Each building is individuated by design as well as size, with common elements such as rich colored masonry, comprehensive landscaping and plaza detailing bringing the ensemble together. Large unobstructed floor areas appropriate for high-density desk work are mixed with a more conventional core-type office building at the center of the complex. The largest building is terraced into two-floor sections which climb the rolling site, with parking adjacent to each section for uncongested and convenient access. It features a ground-floor shopping and pedestrian plaza which extends out-of-doors into an open arcade with public-accessible shopping, benches and public sculpture. The black brick used at ground level becomes red and rose-colored on upper floors of the different buildings, and the narrow upper-floor windows often become open-glass on the first floors to meet the ground in an inviting way.

ACE ARCHITECTS
(see Howard, Lucia and Weingarten, David)

AFLECK, RAYMOND TAIT
(Building Design, Exhibition Design)
Arcop Associates P.O. Box 900 Station H

Max Abramovitz, *Corning Glass Building*, New York City

1440 St. Catherine Street West Montreal Quebec H3G 2L6 Canada

Born: 1922 **Studied:** McGill University **Awards:** Massey Medal; Fellow, Royal Architectural Institute of Canada; Academician, Royal Canadian Academy of Arts **Notable Works:** Place Bonaventure, Montreal; Market Square, Saint John, New Brunswick, Canada; Place Air Canada, Montreal

He begins his sprawling multi-use designs by envisioning the tactile, auditory and volumetric experiences of individuals moving through his spaces, rather than simply arranging objects and surfaces for people to look at. His prime task, he believes, is to design a variety of potential experiential sequences which echo the needs, tastes and norms of the user communities for which he builds. He has worked primarily in the inhospitable environs of Northern Canada, which seems to have had a formative influence on his thick, hulking concrete exterior envelopes. Cavernous underground networks connecting many of his projects to their neighbors sympathetically beckon a weather- and traffic-weary pedestrian population. The convoluted multi-level transport system of his enormous Place Bonadventure—more closely resembling the rambling streets of a medieval village than the tight grids of modern urbia—has had tremendous influence on recent development in such cold weather capitals as Minneapolis and Chicago. He has turned the suburban concept of vertical traffic separation on its ear, ceding the traditional street grid to auto traffic, and burrowing and climbing to make new, temperate channels of pedestrian passage.

AIN, GREGORY
(Building Design)
2830 Francis Avenue Los Angeles CA 90005

Born: 1908 **Studied:** University of Southern California **Awards:** FAIA; *House Beautiful* award; Guggenheim Fellowship **Notable Works:** Dunsmuir Flats, Los Angeles; Mar Vista Housing Development, Los Angeles

He was one of the first West Coast architects to give serious attention to the design of elegant and functional low-cost housing. His interest in group housing for low-income families began in 1937 with his Dunsmuir Flats commission in Los Angeles. The four-building Dunsmuir development was noteworthy for its economical panel-post construction and concealed private porches and patios. In 1939 he began experimenting with pre-fabricated plywood walls which produced even more cost-effective structures. He believes that there is little room for individual virtuosity in architecture or urban planning. A space, he says, is most efficient when it is produced in collaboration with experts from many fields; architecture must "join hands" with other social sciences to purge the mercenary, egotistical spirit which now pervades it. He has always worked closely with artists, craftsmen and contractors both to control construction time and cost and to create integrated, organic structures. His design philosophy for luxury private residences is little different from that which guides modest public projects: frugality and restraint, he believes, are seldom out of place.

ALAMO ARCHITECTS (see Hightower, Irby; Lanford, Michael; Lawrence, Billy; McGlone, Bobby)

ALEKSICH, JOHN
(Building Design)
John Aleksich Associates (213) 202-7811
3440 Motor Avenue Suite 200
Los Angeles CA 90034

Born: 1939 **Studied:** University of Southern California **Awards:** Los Angeles and California Council AIA **Notable Works:** Arlington II Office Building, Los Angeles; Los Angeles Zoo Entrance **COMMERICAL 50%, RETAIL 50%**

His firm probes the specific context, site and program of each project for design parameters. Structural systems aren't necessarily highlighted, and he has no bias for one material over another. His Arlington II Office Building is a speculative, 15,000 square foot office building oriented to and designed around the adjacent Santa Monica Freeway. Set behind an earlier grey stucco building which blocks its street appearance, the building turns its true face to the level of the freeway, where classical forms are combined with the colors of natural foliage, centered around a vivid yellow rotunda. The narrow trapezoidal site suggested the building's organization, with several open courts unfolding and balancing the interior with its freeway surroundings. The building's color relationships are derived from the natural character of its freeway setting, dark green treetops providing the lower colors which shade lighter and lighter up the walls of the building as it climbs toward the sky. Accentuating and contrasting these horizontals and greens, the central curving circulatory tower for the building, containing elevators and stairs, is yellow. The large plaster building forms are further articulated by integrating various exposed structural elements.

ALEXANDER, ROBERT EVANS
(Building Design, Urban Design)
Robert E. Alexander Architect
2909 Regent St. Apt. #3 Berkeley CA 94705

Born: 1907 **Studied:** Cornell University **Awards:** FAIA; AIA Twenty-Five Year Award **Notable Works:** Baldwin Hills Village, Los Angeles (with Wilson Merrill, and Reginald Johnson); Orange Coast College, Santa Mesa CA

He has a diverse practice in which he maintains personal involvement in the conceptual development of each project. His early work, however, centered almost exclusively on developing low-rise residential communities.

The form of an individual house, he wrote in the first years of his private practice, doesn't matter. The only proper level of analysis is the community; the community must have a head, a heart, and a soul. He's known for his concern with user-feedback in the design process. Before formulating plans for the Technology building at California's Orange Coast College, he recruited a well-known area artist to act as color consultant and to prepare color swatches for the approval of teachers and students who would use the building. He calls this interaction "bringing architecture to the people." A

long-time Los Angeles resident, he feels a special responsibility to preserve and renew the city's historic downtown district. Recently he prepared an ambitious plan to restore Bertram Goodhue's picturesque Los Angeles Central Library. He's also expressed interest in designing a central mass transit system for Los Angeles County.

ALLEN, ROBERT E.
Bull Volkmann Stockwell (415) 781-1526
Musto Plaza 350 Pacific Avenue
San Francisco CA 94111

Born: 1939 **Studied:** Cornell University **Awards:** FAIA; Past President, San Fransisco AIA **Notable Works** (also see Henrik Bull): Point Reyes Visitor Center, Point Reyes CA; The Westin at Stanford, Menlo Park , CA; Marin Jewish Community Campus, San Rafael, CA COMMERCIAL 35%, RESORT 35%, HOUSING 15%

His work and that of partners Henrik Bull and Sherwood Stockwell shows a strong respect for the natural features of sites and a dedication to the human qualities which create places for people. He believes that "our buildings should evoke those wonderful emotional responses that prompt the owner, user, and the visitor to remember the buildings with warmth and enthusiasm."

Reminiscent of the grand estates of San Francisco Peninsula, his firm's Westin at Stanford in Menlo Park CA is residential in scale and surrounded by luxuriant gardens and abundant water features. Intimate courtyards are formed as room wings step down a gentle hillside. Expansive roof lines, and generous eaves, dormers and chimneys further an effect of understated elegance. Visitors arriving at the hotel pass through stately gates and up a circular drive to a porte cochere. All rooms have views to the distant hills and/or generously landscaped gardens.

Their design for a visitors center at the entrance to the wildlife preserve at northern California's Point Reyes National Seashore, is made to look "as though it's always been there." Sited on a sloping meadow, silhouetted against rolling hills and a stand of large Douglas firs, its barn-like form borrows from historic dairy farms in the Marin County landscape. Its board and batten cedar exterior is capped with a corrugated concrete panel roof, more durable in the sea air than metal roofs. Fenestration is minimal, puncturing the building at its ends and in the monitor that pops up above the ridge line. The window sash is barn-red, enlivening the otherwise subdued exterior. Inside, heavy timber trusses cross in the light of the clerestory monitor.

AMBASZ, EMILIO
(Building Design)
Emilio Ambasz and Associates (212) 420-8850 636 Broadway New York NY 10012

Born: 1943 **Studied:** Princeton University **Awards:** Seville Competition Award; Former President of the Architectural League of NY **Notable Works:** Private Residence, Cordoba, Spain; Celestial Garden, Houston TX

An "inspired pragmatist," he considers his buildings metaphors of celestial aspiration. He uses nontraditional, primitive and futuristic materials and means, relying heavily on glass; he is strongly influenced by Frank Lloyd Wright and Mies van der Rohe. His structures are attuned to the motion of the "24 hours of the day," the tangible and evocative experience of the lived-in domicile, improved with ornamentation. His work is highly theoretical, drawing from primeval, mythical, subjective and emotional sources. He is less concerned with the appearance of a window, for instance, than he is with the feeling of a window. Some of the materials he uses in innovative ways are earth, air, water, light, and even bales of hay. One of his clients, a family collective, wished to live close to where they could cultivate grapes, and he drew up plans to structure the grape vines on trellises surrounding and overhanging their trailer homes, creating a southern Italian environment. His berm houses are covered on three sides and above with at least four inches of earth. The earth insulates and cools, while the open side faces the sun for maximum warmth.

His proposal for the Museum of American Folk Art, next to the Museum of Modern Art in New York City, houses the museum in a 26-story office building. The museum entrance is faced with a bold portico, so that the overall mass of the building is subordinated to its museum base. He inverts the traditional Manhattan "wedding-cake"-style building, with its rising plateau-like gradations, instead creating an overhanging canopy effect with three blocks forming the structure over the portico. Strong horizontal spandrels framed by a regular outer shell unify the three blocks and entrance.

ARBONIES, GLENN W.
(Building Design)
Centerbrook Architects (203) 767-0175
Box 409 Essex CT 06426

Born: 1947 **Studied:** Washington University **Awards:** AIA; American Wood Council; New England AIA **Notable Works:** Connecticut Water Company Headquarters, Clinton, CT; Sammis Hall & Alfred D. Hersey Laboratory, Cold Spring Harbor Laboratory, Long Island, NY; Cedar Rapids Museum of Art, Cedar Rapids, IA RESIDENTIAL 50%, INSTITUTIONAL/COMMERCIAL 50%

His work and that of his co-principals at Centerbrook is noted for adapting itself to the needs of users and, more broadly, for smoothly blending in with its environment. His award-winning offices for a public utility company on a small-town Connecticut Main Street maintained the original office's low profile, with its New England-residential motifs of grey walls with white trim and pink shutters. Additions were placed in the rear and a new courtyard created a central focus. While most of the office space is straightforward and modest in shape and section, several elements are molded into shapes which give the ensemble the character of a small village encircling the courtyard. The courtyard captures and in turn is dominated by a mature maple tree.

The existing building and the addition have a clear street-like circulation path, open on one side to work spaces and views of the courtyard through continuous window strips. Low partitions divide offices into individual work areas.

Max Abramovitz, *Avery Fisher Philharmonic Hall,* Lincoln Center for the Performing Arts, New York City

Glenn Arbonies, *Connecticut Water Company,* Clinton, Connecticut. Photo: Norman McGrath

ARCHITECTS Di GERONIMO (see DiGeronimo, Louis and Suzanne)

ARDALAN, NADER
(Building Design, Exhibition Design)
Jung/Brannen International
177 Milk Street Boston Massachusetts 02109

Born: 1939 **Studied:** Harvard University **Awards:** Planning Award, *Progressive Architecture;* First Prize, Iran-America Cultural Society Design Competition **Notable Works:** *Sacred Space* exhibition design, Smithsonian Institution, Engineering Sciences

Although the architectural theories of the United States exercise an enormous formative influence over the construction paradigms of developing nations, he argues, they are almost completely bereft of cultural content, and thus their effect is too often divisive and counterproductive. He has strived to develop a holistic architecture which addresses the unbounded needs of the cultural and spiritual spheres, as well as the pragmatic needs of the physical world.

Recently, he has worked with an international panel of architects to design new communities for Iran. These projects clearly reflect his knowledge and respect of Third World planning paradigms. His Teheran Center for Music, for instance, is linked with other nearby cultural institutions through a series of enclosed walkways to create the sense of an integrated, organic entertainment quarter within a village.

BACON, EDMUND NORWOOD
(Building Design)
Edmund Bacon Architect
2117 Locust St. Philadelphia PA 19103

Born: 1910 **Studied:** Cornell University **Awards:** AIA Medal; Philadelphia Award **Notable Works:** Comprehensive Plan for Philadelphia (with Arthur Row); Plan for Market East, Philadelphia (with Romaldo Giurgola); Plan for Lafayette Plaza, Boston (with Romaldo Giurgola)

The condition of man's cities, he believes, is the truest measure of the condition of his civilization. A city's form is determined by the preferences, interactions and decisions of its citizens and administrators. It is not determined by accident or fate. A deep understanding of the variables at play gives us the distance and insight to found and perpetuate truly "noble" cities.

Bacon served the Philadelphia City Planning Commission for twenty-four years, an uncommon tenure in the high echelons of urban planning. Throughout that term he was faithful to his initial vision of a modern series of 'spoke' communities emanating organically from the hub of Philadelphia's historic Center City district. Bacon left the Philadelphia Planning Commission in 1970 to join Montreal-based Mondev International Ltd. His successors have continued to work from the simple, compelling blueprint he crafted for the city's development.

BAIRD, GEORGE
(Urban Design, Building Design, Exhibition Design)
Baird/Sampson Associates, Architects
35 Britain Street Toronto
Ontario M5A 1R7 Canada

Born: 1939 **Studied:** University of Toronto **Awards:** Ontario Renews Award; Fellow, Royal Architectural Institute of Canada; *Canadian Architect* Award of Excellence **Notable Works:** Small Town Arena System, Ontario; Spadina Park, Ontario; Regina Rail Relocation, Regina, Saskatchewan

Conceding that the last quarter-century of Modern architecture was largely anti-urban and simple-minded, he argues that these shortcomings aren't inherent in the Modernist position. He allies himself with Jurgen Habermas in contending that Modernism is a workable "incomplete project." He wants his structures to respond directly to the social character and functional demands of their user communities, expressing those responses through the formal idioms of the International Style and thus contributing to the larger development of the

Modern corpus. The question inevitably arises whether he can fully serve two masters. Though purporting sensitivity to the needs of each project, site and client, there's a growing doubt that the formal and material vocabularies of strict Modernism are too narrow to have meaningful application in every urban social context. The peculiar ethnic and climatic character of Canada may require a more regional and idiomatic architectural approach. Even in its heyday the International Style seemed inappropriate and ill at ease in the culturally distinct cities of the North.

BAKER, F. CECIL

(Building Design)
Cecil Baker & Associates (215) 928-0202
105 S. 12th St. Philadelphia PA 19107

Born: 1941 **Studied:** University of Pennsylvania **Awards:** Silver Medal, Pennsylvania Society of Architects; Architectural Record "In the Public Interest;" HUD Urban Development Excellence Award **Notable Works:** Candy Factory Court, Philadelphia; The Waterworks, New Hope, PA OFFICE 50%, INSTITUTIONAL 25%, RESIDENTIAL 25%

His designs aim for a harmonious balance between basic geometric shapes, site-given opportunities, and functional claims. His home, Candy Factory Court, is a colorful interplay of simple shapes against the backdrop of a former factory. Great Hills Three in Austin TX results from merging a parallelogram and a circle, with a resulting geometry that exploits the site's characteristics. Its atrium is a humanized echo of the abstract exterior shapes. River View Executive Park in Trenton NJ is a mixed-use project crystallized from the orthogonal city grid meeting the sweep of the Delaware River--the city side is angular, while the river side is a gentle sail pulling in. The two sides meet to form a portal to the river.

His Waterworks renovation took nine abandoned mill buildings, built from the 1870s to the 1940s and strung between a local canal and the Delaware River, and converted them to housing while respecting the esthetics of the historic river town close by—and respecting too 100-year flood levels that threatened the ground floors of the buildings. At flood level he put indoor parking for housing units sited above; this enabled him to preserve historic canal walls facing the town. With this traditional facade in place he took a freer hand along the project's Delaware River facade, where he enlarged windows, hung balconies and added occupancy levels oriented toward views across the river. The diverse mill buildings suggested an equally diverse range of living designs—townhomes and triplexes to studios.

BAKER, JOHN MILNES

(Building Design)
John Milnes Baker AIA (914) 232-4903
85 Girdle Ridge Rd. Katonah NY 10536

Born: 1932 **Studied:** Middlebury College; Columbia University **Awards:** *Better Homes and Gardens* Readers' All-Time Favorite Home design; three homes among the magazine's "Top Ten All-Time Favorites;" featured in the US Information Agency's "DESIGN USA" exhibit touring the Soviet Union **Notable Works:** Herzog House, Ridgefield CT; Coker House, Weston CT; Brayton House, Little Compton RI; own home, Katonah NY RESIDENTIAL 100%

Specializing exclusively in residential design, he is author of the recently revised and expanded *How to Build a House With an Architect.* He suggests that we think of houses as people, people with whom we might or might not want to live. By this line of thought a well designed house is above all easy to live with—flexible, tolerant, comfortable.

Regionally sensitive, environmentally sound and highly site-specific, his designs often begin with unremarkable traditional house shapes, especially the familiar New England "salt box." This shape evolved from gable-roofed seventeenth century rectangular homes onto which north-facing sheds were added. The gables became asymmetrical, stretching longer and lower over sheltered sheds at one side. This salt-box style, richly symbolic of safe shelter to Northeasterners, he adapts to contemporary use with open interiors and carefully oriented large windows. Exterior materials are varied but tend to be natural. His bearing walls are often faced with vertical boards whose joints are covered with full-height battens. Horizontal boards tend to lie under windows and spandrels. Such self-explaining structural detail satisfies the eye even when it isn't consciously recognized.

BARNES, EDWARD LARRABEE
(Building Design, Planning)
Edward Larrabee Barnes/John M.Y. Lee, Architects (212) 929-3131
410 E. 62nd St. New York NY 10021

Born: 1915 **Studied:** Harvard University **Awards:** FAIA; Louis Sullivan Award; AIA **Notable Works:** IBM Offices, 535 Madison Avenue, New York City; Rochester Institute of Technology Campus, Rochester NY COMMERCIAL/RETAIL: 50%, HOUSING: 10%, EDUCATION: 15%, PLANNING: 5% MUSEUM DESIGN: 15%

He is a master geometer who uses angle and line to expand and extend his spaces rather than to delimit and enclose them. His strives to create pure forms which intersect at critical points with both the exterior environment and the functional constraints of users, yet maintain uncompromised internal integrity and consistency. His hard, exacting structures have been compared to jewel cases, blending elegantly into their environs while bringing new brilliance to their occupants and interiors.

His range of materials is typically narrow and homogeneous. Frequent changes in massing and materials, he believes, are superfluous, needlessly complicating the visual reading of his elevations. Oversized glass walls topped by equally massive spandrels have become standard features in his recent commissions. He often employs modules as broad organizing tools, but in his finished buildings they are seldom detectable and never overstated. His design for the Plants and Man Building for the New York Botanical Garden relies heavily on the repetitive appearance of hexagonal glass plates. But their shape and distribution is so unusual that he easily avoids the effect of forced and divisive symmetry.

BARNETT, JOHNATHAN
(Building Design)
Johnathan Barnett Architect (212) 594-1650
355 Lexington Avenue New York NY 10017

Born: 1937 **Studied:** Yale University **Awards:** Jesse Neal Award; *Urban Design* Award **Notable Works:** Rapid Transit Corridors Plan for Brooklyn, Queens, Bronx and Manhattan, New York City; Development plan for Gateway National Recreation Area, New York City; Downtown Development Plan, Pittsburgh PA PLANNING: 100%

Although he divides his time between teaching, consulting and writing, all of his energies are directed to the goal of optimally deploying public resources. In contemporary architecture and urban planning, he argues, what is done wrong can almost always just as easily be done right. The problem is that architects, planners and community organizers are often too short-sighted to intelligently address each other's concerns, and so unable to visualize and execute projects of extraordinary size.

In the early days of his association with New York's Urban Design Group, which convened under mayor John Lindsay, he formulated a holistic planning methodology which has set a standard for subsequent urban design work. He began with the premise that an architect can't formulate realistic urban development plans without referring to the myriad political and economic forces within every community. He stressed close interaction with formal and informal political lobbies and the direct involvement of planners in conceptualizing and ratifying public policy. He believes that an urban designer must be a kind of evangelist, thoroughly versed in the practicalities of law, business and power politics. The elements of this philosophy are laid out in the book he co-wrote with John Portman, *The Architect as Developer*.

Since retiring from the Urban Design Group

Edward Larrabee Barnes, *Plants and Man Building*, New York Botanical
Gardens

Edward Larrabee Barnes, *Dallas Museum of Art* (project), *1983*

in 1971 he has consulted on several major development projects, including the plan to renovate and expand Pittsburgh's downtown Golden Triangle district.

BARNEY, CAROL ROSS
(Building Design, Facility Programming, Historic Preservation, Renovation, Interior Architecture)
Ross Barney + Jankowski (312) 663-5220
11 E. Adams Suite 700 Chicago IL 60603

Born: 1949 **Studied:** University of Illinois at Urbana-Champaign **Awards:** Distinguished Service Award, Chicago AIA & Illinois AIA; AIA; Plym Fellowship **Notable Works:** Restoration of Chicago Public Library Cultural Center; Oak Brook Village Hall, Oak Brook IL ; O'Hare Atrium Office Building, Des Plaines IL INSTITUTIONAL/EDUCATIONAL 60%, RENOVATION 40%

In order for architects to control the design and building process that has been abdicated to developers, she thinks that architects will have to become more innovative and forceful in their designs. Architecture has to be brought up to date. To be accurate for its times, it needs to reflect developments in society beyond building techniques—developments in economics, in environmental interplay, in politics and myriad other fields. Conceding that great architecture is built for great clients who realize the importance of their role, she wouldn't want to sacrifice human scale or functional arrangement for the sake of a design statement.

Her work encompasses historical renovation and new innovative design. Her transformation of Chicago's old downtown library into a popular Cultural Center was achieved by both respecting the "spirit of how it was built" and by skillful surgical operations: partitions and multi-tiered library stacks were removed, corridors were eliminated and dead spaces converted into accessible stack and reading areas. New lighting was introduced both for user comfort and to highlight ornamental detailing. Time-darkened Tiffany domes were backlighted using highly efficient newly developed light sources.

The design of Oak Brook Village Mall in the Chicago suburb focuses on a blend of architecture and interior design that create a park-like setting for the municipal center. The maze-like character of many municipal buildings is eliminated by separating public and private functions. Plantings and natural light from clerestory windows enliven public seating areas in the galleria.

BAUHS, WILLIAM
(Building Design, Historic Preservation, Interiors, Renovation)
Bauhs and Dring Ltd. (312) 649-9484
16 E. Pearson, Chicago IL 60611

Born: 1941 **Studied:** University of Wisconsin; University of Illinois **Awards:** Plym Prize; Bronze Tablet; Masonry Institute Excellence in Masonry Awards **Notable Works:** Belden & Geneva Townhouses, Chicago; Lincoln Park house, Chicago COMMERCIAL 30%, OFFICE 30%, RESIDENTIAL 30%

"Appropriate" is the key word for his designs. One of the first of the new-generation contextualists to work in historic urban neighborhoods, his 1978 Belden & Geneva Townhouses in Chicago set an early standard for recycling historic structures. Hired by a community group as site advocate for an abandoned church building, he determined that saving the structure for housing was impractical. But residents of the homogenous historic district surrounding the church were concerned about inappropriate new construction. Ultimately he tore down everything but the church tower, and rebuilt along the old foundation lines a row of Victorian-influenced brick townhomes into which the church tower was integrated.

BAUMEISTER MANKIN ARCHITECTS
(see Baumeister, Terry and Mankin, Haven)

BAUMEISTER, TERRY K.
(Building Design)
Baumeister Mankin Architects
(405) 525-8451
2200 Classen Suite 1120
Oklahoma City OK 73106

William Bauhs, *Belden & Geneva Townhouses,* 1978. Photo: Abby Sadin

Born: 1946 **Studied:** University of Oklahoma **Notable Works:** South Oklahoma City Junior College, Oklahoma City OK; Fashion Value Mall, Amarillo TX COMMERCIAL 50%, RETAIL 50%

Influenced by deeply held religious beliefs, he holds that the human spirit or subconscious is what creates our responses to the built environment. So, manipulations of volume, color, light, and nature should be addressed to "the inner person." His projects bespeak his efforts to communicate to the subconscious so as to engender growth in clients and users of the buildings.

To welcome and to allay uneasiness in students and faculty entering the underground campus of the South Oklahoma City Junior College, two large retaining walls are splayed away from the entry doors "like a pair of greeting arms." This also permits him to bring a large area of well-lit, ground-level landscaping down to the entry doors. Room divider systems and a colorful, casual acoustical system speak fun rather than drudgery to students. And to allay the feeling of being overpowered by the "monumental marble halls of learning," his small building pods house separate subject areas above ground, allowing students to identify themselves from the start with recognizable buildings.

BEEBY, WILLIAM JR.

(Building Design, Planning)
Hammond Beeby and Babka
1126 North State Street Chicago Il 60610

Born: 1941 **Studied:** Yale University **Awards:** National Design Award, 1984; Distinguinguished building Award, Chicago AIA **Notable Works:** Malcolm X College, Chicago; World's Fair Plan, Chicago; Hewitt Associates Building, Lincolnshire, Illinois

He is an "enlightened modernist", who has struggled to reconcile social and aesthetic iconography of the past modern movement with the structuralism and modularity of van der Rohe and the spatial fluidity of Le Corbusier. He is concerned with the expressive transparency of functional elements as well with the identification and perpetuation of cultural and institutional gestalts. After graduation from Yale, he accepte a position with C.F. Murphy, one of Chicago's leading Miesians. Predictably, his early designs adhered closely to the principles of Miesian structural geometry: and relied heavily on prefabricated elements and modular techniques. In his recent efforts, he has continued his dependence on frame construction and prefabricating but there is a marlied movement toward freer plans, curvilinearity and super extra-functional showmanship.

BEATTIE, ROBERT

(Building Design, Site Design)
Robert Beattie Architect (516) 567-8585
131 Homestead Road Oakdale NY 11769

Born: 1924 **Studied:** Columbia University **Awards:** New York AIA; Long Island AIA **Notable Works:** Quadrangle, Suffolk Community College, Selden NY; St. Lawrence the Martyr Roman Catholic Church, Sayville NY; Southhampton Building, Suffolk Community College, Selden NY INSTITUTIONAL 100%

His overriding aim is to integrate his buildings and projects with both site and surrounding context. His work is distinctive, yet harmonious with its environment, reflecting an orderly and restrained handling of form, scale and structure down to the smallest details. He believes buildings should express clearly their overall purpose and function, but he doen't shy away from exploiting the individual expressive potential of particular materials.

His "Hidden Pond Park" is a recreational park in Islip NY which includes a small pond hidden in the woods. The sports facilities—swimming pools, tennis courts, softball field, outdoor ampitheater and recreational buildings—are designed to appear reduced in their visible scale, so as to blend into the natural environment and seem hidden, like the pond. Enclosed structures use warm-colored bricks and exposed laminated wood beams to bring into the spaces the natural themes of the surrounding trees and garden spaces.

BELLE, JOHN

Beyer Blinder Belle, Architects & Planners
(212) 777-7800
41 East 11th Street New York NY 10003

Born: 1932 **Studied:** Portsmouth School of Architecture; Architectural Association of London **Awards:** FAIA; Royal Institute of British Architects; Presidential Design Award; National Endowment for the Arts Design Achievement Award; New York AIA **Notable Works**: Delaware Aqueduct Restoration, Lackawaxen PA; The Limited Building, Madison Avenue NY; Cellular Farm, NY; 305 Second Avenue, Rutherford Place NY; Ellis Island Restoration, New York City

Because today's world is so complicated and full of uncertainties, he considers it important to give people a sense of security, continuity and optimism. Whether the task be designing a new building or restoring an important landmark like Ellis Island, he tries to provide an architecture of context that is aesthetically and functionally appropriate and enduring. More often than not his clues for discovering the best solution are found in researching the past; in using technologies or building materials from other fields; and looking carefully at the building's surrounding context.

The Delaware Aqueduct, erected by John A. Roebling in 1847, spans the Upper Delaware River at Lackawaxen PA and is thought to be the oldest rope-wire suspension bridge in the western world with intact original pier and cable elements. The challenge facing architects, historians and engineers for the restoration was two-fold: first, to accomplish the reconstruction within National Park Service guidelines and second, to satisfy the highly concerned and vocal community in the aqueduct rehabilitation. The design overcame the technical hurdle of the aqueduct functioning as a highway, and satisfied local concerns while adhering to strict restoration parameters based on photo research and Roebling's own notes. The Roebling Bridge was re-opened on June 13, 1987.

BELLUSCHI, PIETRO

(Building Design)

Pietro Belluschi Inc. (503) 225-0131
700 N.W. Terrace Portland OR 97210

Born: 1899 **Studied:** Cornell University **Awards:** FAIA; Knight Commander, Republic of Italy, AIA 25-Year Award **Notable Works:** Portland Art Museum Addition, Portland OR; Alice Tully Hall, Juilliard School of Music, New York City; Kerr-McGee Center, Oklahoma City OK

He believes that contemporary architecture has too many self-aggrandizing tastemakers whose work substitutes ostentation and virtuosity for integrity and aesthetic clarity. In his fifty-year career—in which he has progressed from modest single-family homes to major public commissions—he has strayed little from the orthodox Modernist path. He maintains that designs must derive analytically from functional demands and then be implemented without reference to prevailing aesthetic norms.

In the first decade of his career he developed an elegant, spatially simplified style with Oriental undertones. "Eliminate, refine and integrate" was the credo of those early years, which continued in his design of the Juilliard School of Music at New York City's Lincoln Center. He employed a monolithic travertine facade to conceal the extraordinary internal intricacy of the multi-use structure. His simple exposed concrete design effortlessly accords with the more elaborate structures it adjoins, while conforming closely to an extremely irregular and ungainly site.

BENNETT, ROBERT THOMAS

(Building Design, Engineering, Solar Design)
Robert Bennett Architect (215) 667-7365
6 Snowden Road
Bala Cynwyd PA 19004-2699

Born: 1943 **Studied:** Rice University; Columbia University **Awards:** Owens-Corning Energy Conservation Design Award; "People to Watch" Honoree, Philadelphia **Notable Works:** Chu Solar Biangle House, Thornbury PA; Solar Triangle House, Linwood NJ; Ruf House, West Chester PA RESIDENTIAL 80%, OFFICE 20%

His background in space physics and engineering has provided him with exceptional tools for designing "environmentally sensitive buildings." The idea behind design research into what he calls "dynamic architecture" is that, analogous to our change of clothes in summer and winter, buildings should respond to changes in weather, climate and seasons.

One of his forays into tapping solar energy potential involved a hybrid design combining passive-solar features and superinsulation. Approached from the east, his Chu Biangle House in Thornbury PA appears as a curving white stuccoed north face abruptly halted by a straight cedar-clad south office, looking as if half the house had been cut. The superinsulated northern side is curved to deflect winter winds while the flat southern side, with its many double-glazed widows, collects solar heat. This shape also allows for a minimum surface area for the maximum volume inside.

Elongated like other passive solar houses on an east-west axis to receive maximum southern exposure, it differs from them both in its unusual shape and its avoidance of glass or masonry, which acts as a thermal mass. Putting in more glass and more mass increases construction costs. Using insulation instead, the total annual heating and cooling bill is held to one-third of that of a similar-sized conventional new house in the region.

A pioneer in solar energy, he is one of the founders of the Philadelphia-based Mid Atlantic Solar Energy Association, a group sponsoring energy-saving programs. He is the author of *Sun Angles for Design*, a guidebook to passive solar energy techniques.

BENTLEY, ROBERT
(Computer Drafting, Interior Planning,
Urban Design)
(415) 948-9593
745 Distel Los Altos CA 94022

Born: 1926 **Studied:** University of California at Berkeley **Awards:** Oakland Junior Chamber of Commerce Spark Plug Award; Sunday Section Cover of *Oakland Tribune* **Notable Work:** University of Nations Scheme on Alcatraz Island, San Francisco Bay; Lake Merritt Outdoor Ice Rink, Oakland CA; Lafayette Dome House, Lafayette CA PROPERTY MANAGEMENT 25%, SHOPPING CENTERS 25%, PLANNING 25%

He's a modernist whose philosophy of "form follows function" proceeds from an ideal of geometric purity. He argues that modern architecture's development has been temporarily interrupted by the current fad of postmodernism, which he criticizes for its decorative artificiality. He's fond of using symmetrical forms in his designs, though he also creates interesting structures by breaking symmetries.

His design for a University of Nations would replace the current prison structure on Alcatraz Island, except for its underground foundation. The idea of the University is modelled after the United Nations: each nation contributes students and funds. Students would be housed in 195 spherical 4-story quarters arranged in ring clusters around the island; an electric open-car train would serve as transportation. Bridges from the north, south, east and west parts of the island pass over a fresh-water moat in his design and converge on a concrete platform inside a ten-story conical tower which contains classrooms. The perimeter of the tower base overhangs the moat, so that sunlight hitting the water outside the tower reflects in, lighting the interior. Clusters of circular windows forming larger circles open the outer surface of the dark anodized aluminum cone and light some classrooms, while other classrooms only have windows that face the cone's interior. The cone tip is rounded off by a dome structure with a cross that accords with the cross formed by the four bridges below. Surrounding the island are four piers, each shaped in a quarter circle.

BERG, KARL
(Construction Administration, Specifications)
Hoover Berg Desmond (312) 837-8811
1645 Grant Street Denver CO 80203

Born: 1935 **Studied:** University of Michigan **Awards:** Past President of Denver AIA; Construction Specifications Institute award **Notable Works:** Light of the World Church, Littleton CO; Denver Center for the Performing Arts, Denver CO; Denver Reception and

Pietro Belluschi, *Julliard School of Music*, Lincoln Center, New York City

Pietro Belluschi, Conceptual Design Architect: Sacramento Architects
Collaborative;*Sacramento Community Cente*r, Sacramento, California

Diagnostic Center, Colorado Department of Corrections, Denver CO RESEARCH FACILITIES 20%, EDUCATIONAL 20%, CIVIC 20%, ADAPTIVE RE-USE 10%, COMMERCIAL 10%, RELIGIOUS 20%

His work and that of partner George Hoover draws upon the expressive potential of a Modernist vocabulary through subtly reinterpreting architectural form and other familiar symbols.

Based on the publication *Environment and Art in Catholic Worship*, they developed a design program with parishioners that considerably departs from tradition. The main worship space isn't a typical sanctuary, but a large, simple room with liturgical furnishings on movable platforms that can be rearranged to accommodate dinners and dances. The only fixed liturgical object in the space is the baptismal font which stands prominently in the doorway to symbolize entry to the church. It's also represented on the exterior tower, which is the church's only symbolic form. The baptismal font takes the form of a granite boulder which is split by crossing channels that lead circulating water down to drains. A candelabra mobile hangs above. The floor pattern, like the tower above it, expresses the interplay of cylindrical volumes surrounding the font with the grid of the building as a whole. Locating the font just inside the doors to the main worship space encourages parishioners to reenact their entry into the church.

The play between the church's square grid plan and the circular geometry of the tower results in a marked asymmetrical form. A slightly conical shaft of light shines down from the tower onto the font and can be read as a symbolic "Light of the World." The church features only one fixed cross, an omnidirectional courtyard sculpture which is set at eye level. It repeats the interplay of circles with squares, and a central opening symbolizes, as at the font, passing from the earthly to the spiritual realm.

BERKE, DEBORAH
(Building Design, Modular Housing)

Deborah Berke & Associates (212) 393-9690
64 Fulton St. New York NY 10038

Born: 1954 **Studied:** Rhode Island School of Design; Architectural Association, London; City University of New York **Awards:** Builder's Council; American Wood Council **Notable Works:** The Sward House, Seaside FL; Moosepac, Jefferson Township NJ RESIDENTIAL/HOUSING 80%, COMMERCIAL 20%

Her Sward House is one of ten of her designs in the new town of Seaside FL. She calls the 1800-square-foot wood-frame vacation house "much more diagrammatic" than her earlier Seaside work; living, circulation (in the form of 900 square feet of covered porches), and service spaces are organized into three distinct zones. On the second floor, the porch is the only means of access to the three bedrooms, and the parents' room is separated from the two children's rooms by the stairs. The living room is the most formally 'complete' space downstairs, while upstairs spaces are softer-edged, shading into the open porches. Her Moosepac is a 233-unit, 82-acre residential development in northern New Jersey. Distortions of the imposed regular street grid by existing site conditions create identifiable public spaces: a nature walk; a promenade; a public park; a tree-lined avenue. The houses are made of factory-built modules, or "boxes," which are joined into groups of four to six and fully finished on-site. One attached and four detached house types were developed to adapt to the constraints of modular construction while preserving the integrity of traditional house types.

BERGUM, CHRISTIAN
(Construction Administration, Building Design)
Christian Bergum & Assoc. (619) 241-7742
14455 Park Ave. Suite B
Victorville CA 92392

Born: 1953 **Studied:** University of Pennsylvania, University of Washington **Awards:** Fulbright Professor; Graham Foundation Award; Grand Prize, Sensible Growth Awards,

Housing magazine **Notable Works:** Villa Santa Fe Apartments, Fullerton CA; Victorville Office Building, Victorville CA RESIDENTIAL 40%, COMMERCIAL 25%, INSTITUTIONAL 25%, PLANNING 10%

His design approach is unorthodox, often resulting in unconventional positioning of simple-shaped, cost-effective buildings onto irregular sites. The harsh Southwestern desert region suggests his sparse use of exterior woodwork and his strong affinity for shade-casting stucco forms and small, deeply inset windows.

Original shapes are sometimes suggested by inspirations from the visual arts such as collage and modern painting. He may turn a building at an angle to a strongly rectilinear site, or slightly twist it, or seek an almost sculptural effect in his spatial compositions and his play with interior spaces—for example his Victorville CA Office Building, whose hanging office spaces jut into and overlook other offices on different floors. Yet his desert-sensitive palette and user-oriented siting and detail make these suggestive shapes comfortable to use.

His Santa Fe Apartments in Fullerton CA are subsidized housing on a very long and narrow site. He divided parking and recreation into three pods which nestle among apartment buildings. The buildings form a series of open rectangles which shelter parking and recreation, yet come almost together to shelter pedestrian streets and apartment access.

BETZ, EUGENE W.

(Building Design)
Eugene W. Betz Architects (513) 294-0477
2223 S. Dixie Avenue Dayton OH 45409

Born: 1921 **Studied:** University of Cincinati **Awards:** University of California at Los Angeles/Columbia University/*Architectural Record* Health Facility Honor Award; One of Nation's Ten Best Schools, *Nations Schools;* American Association of School Administrators; Ohio AIA **Notable Works:** Kettering Government Center, Kettering OH; Children's Service Center, Dayton OH; Ambulatory Care Center, Centerville OH MEDICAL 80%, IN-STITUTIONAL 20%

He aims for his buildings to have a central role in shaping their environments, with striking designs and innovative program solutions. His forms are crisp and carefully proportioned, and sensitive to site and environment as well as program demands.

His Kettering OH Government Center was designed to present a strong and positive symbol of the municipality. Its bright white pyramid roof of Tedlar plastic is sculpted with a large window near the apex which contains the Kettering city seal. The pyramid floats above an ivy-covered earth berm which slopes 5 feet into the ground immediately around the Center, giving light and air to windows which illuminate offices that line the outer wall. In the middle of the building the city council convenes on a pedestal which rises into the pyramid's cavity, under the apex window. This open, receptive space encourages public involvement with elected representatives—no doors or walls can close it off. The council meets at the center of subsidiary government activities which line the periphery of the central open space. The whole forms an equilateral triangle. Exterior walls are floor-to-ceiling glass which alternates with precast concrete units. Windows give each department a sitting view into the ivy berm, and a standing view of surrounding woods. The triangular plan ensures minimum walking distance from the main entrance to any department.

BIRKERTS, GUNNAR

(Building Design, Interior Architecture)
Gunnar Birkerts and Associates, Inc.
(313) 644-0604

Born: 1925 **Studied:** Technische Hochschule, Stuttgart, Germany **Awards:** FAIA; Arnold W. Brunner Memorial Prize **Notable Works:** College of Law, University of Iowa, Iowa City IA; Museum of Glass, Corning NY; Federal Reserve Bank of Minneapolis MN INSTITUTIONAL 40%, ACADEMIC 50%

A modernist, he believes that the concept of a building grows organically. Each building has a personality resulting from a synthesis of external and internal factors, such as the design concept's appropriateness to its site; the cost constraints and personal needs of the owner; the innovative use of emerging technology, and energy awareness and conservation. As sensitive as he is to the needs of his clients, he maintains that architecture must avoid being derivative and keep apace of the "zeitgeist," the spirit of the day. He takes a particular interest in the sophisticated use of lighting.

His University of Michigan Law School Addition in Ann Arbor MI extends three floors underground, surrounding the original Gothic structure. A V-shaped glass trough covers the addition at ground level, letting daylight in, offering a view of the old library, and filling the interior with Gothic ambience. His Museum of Glass is derived from the metaphor of glass itself. As glass is heated, it grows soft and bends. The museum's walls similarly mimic the amorphousness of glass with convex and concave glass wall sections. One window section has a periscope effect: when looking into it one sees the outside by reflection of a 45-degree mirror piece.

BJC/KNOWLES ARCHITECTS AND PLANNERS (see Knowles, Brigitte L. and Knowles, John Christopher)

BLACK ATKINSON VERNOOy, ARCHITECTS (see Black, Sinclair and Landes, Robert P.)

BLACK, SINCLAIR
(Building Design, Urban Design, Renovation)
Black Atkinson Vernooy, Architects
(512) 474-1632
212 West 4th St. Austin TX 78701

Born: 1940 **Studied:** University of Texas; University of California at Berkeley **Awards:** *Progressive Architecture* Citation **Notable Works:** Austin Municipal Office Complex; Texas Commission for the Blind URBAN DESIGN 50%, COMMERCIAL 25%, PRIVATE RESIDENTIAL 25%

He specializes in urban design, feasibility studies, concept plans, and public-interest proposals. Committed to quality design that is sensitive to context, user needs and construction economy, he believes as well in the importance of human scale and social atmosphere in public projects.

His Austin Municipal Office Complex in Austin TX illustrates the use of land in creating an integrated mixed-use center with a public social atmosphere. It is a "festival marketplace" which combines a 160-foot square public courtyard and open market with a shopping center, a major hotel and office complex, and City Hall. It centers on pedestrian activity—the square encourages people to congregate and enjoy themselves in the manner of traditional marketplaces. Inspired by the Piazza Navona in Rome as well as Boston's Quincy Market, the plaza contains a fountain and cypress trees for shade, and is surrounded by small shops, restaurants and outdoor cafes, with City Hall predominant among them. The stone-faced 15-story hall has punched openings with deeply recessed windows. A large stairway ascends to City Hall in the style of the Spanish steps in Rome. The square also feeds into the nearby Town Lake Park via a covered "linkage," which avoids the utilitarian feeling of a tunnel by providing a children's museum for leisurely pedestrians.

BLAKE, PETER
(Building Design)
Boston Architects Center (202) 635-5188
320 Newbury Street Boston MA 02115

Born: 1920 **Studied:** Pratt Institute of Architecture **Awards:** FAIA; AIA Architecture Critic's Medal **Notable Works:** Institute Buildings, Max Planck Institute, Berlin; Mental Hygiene Center, Binghamton NY; Roundabout Theatre Stage One, New York City HOUSING: 40% INSTITUTIONAL: 40% PLANNING: 20%

After paying homage to Wright, Le Corbusier and Mics van der Rohe in his 1960 book, *The Master Builders,* he began a slow and painful reassessment of the goals and progress of Modernism. By the early seventies he had

John A. Blanton, *Marsh Residence* (Remodelings in 1974, 1976 and 1982. Street front on 30-foot-wide lot.) Manhattan Beach, California. Photo: Leland Y. Lee.

broken completely with the hard-edged, Miesian functionalism he once trumpeted. In his 1977 polemic , *Form Follows Fiasco: Why Modern Architecture Hasn't Worked* he charges that Modernism has lost touch with human needs; Modernism tells people what's good for them rather than recording and responding to their individual demands. The minimalist ethos, he says, produces merely functional buildings which provide truly minimal comfort and aesthetic nourishment. He has been increasingly attracted to the work of visionary humanists like Alvar Aalto, and has become a populist himself, trying to build as simply and modestly as he can while maintaining a formal, humane "softness."

He has illustrated the economic viability of flexible, humanistic architecture in the construction of the Mental Hygiene Center in Binghamton NY. By rejecting traditional prefabricated materials and instead custom-selecting materials from local distributors, he was able to bring the Center in at nearly ten percent under budget.

BLANTON, JOHN A.
(Building Design)
John Blanton AIA Architect (213) 546-1200
2100 Sepulveda, Suite 14
Manhattan Beach CA 90266

Born: 1928 **Studied:** Rice University **Awards:** AIA; Monterey Design Conference; contributor to *AIA Journal* bicentennial edition **Notable Works:** Marsh residence, Manhattan Beach CA; Chui residence, Palos Verdes CA, Fresno Dental X-Ray and Oral Surgery, Fresno CA RESIDENTIAL 90%

A former longtime collaborator of Richard Neutra, he feels strongly that the architect's responsibility is to respond to the present without counterfeiting the past. "No narrow stylistic image can ever have broad acceptability in our culture, nor sustainability over time," he says. "Every building should be experienced within itself, and designs that are conspicuously in any substyle hamper this perception." So his symbolism is allusive, not intended to be fully recognized and understood.

His diverse architecture emerges from what he calls "feeling myself into my clients' particular esthetic responses." This allows for more creativity even as it fosters client support for successful designs. "It also automatically results in *social* contextualism," he says. "It's my experience that mutual cultural respect could make architecture a popular participating art again, not just a spectator sport." His extensive writing on architecture fosters such mutual respect.

The Chui residence is designed around a panoramic view of Catalina Island and the Pacific. Restrictions allowed only one floor above street level, so bedrooms are dug into the hillside below, where along with the childrens' playroom they open onto an scenic patio.

The Marsh residence, which he remodeled and expanded three times, was a small Southern California beach house on a cramped lot. Building straight up without cutting neighboring sight lines, the remodeled house turns a blank wall to its busy street and opens through a multi-paned picture window to the sea views from the second floor. This blend of intimate detailing and expansiveness also characterizes the patio which separates the two new second floor rooms.

BLESSING, CHARLES ALEXANDER
(Building Design)
RTKL Asoociates Inc. (301) 528-8600
400 E. Pratt St. Maltimore MD 21202
Born: 1912 **Studied:** M.I.T **Awards:** FAIA; First Place Drawing, AIA **Notable Works:** General and scattered site plans for the City of Chicago; general plan for the City of Detroit

He contends that the design of cities is the greatest challenge facing today's architects. Fragmentation and chaos in urban design is the ultimate enemy of architecture, and can only be countered by a level of planning far transcending the scale and style of single buildings. As Detroit's director of city planning for more than a quarter century, he established close links with community and social organizations and came to be known as one of the

Eugene W. Betz, *Kettering Government Center*, 1969, Kettering, Ohio.

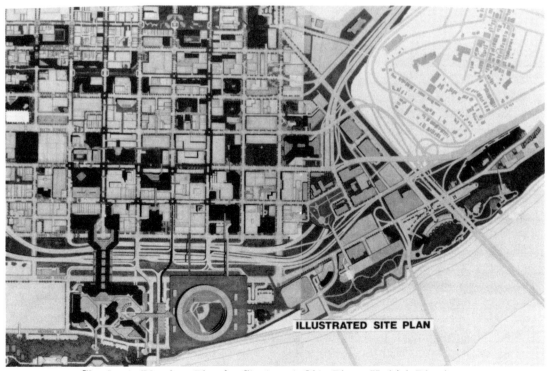

ILLUSTRATED SITE PLAN

Charles A. Blessing, *Plan for Cincinnati, Ohio.* Photo: Hedrich-Blessing.

nation's most conscientious, humane public planners. He's also widely known for his graphic documentations of the architecture of the world's great cities. The AIA presented him with a special medal for his drawings of man-made environments, praising them as the most meaningful and dynamic expressions of urban textures ever created. He is now a professor at the Urban Design Studio of the University of Detroit School of Architecture.

BOEHNING, JOE

(Building Design, Programming, Planning, Construction Administration)
The Boehning Partnership (505) 242-4044
301 Gold Ave SW, Albuquerque, NM 87102

Born: 1931 **Studied:** University of New Mexico **Awards:** New Mexico AIA; Bradley P. Kidder Award, Western Mountain Region AIA; Orchid Awards, AIAAGC (Associated General Contractors) **Notable Works:** University of New Mexico Basketball Arena, Albuquerque NM; PNM Office Building, Albuquerque NM; St. Pius X High School, Albuquerque NM INSTITUTIONAL 40%, COMMERCIAL 30%, OFFICE 20%

Trying to avoid "datable designs," he nonetheless keeps up with new ideas and incorporates them into his work, merging Southwestern regionalism and high-tech. Energy conservation and budget constraints have played key roles in his use of earth berming as a design element in projects ranging from sports facilities to ecclesiastical works.

His basketball arena for the University of New Mexico in Albuquerque is a single-story structure built of pre-cast concrete with sloping walls reminiscent of Indian architecture. The 15,000-seat auditorium is excavated 35 feet into the earth. This earth berming, together with clerestory windows that collect winter heat and natural light, has resulted in significant energy savings since it was built in 1966. More currently, the Albuquerque International Raceway features a two-mile "Indy car" oval with 30,000 open bleacher seats also built on bermed earth, providing acoustical insulation in an economical yet aesthetically pleasing solution.

The PNM building at Alvarado Square in Albuquerque NM is an eight-story structure which resembles a high-rise set on its side. The irregularly shaped building curves on its north end while ribbon windows on its southwest side are stepped back as they descend, providing shade for lower levels. Solar collector panels are set on the south end, which slopes at a 63 degree angle. Built to bridge over a street, the structure features a full-height atrium which offices overlook. Its fountains recirculate water from the air conditioning system, and a synthetic stucco exterior expands and contracts with the changing temperature better than traditional stucco.

BOHLIN POWELL LARKIN CYWINSKI
(see Cywinski, Bernard; Bohlin, Peter Q.)

BOHLIN, PETER Q.

(Building Design)
Bohlin Powell Larkin Cywinski
(717) 925-8756
182 North Franklin Street
Wilkes-Barre PA 18701

Born: 1937 **Studied:** Cranbrook Academy of Art **Awards:** FAIA; National AIA; Silver Medal, Pennsylvania AIA **Notable Works:** (also see Bernard Cywinski) Shelly Ridge Girl Scout Center, Miquon PA; Software Engineering Institute, Carnegie-Mellon University, Pittsburgh PA; Conference Center, Luzerne County Community College, College Center PA EDUCATIONAL 40%, COMMERCIAL 10%, GOVERNMENTAL 15%, NON-PROFIT 15%, CORPORATE 20%

His work has been characterized as "soft, gentle and nuanced." His carefully wrought buildings aim to be pleasing, comfortable and intelligible to viewer and user. Generally modern in design, but employing classical and historical elements, his buildings establish themselves through a disarming friendliness. "They should just quietly be there," he says, adding that too much of contemporary architecture is "trapped intellectually . . . designed to appeal only to other architects."

Charles A. Blessing, RTKL Associates Inc., *Fountain Square*. Photo: Hedrich-Blessing

Wanting to make a collection of buildings for the Shelly Ridge Girl Scout Center in Miquon PA as "strokable, huggable, and joyful as possible," he used Alice-in-Wonderland shapes such as tiny red-framed windows which flank an oversized one on three sides, a giant dormer on one end of a building and other asymmetrical forms.

The main program center is a triangle whose longest elevation, facing south, is a four-inch thick, 25-foot high timber-framed Trombe wall which allows for storage of solar heat during the day and its quick distribution during after-school and evening hours, rather than losing it evenly all night. Two glazed doors give into a small curved hallway flanked by the back wall of a semicircular lobby/sun space at the widest end of a triangle. The sun space has a splendid view, a floor laid out as a sun dial and a stained glass window which doubles as a historic gnomon and shows the area's fauna. Red columns, with undulating gray capitals atop them, mark the entrance. A built-in bench with rounded, outlined arms under the gable such as old doll houses have, leads to the main doorway. Elsewhere the gabled roof is green, and the pediment at the entrance to the swimming pool is marked by a red and yellow sunburst ornament.

BOLTON, PRESTON

(Building Design)
Bolton Associates (713) 522-0827
3010 Phil Fall Houston TX 77098

Born: 1920 **Studied:** Texas A & M University **Awards:** Texas AIA; Past President, Houston AIA **Notable Works:** Bolton Place Townhouses, Houston TX; Pringle Residence, Houston TX

He learned his craft in firms oriented towards designing large-scale buildings, but his penchant for intimate dealings led him into residential design. He has absorbed both the International Style of Mies van der Rohe and the philosophy of Frank Lloyd Wright, combining Mies' crisp squared expansive spaces with Wright's predilection for locally discovered natural building materials.

Many of his houses are faced with earth-toned Mexican brick and floored with terrazzo or terra-cotta tiles. Detailing is restrained, though he might punctuate a well-proportioned box of a living room with a hand-carved limestone fireplace. Lighting is recessed and finely calibrated. Skylights and interior atriums and high shuttered windows illuminate spaces and often offer views of Houston's brushy ravines and pine trees. Spaces are created to fit the needs and living patterns of clients; hallways may broaden to function as art galleries; dining rooms may shrink away altogether or enlarge into magnificence. High ceilings are another trademark.

BONNER, DARCY R.

(Building Design, Interior Design, Interior Architecture)
Himmel Bonner Architects (312) 853-0222
205 West Wacker Drive Suite 305
Chicago IL 60606

Born: 1952 **Studied:** Tulane University, University of Illinois at Chicago **Awards:** Chicago AIA; National Terrazzo and Mosaic Association; American Woodwork Institute **Notable Works** (see also Scott Himmel): Stanley Korshak at the Crescent, Dallas TX; Matthew Hoffman Store, Chicago; 444 N. Michigan Avenue, Chicago COMMERCIAL 35%, RESIDENTIAL 35%, RETAIL 20%

His work and that of partner Scott Himmel proceeds from a "love of materiality." A typical project starts with a material or a detail, then proceeds by exploring new ways of using materials. They tend to use hard and base materials such as stone, glass, and steel, allowing each to be read as a visual treat. In this they have been impressed by the idiosyncratic juxtapositions of materials, finishes and details of the Italian designer Carlo Scarpa. Their taste for layering surfaces and their use of contrasting materials gives warmth to their deployment of Modernist forms.

Their Stanley Korshak specialty store in Dallas is on the first three floors that line both sides of an arcade entrance. Faceted enclosing walls with undulating plates of glass and steel

Darcy Bonner, *Stanley Korshak* (retail space), Dallas, Texas. Photo: R. Greg Hursley, Richard Payne

highlight their departures from traditional Modernist design. The rusticated bays of the arcade are punctuated by crystalline display cases bolted to curved plates of steel which extend beyond the storefront. The focus of the store is a grand, irregularly shaped staircase enclosed in a backlit sandblasted glass cylinder. Precast terrazzo treads rest on slender tracks, making the surrounding glass walls seem to support the assembly. Within the overall design, each boutique has a distinctive design identity.

BOOTH, LAURENCE

Booth/Hansen & Associates (312) 427-0300
555 S. Dearborn St. Chicago IL 60605

Born: 1936 **Studied:** Harvard University; Massachusetts Institute of Technology **Awards:** FAIA; Chicago AIA; Progressive Architecture magazine awards **Notable Works:** Terra Museum of American Art, Chicago; Helene Curtis Industries Corporate Headquarters, Chicago; Krannert Art Museum Addition,Champaign IL; Grace Place Church and Community Center, Chicago RESIDENTIAL 25%, COMMERCIAL 50%, EDUCATIONAL 25%

He calls for an architectural ideology rooted in the democracy of Jefferson which expresses "multiple concerns for energy and flexibility." His entry in the 1980 Chicago Tribune Tower competition is conceived as a metaphor for a free society. His light, open gothic detailing recalls attributes of the original Tower; a glassy membrane enclosing editorial offices opens its operations to public view. Critics praise his "handling of the basic geometries of architecture and allusion to the molecular structure of nature," and his "concern for proportion and color has been rightly called Palladian." He acknowledges a debt to Renaissance villas, because they were a "serious architecture genuinely appealing to people. Those buildings expressed cultural, historical and literary associations with many levels of meaning."

His design for a suburban Chicago house adds to formal Renaissance ideas the logic of modern modular design. Two well-proportioned modern boxes form the main house, gently pivoting around a large column next to the main entrance which softens the crisp geometry of the design. Four strongly defined rooms are connected in a series. Their formal arrangement is emphasized by round openings cut above the procession of doorways that connect the rooms. These windows in turn line up with round windows on both ends of the house. About these windows he says "I have a fantasy of creating a little pavilion on a grassy mound, on eye level with all the circles . . . I could look right through the house and it would become like a Victorian diorama." Its classical organization highlights contemporary design features such as a sculptured white steel staircase in the living room with tubular railings. The simple rectangular windows of the rear facade have expansion joints which suggest in an industrial idiom the traditional pilasters of Renaissance architecture; on the shorter east and west facades the classical symmetry of the rear is amended by alternating rectangular and circular windows. Yellow for the facades and silver-green for doors and trim recall villas designed by Palladio.

BOWEN, RICHARD L.

(Building Design)
R. L. Bowen & Associates Inc.
(216) 491-9300
13000 Shaker Blvd. Cleveland OH 44120

Born: 1935 **Studied:** Case Western Reserve University **Awards:** AIA **Notable Works:** Playhouse Square Hotel, Cleveland OH; First Federal Office Building, Cleveland OH; Cleveland Hopkins Airport RETAIL 40%, INSTITUTIONAL 25%, COMMERCIAL 20%, OFFICE 15%

His roots in the Bauhaus can still be seen in the expressed structure of some of his recent designs, but his practice has been evolving with contemporary tastes. Designs are strongly influenced by client desires, especially those retail and commercial clients with well-defined images to convey.

His Cleveland Hopkins Airport project

Charles William Brubaker, *National Center for Agricultural Education*, Chapingo, Mexico, 1967.

Richard L. Bowen, *Cleveland Hopkins Airport*, Cleveland, Ohio, 1975. Project Achitect: William F. Mason

required tripling the busy airport without impeding operations of the 16 airlines that continued to fly during construction. The old terminal, its ceiling replaced with skylights, became the central lobby and hub of a curved line of ticket counters and baggage facilities. Traffic circulation—car, rapid transit and foot as well as airplane—suggested the shapes taken by new construction, which eventually all but replaced old structures. A new, boomerang-shaped concourse now spreads along the interface between auto and airplane. Access roads are laid out to permit the boomerang to stretch when necessary, and the nation's first airport rapid transit line is extended all the way to the lobby, making it possible to proceed from airplane to downtown hotel without setting foot out-of-doors. Concourses and access roads are double-decked, with upper-level auto traffic bound for ticket facilities driving on the roof of lower-level baggage handling areas, which require more floor space than the ticket windows above.

BOWMAN, OBIE G.
(Building Design)
Obie G. Bowman, Architect (707) 785-2344
1000 Annapolis Rd Sea Ranch CA 95497

Born: 1943 **Studied:** Arizona State University; University of Southern California **Awards:** California AIA; *Builder* magazine; California Coastal Commission **Notable Works:** Brunsell residence, Sea Ranch CA; Spring Lake Park Visitor's Center, Santa Rosa CA RESIDENTIAL 75%

He often uses unusual combinations of material to create works that tie together client considerations, surrounding community, and the larger natural environment. His major aim is to reconcile his desire to build with his "longing to preserve the natural landscape."

His oceanfront Brunsell residence at Sea Ranch CA is concrete and wood, much of it below grade to avoid interfering with neighbors' views. The wedge-shaped portion of the house visible at street level has a sod roof planted with native meadow grasses. A 36-foot solarium gives spectacular ocean views

and works as a passive solar heater, collecting the sun's heat in its brick floor. A brick fireplace serves as sculptural centerpiece: the right half is a traditional grid of bricks; the other side, made of meltdowns and bricks that fused together during manufacturing, seems to erupt from the usual pattern and flow down and out from the fireplace. He explains that the right side of the fireplace represents the husband "who is a warm, rational traditionalist, while the left side represents the wife who could be characterized as possessing a relentless satiric wit."

For his Spring Lake Park Visitor's Center in Santa Rosa CA he built a glass pyramid in an oak woods overlooking a lake. To shade the sun he devised a system of louvres whose texture becomes finer as they climb the structure, echoing surrounding trees whose thick trunks taper into twigs at the top. In the center of this pyramid is a fabric tent-like structure which serves as an exhibit area.

BRANCH, DAN P.
(Building Design, Historic Preservation)
Dan P. Branch, Architect (318) 235-1890
211 Laurence Ave. Lafayette LA 70503

Born: 1931 **Studied:** University of Florida; Columbia University **Awards:** Florida AIA; Tallahassee AIA **Notable Works:** Branch residence, Gainesville FL; Childrens Museum, Tallahassee FL; City Hall and Library, Gainesville FL INSTITUTIONAL 60%, RESIDENTIAL 40%

He has always balanced his architectural practice with teaching, most recently at the University of Southwestern Louisiana. His work reflects a continuing fascination with the vernacular forms of "untrained" architects throughout history. On the academic side of his practice, his book *Folk Architecture of the Eastern Mediterrenean* explores the vernacular traditions of ancient Greece and Italy. His design practice reflects this interest with its simple shapes made of local materials which, following Frank Lloyd Wright no less than architects immemorial, "are of the soil, natural."

As another example of his mix of academic and private design interests, he has collaborated with students in designing a proposed Marine Survival Training Center for workers on Gulf of Mexico ships, oil rigs and planes, to be administered by the University of Southwestern Louisiana on a detached campus in Lafayette, the inland city which is the capital of the Louisiana oil trade. The Center will be located on a 90-foot deep "borrow pit" that was dug for airport runway fill, on an isolated edge of airport property. The pit has filled up with spring-fed clear water, a scarce commodity in southern Louisiana and a great convenience for water training. Architecture students will be designing sea walls, a helicopter pad, boat supports and other real-world necessities as part of their classroom experience.

BRITT, STANFORD R.

(Building Design, Preservation)
Sulton Campbell & Associates, Chartered
(202) 882-6360

Born: 1944 **Studied:** Columbia University **Awards:** William Kinnie Fellowship **Notable Works:** Addison Road Transit Station, Shaw Junior High School, Mt. Sinai Baptist Church INSTITUTIONAL 30% MEDICAL 40% RESIDENTIAL 30%

Working in the variegated environment of Washington, D.C., he attunes his work to both the densely populated urban areas and the relatively open suburban spaces. This contextual sensitivity inspired the construction of the Addison Road Transit Station, among others,, for the Washington Metro system. Riding the subway, one emerges out into the open at the Addison station. The relief and freshness one experiences in coming above ground are bolstered by the light and airy feel of the station. This is achieved by the liberal use of glass and skylights.

The Mt. Sinai Baptist Church makes a statement of drama without overwhelming the largely residential surroundings. The principal colors used are light, bordering on white. Additional touches that soften the appearance include the rounding of corners.

In the design of hospitals and other medical facilities, emphasis has been given to the "circulation patterns," the flows of traffic of different groups of people: patients, visitors, nurses and professional staff. However, the separation of the flow and activity of one group from another has not been done at the cost of claustrophobia. Everyone is able to get a view of the outside and hence feel free.

BRODY, WILLIAM JR.

(Building Design, Planning)
Davis, Brody and Associates   100 East 42nd Street New York New York

Born: 1926 **Studied:** Harvard University **Awards:** Fellow, AIA; Design Award, *Progressive Architecture*; Award of Honor, New York Society of Architects **Notable Works:** (with Lewis Davis) Corning Glass Building, New York; Lambert House, Bronx, New York; Guggenheim Hall renovation, New York City

He is a humanist who works comfortably and fluidly within the often confining idioms of modernism. His works of the last quarter century, with his partner, Lewis Davis, have been most clearly distinguished by their lack of pretention and their attention to the idiosyncracies of their user communities. He is a rationalist who can simultaneously attend to tight budget constraints and tangible sublime aesthetic details which would escape or overtax a shakier hand.

Though he has made significant contributions in institutional and commercial architecture, his most valuable work has been in the field of public housing. Since the early sixties, he and Davis have been developing livable, attractive, and economical alternatives to the antiquated and depressing Pruitt-Igoe low income prototype. Typically, he has combined standard masonry techniques with sophisticated, intricate massing patterns, to create inexpensive but highly sculptural, attractive structures.

BROMLEY, R. SCOTT

(Interior Architecture, Furniture Design)
Bromley/Jacobsen Design Inc (212) 620-4250

242 W. 27th St. New York NY 10001

Born: 1939 **Studied:** McGill University **Awards:** "10 x 10: The Critics' Choice" Exhibition; New York AIA; New York City AIA **Notable Works:** Abitare Store, New York City; Private Residence, New York City; Studio 54, New York City RESIDENTIAL 60%, COMMERCIAL 20%, OFFICE 20%

His spaces are functional, visually interesting and exactingly detailed. His approach might seem sleekly minimal but for its site-specific effect in Manhattan, where space is coveted as the ultimate luxury.

This emphasis on openness figures in his commercial as well as residential designs. His New York City Arbitare Store features free-standing furniture displays delineated only by light from mobile theatrical lighting masts. Its original facade was stripped to create large window bays, and floating stairs lead up to a glass-walled conference room.

He often eliminates interior walls in his residential designs, sometimes replacing them with full-height pocket doors, colonnades, or panels of etched glass. Remaining walls are used for display and storage and are emphatically sculpted. His New York City Private Residence, a converted loft, features mirror-image guest bedrooms at each end of a large open interior, from which they are separated by full-wall electric pocket doors which retract to incorporate the rooms into the open area between them. Around the perimeter of the space he has put wiring, audio speakers and radiators behind aluminum grilles, creating simple electrical access and comfortable seating ledges. Lighting throughout may be computer controlled for instant comprehensive effects. Weight sensors are located in the floor of any carpeted areas for optional automatic illumination.

BROOKS, TURNER
(Building Design)
Turner Brooks, Archtitect (802) 658-0261
4 Howard Street Burlington VT 05401

Born: 1943 **Studied:** Yale University **Awards:** Rome Prize, American Academy in Rome **Notable Works:** Fuisz House, Narazeth PA; house for two artists, Litchfield CT; Brooks/McLane House, Starksboro VT RESIDENTIAL 75%, INSTITUTIONAL AND COMMERCIAL 25%

His buildings use materials associated with vernacular architecture, but often have shapes suggested by trains, cars, or planes. His houses contain areas where the inhabitants feel as if they're moving through the landscape, rather than being rooted in it. He also uses animal metaphors to describe his work, saying that "all great buildings are essentially bestial"— they seem as if they could spring to life if aroused.

His own house in the foothills of the Adirondacks in Starksboro VT looks as if it's ready to race off into the mountains. The bulk of the building is to the rear. The roof slopes down to the front of the clapboard- and asphalt-shingled house, while the walls taper in, giving the structure an aerodynamic look. Windows line the three walls of the front of the house and bring the country inside. Overhanging the large open living area, supported by thin pillars, is the master bedroom. The bedroom wall facing the mountains is cut away to allow light from a dormer and to give another view of the countryside.

BROWN, BILL
(Building Design)
Bill Brown AIA Professional Corporation
(303) 473-8138
102 S. Tejon Suite 1100
Colorado Springs CO 80903

Born: 1950 **Studied:** University of Notre Dame **Awards:** HUD National Design Award, Reynolds Aluminum Design Award **Notable Works:** *Building and Renovation Kit;* Downtown Three Rivers MI

He designs in close partnership with the congregation and clergy who will use his buildings. This commitment is exemplified in the popular guidebook for which he was editor and primary author, *Building and Renovation Kit for Places of Catholic Worship,* which won *Modern Liturgy* magazine's national "Bene"

Charles William Brubaker, Perkins & Will and Mimbles, Inc., *Capital High School*, Santa Fe, New Mexico

award. The book is written for lay building committees and busy pastors, not architectural professionals, with the aim of helping these 'end-users' to discover and articulate their unique architectural needs. He works in materials appropriate to local climates and environments, often informed by regional vernaculars and historical roots. He disrespects iconoclasm, and works with art and craft as integral elements of architecture.

BRUBAKER, CHARLES WILLIAM
(Building Design)
Perkins and Will Architects (312) 977-1100
123 North Wacker Street Chicago IL 60606

Born: 1926 **Studied:** University of Texas at Austin **Awards:** FAIA; Member, National Urban Planning and Design Committee; Vice-President, Chicago Architecture Foundation **Notable Works:** National College of Agriculture, Chapingo, Mexico; First National Bank (and Plaza), Chicago; Woodbridge High School, Irvine, CA COMMERCIAL/RETAIL: 40%, HOUSING: 10% EDUCATION: 25%, PLANNING: 10%, OTHER: 15%

The buildings that house educational institutions, he believes, are the most important architecture in any proper community. In the evolving American landscape public schools have become *de facto* community centers, while colleges have become cultural touchstones. While he has concentrated his energy on spaces which promote and intensify the learning experience and its effects, the apogee of his humane, unmannered modernist approach is his 1968 First National Bank and Plaza (with C.F. Murphy and Associates). The curving tower silhouette is an elegant response to the divergent needs of the bank's public service and executive departments. Large, open ground floors provide service space for the major metropolitan banking center, which then tapers up to smaller, more segmented upper floors which provide articulated space for managers and clerical support staff. To augment the spacious feeling of the lobby floors, elevator banks were separated and isolated against opposite walls. The granite and glass tower is set in a large sunken plaza, also with

a slope-walled motif, which attracts constant foot traffic in fair weather. The plaza is built around a square fountain which subsumes nine square steps, and is highlighted by Marc Chagall's pastoral *Four Seasons* mural .

BULL VOLKMANN STOCKWELL (see
Allen, Robert; Bull, Henrick; Stockwell, Sherwood)

BULL, HENRICK
(Building Design)
Bull Volkmann Stockwell (415) 781-1526
Musto Plaza 350 Pacific Avenue
San Fransisco CA 94133

Born: 1926 **Studied:** Massachusetts Institute of Technology **Awards:** FAIA; Federal Design Achievement Award; Design Award, Honor Award for Sensitivity to Handicapped Access, California Department of Rehabilitation; People in Architecture Award, California AIA **Notable Works:** The Inn at Spanish Bay, Pebble Beach CA; Stanford Shopping Center, Stanford CA Bear Valley Visitors Center, Point Reyes CA; Student Center, University of California at Santa Barbara COMMERCIAL 35%, RESORT 35%, HOUSING 15%

"Architects have a responsibility to build with rather than on land," he says. What architects decide to do or not to do can preserve and enhance our natural environment as much as any regulations.

His handsomely composed Inn at Spanish Bay is a luxury hotel situated on the beautiful Pebble Beach drive near Monterey CA. The building comports well with its surroundings— between blue, emerald, and turquoise waters and pine and cypress trees and alongside other quasi-Mediterranean mansions. It is rich in regional characteristics: sweeping hip roofs and wide overhangs recall San Francisco Bay-area domestic architecture; adobe-like walls and hefty arches borrow from California mansions. A ridgetop section of the hotel especially fits into its larger site. Facing the water the hotel is four stories high, the fourth story made up of dormer rooms cut into the roofs. Gently sloping roof planes echo the

John Burgee, Philip Johnson, *AT&T Headquarters Building,* New York City

surrounding dunes which were carefully sculpted for a golf course. From a distance, the hotel reads as a series of pavilions and towers in the woods. From the entry side it seems a modest if extensive structure nestled in dunes and trees. Its long corridors are punctuated by stunning views and furnished with alcoves at each turn for respite.

Selected by a student committee on the strength of his firm's reputation for designing comfortable and warm buildings, His Student Center for the University of California at Santa Barbara is a wooden pavilion which bridges an existing concrete building and the site for a future theatre. Its pavilioned shelter retains a sense of open, landscaped outdoor space. Wood trusses frame a large Brazilian pepper tree, retained in its original setting. Heavy wood sunscreens of 2 x 4-foot redwood lattice-work give protection from the sun. A similar wood lattice detail is used in the railings. The six- and ten-foot deep trusses are fabricated from glu-lam wood beams, as are the railings.

BUNSHAFT, GORDON
(Building Design)
Skidmore Owings and Merrill (212) 309-9500
400 Park Avenue New York NY 10022

Born: 1909 **Studied:** Massachusetts Institute of Technology **Awards:** FAIA; Medal of Honor, New York AIA; Fellow, Academy of Arts and Sciences **Notable Works:** Lever House Corporate Headquarters, New York City; Hirshorn Museum and Sculpture-Garden, Washington DC; New Jeddah International Airport, Saudi Arabia COMMERCIAL/ RETAIL: 45%, HOUSING: 15% INDUSTRIAL: 10%, EDUCATION: 5%, PLANNING: 10% OTHER: 15%

After thirty years his name has become inseparably associated with the the world's largest architectural firm, Skidmore, Owings and Merrill. He has always worked out of SOM's New York office, but his influence has reached to all of the firm's branches. In the early 1950s he wooed and won many of the nation's largest corporations with his argument that contemporary American architecture could give their national headquarters a distinctive cachet,

hence a subtle but valuable competitive edge. The monumental glass box he built for the Lever Brothers Corporation in 1952 put the Miesian aesthetic in the corporate mainstream.

In a long and prolific career he has avoided adventurism and searched for crisp, functional design solutions which aren't sterile or ritually fixed. In his recent design for the Hirshorn Museum and Sculpture Garden the main museum building is a circle; yet the overall effect of the installation is traditional and dignified.

BURGEE, JOHN
(Building Design)
John Burgee Architects with Philip Johnson
375 Park Avenue New York NY 10152

Born: 1933 **Studied:** University of Notre Dame **Awards:** Honor Award, AIA, 1975; Chicago Architecture Award, 1984, AIA Chicago Chapter; Reynolds Prize, 1978 **Notable Works:** O'Hare International Airport, Chicago; The Crescent, Dallas (with Philip Johnson); American Telephone and Telegraph Headquarters, New York City (with Philip Johnson)

Although he has shared little of the attention that the popular media have given recently to his long-time partner, Philip Johnson, both men describe their working relationship as a true symbiosis. On a typical project, he prepares a detailed design 'rebuttal' after Johnson completes initial conceptual work. Eventually a synthesis is reached, and the two prepare a broad consensus plan. Throughout the project, each freely edits the other's work. Ironically, his most frequent criticisms involve Johnson's excessive attention to "Miesian details," and his occasional tendency to cannibalize his own effforts.

He is an adventurous geometer, whose formal flexibility is well displayed in his admixture of rectangular and cylindrical forms in his design for Boston's Fort Hill Square. His greatest contribution to contemporary architecture, however, is his reintroduction of ornamentation and vernacularism to large-scale commercial and institutional commissions. His "maximalist" gestures include his well-known crest to New York's AT&T Headquarters Building (modeled after the sinuous curves of a Chippendale cabinet), and the overscaled, cast metal, neo-Victorian lamps and crestings at Dallas' Crescent Center.

BURNS, MICHAEL

(Building Design, Construction Administration, Facility Programming, Interior Architecture)
Micheal Burns, AIA (609) 921-6044
P.O. Box 314, 909 State Road
Rocky Hill NJ 08553

Born: 1951 **Studied:** Drexel University **Awards:** New Jersey AIA; Somerset County Land Planning Award **Notable Works:** St. Luke's Housing for the Elderly, Gladstone-Peapack NJ; Rosko Junction Industrial Park, Metuchen NJ RESIDENTIAL 45%, COMMERCIAL 30%, OFFICE 25%

His designs are drawn from traditional philosophies and ideals that have stood the test of time. Their spatial planning is classically inspired, aiming to create orderly progressions of spaces in clear relation to one another. Detailing, however, is drawn from each project's surrounding vernacular; a large part of his practice is devoted to contextually sensitive infill projects in smaller, older urban centers.

His St. Luke's Elderly Housing in Peapack-Gladstone NJ incorporates an existing house into a low-impact complex of 16 apartments. The new buildings too emulate surrounding single-family home shapes, and the imagery of the complex—clapboard siding, shingled roofs and Colonial green trim—reflects the old town's architectural vocabulary. The progression of spaces attentively reflects program requirements, especially the continuing need for human contact of old people who commonly live far from family. The single entrance channels all residents into a purposefully small greenspace which is overlooked by porches from both buildings. Four apartments share each entry vestibule, and second-floor units overlook them. Recognizing the unique needs of the elderly, he actually *increased*

density to create a more satisfying community.

BUTLER, GEOFFREY H.

(Construction Administration, Cost Estimating, Building Design, Facility Programming)
Butler Group AIA (417) 887-0340
1550 B East Battlefield Springfield MO 65804

Born: 1953 **Studied:** University of Kansas **Awards:** AIA; Springfield AIA **Notable Works:** Acura of Springfield, Springfield MO; US Courthouse, Springfield MO; Galleria Shopping Center, Springfield MO OFFICE/COMMERCIAL 35% INSTITUTIONAL 25%, MEDICAL 25%, GENERAL SERVICES 15%

Viewing his firm as a service organization, he takes architecture a step further by making the economics of a project work towards its creativity. His showroom for Acura was built from a burned-out waterbed warehouse that other architects had proposed razing. His solution was to gut the interior, leaving the roof structure exposed, which created a high-tech showroom for a high-tech car that also respected the history of the neighborhood. And it enabled the owner to buy the building and property for the same cost as building a new showroom.

In his role as developer and designer for the Springfield MO Galleria Shopping Center, he proposed a two-building structure with large vaulted ceilings cantilevered up to 28 feet. The project was attractive to businesses in part because of the dramatic interior, which featured glue-laminated timber ceilings, and in part because only ground floor space was leased and paid for, leaving tenants the option of build mezzanines and doubling their square footage for the same price.

CADLE, WILLIAM R.

(Facilities Design, Interior Design, Construction Management)
Harrison & Spencer, Inc. (912)742-5751
483 Cotton Avenue Macon GA 31201

Born: 1936 **Studied:** Georgia Tech **Awards:** AIA, Georgia AIA **Notable Works:** Woodland Christian Church, Macon GA; Cross Keys Baptist Church, Macon GA; Historic

Restoration of Alexander II Elementary School, Macon GA COMMERCIAL 50%, GOVERNMENT 50%

A conservative Postmodernist, he has much experience with churches, schools and residences as well as diverse other structures. He believes that architecture should harmonize with its locale, which for him is largely conservative southeast Georgia. Since his clientele prefer the classical, ante-bellum southern style, his subtle Postmodern classicism is well suited to his clients, and offers a contemporary solution to what can be perceived as the architectural constraints of regional conservatism.

His restoration of the Alexander II Elementary school in Macon GA saved much of the exterior walls. The result is true to the original but accommodates modern air-conditioning. The former light well is now a solarium which distributes stored greenhouse heat in the winter and expels building heat in the fall and spring. The late-Victorian high ceilings have been lowered with improved lighting, and walls are now fire-retardant. His Woodland Christian Church in Macon GA consists of a laminated wooden frame in exploded-triangle form. The walls stand upright at ninety degrees instead of the usual sixty degrees, and sweep upward convexly, to give the appearance of a triangular structure that has been inflated. But the three-sided triangular roof is concave in shape. Mondrian-style stained glass windows are another contemporary feature.

CALLISTER, PAYNE AND BISCHOFF
(see Callister, Charles Warren)

CALLISTER, CHARLES WARREN
(Building Design)
Callister, Payne and Bischoff
1865 Mar West Tiburon CA 94920

Born: 1917 **Studied:** University of Texas at Austin **Awards:** Lecturer-Designee, Stanford University **Notable Works:** Field House and Playing Grounds, University of California at Santa Cruz; Pier 45, San Francisco; Amherst fields development, Amherst, Massachusetts

While the focus of his practice has shifted from single-family luxury residences to major community developments, he has maintained the almost obsessive attention to siting details for which he is known. In his first residential commissions he synthesized traditional Japanese and New England colonial motifs with the more progressive idioms of the San Francisco Bay area. These structures made a distinctive aesthetic statement while harmonizing with existing development and avoiding ostentation.

His Field House for the University of California at Santa Cruz demonstrates his sensitivity to siting constraints in institutional contexts. The main building is nestled on a gradual slope to avoid obstructing magnificent ocean views from the school's central quadrangle. The roof of the locker room extension of the Field House doubles as a grandstand for playing fields at the hill's base, adding to the building's visually compact effect.

CAMPBELL, DOUGLAS AND REGULA
(Building Design, Landscape Architecture, Urban Design)
Campbell and Campbell (213) 458-1011
1425 Fifth St. Santa Monica CA 90401

Born: 1947, 1948 **Studied:** University of California at Berkeley, University of California at Los Angeles **Awards:** Honor Award, California AIA; National Award of Merit, American Society of Landscape Architects **Notable Works:** Imperial Beach Pier Plaza, Imperial Beach CA; Los Angeles State and County Arboretum Education Center INSTITUTIONAL 50%, CIVIC 25%, COMMERCIAL 20%, RESIDENTIAL 5%

Grounded equally in the disciplines of architecture, planning and landscape architecture, and growing out of their commitment to a collaborative design process, their work has a strong affinity for natural landscapes and seeks to give expression to collective memory and imagination. Their Los Angeles State and County Arboretum Education Center builds on the existing character of the arboretum, which is in the Southern California tradition of interior and exterior closely linked together in powerful spatial sequences. The buildings are organized around a series of outdoor rooms configured not only to accommodate various functions but also to provide beneficial microclimates for people and plants. The separate pavilion of the Lecture Hall is designed to support a great variety of events, from formal talks to conferences. Its entry courtyard is scaled to act as an informal gathering place before, after and between events. It's defined on the north by the arcade of the classroom court, the east by the facade of the hall accented by specimen trees, the south by plantings and the west by views out to the Arboretum.

CANDELA, FELIX
(Building Design)
Candela Architects
Avenida America 14 Madrid Spain

Born: 1910 **Studied:** Academia de Bellas Artes de San Fernando, Spain **Awards:** Fellow, American Concrete Institute; Honorary Member, AIA; Lindau Award, American Concrete Institute **Notable Works:** Cosmic Ray Center, Mexico City; Church of the Miraculous Virgin, Mexico City; Texas Instruments Factory Building, Dallas, Texas

He is a builder and designer who has pioneered the use of thin-shelled concrete in vaulted roofs. As a student in Madrid (he emigrated to the U.S. in the early seventies) he witnessed the construction of the La Zarzuela racecourse and the Fronton Recoletos, Eduardo Torroja's seminal barrel-vaulted masterpieces. He did not undertake a thin-concrete project of his own until 1949. Two years later he secured his international reputation with a revolutionary design for the Cosmic Ray Center of the University of Mexico, built around a hyperbolic paraboloid. The shell's thickness was kept to a mere 15mm to permit the penetration of low-energy waves. The advantages of his paraboloid construction were its compatibility with conventional planar shuttering, and its lyrical sculptural effect. Often, however, the technique proved incompatible with the conventional interior layouts required in commercial and institutional commissions.

CARDINAL, DOUGLAS JOSEPH
(Building Design)
Douglas J. Cardinal Architect Ltd. #1601-8830 85th St. Edmonton Alberta Canada

Born: 1934 **Studied:** University of Texas at Austin **Awards:** Award of Excellence, *The Canadian Architect;* Province of Alberta Achievement of Excellence Award **Notable Works:** St. Mary's Church, Red Deer, Alberta; Keliewen School, Alberta; Grotski House, Edmonton

He believes that the fundamental purpose of architecture and all professions is to better the human condition. In his work he identifies the needs of relevant individuals and with their inspiration creates designs that affirm users' "collective humanness." Placing the concerns of people before the formal strictures of system design, he aims to ensure that man is served by his structures rather than imprisoned in them.

Throughout his career he has tried to interweave the simple design philosophy of North America's Plains Indians with the technologies and intellectual sophistication of imported Euro-American culture. He argues that by adopting the Indian design bias toward circles and curves we can create structures and communities which radiate out from a central space and motif, and so continually address the evolving needs of whole populations. In his design for St. Mary's Church in Red Deer, Alberta, he achieved unprecedented curvilinearity and formal looseness by using advanced reinforcement techniques and computer stress analysis.

CARLISLE, PAT
(Landscape Architecture)
Royston, Hanamoto, Alley & Abey
(415) 383-7900
225 Miller Avenue
Mill Valley CA 94942-0937

Studied: Pennsylvania State University

Awards: Honor and Merit Awards, Northern California American Society of Landscape Architects; Honor and Merit Awards, American Society of Landscape Architects **Notable Works:** Father Alfred Boeddeker Park, San Francisco CA; Sun River Master Plan, Sun River OR; Santa Clara Central Park, Santa Clara CA PARKS AND RECREATION 75%, OTHER 25%

Her landscaping of San Francisco's Boeddeker Park exemplifies her design philosophy: she creates works of lasting beauty by working closely with the people who will use and appreciate them. The city had set aside 8/10 of an acre, split into two parcels by existing buildings and connected by a thin strip of land. After holding a number of town meetings to determine community needs in the diverse neighborhood, her firm came up with four site plans. Elements of the two most popular plans were merged to create a park with something for everyone that retains a distinctive identity.

All of the distinct areas of Boeddeker Park branch off of a diagonal red-brick walkway, including a tot lot with swings, slides, sand and shelter; a basketball court; and arbors in sunny areas with tables for picnicking. The park rises ten feet in elevation from end to end, but a series of ramps traverses the park without using any steps. A Victorian clock and the work of three sculptors decorate the park, which is planted with evergreen ash and accented with flowering trees. Pines and poplars are placed against adjacent buildings to soften their walls.

CARLSON, VAN J.
(Building Design, Ecclesiastical Design, Educational Design)
Van Carlson, Architect, AIA, P.C.
(203) 735-2677
159 Center Street Shelton CT 06484

Born: 1928 **Studied:** Rensselaer Polytechnic Institute; University of Connecticut **Awards:** AIA; NSBA **Notable Works:** Hillcrest High School, CT; Connecticut Valley Hospital CT EDUCATIONAL 25%, ECCLESIASTICAL 25%, MEDICAL 25%, HOUSING 25%

He works with equal facility in the contemporary, traditional and colonial styles common to the Northeast, in line with client desires and restrictions. He often uses dramatic design features such as textured materials, natural lighting, solar heating and colored glass, and strongly emphasizes courtyards, greens and shrubbery. His frequent renovations aim to minimize site impact by locating additions carefully and adorning them in appropriate styles, whether Romanesque, Gothic or Georgian.

His Hillcrest High School is structured from vertical granite panels. Simultaneously contemporary and Romanesque, it features a barrel-vaulted swimming pool and a domed planetarium. High library windows and expanses of glass in the courtyards give an airy Romanesque effect while admitting winter sunlight for energy efficiency. Yet classrooms are quietly lit, creating an intimate, human atmosphere, which counterbalances the Romanesque starkness: he believes that regional styles shouldn't overpower the individual and should maintain a human scale. His Immaculate Conception Church in Waterbury CT is a pure renovation of a 1912 Romanesque structure, but it also exemplifies his use of highly textured concrete panels, copper-covered domes, and natural stone which lends solidity and warmth.

CARLSON, WALTER
(Building Design)
Walter C. Carlson Assoc., Inc. (312) 940-9422
1121 F Lake Cook Road, Deerfield IL 60015

Born: 1934 **Studied:** self-educated **Awards:** Award of Excellence, SARA **Notable Works:** Arnold T. Olson Chapel, Deerfield IL; First Evangelical Free Church, Rockford IL. RELIGIOUS 65%

Church design is the major part of his practice, both protestant and Catholic. In designing for each denomination, form follows faith, which decrees such functional constraints as the location of baptismal fonts, the relative importance of pulpit and altar, and the nature and significance of doctrinal displays. Working especially with masonry, he strives for a timeless quality that will look good today as well as in 50 years and beyond.

"Architecture for churches is a matter of gospel," he says. "If the gospel of Christ is worthy of accurate verbal proclamation week by week, it is also worthy of accurate architectural representation, where its message speaks year after year. Every aspect of the building, its form, materials, budget and plan, must be an accurate representation of the gospel."

CARTER, JOHN A.

(Building Design, Construction Administration, Programming and Institutional Planning)
John A. Carter, Architect, P.A.
(603) 883-6443
7 Concord St. Nashua NH 03060

Born: 1924 **Studied:** Yale University **Awards:** FAIA; New Hampshire AIA; First Prize, Church Architectural Guild of America **Notable Works:** Eaglebrook School, Deerfield MA; First Baptist Church, Keene NH

Influenced by Eero Saarinen, he tries to design buildings that show the "generational thread" or evidence of the function of the building. He chooses his building materials carefully and gives great consideration to the shape of architectural space, believing that these elements are the ones which please and excite the eye.

His Keene NH First Baptist Church has a poured concrete and ceramic tile immersion baptismal tank which parishioners walk by upon entering. The ceiling rises to forty feet over a central area, where lectern and pulpit are surrounded on four sides by a diamond-shaped seating arrangement. Lighting for the steel-framed church comes from a large glass lantern over the center. A low window over the baptistery and lantern vertical-slit windows at the edges provide natural light.

In the Eaglebrook School Dining Facility in Deerfield MA he constructed a steel frame building with water-struck brick to house a dining room, kitchen and boiler for the central campus, with service facilities, loading dock and storage space hidden under a concrete deck balcony. Southern-facing sun scoops let

in sunlight. The dining room, overlooking a valley, has carpets and an acoustic wooden ceiling to absorb sound.

CASBARIAN, JOHN

(Building Design)
Taft Architects (713) 522-2988
807 Peden St. Houston TX 77006

Studied: Rice University **Awards:** AIA; Interiors Magazine "40 under 40" Honoree; Texas AIA **Notable Works** (also see Robert Timme & Danny Samuels): YWCA Masterson Branch, Houston TX; Springer Building, Galveston TX; River Crest Country Club, Fort Worth TX

His work and that of partners Danny Samuels and Robert Timme is a collective process which fosters exploration and results in work of divergent character. Their early experiences at Rice University and in Houston provided them with an abstract conceptual process for exploring two- and three-dimensional structures. This rationalist background was gradually influenced by their Rice University campus, which he describes as "appropriate hot-climate Gothic style, almost Venetian in scale, texture, and color." With this background they are attracted to "examples of work from architectural history in which two sets of seemingly conflicting concerns coexist, allowing aspects of each position to occur at various scales."

The Grove Court Townhouses in Houston illustrate these twin interests in abstraction and continuity. They combine functional loft-like volumes with a layered ordering system which delineates a hierarchy of public to private spaces. The undulating stucco wall, a sign of informality and depth in all their work, is stepped and modulated to let the formal architecture rise above it in contrast. Elsewhere, as in the Municipal Control Building in Missouri City MO, an overscaled planar facade makes the building an abstract representation of its building type, in the style associated with WPA public buildings of the 1930s. Their works consciously explore contrasts between public and private, courtyard and figural gateway, utilitarian and symbolic, building and architecture, vernacular and international Post-Modern Classicism. The explorations result in an eclectic and interesting body of work.

CATALANO, EDUARDO
(Building Design)
Eduardo Catalano, Architects and Engineers
(617) 491-8386
300 Franklin St. Cambridge MA 02139

Born: 1917 **Studied:** University of Pennsylvania **Awards:** North Carolina AIA; *Progressive Architecture* award **Notable Works:** Civic Center, Portland ME; Architecture Building, University of Buenos Aires (with H. Caminos); Juilliard School of Music, New York City

As one of the leading critics and gadflies of contemporary architecture, he argues that in the last century the discipline has seen great movement but little progress. He sees the future of architecture lying with those who forsake the haughty traditions of custom construction, which pander to the mercurial or illusory needs of a handful of people and create useless "museum pieces." The new architect will be wholly indoctrinated in the quantum advances of science and industry. He'll recognize that in order to provide long-lasting and flexible housing for the world's growing population, he must think in terms of community-wide systems rather than individual shelters. The focus of the design process must be shifted from the narrow demands of individuals to the broad needs of the social collectivity. In his own commissions—most notably the Juilliard School of Music at New York's Lincoln Center—he has achieved geometric simplicity and functional flexibility in structures designed for a multitude of mass activities.

CAVAGLIERI, GIORGIO
(Building Design, Historic Preservation, Interior Architecture)
Giorgio Cavaglieri, FAIA Architect
(212) 245-4207
250 West 57th St. Suite 2016
New York NY 10107

Born: 1911 **Studied:** School of Engineering, Milan, Italy; School of Architecture, Rome, Italy **Awards:** FAIA; Bard Award of Merit, City Club of New York; AIA; Distinguished Architecture Award, New York AIA **Notable Works:** Restoration of Jefferson Market Branch Library, New York City; New York Shakespeare Festival Public Theatre, New York City; Renovation of New York Public Library, New York City; Renovation of National Museum of the Building Arts, Washington DC INSTITUTIONAL/MUSEUM/LIBRARY 100%

In principle he believes in the "modern moment," the "moment" that heralded rational, functional form. But as a technology and a way of life, architecture can't be mere visual decoration. It should be valid and usable, at ease with its civilization. Civilization spans the generations, and the architecture of the past reminds us of our origins and our inheritance; it binds us to our traditions and even to our own selves. But preserving the past does more than make us think about the past. The great architecture of the past speaks to the human condition, and its forms and aesthetics can evoke feelings and emotions that have stirred through the ages. His restoration work has been marked by this civilized awareness that the best is eternal in every moment.

His restoration of New York City's Jefferson Market Library, a former Greenwich Village courthouse, was an oft-cited example in the inauguration of the municipal Landmark Preservation Commission. He blends the old and the new in his design, so that both the "literature of architecture"—cut stone faces and flowers, spiral stairs, soaring stained glass windows—and new and necessary functions, are respected. The nineteenth century courthouse was inspired by a fourteenth century Venetian building. With a compelling frankness, he adds elements that in their contrast bring older forms, adornments and colors to new life: new fluorescent lighting is suspended in articulated black boxes, and a modern, austere railed catwalk crosses the main 37-foot hall without violence to Gothic stained-glass windows nearby. The entrance to a circular

Eduardo Catalano, *Greensboro, North Carolia Government Center/Court House.* Photo: Gordon H. Schenck, Jr.

stair tower now passes through a sleek glass door which is set into the old carved limestone. A wheel of ornamented Victorian tie-rods is spotlighted at the top of the stairs. The low-vaulted basement chamber, with its softly aged salmon-pink brick columns and arches sand-blasted clear of a century's accretions, is a bookworm's dream come true.

CECIL, RUSSELL C.
(Building Design)
Cecil, Pierce and Associates (212) 308-5060
330 E. 59th St. New York NY 10022

Born: 1926 **Studied:** Yale University **Awards:** New York City AIA; American Society of Landscape Architects **Notable Works:** Chappaquonsett proposed resort community, Martha's Vinyard MA; Charles Pratt house, Ile au Haut ME; Revere Sugar Corporation offices, Lyndhurst NJ RESIDENTIAL 35%, OFFICES 30%, RESORTS 20%, SHOWROOMS 15%

His particular interest is in the sequence and variety of spaces experienced in buildings. Working with the tension between activity and serenity, he contrasts architecturally active and dramatic circulation "spines" with restful private rooms. The shape of stairs and hallways respond to nuances in direction and intensityu of traffic flow. Wherever possible, rooms are entered through small transitional spaces. Windows in halls and stairs are a favorite grace note: the play of their light and shade on facing walls and floors is no less a design motif than the views they capture at points of pause.

Thehouse at Mamaroneck NY has a low entry hall , but the ceiling rises to take in bright clerestory windows whose light plays on high facing walls. Sunlight is filtered through high openings in these walls before it passes into adjoining rooms, thus admitting light to the major rooms without uncomfortable glare. The rooms are in close relationship with their surrounding landscape, and ocharacteristically contain semi-discreet spaces defined by such features as window seats, flat vs. sloping ceilings, and level changes. Windows are seldom set in the plane of the interior wall, but rather are projected out in window bays or enveloped with comfortable features such asboookshelves, cupboards or fire-place hearths that define a seating nook, as in the Mamaroneck master bedroom. Such details evoke a quiet traditional recall without pastiche or self-conscious architectural witticisms. His preference in houses is for materials with soft, lustrous, non-reflective surfaces. His commercial work also is characterized by softness in light and colors and the use of natural wood in key details. A lifelong interest in paintings and collecting has currently led him to experiments integrating the work of painters and sculptors into the design process and thereby into the permanent fabric of the building. `

CELLI, THOMAS C.
(Building Design, preservation, renovation)
Celli-Flynn & Assoc. (412) 281-9400
931 Penn Ave. Pittsburgh PA 15222

Born: 1944 **Studied:** Cornell University **Awards:** Arthur Ross Award from Classical America **Notable Works:** Completion of the Pennsylvania Capitol, addition to Blessed Sacrament Cathedral, Greensburg PA EDUCATION 45%, GOVERNMENT 15%, RELIGIOUS 15%, RESIDENTIAL 15%, TRANSIT 10%

Though trained in modernist design, he takes great pleasure in the last decade's return toward the classical aesthetic. The completion of the Italian Renaissance Pennsylvania Capitol centers on a $125 million dollar addition that blends neoclassical and postmodern elements. Interior atria are put to uses both new and old, serving as a public dining conservatory in one setting, as a contemplative garden for senators in another. Office spaces too show this blended conception of new and old, with elected representatives enjoying private panelled offices in one location, while staff and caucus areas are entirely open in another.

His addition to Pittsburgh's Taylor-Allderdeice High School, the city's public school for gifted students, similarly protects a familiar structure while updating it. Leaving the neoclassical facade inviolate, he built an under-

Philip Johnson and **John Burgee,** *AT&T Center* (with surrounding cityscape), New York City

Russell E. Cecil, Cecil, Pierce & Associates, Architects, *Private Residence*, Mamaroneck,New York, 1989.

ground addition entirely under the school's sloping front lawn, containing gymnasium, Olympic swimming pool and team rooms, all grade-accessible and nowhere rising more than 12 feet above grade. The new entrance features postmodern brick pilasters which sympathize with the older brick detailing of the main building.

CENTERBROOK ARCHITECTS (see Arbonies, Glenn; Floyd, Chad; Grover, William; Harper, Robert; Riley, Jefferson; Simon, Mark)

CERALDI, THEODORE M.

Theodore M. Ceraldi Architect (914) 353-1199
48 Burd Street Nyack NY 10960

Born: 1945 **Studied:** Cooper Union **Awards:** New York AIA; Contributor, American Graphics Standards, Eighth Edition; AIA **Notable Works:** Gainesway Farm, Lexington NY; Chancen Residence NY; Palace for Saud Bin Khalid, Riyadh, Saudi Arabia RESIDENTIAL 50%, COMMERCIAL 25%, FARMS 25%

His work is in vernacular idioms, including our American Indian traditions. He's delighted that the bombastic and aggrandizing ambitions of Modernism have been by and large relinquished. Modernism's monuments had become sculptures, not buildings "designed by people for people." He sees honesty and elegance in simple, well-proportioned structures and aims for the same in his own work.

Commissioned by horse breeder and art patron John Gaines to design a state of the art equine covering yard, he created a harmonious ensemble of buildings. The yard is made up of eight identical four-horse barns (for safety and grooming reasons), an exercise building and a large renovated barn to which a breeding shed is attached. Mares enter the breeding shed directly from transport vans at one end, and their partners come in from the opposite side.

The roof loads of the four-horse barns are carried on three-hinged laminated timber frames that provide clear-span interiors. These are separated from the masonry walls. At the base of the steeply pitched clay tile roofs, horizontal window slots are carefully positioned slightly above the horse's eye so that he can lift his head to look out, exercising his neck at the same time. Detailing is carefully wrought. He writes, "The only manifesto architecture requires is freedom; the only limitation is that of gravity. To understand freedom takes wisdom; to understand gravity takes time."

CHANN, EARL KAI
(Building Design)
Earl Kai Chann & Assoc. Ltd. (602) 325-5847
5232 East Pima St., Tucson AZ 85712

Born: 1933 **Studied:** North Carolina State University **Awards:** Arizona Society of Architects Energy Award; National Association of Minority Architects **Notable Works:** Mezo Environmental Quadruplex Unit; Crash Fire Rescue Facility-Tucson International Airport, AZ COMMERCIAL 50%, GOVERNMENT OR INSTITUTIONAL 40%

The southwestern deserts make unique functional demands, which he enjoys responding to. His Environmental Quadruplex Unit and the Marine Corps Air Station at Yuma solves two problems in a single stroke: Desert sun and airport noise both posed difficult housing problems on this marine base. He dug his quadruplex 5 feet into the earth, in an atrium design opening into sunken courtyards, with 20 inches of earth on top of the block and reinforced concrete structures. This design lowered energy consumption by 50 percent and eliminated complaints of airport noise.

CHARNEY, MARVIN
(Building Design, Exhibition Design)
3620 Marlowe Avenue Montreal Quebec H4A 3L7 Canada

Born: 1935 **Studied:** Yale University **Awards:** Member, Royal Architectural Institute of Canada; Member, Ordre des Architectes du Quebec **Notable Works:** proposed Canadian Air Force Museum, Trenton, Ontario; *Streetwork,* Art Gallery of Ontario, Toronto; *Corridart* street exhibition, Montreal

Russell E. Cecil, *Rapaport House,* Rye, New York, 1977. Photo: Russell E. Cecil

In 1969, he shocked the Canadian architectural community with his unorthodox deconstructed submission to the design competition for the Air Force museum at Trenton, Ontario. Rather than working toward a "Memorial Hall of History" as the competition guidelines had specified, he outlined a diffuse network of extant buildings, relics and sites which would collectively and organically represent the history of Canadian military aviation. Since 1970 he has extended the scope of his architectural experiments, moving well beyond the pale of conventional practice. Perhaps his most successful and provoking work was the mammoth Corridart exhibition, staged in Montreal during the 1976 Olympic Games. Buildings along five miles of Montreal's Sherbrooke Street were fitted with huge graphics, mounted on scaffolding, which portrayed the area's social and architectural history. Enormous pointing hands flagged significant but hidden features of the historic community. The project involved a dozen prominent local artists, and was so controversial that the Mayor of Montreal eventually ordered that it be completely destroyed.

CHERMAYEFF, SERGE IVAN
(Building Design)
Serge Chermayeff Architect (508) 532-4499
Box NN Gross Hill Road Wellfleet MA 02667

Born: 1900 **Studied:** Royal Drawing Society, London **Awards:** FAIA; Fellow, Royal Institute of British Architects **Notable Works:** Walter Horn House, Richmond CA; British Railways Office, Rockefeller Center, New York City; Chermayeff Studio, Wellfleet MA

In the 1920s he emerged as one of England's foremost modernists with the construction of several of that nation's first International Style buildings. He emigrated to the United States in the late 1930s and began a distinguished career as an academic and critic of architecture while continuing his professional practice. In his books, *Community and Privacy* and *The Shape of Community* (co- authored respectively with Christopher Alexander and Alexander Tzonis) he argued that the fundamental problem for architecture and community planning is the proper interrelation of public and private spaces. His primary design goal is to create separate, strongly delineated spaces for public and private (which is to say communal and solitary) functions which communicate with minimal friction. The fundamental function of the *community*, he asserts, is *communication*. Architecture is ultimately the design of spatial nodes and the communication channels that connect them. His own house embodies his design philosophy. It is assembled from a series of courtyards and pavilions which create a rhythmic alternation of public and private— open and closed—spaces.

CHONG, RICHARD D.
(Building Design, Programming, Historic Preservation, Redevelopment Planning)
Richard D. Chong & Associates
(801) 364-1797
248 Edison St. Salt Lake City UT 84111

Born: 1946 **Studied:** USC, UCLA **Awards:** Utah Heritage Foundation Project Award; AFLC Top Honor Award, US Air Force Design Awards Program **Notable Works:** Renovation of Independent Order of Oddfellows Hall, Salt Lake City, UT; Evanston, Wyoming Wastewater Treatment Facility MILITARY 40%, INSTITUTIONAL 20%, MEDICAL 20%, INDUSTRIAL 15%

He has no signature style, rather allowing each project's aesthetic to emerge from functional needs, influenced by his strong contextual sympathies. His Baker Shoe Building renovation, located next to a large municipal office building in downtown Salt Lake City, presented him with an old shoe store and warehouse, in the shade of a much larger building, which was to be converted to speculative office space. He hung a curtain wall three feet out from the the former face, which gave an interior view out over the street while creating a single glass element on the outside with visual weight to counterbalance its larger neighbor. He added articulated seismic bracing, and recessed the ground floor glass line by one full bay, thus opening the basement to natural light and exposing trusswork.

His Evanston, WY Wastewater Treatment Facility is in high plains desert, well out of town. The main buildings, enclosures and tanks are all in panelized natural concrete. Though natural surfaces tend to mottle and discolor unevenly, his strong shadow lines unify the structures and reduce such imperfections, while serving as expansion joints. Metal trim, both interior and exterior, is deep red, royal blue and bright yellow, thus uniting the program requirement for corrosion-resistance with human goals: the paint provides a lively motif for interior painting, and also creates a colorful showplace in which touring schoolchildren are introduced to the realities of waste management.

CIAMPI, MARIO JOSEPH
(Building Design)
Mario J. Ciampi and Associates
(415) 461-1683
617 Front Street San Francisco CA 94111

Born: 1907 **Studied:** Beaux-Arts Institute of Design, Paris **Awards:** FAIA; Collaborative Medal of Honor, Architectural League of New York **Notable Works:** Westmoor High School, Daly City CA; St. Peter's Roman Catholic Church, Pacifica CA; Art Museum, University of California at Berkeley

By the early 1950s an identifiable Bay Area regional style had emerged for residences and small public structures. But a comparable local architectural style for larger institutions was conspicuously absent until he undertook a series of public buildings in the San Francisco suburbs of Pacifica and Daly City. He exchanged the dark wood frames and pink stucco of his predecessors for colorful, durable materials like ceramic tile, steel and concrete-folded plates.

His Westmoor High School and Oceana High School buildings brought a taste of sophistication and international context to the architectural community of the Bay area, which some thought had become complacent and self-absorbed. He brought vitality, color and spaciousness to the designs of nearly a dozen Bay area educational institutions. Then the tides of fashion shifted again, bringing a flood of more orthodox, East Coast-inspired educational designs that pushed his work from favor.

He has gone on to design a number of major entertainment and exhibition spaces. The linked, clover-shaped galleries of his monolithic concrete Art Museum at the University of California at Berkeley are particularly noteworthy.

CLARK, H. STEVE
(Building Design, Renovation)
Dave Robinson (407) 567-5224
Vero Beach FL 32960

Born: 1947 **Studied:** Texas Tech University **Awards:** National School Board Association Conference **Notable Works:** Temple Baptist Church, Odessa TX; Ratliff Stadium, Odessa TX; First Savings and Loan Building, Odessa TX

He is a regionalist who makes use of modernist techniques where appropriate, to improve a building's aesthetic value and 'workability.' Opposed to egotism in architecture, his first priority is the owner. He believes that a building should be adaptable to growth and evolution; his designs often foresee and provide for subsequent additions. But, like growing crystals, his buildings are designed to hold their own forms even while they may grow, maintaining their identities down to the fine-tuned details experienced by visitors.

His Odessa TX Temple Baptist Church is a renovation of a 1950s church with a barrel-vaulted roof. He made the building's appearance more striking by extending it to the roadway, at the same time enlarging the bottom floor and interior space. The nave reaches up to a five-panelled glass block masonry unit which replaces a lobby partition. Four inches thick and translucent white, the glass block rises upward in full exterior view and frames a twelve-foot chrome cross. At night the glass glows from within when viewed from the highway; during the day sunlight penetrates the glass to illuminate the interior.

CLOVIS HEIMSATH ASSOCIATES (see Heimsath, Clovis and Maryann)

COBB, HENRY NICHOLS
(Building Design, Master Planning)
I. M. Pei & Partners (212) 751-3122
600 Madison Ave. New York NY 10022

Born: 1926 **Studied:** Harvard College; Harvard Graduate School of Design **Awards:** FAIA; Brunner Memorial Prize; NY AIA Medal of Honor **Notable Works:** Charles Shipman Payson Building/Portland Museum of Art, Portland ME; John Hancock Tower, Boston; Johnson & Johnson World Headquarters, New Brunswick NJ; Allied Bank Tower (now First Interstate), Dallas TX COMMERCIAL/CORPORATE 50%, INSTITUTIONAL/PUBLIC 35%, DEVELOPMENT PLANNING/URBAN DESIGN 15%

A recent Department of Architecture chairman at Harvard's Graduate School of Design, he has articulated in writing and teaching as well as building his philosophy that "every design initiative, at whatever scale, is a fragment embedded in a larger context, and neither the fragment nor the context can be well understood without reference to the other." In other words, buildings are creations and mirrors of social forces. They should be understood and designed as such. Some buildings have such hierarchic importance that their designs are properly 'autonomous' from, uninfluenced by, surrounding context. Other lesser buildings may be shaped entirely by their 'contingent' status with respect to neighbors.

His landmark John Hancock Tower in Boston exemplifies the play of these contradictory qualities. The Hancock Tower, 790 feet tall, is preeminently an assertion that Boston's largest private employer has a right to grow larger, even in the heart of a dense city. But in its form and conception the Tower responds to contradictory, almost equally powerful assertions made 700 feet below its summit, where historic Copley Square and Trinity Church had enjoyed primary status for 80 years. From lobby to summit the Tower defers to its relatively miniscule neighbors by presenting its mass as a pure surface, just a narrow, reflective two-dimensional plane which contrasts with and flatters Trinity Church's rich volumes and form. Yet the Tower's scale makes it a regional as well as a neighborhood presence. At the regional scale its local design contingencies have an ethereal, at times immaterial effect among metropolitan clouds and sky. Cobb says, "The Hancock Tower is significant not just because it solves a problem but equally because it *illustrates* a problem. I believe this is a legitimate role for architecture—to illustrate, with eloquence and precision, the uncomfortable paradoxes of our human condition."

CODY, GEORGE
(Building Design, Facility Programming, Interior Architecture, Renovation)
Cody Associates (415) 328-1818
941 Emerson Street Palo Alto CA 94301

Born: 1933 **Studied:** Stanford University **Awards:** AIA/Housing Magazine Award; *Sunset* magazine Western Home Award; National Merit Award, American Wood Council **Notable Works:** Cinnabar Winery, Saratoga Skyline Vineyards, Saratoga CA; 365 Forest Avenue, Palo Alto CA; 480 San Antonio Road, Mountain View CA COMMERCIAL 50%, RESIDENTIAL 50%

Besides client needs and budget restrictions, he concentrates on sites—what they offer and what they will become. He isn't interested in building "the jewel box that is the goal of a great many egos," and he tries to emphasize the good in surrounding architecture and create buildings of appropriate scale.

The five-story 365 Forest Avenue building in Palo Alto CA is set back from the sidewalk and leaves an L-shaped open area on the corner reflecting a similar opening in the building across the street. To give the long facade variety and movement, and to keep it from overwhelming surrounding buildings, three windows types are used, and balconies and projecting sections are varied with recessed sections. The site's narrow depth suggested a novel floor plan in which apartments are laid

Stuart Cohen, *Residence in Highland Park, Illinois* (with Anders Nereim).

out at a forty-five degree angle to the street front. The varied and adaptable rooms "read through" other spaces. The unusual layout gives the unit the charm of an old house, and the newcomer always wonders what's around the next corner.

COHEN, STUART E.

(Building Design, Interior Design, Urban Design)
Stuart Cohen & Associates (312) 939-2992
644 South Clark Street Chicago IL 60605

Born: 1942 **Studied:** Cornell University **Awards:** FAIA; Chicago AIA; Progressive Architecture award; One of 20 architects selected to represent the U.S. at the 1980 Venice Biennale **Notable Works:** Private Residences, Chicago's North Shore IL; 175 N. Franklin Building, Chicago RESIDENTIAL 85%, COMMERCIAL 15%

The term contextualism was first applied to architecture in the mid-1960's by Steven Hurtt and him. It was used to describe an aspect of the urban design teachings of their mentor at Cornell University, Colin Rowe. Modernism's utopian aspirations, exemplified in freestanding private, non- institutional buildings, were seen as destructive to the 'public domain' of streets, courts, plazas, greens, and courtyards. Contextualism arose out of seeing cities as both buildings and spaces; it was conceived as a set of strategies for building in cities and it proposed the continuity between adjacent buildings. Derived from the Latin contextus, meaning connection, contextualism eschews any a priori preference for particular architectural forms.

Traditionally a hierarchy of meanings in the city was provided by prominent building types which housed different, important functions. But virtually any function may now be contained in the preferred forms and types of modern architecture—the point block, the tower and the slab have eroded our hierarchy of symbolic function. Contextualism suggests that bold and monumental forms be reserved for structures that celebrate important public functions, and that private buildings be de-

signed as accretions to their surrounding environment. Forms, materials and details then emerge as extensions of the visual characteristics of the enveloping natural and built context. In the absence of a built context, one can explore local building traditions, vernacular forms and indigenous materials; in the absence of any architectural history one can proceed by analogy. In this light, contextualism is an empirical method for determining architectural form. It focuses formal typology and generously expands the limits of precedent.

His own work is deeply informed by the theory of contextualism. Concerns that inform much present architectural practice—the exploration of modern spaces, the passage of private to public space, and the effects of light and lighting—are very much his own also.

COLE AND GOYETTE, ARCHITECTS AND PLANNERS (see Cole, Doris; Goyette, Harold)

COLE, DORIS

(Building Design, Interior Architecture, Renovation)
Cole and Goyette, Architects and Planners Inc.
(617) 491-5662 540 Franklin St.
Cambridge MA 02138

Born: 1938 **Studied:** Harvard Graduate School of Design, Radcliffe College **Awards:** Illumination Engineering Society of North America International Illuminating Design Award; National Endowment of the Arts grant **Notable Works:** Damson & Greengage, Boston; Rafael Hernandez School Renovation, Roxbury MA; Private Residence, Westwood MA COMMERCIAL 25%, OFFICE 25%, RESIDENTIAL 25%, EDUCATIONAL 25%

With customized designs she aims to give physical form to the aspirations and feelings of her clients. Their styles of living and working are the genesis of her designs, which are informed as well by site and material constraints.

Her Scott/Jabaily residence in Westwood MA is a large renovated New England barn whose structural members dictated much of the finished design. The upper living floor is

Doris Cole, Cole and Goyette, Architects and Planners Inc., *Damson and Greengage at Boston Design Center*, 1987. Photo: William T. Smith

Eduardo Catalano, *Juilliard School of Music at Lincoln Center for Performing Arts* (With Pietro Belluschi), New York City. Photo: ESTO.

nestled among sloping walls and bearing beams whose pattern gives form to the arrangement of small activity centers—sleeping room, dressing room, sitting room and bath. But the central area of the upper level is open, exposing soaring structural beams to the living room below. A bridge crosses this space, connecting to a study at the other end of the house on the same level. Her renovation for the Rafael Hernandez School in Roxbury MA is a sensitive restoration of a 1920s public school building to meet the contemporary educational requirements of a bilingual elementary school. The classrooms, gymnasium, auditorium and cafeteria have brightly colored walls and refinished natural floors. Its original globe lights are incorporated into new custom designed lighting fixtures that retain the character of the historic school.

CONKLIN, WILLIAM

(Building Design, Historic Preservation)
Conklin Rossant (212) 777-2120
251 Park Avenue So. New York NY 10010

Born: 1923 **Studied:** Harvard University **Awards:** FAIA **Notable Works:** Butterfield House, New York City; Myriad Gardens, Oklahoma City OK RESIDENTIAL 50%, INSTITUTIONAL 50%

An architect, preservationist and archaeologist, he believes that architecture should integrate itself into the urban structure and fabric, providing space for social activities and meaning for human communities.

His New York City Butterfield House is integrated into its street context by capturing neighborhood essences rather than copying surrounding building features. Adapting the classic bay-window design of a nearby cast iron building, the house offers streamlined bay windows in vertical formation, highlighted by bands of limestone that run between window columns. Narrow limestone spandrels mark the floors between the windows, but the height of the windows dominates the spandrels, and in Modern fashion gives an effect of vertical columns of glass running the height of the seven-story structure. Within the building there is a landscaped interior garden. His

Oklahoma City OK Myriad Gardens is a four-block park in the downtown area which is sunken below grade to avoid strong winds. The excavated area provides civic facilities, plazas, waterways, and a lake. A cylindrical glass botanical bridge spans the lake. The overall effect of the park is of stylistically abstract buildings set in a modern oasis.

COOPER, ALEXANDER

(Building Design, Urban Design)
Cooper Robertson + Partners (212) 247-1717
311 W. 43rd St. New York NY 10036

Born: 1936 **Studied:** Yale University **Awards:** FAIA; Progressive Architecture award; Certificate of Merit, Municipal Arts Society; Bard Award **Notable Works:** Battery Park Proposal, New York City; City Front Center, Chicago; International Trade Center, Mount Olive NJ COMMERCIAL 50%, INSTITUTIONAL 50%

Current architecture, he feels, is withdrawn and insensitive to society, with the result that city life isn't improving. Since an increasing number of planners are trained in administrative rather than in engineering skills, contemporary urban planning has lost touch with the physical environment. He stresses the need for three kinds of practice: public sector experience, academic experience, and sensitivity to the owner's point of view. Art is a major influence on his designs, and his company frequently works with artists, for example when ideas are needed for park sculptures or interior paintings. His career has moved from an interest in buildings to a concentration on background architecture—architecture that emphasizes urban spaces and streets.

His proposal for Battery Park City in New York approaches Battery Park as an extension of lower Manhattan. A road and park system, covering a mile and a half of landfill, establishes graceful streets and open spaces as the primary quality to which future building projects will be subordinated. The design also calls for combining residential living and workplaces. Public walkways extend from the Battery Park esplanade to lower Manhattan. A

Warren J. Cox, *National Permanent Building,* Washington, D.C. Photo: Robert Lautman.

large performance area contains recreational fields and a spectator area, surrounded by a heavily wooded ring of parkland which is punctuated with battlement-topped towers and colonnades. Artists will work with architects and landscape architects in ongoing improvements of Battery Park City.

COX, WARREN JACOB
(Building Design)
Hartman-Cox Architects (202) 333-6446
1071 Thomas Jefferson Street NW
Washington DC 20007

Born: 1935   **Studied:** Yale University **Awards:** FAIA; Louis Sullivan Prize **Notable Works:** Dodge Center, Washington DC; National Humanities Center, Raleigh NC; Folger Shakespeare Library, Wahington DC COMMERCIAL: 40%, INSTITUTIONAL: 35%, EDUCATIONAL: 5%

His work is distinguished by its diversity rather than any set design vocabulary. His commissions with partner George E. Hartman have ranged from hotels to houses, libraries to jails. Each requires a unique treatment, he believes, specific to its peculiar demands. To extend an overarching aesthetic lexicon to unrelated projects seems to him arrogant and irresponsible.

He and Hartman were among the first and most prominent defectors from the modernist camp, but they shrink from the label 'postmodernist.' Their aim is to work comfortably with a wide variety of idioms, as architects did in past eras. Modernism, he complains, relies on an inadequate spatial vocabulary of only five basic shapes. This artificially narrow lexicon makes it impossible to achieve optimal designs. But postmodernism's self-conscious frippery isn't an appropriate response to the problem.

They eschew radically unstructured design approaches, preferring molded spaces to free-flowing forms which they perceive as ill-defined. The barrel vaulted spine of their Folger Library is at once a rejection of modernism and an endorsement of classical spatial delineation.

CRANE, DAVID ALFORD
(Urban Design)
David A. Crane and Partners
1316 Arch Street Philadelphia PA 19107

Born: 1927   **Studied:** Harvard University **Notable Works:** General Plan for Boston and the Boston Regional Core, 1961- 65; Master Plan for Fort Lincoln, Washington DC; Plan For Sadat City, Egypt

As Director of Planning for the city of Boston he was responsible for several site developments, but the bulk of his energies went toward the creation of the General Plan for Boston and its regional core. This plan was exceptional for targeting areas well beyond Boston's city limits, for including a great number of practical financial details as well as physical plans, and— most exceptional—for being ratified and widely implemented.

In 1965 he became a professor at the University of Pennsylvania, where he chaired the graduate department of Civic Design. Shortly afterwards he founded David A. Crane and Partners with several junior associates and went on to complete a number of well-known large-scale urban design projects, including the new community of Fort Lincoln outside Washington DC. Recent projects contain a number of distinctive common elements, including the use of a strongly diagonal grid system.

CYWINSKI, BERNARD
(Building Design)
Bohlin Powell Larkin Cywinski (215) 592-0600
12 South 12th Street Philadelphia PA 19107

Born: 1940 **Studied:** Columbia University **Awards:** Silver Medal, Pennsylvania AIA **Notable Works** (also see Peter Bohlin): Software Engineering Institute,Carnegie Mellon University, Pittsburg PA EDUCATIONAL 40%, GOVERNMENTAL 15% ,COMMERCIAL 10%, NON-PROFIT 15%, CORPORATE 20%

His architecture and that of his firm is broadly contextualist. It is exemplified in their recent

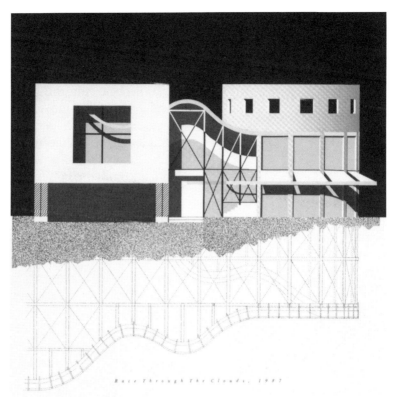

Race Through The Clouds, 1987

Steven D. Ehrlich, *Windward Circle* (Sketch), Venice, California

Warren J. Cox (with Craig Hartman), *National Humanities Center*, Washington, D.C. Photo: Robert Lautman

award-winning design (in conjunction with Burt Hill Kosar Rittlemann Associates) for the Software Engineering Institute, located in Pittsburgh's academic and cultural center. Of comparable scale to its neighbors, their design employs a massive granite base punctuated with vertical windows. The base parallels the rhythm and scale of the adjoining Mellon Institute, with its limestone colonnade and entablature atop a granite podium. The first floor walls are covered with limestone cladding. Above it stands a segmented two-color glass curtainwall aligned with the cornice of the Mellon Institute. The SEI's facade employs various mullion sizes and glass colors to repeat the rhythm established by Mellon Institute's massive vertical columns. However, because this rhythm has been rendered in glass curtain wall, it achieves a lightness and delicacy of scale that relates to the tracery of St. Paul's Cathedral across the street. As a contrasting response to St. Paul's Cathedral, a curved inflection in the SEI's northeast corner creates an open space and provides a suitable backdrop for the limestone entrance pavilion.

The entrance pavilion, with doors at either end, serves as both the front and rear entrance to the building. The pavilion is aligned axially with St. Paul's Cathedral and is clad in similar limestone. A wisteria-covered arbor enhances the stone, metal, and glass environment. Joining the arbor columns are rolled structural shapes with exposed bolts, an allusion to the heavy industry so central to Pittsburgh's past.

DATTNER, RICHARD
(Building Design, Exhibition Design, Interior Architecture)
Richard Dattner Architect P.C.
(212) 247-2660
Carneigie Hall Studios 154 W. 57th St.
New York NY 10019

Born: 1937 **Studied:** Massachusetts Institute of Technology; Architectural Association, London **Awards:** FAIA; AIA; New York City Art Commision award; Computer Images in Architecture Award, New York AIA **Notable Works:** Estee Lauder Laboratories, Long Island NY; Public School, PS-234, New York City; Consolidated Edison Offices, Bronx NY COMMERCIAL 20%, EDUCATIONAL/INSTTUTIONAL 20%, PUBLIC 60%

It has become more difficult to practice architecture, he feels, though it remains vitally important to the quality of our lives. The complexity of architectural practices arises from factors that once were relatively unimportant: proliferating regulations, greater environmental sensitivity, new zoning requirements, etc.; yet limits can inspire creative solutions.

Commissioned to build a "simple functional design—avoiding any impression of wasteful expenditure of customer's money" by Consolidated Edison, he designed a "not groovy" yet sturdy two-story structure in the thriving working class neighborhood of Westchester Square in the Bronx. The scored-concrete-block building acknowledges public and private functions with separate entrances: a mildly grand, brightly daylit double-height vestibule is for customers and office workers, and a less grand stairway goes to a basement area for meter readers. Aluminum brise-soleil on the top- floor windows, and deep recesses for the big ground-floor windows on the south facade, announce Con Ed's advocacy of energy-conscious design.

Appointed by a mayoral task force in New York City to create a school design appropriate for various sites, he proposed an innovation in the design of classroom modules. He substituted a curving wing for the usual rectangular element so that it could be set against a larger rectangular central wing to create an intimate courtyard. His design promises to reassert the civic and architectural importance of school buildings without being alienating or overbearing.

DeMARS, VERNON ARMAND
(Building Design, Landscape Architecture, Urban Design)
Vernon DeMars Architect (415) 654-5078
240 The Uplands Berkeley CA 94705

Born: 1908 **Studied:** University of California

at Berkeley **Awards:** FAIA; American Society of Landscape Architects; Association of American Universities **Notable Works:** Golden Gateway Redevelopment, San Francisco; Student Center, University of California at Berkeley; Aster Park, Sunnyvale CA

He tries to design settings for social events, interactions and activities that will work as do stages that provide settings for shows. A proper stage, he believes, isn't completely self-effacing. It should provide an accent or enhancement to any proceeding, but stop short of novelty which calls attention directly to itself.

He argues that early modern buildings were successful because they contrasted sharply with their environs. Today's homogeneous blocks of glass boxes, sadly lacking that contrast, have become boring. He self-consciously works toward a broader formal vocabulary and a design methodology which leaves room for "accidental," seemingly spontaneous features. His best-known experiment with this unity in diversity is his four-building Student Center at the University of California at Berkeley. The four buildings—a student union, a 2000-seat theater, a central cafeteria and an 8-story office tower—are sited symmetrically around a huge sunken square and plaza, each maintaining a strongly separate stylistic identity. None of the buildings dominates; scales, geometries, and materials diverge in direct response to functional roles and each building's relations with adjacent structures and landscape breaks. The effect of this controlled chaos within the larger architectural palimpsest of UC Berkeley is to distract focus from particular buildings, whether they be virtuosic or merely necessary, and to direct attention instead into the plaza which has become the social center of the warm-weather campus.

DeSTEFANO, JAMES R.
(Building Design)
Skidmore, Owings and Merrill
(312) 641-5959
230 East Ohio Street Chicago IL 60602

Born: 1938 **Studied:** Illinois Institute of Technology **Awards:** FAIA; Restoration Award, Chicago AIA **Notable Works:** Caterpillar Training Center, Peoria, Illinois; Masterplan, University of Illinois at Chicago; Orchestra Hall Renovation, Chicago

He is a versatile and resourceful designer, who has risen to the rank of general partner in his twenty-five year association with Skidmore, Owings and Merrill. Since his collaboration with Walter Netsch on the masterplan for the commuter campus of the University of Illinois at Chicago Circle, in 1965, his work has displayed an increasing tendency toward modularity. This is particularly evident in his 1981 design for Caterpillar Tractor Corporation's headquarters in Peoria, Illinois. The complex is centered around a long, two-story structure whose space is largely devoted to laboratory facilities. Identical modules housing offices, classrooms and individual labs are lined symmetrically along a diagonal spine, which is skylit to emphasize its status as the building's primary thoroughfare.

De VIDO, ALFREDO
(Building Design, Renovation, Interior Architecture)
Alfredo De Vido Associates (212) 355-7370
699 Madison Ave. New York, NY 10021

Born: 1932 Education: Carnegie-Mellon University; Princeton University **Awards:** FAIA; New York AIA; Bard Award, City Club of New York **Notable Works:** Matthews House; 222 Columbia Heights, Brooklyn Heights NY; Community Church of Astoria, Queens NY

While acknowledging that one can't invent the wheel every week, he aims to find solutions that are innovative and buildable on a reasonable budget and timetable. Working in high-density urban areas, he feels that one shouldn't mimic historical styles, but promote liveliness in facades by recalling traditional details. This may mean pulling out elements such as pitched roofs for residences and emphasizing them through strong geometric shapes.

His Community Church of Astoria in Queens NY is in a poor neighborhood with a high rate of vandalism. Faced with the challenge of building a symbolic structure on a small budget, he used concrete block in a variety of textures and glazes for both interior and exterior. In lieu of fragile stained glass the church is illuminated using translucent white fiberglass with a tracery design in its reinforced ribs. In the four years since its completion, the church has yet to be damaged.

In his residential work he prefers natural materials, especially wood. The exterior of his Matthews house is designed around an articulated interior, while the DeVido residence is centered around a rough-hewn living room which influences the design of the rest of the rooms.

DIAMOND, ABEL JOSEPH
(Urban Design, Building Design)
A.J. Diamond and Associates
322 King Street West
Toronto Ontario M5V IJ4 Canada

Born: 1922 **Studied:** University of California at Los Angeles Extension Division **Awards:** Member, Royal Architectural Institute of Canada; Canada Council Grant **Notable Works:** Innis College, University of Toronto; York Square, Toronto; Le Breton Flats, Ottawa

He takes on a wide variety of projects, from major urban planning to small-scale residential interior renovations. He's particularly noted for pioneering designs of infill housing for tightly restrictive sites, for reconfiguring existing structures for new uses and for his innovative high density yet low-rise group housing for sensitive communities. He pays attention to the social meaning and impact of his work, maintaining that buildings must be viewed as organic consequences of the needs and habits of users, rather than analytic extensions of physical and aesthetic principles. He's committed to preserving the human scale in buildings of all sizes, and to signalling their continuity with the American agrarian architectural tradition. His recent work is distinguished by its functionalism. His La Cantinetta restaurant in Toronto makes graceful use of exposed brick- and duct-work and large industrial lighting.

Di GERONIMO, LOUIS AND SUZANNE (Building Design, Interior Architecture, Planning)
Architects DiGeronimo (201) 670-9200
12 Sunflower Ave. Paramus NJ 07652

Born: 1941, 1947 **Studied:** Cooper Union, Columbia University **Awards:** NJAIA **Notable Works:** Lincoln Tunnel Emergency Garage Extension, Weehawken NJ; Mantoloking residence, Mantoloking NJ; US Post Office, Pompton Plains NJ INSTITUTIONAL 40%, COMMERCIAL 30%, OFFICE 20%, INDUSTRIAL 10%

They work in a densely urban environment where green-field design isn't possible. Sensitive to the communities, streets and neighbors that their buildings will stand among, they like to use building materials as well as design motifs from the locales they're building for. They once reopened a local quarry for a purple pudding stone church project.

Their Mantoloking residence restoration is on the shore of a Victorian-era beach community whose huge homes are too big for modern families. A large frame house surrounded by similarly massed structures, the Mantolokin residence was adapted to contemporary tastes by carving long balconies *into* the original exterior wall line. From the living spaces within, glass walls give onto these inset balconies and the shore views beyond.

Their Lincoln Tunnel Emergency Garage Extension in Weehawken NJ is located at the mouth of the heavily used tunnel, where police personnel and emergency vehicles have immediate access. But its location at the inland base of a coastal hill cradles heavy car exhaust, and a positive-pressure fresh air system for the new facilities was necessary. Air is brought from the hilltop via a hollow fluted granite tower which duplicates the tunnel's two landmark light towers. The new tower stands between them.

DINSMORE, PHILIP W.

Louis and Suzanne Di Geronimo, *Lincoln Tunnel Emergency Garage Extension*
1983, Weehawken, New Jersey.

(Building Design, Facility Programming)
Architecture One, Ltd. (602) 722-0400
6303 E. Tanque Verde Tucson AZ 85715
Born:1942 **Studied:** University of Arizona
Awards: AIA **Notable Works:** Southern
Arizona Operations Center, Southwest Gas
Corporation, Tucson AZ EDUCATIONAL
50%, COMMERCIAL 25%, INDUSTRIAL
25%

He makes extensive use of current technology.
His buildings respond to the desert environment and materials used are energy- efficient
and comfortable. Shades and shadows figure
prominently in his designs, and the south sides
of his buildings tend to be recessed behind
overhanging roof or floor lines to shield them
from the sun. Dramatic visual effects are also
created by the calculated play of shadows. But
his projects are diverse in style, because he
believes that buildings develop different "vocabularies" depending on client needs.

His Tucson AZ Operations Center consists
of two buildings, one housing public and
administration functions, the other maintenance and workshop areas. In both buildings
the organizing element is the spine, which is a
long vaulted corridor in the administration
building. The glass- and steel-framed vault
expresses the building's structural frame as
well as organizing circulation and collecting
sunlight. Open offices complement the airy
spaciousness of the corridors.

DORMAN, RICHARD L.
(Building Design, Interior Architecture, Landscape Architecture)
Dorman/Breen (505) 982-9196
1512 Paseo de Peralta Santa Fe NM 87501

Born: 1922 **Studied:** University of Southern
California **Awards:** AIA; Western States AIA
Notable Works: Sperry Flight Systems, Al-
buquerque NM; First Interstate Bank, Sante Fe
NM; Channel Two Television Station, Santa
Fe NM MIXED COMMERCIAL/RETAIL
70%, RESIDENTIAL 10%, RECREATION
10%

For thirty years a Los Angeles architect with a
glass and steel Modernist vocabulary, in 1975
he moved to the small "Flintstone Modern"
city of Santa Fe NM, whose adobe origins are
expressed in increasingly aggressive regionalist zoning. Flat roofs, small window openings,
white stucco and exposed wood trim are among
the design elements which are awarded necessary zoning points throughout Santa Fe county.
His Channel Two Television Station in Sante
Fe sculpts negative spaces from its 3-level
white stucco mass by insetting ground floor
walls behind columns at the upper wall line.
The south wall has a solar panel which assists
the heating of an interior two-level entranceway. Not visible from the outside, the lofty
entrance and other interior spaces feature
exposed metal joists and ductwork.

DOWNING, WILLIAM S.
(Building Design, Historic Preservation,
Renovation)
Downing/Hascup Associates (607) 273-6464
215 N. Cayuga St. Ithaca NY 14850

Born: 1920 **Education:** University of Vir-
ginia; New York
University **Awards:** New York AIA; DuPont
Teaching Fellowship OFFICE 60% INDUS-
TRIAL 20% INSTITUTIONAL 20%

A regionalist, his approach is contextual, responding to the immediate community and to
the contemporary demands of the small city
where he lives.

For his Ithaca NY Youth Bureau, he wanted
to combine the community's rural yet sophisticated university setting with an expressive-
ness inviting to youth. He chose a gabled roof
and glass and stucco exterior. Neither new
wave nor postmodern, this selection instead
strives for coherency in its references to other
nearby buildings and its deemphasis on institutional characteristics. Siting the gabled ends
to overlook Cayuga Lake, the interior is organized around a courtyard pavilion. This 2-story
mezzanine contains a skylit winter garden and
is adjacent to a theater and multi-purpose room
which houses sports facilities. An exterior
amphitheater provides seasonal alternatives

Louis and Suzanne Di Geronimo, *Lincoln Tunnel Emergency Garage Extension*
1983, Weehawken, New Jersey.

Robert Ferris, *Keiller Elementary School*, San Diego, California, 1965.

for programming activities.

His design for the Tompkins County Mental Health Services Building, also in Ithaca NY, combines contemporary expression with historic references to the work of William Henry Miller, Cornell's first professor of architecture and a major influence in downtown Ithaca. Miller's use of red brick and limestone is combined with a contemporary tower which celebrates the corner entranceway. Considering well-lit interior space as essential to mental health, a winter garden with a skylight was designed as a one-story addition to the 6-story building.

DOWNS, BARRY
(Building Design)
Downs/Archambault
1272 Richards Street
Vancouver British Columbia Canada

Born: 1929 **Studied:** University of Washington at Seattle **Awards:** Fellow, Royal Architectural Institute of Canada; Academician, Royal Canadian Academy of the Arts **Notable Works:** North Vancouver Civic Center; Lester Parson College of the Pacific, Vancouver Island BC; Gymnasium/Arts Complex, York School, Vancouver

Architecture, he argues, can't be cloistered from social and human demands. To plan any design program end-users as well as clients and planning authorities must see their needs identified and met. His firm maintains a continuing dialogue with users in which project architects and engineers make basic suggestions about overt design features and provide information about physical and financial resources and construction techniques. This sharing, he believes, helps his work to stay fresh and malleable, and lends a human scale even to his largest undertakings. A sense of the cozy and homelike within the large characterizes his work. His work with such an identifiable design-gestalt has led to charges that he superimposes his own preconceived ideas of social needs on his projects, rather than polling affected communities sincerely.

DOYLE, DEBORAH
Born: 1952 **Studied:** Illinois Institute of Technology **Notable Works:** Tackbary House, Walner House and Walner House Addition, London; Kanarish Residence, Deerfield IL

Her architectural training and experience includes work and teaching not only in the United States but in England and France as well; her designs reveal a similarly eclectic style. In the design for the Kanarish residence in Deerfield, Illinois, she presents seven alternative approaches to the problem of adding to a private residence. Each of the seven alternatives offers unique design features within a consistent Post-Modern style emphasizing the square and the circle. Several of the alternatives include sympathetic, symmetrical landscaping in addition to the cubical structure to be added to the house. This approach from many angles to a solitary problem simultaneously allows the client a number of possibilities, reveals a facility and flexibility with the medium and an impressive breadth of knowledge, and deals with the issue of making a distinctive architectural statement with an addition to a fairly commonplace residential structure in a mundane suburban setting.

DUBOIS, MACY
(Building Design)
Dubois and Associates 76 Richmond Street East Toronto Ontario Canada

Born: 1929 **Studied:** Harvard University **Awards:** Fellow, Royal Architectural Institute of Canada; Academician, Royal Canadian Academy of the Arts **Notable Works:** Toronto City Hall (with John Andrews); Sarnia Opera House, Sarnia, Ontario; Joseph Shepard Building (Government of Canada Offices)

His goal is to satisfy particular practical requirements while extending the state of the art. His design process reacts to the physical demands of a site, prevailing climate, and available indigenous materials as well as financial and physical restrictions. He often uses 'found' materials from the communities surrounding his sites, giving many buildings a distinctive Northwestern regional character.

Since temperature and precipitation are usually severe in his work areas, he avoids fashionable flourishes and searches for durable and predictable materials and methods. He feels great admiration for the creative work of past eras, but little temptation to duplicate it. He's committed to building socially responsive structures and argues that a social concept must always precede an architectural one, for a project can only succeed if it benefits its full community. In his design for the Government of Canada office building in Ontario his enormous open atrium has long, low overhangs that suggest a series of lushly forested terraces.

DURA, ARTHUR U.
(Building Design, Specifications)
Dura & Associates (701) 251-2284
400 2nd Ave SW Jamestown ND 58401

Born: 1931 **Studied:** North Dakota State University **Awards:** AIA; 1st Place, State of North Dakota Barrier Free Design **Notable Works:** Stutsman County Courthouse, Jamestown ND; City/County Law Enforcement & Correctional Center, Jamestown ND; First Federal Savings & Loan, Jamestown ND COMMERCIAL 40%, INDUSTRIAL 20%, INSTITUTIONAL 40%

His buildings are designed with both efficiency and sense of purpose in mind. Preferring masonry and pre-cast concrete as materials, his low-lying structures use a modernist aesthetic, their form embodying the function they are intended to perform.

His Stutsman County Courthouse and adjacent City/County Law Enforcement & Correctional Center in Jamestown ND, like his projected Jamestown City Hall, are designed to emphasize their individual roles in the community. The Correctional Center's bronze-tinted strip windows obscure their inside bars, yet its substantial pre-cast concrete massing conveys a sense of containment. Warm bright colors inside counteract the building's institutional nature and a recreation area on the roof provides fresh air for inmates while maintaining downtown security.

His Courthouse design is monumental, with an emphasis on efficiency and modernity as well as forthrightness. High-ceilinged interiors give a sense of grandeur and paneling in the courtrooms are a traditional means of evoking the dignity of the proceedings.

ECKBO-KAY ASSOCIATES (see Eckbo, Garrett; Esherick, Joseph; Wolf, Harry Charles)

ECKBO, GARRETT
(Landscape Architecture)
Eckbo-Kay Associates
1045 Sansome Street Suite 302 San Francisco CA 94111

Born: 1910 **Studied:** Harvard University **Awards:** Fellow, American Society of Landscape Architects, International Federation of Landscape Architects, and American Institute of Planners **Notable Works:** Jose' del Valle Park, Lakewood CA; Master Plan for Baylands, Palo Alto CA (with Kenneth Kay); Plan For Sausalito CA waterfront

One of the nation's foremost theoreticians and practitioners of landscape architecture, his design philosophy for gardens, plazas, parks and other urban landscapes always stresses the interpenetration of natural and crafted elements. He is a harsh critic of the rapid and often mercenary high-density urbanization of the post-war era, but finds suburbanization a sterile alternative. His design goal is to link the modern, over-industrialized urban sprawl to its rural past through a series of accessible and strategically located common meeting areas.

He is often credited with developing the 'California-style' park, which uses trees, fences and posts to screen visual and aural intrusions of urban turmoil, while suggesting leisure living with long patios and small, rolling hills. His Jose' del Valle Park in Lakewood CA is perhaps his prototypical 'oasis within the city.'

EDWARDS, RICHARD W.
(Building Design, Construction Administration, Specifications, Project Management)
Langwith, Wilson, King Associates, Inc.

(713) 621-1890
17 S. Briar Hollow, #100 Houston TX 77027

Born: 1947 **Studied:** University of Arkansas **Awards:** selected for school architecture exhibition by American Association of School Administrators and AIA **Notable Works:** Waterford Harbor Yacht Club, League City TX; TPC Golf Clubhouse, The Woodlands TX INSTITUTIONAL 60%, COMMERCIAL 20%, OFFICE 10%, RESIDENTIAL 10%

He has no signature style, rather discovering his designs by listening to his clients' needs and actively involving them in every phase of their project from conception to completion.

His TPC Clubhouse was built in two phases. This satellite clubhouse for a new golf course first required cart storage space and car parking; a year later the cart parking became a platform for the new clubhouse, which is designed to blend in with its woodland setting. The cart park below is concealed with natural stone walls and columns, and fences and siding on the golf course side, while on the parking-lot side the lot itself is bermed up above the cart park, with pedestrian access to the clubhouse via a bridge over the cart track. Nestled among surrounding woods, the clubhouse is composed of long, low elements in glass and wood, with broad overhanging eaves protecting low glass windows from the sun. A strong band of high windows along the clubhouse second floor also emphasizes its low and horizontal character.

EHRENKRANTZ, EZRA
(Building Design)
The Ehrenkrantz Group (212) 730-1950
19 West 44 Street New York NY 10036
855 Front Street San Francisco CA 94111

Born: 1933 **Studied:** University of Liverpool **Awards:** *American Builder* Innovation in Building Award; *Engineering News Record* Construction Man of the Year **Notable Works:** School Constructions Systems Development Pilot Unit, Stanford CA; Delaveaga Elementary School, Santa Cruz CA; Interdisciplinary Resource Center, Pratt Institute, Brooklyn NY COMMERCIAL/RETAIL: 19%, HOUSING: 14% INDUSTRIAL: 3%, EDUCATION: 4%, PLANNING: 15% CRIMINAL JUSTICE: 23% OTHER: 22%

He gained international attention in 1964 with his scheme to use standardized, pre-fabricated components to assemble affordable buildings for California's public school system. Easily adaptable, they retained a sense of solidity and architectural uniqueness. The prototype for his School Construction Systems Development in Stanford was hailed as something of an aesthetic marvel. It was quickly followed by full-scale installations at Santa Cruz and San Jose. Non-standard exterior walls gave a custom finish to each building, while pre-fab interior wall systems ensured easy adaptability at minimum expense. In the 1970s he expanded his horizons with three commissions for major multi-use college sites. The most challenging and interesting of these projects was his Interdisciplinary Resource Center at Brooklyn NY's Pratt Institute. His design featured a massive hyperbolic paraboloid roof which covered the clear span of an upper-level gymnasium, and an innovative cooling system which conserved energy by tapping the icy waters of an underground stream.

EHRLICH, STEVEN
(Building Design)
Steven Ehrlich Architects (213) 399-7711
76 Market St. Venice CA 90291

Born: 1946 **Studied:** Rensselaer Polytechnic Institute **Awards:** California AIA; Los Angeles AIA; one of *LA Times Magazine*'s "89 For 89" **Notable Works:** Miller House, Los Angeles; Kalfus Studio, Los Angeles; Windward Circle, Venice CA COMMERCIAL 40%, RESIDENTIAL 40%, CIVIC 20%

In his designs he looks for intrinsic, pure solutions to design problems, which point the way to the future. His residential designs seek to create Zen environments of serenity and replenishment, using for example waterfalls threading indoors and out which wash over the noise pollution of the congested Los Angeles basin. His commercial designs tend in the opposite direction, recapitulating the commercial chaos that is also Los Angeles. His Windward Circle commercial revitalization development in downtown Venice CA is a collage of elements from the site's past brought together in a contemporary composition. The site, around what was once a lagoon at the intersection of several canals, is now a traffic circle. In Venice's salad days an amusement park was on the site; he has recreated roller coaster tracks through one store and around the development. The Ace Market Place 3-story retail center, facing the circle, is topped with a large mechanical device reminiscent of the steam shovels used to dredge the Venice canals. Now the motif is redefined as a marquee which announces stores inside.

EISENMAN, PETER

(Building Design)
Eisenman Robertson Architects
(212) 645-1400
560 Fifth Avenue New York NY 10036

Born: 1932 **Studied:** Columbia University **Awards:** Brunner Prize; Guggenheim Fellowship; Graham Foundation Fellowship **Notable Works:** Frank House, Cornwall CT; House lV, Falls Village CT COMMERCIAL/RETAIL: 35%, HOUSING: 5% INDUSTRIAL: 35%, EDUCATION: 5%, PLANNING: 15% OTHER: 5%

As founder of New York City's Institute for Architecture and Urban Studies he has been one of the most influential and caustic critics of contemporary architecture. He believes that the bitter fruits of 'machinism,' such as modular design and production, repetition, and prefabrication, have ritualized and trivialized man's environment, leaving us unexpectant and numb. His architecture attempts to reawaken humanity's dormant awareness of our physical world. He uses discomfort, shock, abrasion and incongruity to achieve his effects, forthrightly designing against the basic comfort and needs of clients. He builds columns that hang inches short of the ground, lampooning their usual structural role; stairs without railings; and glass walls facing hot southern exposures. Such "niceties" as show-

ers and kitchens are often omitted.

His 1972 Frank House is typical of his confrontational approach. It has doorways that can only be penetrated sideways, stairs too low to climb without ducking, and obtrusive columns which parse already small rooms into virtually unusable spaces. Only by creating a tactilely hostile architecture, he believes, can we awaken ourselves to the made spaces which we will always inhabit.

ELLWOOD, CRAIG

(Building Design, Cost Estimation)
7488 Mulholland Drive
Los Angeles CA 90046

Born: 1922 **Studied:** University of California at Los Angeles **Awards:** First Prize, Collective Dwellings, International Exhibition of Architecture; AIA; Los Angeles Beautiful Award **Notable Works:** Arts Center College of Design, Pasadena CA; Courtyard Apartments, Hollywood, Los Angeles; Scientific Data Systems manufacturing plants, El Segundo CA

He began his career as a cost estimator for a major construction company. After two years he shocked his employers by establishing his own design practice. Within another five he was recognized as one of the most world's most creative architects. It's been said that much of his success derives from the consummate mastery of materials that he brought to his second profession. His fluency with steel and glass construction freed him to develop a cohesive aesthetic while others struggled with technicalities. Hale House, one of his earliest commissions, was a virtuoso study in steel which used extensive flash-gap detailing. But his four-building Hollywood CA Courtyard Apartments is considered his first truly mature work. It was his first use of the exposed warren trusses which were to became his signature.

In the 1960s, in the face of the gathering reaction against hard-edged modernism, he immersed himself in Miesian functionalism. He solicited large-scale commissions and began building externally trussed steel cages in earnest. His most remarkable effort was the strongly horizontal Art Center College of Design in Pasadena CA, which gently crosses a flat landscape until it juts across a shallow valley, bolstered by two sets of parallel warren trusses.

ERICKSON, ARTHUR CHARLES
(Building Design, Urban Planning)
Arthur Erickson Architects (213) 278-1915
125 North Robertson Blvd.
Los Angeles CA 90048

Born: 1924 **Studied:** McGill University **Awards:** Honorary FAIA; Fellow, Royal Canadian Academy of Arts; Companion, Order of Canada **Notable Works:** Simon Fraser University, Burnaby, British Columbia; Sikh Temple, Vancouver; Arts, Sciences and Technology Centre, Vancouver COMMERCIAL/RETAIL: 68%, HOUSING: 2% OTHER INSTITUTIONAL: 25%, PLANNING: 5%

Philip Johnson dubbed him "the greatest architect in Canada," suggesting that he may also be the greatest on the continent. He draws this praise for a consistent material and formal austerity, rather than obvious virtuosity or ostentation. He is opposed to all exterior ornamentation, even simple board frameworks, which he regards as a subtle brand of aesthetic subterfuge. Like many of his contemporaries, he believes that a building's design should follow directly from its function and its context—what he would call respectively the 'pressure from within' and the 'pressure from without.' He's exceptional in giving these pressures equal importance. A site so colors and pervades what is built on it, he feels, that any building form is meaningless without considering it. His work is characterized by spare facades and sweeping, dominant horizontals. His most famous design, a covered mall for Simon Fraser University (with Simon Fraser and Jeffrey Lindsay), established his talent for elegant, planar construction. The primary mall complex, built of composite wood, steel and glass, juts across the twin peaks of a small mountain. Between the peaks he concealed a vehicular underpass and a pared-down entrance to the pedestrian campus which adjoins the mall.

ESHERICK, JOSEPH
(Building Design)
Esherick Homsey Dodge and Davis
(415) 285-9193
2789 25th Street
San Francisco California 94110

Born: 1914 **Studied:** University of Pennsylvania **Awards:** Fellow, AIA; *Progressive Architecture* Award, 1974; Associate, National Academy of Design; Gold Medal for Lifetime Achievement, AIA **Notable Works:** Wurster Hall, University of California, Berkeley; Pan American Boarding Office B, San Francisco; United States Embassy, La Paz, Bolivia COMMERCIAL/RETAIL: 18%, HOUSING: 5%, EDUCATION: 25%, MEDICAL: 2% PLANNING: 20% OTHER: 5%

He disputes the Bauhaus assertion that modernist design methodologies are analogous to industrial processes. He argues that their approaches derive from machinist aesthetics, not meaningful functionalism. A truly scientific and systematic approach to architecture, in his view, can't prescribe modular construction or any other normative program. The solutions to architectural problems must flow analytically from the peculiar circumstances of each task. So his approach to real-world design tasks is utilitarian, even opportunistic. He scorns the use of aesthetic metrics in the primary design process, yet this very inattention creates a distinctive, incongruous aesthetic of its own. In his Wurster Hall at the University of California at Berkeley the interaction of exposed plumbing, ventilation and electrical conduits with cool, smooth, unadorned concrete walls in the main hallways creates a tangled, urban jungle-scape.

EVERTON, GARY L.
(Building Design, Architectural Delineation, Facility Programming, Renovation)
Tuck Hinton Everton Architects
(615) 320-1810
1810 Hayes St. Nashville TN 37203

Born: 1953 **Studied:** University of Tennessee

Awards: Tennessee AIA; Builder's Choice Grand Prize; Metropolitan Historical Commission awards **Notable Works:** The Village at Vanderbilt, Vanderbilt University, Nashville TN; Customs House rehabilitation, Nashville TN; Schulman, LeRoy & Bennett offices, Nashville TN RESIDENTIAL 30%, OFFICE 25%, COMMERCIAL 20%

He aims to draw and exemplify lessons from the continuum of human history in his approach to design. His Village at Vanderbilt is an urban-scale mixed-use complex with a 95,000-square-foot office/retail structure, 187 apartment units and underground parking structures for both. The project is adjacent to Vanderbilt University, and so architectural forms and elements from the Peabody campus—domes, brick arches, stone details and pitched roofs—are integral to the design. Sympathetic scale relationships along site edges are thoroughly explored, and compatible materials, strong organizational axes, and heavily landscaped areas give a finish and flow to the project. Vehicles and pedestrians are separated throughout, and underground parking protects the visual character of the site without sacrificing convenience.

FERRIS, ROBERT D.

(Building Design, Historic Preservation, Renovation)
Robert Donald Ferris (619) 297-4659
3776 Front St. San Diego CA 92103

Born: 1926 **Studied:** University of Oregon **Awards:** AIA **Notable Works:** Keiller Elementary School, San Diego; Palace Garden Mobile Home, Chula Vista CA; Anza-Borrego Desert State Park Visitors Center, Borrego Springs CA EDUCATIONAL 20%, MUSEUMS 20%, RELIGIOUS 20%, COMMERCIAL 20%, RETAIL 20%

His work is varied—his Palace Garden Mobile Home in Chula Vista CA is contemporary American with Oriental overtones to suit its Japanese owner. His San Diego Keiller Elementary School on a narrow and sloping site features cluster classrooms with hyperbolic paraboloid roofs and vented cupolas. The unusual roof provides natural ventilation, and also high interior ceilings for superior acoustics. The simple wood frame which supports the roof hangs wide and low over outside walls, creating an intimate, child-size scale and a feeling of shelter.

His Anza-Borrego Desert State Park Visitors Center follows the example of many desert animals by burrowing into the desert floor for efficient comfort. With a program of interpreting the surrounding desert while introducing visitors to it, the earth-sheltered Center is landscaped exclusively with native plants which are identified for browsers. The predominant design element is field stone gathered from the desert floor, and the parking area is unpaved, left in indigenous gravel and sand. Stairs, also faced with local stone, lead to a viewing area atop the Center where visitors can see and identify surrounding mountain peaks as well as plants.

FISK, HALSEY, B

(Construction Administration, Building Design, Facility Programming)
Burgess & Niple, Limited (606) 331-8288
2734 Chancellor Drive
Crestview Hills KY 41017

Born: 1920 **Studied:** University of Cincinnati **Awards:** AIA; Kentucky AIA; C. Julian Oberwath Award **Notable Works:** Northern Kentucky University Master Plan, Highland Heights KY; W. Frank Steely Library, Highland Heights KY INSTITUTIONAL 80%, INDUSTRIAL 20%

He's sensitive to client needs and dedicated to professional service as well as local, regional and national civic and church involvement. A pragmatist who never stopped to consider whether he was a Modernist, he believes that a good functional plan will produce a good building and cutesy things only add to the cost. While anyone can do a complex building, his talent lies in making it simple.

His work as master planner at Northern Kentucky University in Highland Heights started when the school was chartered by the Kentucky legislature in 1969. He advocated board-formed concrete for the initial building, as the one material which would be compatible for future architects at the campus. Subsequently his firm designed eight of NKU's twelve buildings, resulting in a unified campus.

His design for Newport High School in a depressed neighborhood of Newport KY aimed to make the school a sanctuary for students. Built around a great hall with a minimal amount of windows, the building turns in on itself, relating to itself rather than to its immediate neighborhood. The absence of a playground led to using the dining hall and library as central core areas for traffic and congregation. His design's success can be measured by its 7 years of vandalism-free existence.

FITZWATER, JAMES
(Cost Estimating, Building Design, Renovation)
Design Automation (713) 528-7308
6100 Corporate Drive Suite 110
Houston TX 77036

Born: 1949 **Studied:** University of Oklahoma; University of California at Berkeley **Awards:** Royal Institute of Dutch Architects; National Convention of the Society of American Registered Architects Notable Work: Klein Residence, Houston TX; Dunlop Residence, Houston TX COMMERCIAL 50%, INDUSTRIAL 50%

His first aim is to produce architecture whose quality lasts and lasts; he's willing to sacrifice design to achieve durability. For example, he builds roofs that slope forward rather than together in gable fashion, to avoid gutter leakage during heavy rainfall. He avoids traditional Texas styles of architecture, favoring a more organic approach which employs wood and other natural materials. He also avoids the commonly seen stucco, because it decays easily in humidity. He is influenced by Frank Lloyd Wright in believing that architecture can be multi-faceted. Materials, context, and structure should "dance together" rather than fade into an imposed formal harmony. He is unsympathetic to Postmodernist trends and other faddish styles that come and go. His addition to the Houston TX Klein Residence was commissioned after Hurricane Alicia partially destroyed the house. It is U-shaped with a courtyard in the middle. Along one side he solved the problem of a narrow bathroom corridor by putting in a 20-foot glass block wall of six-inch translucent glass whose airiness makes the corridor more spacious. As a counterpoint to this glass block he placed a second short, curved glass block in beaux-arts style across the courtyard in the facing wall.

FLOOD, DAVID JAY
(Building Design, Programming, Master Planning)
David Jay Flood Architects (213) 451-1384
1408 Third Street Mall
Santa Monica CA 90401

Born: 1933 **Studied:** UC Berkeley **Awards:** Award for Excellence, Urban Land Institute; California Council AIA Masonry Award **Notable Works:** Blacktop Office Building; Sea Colony, Redondo Beach CA OFFICE 45%, RESIDENTIAL 40%, INDUSTRIAL 15%

A design regionalist whose practice ranges from Colorado ski resorts to seaside Florida shopping centers, his contextual bias responds both to natural forms of mountain and land, and to the built environment around his buildings. The resulting architecture reflects indigenous qualities. His Sarasota Quay, a multi-storied mixed-use 200,000-square-foot office and specialty shopping center on the water in Florida is designed with a Mediterranean and Bermuda palette, abstracting traditional architectural elements and materials to capture and express the local spirit.

His Blacktop Building responds to a very different environment, a California blacktop plant. The multistory office building is oriented around an interior atrium; the outside is frankly industrial and utilitarian. The materials—concrete block, corrugated steel panels and glass block covered with exosed and articulated ventilation piping—blends in with the factory setting, while the palm-lined atrium

David Jay Flood, *Blacktop Office Building*, Sun Valley, California 1983.

with its exposed wood trusses makes both plant workers and office staff feel comfortable inside.

His Seascape renovation represents a continuation of strong Shindler and Neutra influences, with building materials and design function strongly expressed. This development of view-oriented, self-contained apartments and townhouses surrounding a landscaped central courtyard also features detached exterior circulation elements, in this case articulated from floor to floor. Architectural elements such as plaster and piping are layered rather than simply plastered over for an articulated, unifying effect.

FLOYD, CHAD

Centerbrook Architects & Planners
(203) 767-0175
Box 409 Essex CT 06426

Born: 1944 **Studied:** Yale University **Awards:** AIA; American Wood Council award; Connecticut AIA **Notable Works:** Hood Museum of Art, Dartmouth College, Hanover NH; Watkins Glen Pier Pavilion, MA; Key Plaza, Roanoke VA INSTITUTIONAL 60%, RESIDENTIAL 30%, COMMERCIAL 20%

Broadly a contextualist, he allows his work to emerge from a feel for site, purpose and user needs. Setting up offices at Dartmouth College in Hanover NH, he and fellow architect Charles Moore held a series of meetings with the university community to explore options for the siting and features of an art museum. Concern for coordinated programming and symbolic decorum dictated that the Museum be hemmed in between the Modernist Hopkins Center for the Performing Arts and Wilson Hall, a Romanesque building. Other site constraints included lack of space, a heating plant to the immediate east, and requirements that the Museum be connected to the performing arts center while establishing a physical presence on the nearby college green.

To fit into the site the Museum recedes, with only a low connector and an outdoor gateway linking Wilson Hall and the Hopkins Center.

On the other side of this gateway the Hood Museum rises to its tallest height. Built of brick with a standing seam copper roof, the Museum's informal gabled forms are reminiscent of New England architecture. A concrete frame supports the first two floors, and lightweight steel supports the third. Two types of veneer brick clad the building; over most of the wall height a water struck red brick is laid up in stacked bond in bands of varying width. With these features the Museum mediates between the Romanesque vigor and Modern lines of its different neighbors.

It sets up a "processional experience" in its twist and turns. One passes from an oval granite forecourt on the north to a pastoral, "Medieval" courtyard on the south. The ramp to the gallery entrance on the northern end has a stepped parapet, envisioned as a pedestal for sculpture. A second bridge links the museum to a newly created popular cafe that curves around the back of the Hopkins Center to help shape an amphitheater-like garden that welcomes visitors arriving from the south. Inside are different varieties of room shapes and degrees of luminosity congenial to different kinds of art. One chamber evokes a reliquary; another skylighted barnlike chamber slices diagonally through an enfilade of cove-ceilinged spaces modelled loosely on the long galleries of English country houses. Another is crossed at its gabled ceiling by a catwalk below a skylight, which spills daylight onto gallery walls dominated by a large Frank Stella metal collage.

FORBES, PETER

Peter Forbes Associates (617) 542-1760
144 Lincoln St. Boston MA 02111

Born: 1945 **Studied:** University of Michigan; Yale University **Awards:** FAIA; AIA; "Emerging Voices" invited lecturer, Architectural League of New York; Tucker Architecture Award, Building Stone Institute **Notable Works:** Wenglowski House, Deer Isle ME RESIDENTIAL 80%

His architecture is disciplined by pursuing a theme within an economy of means. Ener-

Peter Forbes, *Wenglowski Vacation House*, Deer Isle, Maine, 1983

gized by a spartan design vocabulary, it exudes energy and serenity.

Of a number of retreats designed on the New England coast, his Wenglowski House on a rocky little island which overlooks Maine's Penobscot Bay, features three barn- or basilica-like pavilions. Two house a living/dining room and a bedroom, and are anchored by oversized granite fireplaces. These two are at an angle to each other, opening up a triangle that offers a view to the ocean. This triangle also points away to the third pavilion, a wood-sided children's cottage. The three pavilions together form a triangle enclosing a courtyard adorned with paved granite, grass, fir and birch trees.

The two adult pavilions are made of a rigid welded framework of white steel tubes resting on four massive round concrete columns. The steel frame supports the rafters and decking of the gray copper hip roof with little steel clips. Walls are sliding glass panels that open onto wood decks except where the fireplaces fill the far ends of the rooms. The living room pavilion has a miniature wooden cottage housing the kitchen and a semi-circular freestanding wall which encloses the dining table.

FORT-BRESCIA, BERNARDO
(Building Design)
Arquitectonia (305) 442-9381
4215 Ponce De Leon Blvd.
Coral Gables FL 33146

Born: 1951 **Awards:** Progressive Architecture citation; Florida AIA **Notable Works:** Overseas Tower, Dade County FL; Atlantis Condominium, Miami FL; Square Shopping Center, Key Biscayne FL COMMERCIAL 40%, HOUSING 35%

With the other architects of Arquitectonia he's creating architecture that matches the colorful splendor of south Florida. He doesn't hold himself to preconceived ideas of 'proper' forms for his structures, but works in a large vocabulary of less rigid shapes. He works by sketching design ideas, coloring them, then examining each separate piece to see how it works on its own.

The Overseas Tower, the Dade County FL headquarters for a trading and finance company in the Fingerlakes Commercenter industrial park, is an example of his geometric legerdemain. A seven-story glass cylinder holds 38,000 feet of office space which looks out over man-made lakes. The cylinder is cut by a plane housing the service features of the building. This plane extends beyond the cylinder, forming a rectangular entrance arch for the parking lot. The fifth-floor landing has a two-story terrace formed by a cut-out in the plane. On the other side of the structure, a glass wedge forms a bank entrance and contains a 24-hour teller.

FRANZEN, ULRICH
(Building Design)
Ulrich Franzen and Associates
(212) 489-1414
881 7th Avenue 10019 New York NY 10017

Born: 1921 **Studied:** Harvard University **Awards:** Fellow, AIA **Notable Works:** MVR Hall, Cornell University, Ithaca, New York; Paraphernalia Shops, New York, New York; New Academic Facilities, Hunter College, New York COMMERCIAL/RETAIL: 25%, HOUSING: 20% INDUSTRIAL: 5%, EDUCATION: 15%, PLANNING: 20% OTHER: 15%

Contemporary architecture, he says, no longer has an identifiable mainstream. In its place is a parched and braided babble of voices. Intellectuals generally recognize the reductive qualities of the modern movement, and acknowledge that buildings of any style are reflections of strong and often unreconciled voices within the societies that build them. But they haven't recognized that the modernist ethos itself was born of conflicting paradigms whose upstream sources were Marxism, Futurism and fascism. Ultimately, he says, a building is a snapshot of the society and epoch in which it's erected. So an enlightened architect is transparent; his design presents a crystal reflection of many dissonant voices. His own designs typically include several architectural vocabularies, each of which is suggested by

Ulrich Franzen, *University Center, University of Michigan*, 1982, Flint, Michigan.
Photo: Peter Aaron.

Ulrich Franzen, *Multicategorical Research Tower, College of Veterinary Medicine
Cornell University*, 1978, Ithaca, New York. Photo: Norman McGrath

the dominant organizing geometry of each individuated subsection. His production is remarkably varied, but his experimentalism and eclecticism invariant. Perhaps his most extreme attempt to express current "cultural context" was his design for a series of New York City Paraphernalia shops. He was so taken with the 1970s cult of video that he replaced traditional merchandise cases and window displays with fixed television banks which flashed images of available items.

FREED, JAMES INGO

(Building Design, Master Planning when appropriate to design) I.M. Pei & Partners
(212) 751-3122
600 Madison Ave. New York NY 10022

Born: 1930 **Studied:** Illinois Institute of Technology **Awards:** FAIA; American Academy and Institute of Arts and Letters' Brunner Memorial Prize; New York AIA Medal of Honor Associate, National Academy of Design **Notable Works:** Jacob K. Javits Convention Center, New York City; U. S. Holocaust Memorial Museum, Washington DC; First Bank Place, Minneapolis MN INSTITUTIONAL 40%, OFFICE 35%, MASTER PLANNING 15%, RESIDENTIAL & HOTEL 10%

An urbanist by inclination no less than profession, he enjoys working on large city projects that contribute to the transformation of urban areas. While solving the program needs of users he aims to act in the public interest as well, addressing the unarticulated need of every citizen to live in a meaningful and delightful world. He looks for large or difficult commissions (for example the Holocaust Museum) whose program requirements and contradictory constituencies commonly seem too unwieldy to be resolved 'architecturally.'

Convention centers, a recent focus, require vast service, circulation and parking facilities in such controlled circumstances that to non-conventioneers they become 'black boxes' isolated across asphalt acres. His Los Angeles Convention Center is designed to enrich the experience of passers-by no less than users by

addressing all comers on their own terms. While its pedestrian side is scaled for human contact, many more people experience the Center from the freeway curve in which it's sited. He counter-curves back to the freeway a wall of repetitive lights and canopies, offering a public identity that can be seized and remembered in freeway glances. He integrates an existing building into his new facility by means of an open-glass row of conference rooms and public passage that highlights the flow of people within, making a design feature of its connective function. The two separate halls, one square and the other a partial arc, are topped by towers of light visible from a distance down the freeway. They provide an old-fashioned focus of expectation and arrival for convention-goers, and stand as landmark and remembered delight for travelers still on their way.

FRIEDBURG, MARVIN PAUL

(Landscape Design, Urban Design)
M. Paul Friedburg and Partners
(212) 477-6366
41 East 11th Street New York NY 10023

Born: 1931 **Studied:** Cornell University **Awards:** Fellow, AIA; Downtown Achievement Award, New York, 1982; Fellow, American Society of Landscape Architects **Notable Works:** Fifth Avenue Restoration, New York; Hall of Science, Flushing Meadow Park, New York; James Center, Richmond, Virginia

The process of design, he says, at first blush appears orderly and rational, but closer examination only obscures the true sources of spatial ideas. In the end, in his view, architectural and landscape design is intuitive and largely incomprehensible, at best an attempt to translate verbal parameters into three-dimensional forms.

He aims to design parks, plazas and monuments which are accessible, appropriate and responsive to client needs, but which also continually provide them with new insights and an "expanded world view." His outdoor environments are conceived as stage settings where people become simultaneously specta-

James Freed, *U.S. Holocaust Museum*, Washington, D.C.

James Freed, *Los Angeles Convention Center*

tors and participants, giving a wide range of possible interpretations and opportunities for user participation.   Though his designs may proceed from "irrational" inspirations, his progress toward a finished product is extremely measured and disciplined. He begins by breaking each site into smaller, human-scale areas, using hard, durable materials to define their borders. His spaces don't encourage cross-navigation. The ideal public meeting place, he believes, is a series of connected but discrete sites for a variety of activities. His urban installations bear little resemblance to the quasi-rural parks of the last century. He prefers the durability of asphalt, concrete, granite and steel to the transience and complexity of earth, grass and trees.

FRIEDMAN, ANDREW
(Building Design)
Born: 1960 **Studied:** Cooper Union
Notable Works: The Beach House, Long Island NY

He says the decisive issue in architecture is the unity of design and structure. He tries to proceed from a "strong, clear and balanced plan" and to allow site, materials, and structure to have a play in the design.

His Beach House, on a site in Bridgehampton in eastern Long Island NY, is located on a narrow tract of flood plain bounded on the north by a bay and on the south by an ocean-front road and high dunes. Zoning permitted construction on only a small area of the site.

A primary decision was to allow the landscape to dominate the house. The house is conceived as a platform raised above the dunes, and its axis is emphasized to provide views of the ocean and bay. To free the platform from the dunes, the wood-friction piling foundations are exposed to reduce their impact on the open landscape. The 2000-square-foot house sits on the platform, enclosed principally by sliding panels that hold out the elements in winter. It has a further 3000 square feet of decks, including a rooftop terrace. The house is intersected by its view axis, and on the ground level the axis is marked by a walkway

that leads from the house to the bay. The transition between inside and outside is treated as a sequence of covered, sunscreened, and open spaces. The simple exposed wood-frame platform construction is contrasted with the more carefully finished wood of the deck railings, sliding panels and stairs.

FURNO, ROBERT
Furno/Dowling Architects (203) 869-1839
333 Taconic Road Greenwich CT 06831

Born: 1937   **Studied:** Cornell University
Awards: New York AIA **Notable Works:** Highview Office Building, Norwalk CT; Perdue Frederich Corporation Headquarters COMMERCIAL 60%, RESIDENTIAL 40%

His larger projects have been accomplished within rigorous budgets. His basic philosophy is to use few and natural materials, preferably indigenous. He prefers a simple approach, embellished with elaborate detail. But he believes that his primary responsibility is to comply with the requirements of his clients.

Much of his work is adaptive re-use. One such award-winning project, the Highview Office Building in Norwalk CT, required converting an old factory into office space. A courtyard was taken over to create the large amount of office space needed. Executive offices were established behind a low perimeter wall, and natural light filters in through retained monitors. The simplicity and precision of the adaptation is counterpointed by carefully wrought interior landscaping.

GEDDES, ROBERT
(Building Design, Planning)
Geddes Brecher Qualls Cunningham
(609) 520-0808
120 Alexander Street
Princeton New Jersey 08540

Born:1923   **Studied:** Harvard University
Awards: Fellow, AIA; Member, National Academy of Design; First Design Award, *Progressive Architecture*, 1960 **Notable Works:** Humanities and Social Science Center, Southern Illinois University; Fotteral Square, Philadelphia; Dormitories, McGuire

James I. Freed, *Jacob K. Javits Convention Center*, New York City

Airforce Base, New Jersey COMMERCIAL/RETAIL: 34%, INDUSTRIAL: 5%, EDUCATION: 9%, MEDICAL: 36% INTERIOR DESIGN: 1% PLANNING: 15%

Architecture, he insists, isn't a personal expression but a "public art." In his view, a society's zeitgeist—its economy, culture and political structure—is reflected in its buildings. In the microcosm of his specialty, institutional architecture, he argues that a building should reflect the purpose, qualities and ambitions of the institution it shelters. Though the institutional architect should provide flexibility for growth and reorganization, his primary responsibility must be the immediate satisfaction of the community of users. A compelling building, he believes, should be formally complex but always coherent. It should be colorful and stimulating to the senses. He hopes that it will also make a major social and aesthetic contribution to its community. His buildings are typically marked by intricate, interlocking volumes. His Humanities and Social Science Center for Southern Illinois University at Carbondale makes particularly clever use of alternating curved and plane panels to give an undulating, fluid feeling to long and otherwise plain horizontal expanses.

GEHRY, FRANK O.
(Building Design)
Frank O. Gehry and Associates
(213) 392-9771
11 Brooks Avenue Venice California 90291

Born: 1929 **Studied:** Harvard University **Awards:** FAIA; Brunner Memorial Prize **Notable Works:** The Temporary Contemporary (Museum of Contemporary Art), Los Angeles; California Aerospace Museum, Los Angeles; Frances Howard Goldwyn Regional Branch Library, Hollywood, California

His approach to design is atypical. Ideas often result from the adaptation of building materials to cost constraints. For example, he has used materials which were not generally considered acceptable as serious design elements such as corrugated iron, chain-link fence, asbestos shingles, and raw plywood, which he

has left exposed. Unusual materials are also used for creating furniture from corrugated cardboard, and decorative lamps from broken chips of plastic laminate. Notable buildings include his own house, an ordinary bungalow surrounded by another house made of corrugated metal, plywood and glass. The Loyola Law School features a plaza defined by small structures variously clad in stucco, metal and prefinished "finn-ply" plywood, set against a three-story yellow stucco classroom building as a backdrop. The California Aerospace Museum is an eighty-foot high building, characterized by a plain stucco box juxtaposed against a metal polygon joined by a wedge-shaped clerestory above, with an F-104 Starfighter thrusting upward on the facade. "The extreme end of unorthodoxy," is a term which has been applied to his unique approach to design, form, and especially to materials, be they "cheapskate," as one critic coined them, or very opulent when appropriate.

GIBSON & RENO ARCHITECTS (see Gibson, David; Reno, August)

GIBSON, DAVID
(Building Design)
Gibson & Reno Architects (303) 925-5968
418 E. Cooper Aspen CO 91611

Born: 1945 **Studied:** Yale University **Awards:** Colorado West AIA; Colorado AIA; Aspen Historic Preservation Committee award **Notable Works:** Battlement Mesa Public Safety Building; Wildwood School RESIDENTIAL 30% INSTITUTIONAL 30% OTHER 40%

Collaborating with partner August Reno he aims to mold client desires and input into a shape of art that works technically while being more exciting than "normal" architecture.

This goal is exemplified in his design for the Wildwood school, which draws its inspiration from J.R.R. Tolkien's novel *The Hobbit*. Its undulating structure is partially earth bermed and made of lightweight sprayed cement. Built on a child's scale with smaller doorways and amenities, the different pods housing class-

Robert Geddes, *Trexler Library*, Muhlenberg College, Allentown, Pennsylvania

Robert Geddes, *Southern Illinois University*, Carbondale, Illinois. Photo: George Cserna

room areas contain portholes, skylights and even a tree trunk. This provides unique access to nature both indoors and out, and preserves the natural environment of the valley while conserving energy.

His design for the Andress residence, in Snowmass CO is also an atypical structure, reminiscent of the ancient dwellings of Mesa Verde in its materials and massing.

GILBERT, MOWRY C.

(Development Architecture, Facility Programming)
Mowry C. Gilbert & Assoc. (719) 599-3326
1019 Ellston St. Colorado Springs CO 80907

Born: 1928 **Studied:** Kansas State University **Awards:** Annual W.O.O.D. Award, Wood Association **Notable Works:** First Valley Bank, Colorado Springs CO; Blair Business College, Colorado Springs CO; 625 Cascade Professional Building RESIDENTIAL 30%, OFFICE 50%

His buildings are warm and inviting without being identified with any particular style. He tries to be expressive in contemporary idioms using locally available materials. His First Valley Bank in Colorado Springs is a glue-laminated, two-story building with a stucco and brick exterior. It features a wood deck and an atrium that opens through two doors, imparting a soaring character to the building. His Professional Building, made of structural brick and pre-stress concrete uses Western red cedar on the exterior.

GIURGOLA, ROMALDO

(Building Design, Planning)
Mitchell/Giurgola Architects (212) 663-4000
170 West 97th Street New York New York 10025

Born: 1959 **Studied:** University of Rome **Awards:** Fellow, AIA; Fist Honor Award, 1977, Pennsylvania Society of Architects; Design Award, *Urban Design*, 1978 **Notable Works:** Liberty Pavilion, Philadelphia; Mitchell House, Lafayette Hill, Pennsylvania; Parliament House, Canberra, Australia COMMERCIAL/RETAIL: 40%, EDUCATION:

20%, INTERIOR DESIGN: 5%, PLANNING: 10% OTHER: 25%

He is interested in gracefully extending the continuum of historical architecture. An architect's key concern, he believes, should be how his designs relate to reality: to the physical features of a site, the architectural texture and traditions of adjacent communities, and the expressed and implicit needs of clients and users. He and partner Ehrman B. Mitchell stress the need to view each project in its largest possible context. Because of his reputation for extreme sensitivity to historical nuance and decorum, in the last two decades he's worked on more than a score of delicate renovation, expansion and build-in projects. In his 1971 addition to the University of Pennsylvania Museum in Philadelphia he designed a brick wing which deferentially followed the original Lombard Renaissance section of the museum, designed by Wilson Eyre, in materials, tone and proportions. The glass and steel of his dominantly horizontal pavilion for the Liberty Bell, however, gives the effect of an enormous, ahistorical display case, preserved from the stylistic taint of either the colonial meeting house at hand or the skyscraper that rises behind it.

GOLDBERG, BERTRAND

(Building Design)
Bertrand Goldberg Associates
(312) 431-5200
800 South Wells Street Chicago 60610

Born: 1913 **Studied:** Bauhaus, Berlin **Awards:** Fellow, AIA; Silver Medal, Architecture League of New York, 1965; Award of Merit, Society of Registered Architects, 1982 **Notable Works:** Marina City, Chicago; River City, Chicago; Affiliated Hospital Center, Boston COMMERCIAL/RETAIL: 3%, HOUSING: 10%, EDUCATION: 10%, MEDICAL: 70%, INTERIOR DESIGN: 2%, PLANNING: 5%

His work challenges the linear character of traditional spatial layout. Working with Edward Hall, anthropology professor at the University of Illinois, he pioneered the study of

Joseph A. Gonzalez, *303 West Madison*, Chicago. Photo: Hedrich-Blessing

how people actually use space. This work has led to many design innovations. His Marina City in Chicago was the first mixed-use complex in the center of a large city, and the highest reinforced concrete structure at the time of its completion. Its adventurous use of concrete led him away from Miesian boxes toward more "biological" forms, first in Marina City spirals and circles, and more recently in his serpentine River City Complex, another mixed-use downtown development in Chicago.

In health care too, his building forms are conceived as biological shells, within which human activities are free to evolve. His State University of New York Health Sciences Campus at Stony Brook is built on a million-square-foot megastructure of seven stories, partly underground, on which several towers of various heights and forms, which interconnect with bridges as well as basements, collect related and interconnected disciplines and services in a matrix of unrestricted open space for future use evolution.

GOLDSMITH, MYRON
(Building Design, Urban design)
(312) 251-8260
503 Central Avenue Wilmette Illinois 60091

Born: 1918 **Studied:** Illinois Institute of Chicago **Awards:** Fellow, AIA; *Progressive Architecture* Award, 1979; Award of Merit, Chicago Lighting Society **Notable Works:** San Francisco Airport Hangars; Harlem Station, Chicago; Stellar Telescope, Kitts Peak, Arizona COMMERCIAL/RETAIL: 45%, HOUSING: 15% INDUSTRIAL: 10%, EDUCATION: 5%, PLANNING: 10% OTHER: 15%

Working in the Chicago offices of Skidmore, Owings and Merrill since 1958, he's regarded as a key theorist of the Chicago School. He came out of long apprenticeships with Mies van der Rohe and the great engineer Pier Lugi Nervi a fervent structuralist. In addition to his many important designs as principle architect, he's acted as a design catalyst and guru of sorts in the huge SOM firm, collaborating officially or informally with Gordon Bunshaft, Charles

Basset, Walter Netsch and many other architects of international stature. His first commission for SOM, a series of airplane hangars for San Francisco Airport, set the tone of much subsequent work. The main hangar is a gloss on Nervi's Turin Palace of Labour, with boldly modeled exterior surfaces and supports which reveal and accentuate internal stresses. But his economical, unforced arrangement of a smaller wash hangar is more methodical, less mannered.

GONZALEZ, JOSEPH A.
(Building Design, Urban Planning)
Skidmore, Owings and Merrill
(312) 641-5959
33 West Monroe Chicago IL 60603

Born: 1950 **Studied:** Oklahoma State University **Awards:** Progressive Architecture; Chicago AIA **Notable Works:** 303 West Madison, Chicago; Park East Development, Milwaukee WI; ABC/WLS-TV Renovation, Chicago

Working within the SOM tradition of straightforward architecture, he thinks it's a mistake to dismiss the modern movement, although "balance" is more important than over-abstraction and the expression of buildings as machines. Fenestration proportions and ground floor space articulation are fundamental concerns in projects ranging from a mixed-use development in Cincinnati OH, where three high-rises with hotel rooms, offices and apartments are designed to provide interesting views from the streets, to the nine-block Park East Development in Milwaukee WI which uses the extant urban grid as the foundation for "neighborhood retail centers," town houses, apartment buildings, and a park.

For his 303 West Madison design he studied Chicago and Prairie School buildings to create a synthesis that would make a quiet statement in Chicago office building. Two-story oriel windows with stainless steel spandrel ornamentation give a glassy, contemporary look that also articulates the building's middle. A loggia, playing in light and shadow, caps the building's top, mechanical floor. At ground level the building's long facade, punctuated with individual storefronts, respectfully echoes the nearby landmark Monadnock Building.

GOODY, JOAN
(Building Design, Urban planning)
Goody, Clancy and Associates
(617) 262-2760
334 Boylston Street Boston MA 02116

Born: 1899 **Studied:** Cornell University **Awards:** Fellow, AIA; Urban Planning Award, Progressive Architecture, 1983; Architectural Record Award, 1979; Housing Award, Boston Society of Architects **Notable Works:** Summer Street Housing for the Elderly, Hyde Park, Massachusetts; Paine Webber Building, Boston; Harbor Point Housing, Boston COMMERCIAL/RETAIL: 35%, HOUSING: 15%, EDUCATION: 15%, MEDICAL: 20%, INTERIOR DESIGN: 5%, PLANNING: 5%, OTHER: 5%

She is known throughout New England for her commitment to making space in her designs for the community to meet and gather. Her fundamental complaint, she says, is the epic scale at which she's usually asked to build. Her recent commissions demand more space, capital and resources than the buildings that antedate and adjoin them. She takes special pains to avoid overwhelming surrounding cityscape, finding the richest urban textures created by accretions of respectful, continuous change which integrate past and present. Having worked almost exclusively in architecturally traditional and climatically harsh New England, she works in a comparatively narrow range of materials and forms. Her commercial work generally features continuous brick or granite skins which obscure structural detail. Smaller- scale residential projects most frequently incorporate bricks from local yards and pitched roofs which evoke neighboring clapboard houses. In her community planning she bows to the power of nature, usually providing sheltered atriums where open parkland might otherwise prevail. Her attention to historical, social and environmental

contexts is most evident in her Massachusetts Department of Transportation Building in Boston. The eight story building's slightly concave brick perimeter follows the existing curvature of the site, and closely matches exterior textures of the historic buildings nearby. Extensive retail space is provided at street level to attract foot traffic and revitalize the local commercial district. A revolutionary heating and refrigeration system draws 80% of its hot water needs from solar panels and makes use of heat generated by people, electrical systems and moving equipment.

GOYETTE, HAROLD L.
(Building Design, Facility Programming, Master Planning)
Cole and Goyette, Architects and Planners Inc.
(617) 491-5662
540 Franklin St. Cambridge MA 02139

Born: 1927 **Studied:** Auburn University; Harvard Graduate School of Design **Awards:** *Progressive Architecture* design awards; Second Place, Boston Architectural Center design competition **Notable Works:** Glover Landing, Marblehead MA; Louisville KY Urban Renewal; Harvard Square Branch Bank, Bank of Boston, Cambridge MA MASTER PLANNING 30%, INSTITUTIONAL 30%, RESIDENTIAL 20%, COMMERCIAL 10%, OFFICE 10%

He points out that everything that can be said about design has already been said and will be said again with different words. He refers back to Palladio to describe his own design approach and notes that Palladio was restating Vetruvius. He aims to trade off Palladio's three key elements—economy, function and beauty—in such a way that proper attention to each leads to discoveries for each of the others. Architecture exists in four dimensions, including the time dimension in which we experience a progression of architectural effects. That fourth dimension, like the other three, should create uplifting and exciting experiences.

His Glover Landing residential complex is at harborfront in Marblehead MA, sloping up rocky outcrops and terraces toward the historic clapboard and shingle village which surrounds the harbor. He achieves high density with low impact by clustering residences in loosely organized groups on accomodating ledges and terraces, thus saving money while rooting his new construction in the old landscape, and offering many more harbor views in and around the site. With no through-circulation he was able to put cars and pedestrians on single narrow lanes that access some small clusters of homes, while in other areas pedestrian-only courts are provided. This capillary circulation pattern breaks up the parking and service areas that so often dominate such projects.

GRAHAM/MEUS, INC. (see Graham, Gary; Meus, Daniel L.)

GRAHAM, BRUCE
(Building Design)
Skidmore, Owings and Merrill
33 West Monroe Street Chicago Illinois

Born: 1925 **Studied:** University of Pennsylvania **Awards:** Fellow, AIA; Member, Royal Architectural Institute of Canada **Notable Works:** John Hancock Center, Chicago; Sears Tower, Chicago; Hyatt International Hotel, Cairo COMMERCIAL/RETAIL: 45%, HOUSING: 15%, INDUSTRIAL: 10%, EDUCATION: 5%, MEDICAL: 10%, INTERIOR DESIGN: 5%, PLANNING: 10%

He is one of the most prolific and innovative high-rise designers of the post-war era. In his twenty-five year association with Skidmore, Owings and Merrill he has been responsible for many of the nation's tallest and most visible buildings.

He first attracted attention in 1958 when he led the team responsible for designing Chicago's Inland Steel Building, the first major office project in the heart of the business district since World War II. The Inland Building was the Midwest's introduction to the spare, functionalist style that Mies van der Rohe had made internationally popular. Chicago's commercial architecture of the next decade closely followed this prototype. In the mid-1960s he designed a number of skyscrap-

ers in collaboration with SOM's Bangladesh-born engineer Fazlur Khan which were primarily supported by revolutionary tubular steel exterior skeletons. Although the Sears Tower, the world's tallest building, is probably his most recognized project from that period, the John Hancock Center, also in Chicago, represents his most sensitive and harmonious use of the new technology. The building's fundamental form is an elongated pyramid. Six vertical tubular supports are superimposed on each of the structure's four nearly triangular exterior faces. These vertical supports are criss-crossed by pairs of intersecting diagonal supports, which form ever-narrowing diamonds and incidental quadrilaterals as they ascend.

GRAHAM, GARY
(Building Design, Facility Programming, Interior Architecture)
Graham/Meus, Inc. (617) 267-9399
224 Clarendon St. Boston MA 02116

Born: 1944 **Studied:** University of Virginia; University of Manchester, UK **Awards:** New England AIA; Massachusetts Department of Capital Planning & Operations Design Award **Notable Works:** Arbour Hospital, Boston; Back Bay Racquet Club, Boston; House on New England Coast MEDICAL/INSTITUTIONAL 50%, RESIDENTIAL 10%, RECREATION FACILITIES 20%

His background in medical architecture helps him to understand the complex regulatory requirements in his chosen speciality of psychiatric design. Sensitivity to patient interaction and group activities, and the supervision and support requirements of staff, determine efficient functional layouts. But his concern for patient perceptions and psychological needs are the most important determinants in establishing effective and appropriate architecture.

Arbour Hospital in suburban Boston integrates his interest in physical setting with his awareness of the needs of the behaviorally impaired. A prototype for subsequent projects relating to psychiatric or chemical dependency treatment, it is sensitive to regional and local architectural influences, which makes

Inside the photo: John Hancock Center
Chicago, Illinois

Bruce Graham, *John Hancock Center*, Chicago. Photo: Timothy Hursley

for comfortable transitions both for patients and the surrounding community. De-emphasizing patient rooms and focussing attention on public spaces that are safe and secure while retaining a residential character, many of his facilities have a campus-like atmosphere in which free- standing facilities are integrated within landscaped grounds.

GRAVES, MICHAEL

(Building Design, Furniture Design)
Michael Graves Architect (609) 924-6409
341 Nassau Street
Princeton New Jersey 08540

Born: 1934 **Studied:** Harvard University **Awards:** Fellow, AIA; *Progressive Architecture* Award, 1970, 1976, 1977, 1978, 1979 **Notable Works:** Municipal Services Building, Portland, Oregon; Whitney Museum Addition, New York; Mezzo House, Princeton, New Jersey COMMERCIAL/RETAIL: 60%, HOUSING: 5%, INDUSTRIAL: 10%, EDUCATION: 5%, INTERIOR DESIGN: 15% OTHER: 5%

He was one of the first young, prominent American designers who attempted to reestablish contextualism, wit and sculpturalism as virtues in center-city office architecture. His work reacts against the formal restrictiveness, material hardness and somewhat imperial presence of modernist and International Style design. Yet he shuns the label of Postmoderism as he does any other doctrinnaire categorization. His designs draw from Art Deco skyscrapers of the 1920s and 1930s, yet technically he is strongly indebted to his Miesian forebears.

In many cases his designs have been selected to bring harmony to urban areas where reckless development in the 1950s and 1960s had created logistical and aesthetic chaos. The Municipal Services Building in Portland OR was one of his first such efforts and remains his most controversial.

Portland's downtown is on a tight, square grid, situated between the Willamette River and a stretch of massive bluffs. A number of earlier International Style buildings had ig-

nored the scale of the bluffs and the situation of their plazas disrupted the order of the street grid. His almost cubical design responds to these neglected site considerations: it imitates the scale of the bluffs and fits squarely within the established grid. The structure's lowest floors are formally and materially continuous with the existing street level. Upper floors, however, are accented with a series of rectangular and trapezoidal areas of primary color, capped by a pair of wedges in high relief. The building conveys much of the whimsy and elegance of the high Deco period, while working within the technical and financial confines of a rather less spacious era.

GREENBERG, ALLAN

(Building Design)
Allan Greenberg Architect (203) 776-2006
31 High Street
New Haven Connecticut 06510

Born: 1938 **Studied:** Cornell University **Awards:** First Prize, Art Center Competition, Thibodeaux, Louisiana **Notable Works:** Marshall Reception Room, Washington, D.C.; Bergdorf Goodman Facade, New York; Trellis Room Proposal, White House, Washington, D.C.

His work marks a return to the neo-classicism of the late nineteenth century, which reached its apex in the public commissions of Englishman Sir Edwin Lutyens. Unlike Robert Venturi and Thomas Gordon Smith, who have attracted international attention with their highly selective and idealized use of classical idioms, he attempts to work wholly within the formal vocabulary that Lutyens distilled from his study of the high Renaisannce. Appropriately, he has worked predominantly on major, authority-laden public commissions: courthouses, judicial buildings, war memorials, libraries, and recently his design for the Trellis Room of the White House. But in 1984 he submitted a striking design for a monument to the victims of the Holocaust in New York City's Battery Park: a short, stout chimney rises from two mighty pairs of arches. The monument's eloquent evocation of tremen-

Michael Graves, *The Portland Building*, Portland, Oregon, 1980. Photo: Paschall/Taylor

dous public forces, ponderous, crushing weight, and finally the wild upsweep of fire—all argue with him that the formal phrases of classical architecture provide mankind's most sensitive and complete language for symbolic expression.

GREENE, HERBERT
(Building Designer)
1218 Queens Road   Berkeley
California 94708

Born: 1929 **Studied:** University of Oklahoma, Norman **Awards:** Senior Fellow, National Endowment for the Arts; **Notable Works:** Prairie House, Norman, Oklahoma; Lurie House, Houston, Texas; Dubou House, Lexington, Kentucky

His 1961 Prairie House, built for his own family in Norman OK, confirmed him as the dominant voice of the American organic movement which took root in the late work of Frank Lloyd Wright, and found contemporary expression in the works of Bruce Goff and thousands of enlightened "do it yourself" architects of the 1960s and 1970s.

His Prairie House harkens to Wright's original Prairie School in using natural, native materials, in smoothly joining foundation to ground and site, and in its "addressable," human-scale interior partitioning.   But the reprise isn't slavish. His houses also radically depart from Wright's simplified, geometric, Oriental-influenced formal vocabulary. While Prairie House doesn't submit easily to formal analysis, its overall effect is of a great wooden bird perched astride a cone or softened pyramid.   Fantastical, totemic, enormously idiosyncratic, in the end it's a house that could only have been built by an architect for himself. Yet it's served as an inspiration and call to hundreds of others to encode their personal inconography in wood, stone and space.

GREGORY, RONALD
(Landscape Architecture)
Ronald Gregory Assoc., Inc. (619) 568-3624
73960 Highway 111 Suite 2

Palm Desert CA 92260

Born: 1949 **Studied:** University of California at Berkeley **Awards:** Awards of Excellence, Landscape Architectural Foundation/California Landscape Architectural Student Scholarship Fund **Notable Works:** Mission Hills Resort Hotel, Rancho Mirage CA; Desert Falls Country Club, Palm Desert CA; Norton Residence, Indian Wells CA RESORT 40%, COMMERCIAL 25%, RESIDENTIAL 25%

In his landscape designs he strives for an uncontrived, natural-looking plan with asymmetric plant groupings, flowing lines and massed elements balanced by open areas. He often uses native plants for ease of maintenance and annual plants for color.

His Oasis Water Park in Palm Springs CA is a water-recreation park built and landscaped atop an eighty-foot man-made mountain. The mound was made of compacted earth and covered with a concrete and artificial-rock shell to prevent erosion on the steep slopes. Openings in the casing are planted with trees and a mixture of native and desert plants—brittle bush, cassia, verbena, clumping bougain villa and other plants—to give the illusion of a real mountain. A low pressure, water conserving drip irrigation system is installed between the concrete and the earth.

His landscaping for the Magnet Resonance Imaging building in the Rancho Mirage CA Eisenhower Medical Center is designed to keep people away from areas where magnetic pull could be felt. Half of the building is surrounded by a lake which works as a moat. The lake is part of a low-maintenance desert landscaping composed of yucca, saguaro, Texas Rangers and ocotilla in raked earth and gravel fines.

GROSSMAN, IRVING
(Building Design)
7 Sultan Street Toronto
Ontario M5R Il6 Canada

Born: 1926 **Studied:** University of Toronto **Awards:** Fellow, Royal Canadian Institute; Annual Design Award, *Canadian Architect*, 1978; Canadian national Design Award, 1971

One Magnificent Mile
Chicago, Illinois

Bruce Graham, *One Magnificent Mile*, Chicago

Notable Works: Crombie Park Housing, Toronto; Flemingdon Park, Toronto; Edgeley, Toronto

He's completed a number of highly experimental 'one-off' projects, but he remains deeply committed to the design of cost-effective, multifamily residential groupings. In the early 1960s he concluded that even with the steady stream of innovative designs from the architectural community, builders were wedded to a handful of archaic and unattractive paradigms. His Flemingdon Park in Toronto offered a new prototype for low-cost, medium-density, mixed-use subsidized housing of considerable aesthetic sophistication. Flemingdon Park repopularized linearly attached multi-family row houses, re-christened townhouses, around wide, closed pedestrian spines.

His later Edgeley community, also in Toronto, employed a similar linear arrangement for its four-story stacked townhouse units and added an equal number of unsubsidized free-market houses. Garage substructures were built into the foundations of townhouse units, and the development centered around a large communal park and recreation center. Despite a development density of more than sixty units per acre, cross ventilation and multiple light exposures were maintained in the great majority of dwellings.

GROVER, WILLIAM H.
Centerbrook Architects & Planners
(203) 767-0175
Box 409 Essex CT 06426

Born: 1938 **Studied:** Cornell University; Yale University **Awards:** FAIA; Connecticut AIA; Builder's Choice award; International Competition Credit Award, Parc de la Villette, Paris, France **Notable Works:** Grace Auditorium, Cold Spring Harbor Laboratory, Long Island NY RESIDENTIAL 50%, INSTITUIONAL/COMMERCIAL 50%

Whether creating an office building, a laboratory or a house, he considers the design of space and light down to the smallest detail.

Working at Cold Spring Harbor Laboratories for 12 years, his research spaces incorporate up-to-date technology but always recognize and even celebrate the human needs of the scientists who use them.

His award-winning Grace Auditorium is partly built into a hillside, which moderates interior temperatures year-round. A covered piazza along the south facade also shades the auditorium in the summer months. Four dormer windows, piercing the roof in a highly asymmetrical fashion, are positioned to receive directly the rays of the winter sun. Solar warmth from these windows strikes and is stored in two solid masonry interior walls. The building is framed in steel with a veneer of dark brown and terra-cotta colored bricks, set in alternating courses. The entrance portico features a roof which extends the shallow hipped roof of the building itself, now enlivened by the four scattered dormers. Out-of-doors colors are used in the interior. Pale walls trimmed in dark green rise to a band of midnight blue which is decorated with a frieze representing DNA.

GUND, GRAHAM
(Building Design, Interior Architecture, Planning)
Graham Gund Associates (617) 577-9600
47 Thorndike St. Cambridge MA 02141

Born: 1940 **Studied:** Harvard University; Rhode Island School of Design **Awards:** FAIA; AIA; One of *Time* Magazine's "Best Designs of 1983"; Builder's Choice Grand Award **Notable Works:** Church Court Condominiums, Cambridge MA; Bullfinch Square, Cambridge MA; Connecticut College Humanities Center, New London CT INSTITUTIONAL/LIBRARIES/SCHOOLS 75%, COMMERCIAL 25%

Just as the Hancock Tower in Boston exemplifies the abstraction and minimalism of Modernism, his Church Court Condominiums in the same city embody common Postmodern qualities: contrast, color, ornament and urban context. Sited at the head of the Harvard Bridge, this cluster of condominiums in and

William B. Bauhs, *Executive Drive Office Building*
(entrance), 1986. Photo: Hedrich-Blessing

John A. Blanton, *Chui Residence*, (Garden side with view of Pacific Ocean). Photo:
Leland Lee.

Russel C. Cecil, *Slavin House*, Rye Brook, New York.

Richard L. Bowen, *Playhouse Square Hotel* (drawing).   Senior Designer: Dominick Durante. Project Architect: Robert A. Fiala

Louis and Suzanne Di Geronimo, *Alterations to the Goldin Residence* (Beaux-Arts rendering), Mantoloking, New Jersey, 1983.

Robert Donald Ferris, *Anza-Borrego Desert State Park Visitors Center*, California

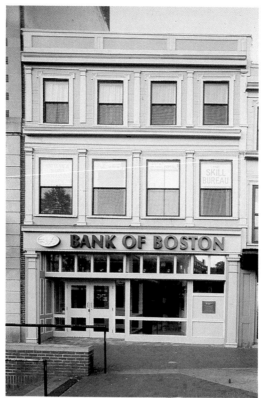

Harold Goyette, Cole and Goyette, Architects and Planners, Inc., *Bank of Boston, Harvard Square Branch*, Cambridge, Massachusetts, 1987. Photo: William T. Smith

David Jay Flood, *Seascape III*, Redondo Beach, California

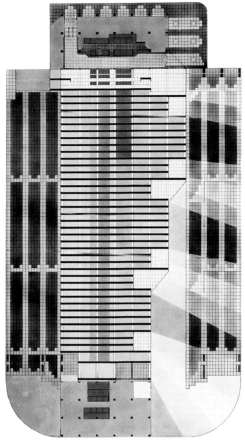

Helmut Jahn, *1 South Wacker*, Chicago,
1983. Project Architect: James Goettsch

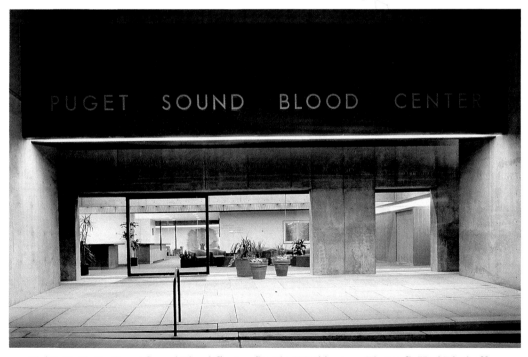

Keith R. Kolb, *Puget Sound Blood Center*, Seattle, Washington. Photo: G. Karl Bischoff

William Kessler, *Industrial Technology Institute*, Ann Arbor, Michigan, 1987. Photo: Balthazar Korab, Ltd.

Julian F. Kulski, *G. Kimball Hart Residence*, 1988. Photo: Gordon Beal.

Wendell H. Lovett, *Proctor House,* Kirkland, Washington, 1987.

Julian E. Kulski, building design, interiors and landscaping, *Kulski Residence* , 1973. Photo: Robert Lautman.

Avinash K. Malhotra, *The Archive,* 1988. Project Architects: Daniel Margulies, Vinod Devgan.. Photo: Richard Saunderson.

Bernard A. Marson, *Lowengrub Townhouse renovation,* 1982. Photo: Wolfgang Hoyt/ESTO

around a ruined church marks the considerable distance he has travelled from his training under Walter Gropius to arrive at a unique idiosyncratic Postmodernism. The building's units are partly tucked into and around the ruin of a an L-shaped Richardsonian Church. It rises seven stories at a little distance from the church, separated by a courtyard sanctuary. The renovated church has glazed doors and windows to insulate the courtyard acoustically and permit views into the courtyard. The former bell tower, anchored in the corner, is now an apartment. Newer apartments are peppered with bays and bumps permitting many views of the Charles River.

Facade patterning is bold and delightful. Banded horizontally in a traditional ordering of base, middle and top with contrasting colors of brown, red and buff brick, dark and light granite, and reflective orange tile, they dramatically articulate its flat skin. The whimsy and play is accentuated by a gentle parody of surrounding Back Bay facades: he shifts the traditional banding which connects lintels and sills down to new lines which he draws midway between stories. The windows themselves, many outlined in white, call attention with their size and simple panes, hinting at contemporary construction while alluding to the old.

A well-known art collector, his interests are reflected both in patterning which is inspired by Frank Stella, whose color experiments have sought to create optical depth with flat surfaces. He also commissioned tapestries and sculpture throughout the building. A bronze angel, executed in the Beaux-Arts manner by sculptor Gene Cauthern, sits atop the Church wall looking down at the newly widened and landscaped sidewalk on Massachusetts Avenue.

GWATHMEY, CHARLES
(Building Design)
Gwathmey Siegel and Associates 475 Tenth Avenue New York New York 1018

Born: 1938 **Studied:** Yale University **Awards:** FAIA; Design Award, *Interiors* magazine, 1983; Product Design Award, 1981

Notable Works: Francois de Menil House, East Hampton, New York; Guggenheim Museum Addition, New York; Museum of Moving Images, Astoria, New York

His work is an indomitably American interpretation of the International Style of Le Corbusier. His formal vocabulary is almost exclusively limited to cylinders, semi-cylinders and most commonly close derivatives of the cube. His architecture is in many ways analogous to Cubism and Constructivism in art. His basic space-organizing unit, the cube, is invaded, adjoined and abridged by shooting columns, obtuse diagonal stairways and ribbon windows, creating an enormous geometric conflagration. Yet his work has unmistakable order and unity; its attraction is in its tension between movement and control. His materials of choice depart sharply from the International School's industrial-age standards. He borrows heavily from native crafts houses of early New England and the Shingle School, creating smooth, elegant wooden enclosures that belie the drama unleashed within.

GWIN, WILLIAM R.
(Building Design, Historic Preservation)
William R. Gwin, Architect (205) 887-7833
439 North College Street Auburn AL 36830

Born: 1941 **Studied:** University of Pennsylvania; Auburn Unviersity **Awards:** Alabama AIA **Notable Works:** West Church Street Condominiums, Mobile AL RESIDENTIAL 100%

His contextualism aims to situate a building in its appropriate physical and intellectual environment. He thinks that architects should produce as full and complete an experience as possible by weaving elements of the surrounding neighborhood into the building site. To achieve this, he takes into account the land in its original geological status, the land as it has been changed by man, the rhythms of zones and property lines, and the surrounding types and styles of buildings. If successful, the result will be a structure that exhibits integrity of function and appropriateness to its context.

His West Church Street Townhouses

Sears Tower
Chicago, Illinois

Bruce Graham, *Sears Tower,* Chicago.

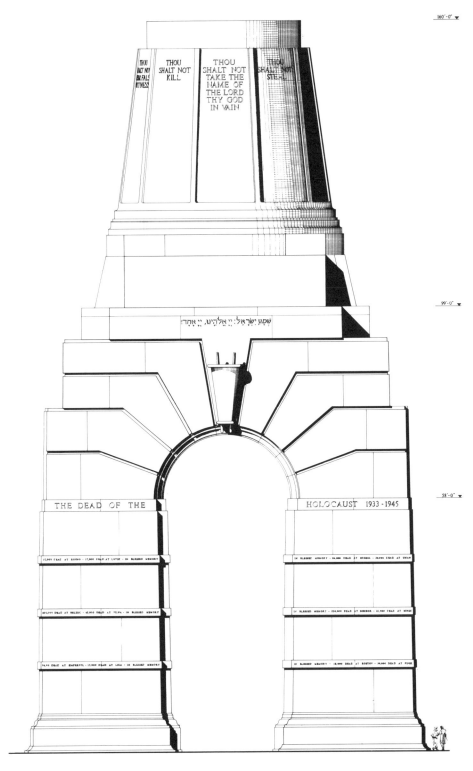

160'-0"

THOU
NOT NOT
BE FALSE
WITNESS

THOU
SHALT NOT
KILL

THOU
SHALT NOT
TAKE THE
NAME OF
THE LORD
THY GOD
IN VAIN

THOU
SHALT NOT
STEAL

99'-0"

שְׁמַע יִשְׂרָאֵל יְיָ אֱלֹהֵינוּ, יְיָ אֶחָד׃

58'-0"

THE DEAD OF THE

HOLOCAUST 1933 - 1945

ELEVATION · MAJOR AXIS

Allen Greenburg, *Drawing for Proposed Holocaust Memorial*

107

occupy three irregularly shaped blocks in an historic area of Mobile AL. Most of the area consists of preserved "shotgun" houses (so named because each house's simple row of rooms, connected by centered doorways in a line from the front door through the back door, suggested that one could fire a shotgun through the house from front to back without hitting anything) originally inhabited by lower- income residents. His project was designed to fill an empty corner of the historic area with townhouses that respected the surrounding neighborhood and the regional flavor of Mobile. A total of 30 townhouses are clustered in the three the blocks, facing green squares. The squares were modelled after several historic squares in downtown Mobile, with their pockets of live oaks and their functional networks of walkways, and also inspired by the ancient Greek idea of the square as public space. The houses feature pastel-colored opaque stained wood, double-hung shingled windows and porches. Although there are four different prototypes, houses are unified stylistically. They are reminiscent of the southern "raised cottage"-four rooms surrounding a central hall—and the 1920s bungalow.

HAID, DAVID
(Building Design, engineering)
David Haid + Associates PC Architects
(312) 644-2570
415 N. State St., Chicago IL 60610

Born: 1928 **Studied:** University of Manitoba; Illinois Institute of Technology **Awards:** AIA Citation of Merit, James F. Lincoln Arc Welding Foundation Award **Notable Works:** Pavilion, Highland Park IL; Walter H. Dyett Middle School, Chicago

He worked for nine years with Mies van der Rohe, from whom he received strong guidance and direction that has informed his subsequent work. "Mies never set a style. He only gave us a working method," he says, holding himself aloof from postmodern stylists. He sees buildings as complete entities that will serve and adapt to evolving uses for 50 or 100 years, and so strives for purity and simplicity of expres-

sion. His diversified practice includes many large projects. He and his relatively small office enjoy collaborating together on all the elements that converge in a successful design.

HALPRIN, LAWRENCE
(Landscape Architecture)
Lawrence Halprin Architect (415) 546-1952
1620 Montgomery Street   San Francisco
California 94111

Born: 1916   **Studied:** Cornell University **Awards:** Fellow, AIA; Fellow, American Society of Landscape Architects; Industrial Design Award of Excellence, Smithsonian Institution, 1968   **Notable Works:** Master Plan, University of California at Davis; Bay Area Rapid Transit design, San Francisco Bay area; Portland Civic Auditorium

He has always been concerned with linking public and private spaces in urban and suburban communities. In the first years of his career he concentrated on single-family houses and small private gardens. Soon he became interested in ways to link these together without diminishing their individual effects. Plans for group houses, suburban communities and shopping malls followed. These mid-scale projects gave way to larger ones, and his attention was eventually drawn to the problems of free communication and transportation between cities and suburbs. After designing freeways and subway systems in the San Francisco Bay area, he began to explore ways to recreate a feeling of connectedness and community in America's urban cores. His work emphasizes pedestrian networks, central parks that stimulate the senses, and old buildings recycled for new uses. Involved in a remarkable range of design activities, he's perhaps best known for his exuberant, geometrical plazas and fountains. His forecourt fountain for the Portland OR Civic Auditorium is a complex arrangement of falls and pools which evokes the falling waters of the nearby Cascade Mountains. The largest of the falls is more than a hundred feet high, while the lowest pool is depressed ten feet beneath the sidewalk. The roar of the fountain overcomes

Allan Greenburg, *George C. Marshall Reception Room*, State Department. Photo: Richard Clark

even the clamor of surrounding traffic.

HAMMOND BEEBY and BABKA (see Beeby, William Jr.)

HANSEN, ALAN L.
(Building and Graphic Design, Interior Architecture, Historic Preservation)
Hansen Architects & Associates PC
(703) 450-6634
2 Pidgeon Hill Drive Suite 560
Sterling VA 22170

Born: 1951 **Studied:** University of Maryland **Awards:** Northern Virginia AIA; AIA/*Housing* magazine First Honor Award Notable Work: South Concourse, Washington National Airport, Arlington VA; Lenkin Residence, Foggy Bottom, Washington DC; Chairs & Company, Washington DC COMMERCIAL 75%, RESIDENTIAL 25%

In keeping with the general flight of architecture from the heroism and monumentalism of 30 and 40 years ago, his work has moved from pure expression and form-making—what he calls "architectural athletics"—to more contextualist idioms. He believes that the future will see a return to "pattern-book classicism" and a renewed commitment to technique.

His Lenkin Residence in Foggy Bottom, Washington DC blends contemporary and Federal architectural styles and bows to the neighborhood with its masonry walls and traditional exterior detailing. Interior spaces are defined with cypress-clad forms that float in and out of the masonry container. A lead pan under the roof sheathing and triple-insulated shaded glass insulate the house from overhead traffic bound for nearby National Airport. A spiral stair ascends to the third floor where a radial layout takes in views to the Potomac river.

His South Concourse at Washington National Airport close by in Arlington VA is in keeping with the pre-war styling of other connecting parts of the airport but has been freshened with architectural neon lighting. Cobalt blue tubing provides a color accent on clear anodized aluminium, while white tubing silhouettes informational ribbon-style aluminum lettering and backlights each glass bay.

HARDY HOLAMAN PFEIFFER (see Pfeiffer, Norman; Hardy, Hugh Gelston)

HARDY, HUGH GELSTON
(Building Design)
Hardy Holaman Pfeiffer Associates
(212) 677-6030
902 Broadway New York NY 10010

Born: 1899 **Studied:** Cornell University **Awards:** Fellow, AIA; Honor Award, New York AIA, 1976; Bartlett Award, 1977 **Notable Works:** Brooklyn Children's Museum, New York; Simon's Rock Art Center, Great Barrington, Massachusetts; WCCO-TV Building, Minneapolis COMMERCIAL/RETAIL: 15%, HOUSING: 15%, INDUSTRIAL: 5%, EDUCATION: 10%, PERFORMING ARTS: 40%, PLANNING: 10%, OTHER: 20%

He describes his long partnership with Malcolm Holzman and Norman Pfeiffer as noisy and often redundant, yet he believes that collaboration and compromise are indispensable to responsive architecture. Good ideas, he says, can come from anywhere in his firm, so he's hostile to the idea of "designer-tyrants" disseminating and delegating ideas to obedient junior functionaries.

His flamboyant Hardy/Holzman/Pfeiffer team has been criticized as being excessively eclectic, even pranksterish, yet it has evolved from small, experimental adaptive re-use commissions to designing major multi-use entertainment centers. He and his associates are committed to establishing a more pluralistic architectural idiom, but his mannered choices of forms and materials are far from arbitrary. He believes that architecture and other arts should incorporate the materials that permeate everyday reality. Further, architectural elements needn't be uniform nor classically harmonious to provide order.

From the outside his buildings are most conspicuous by their absence or obscurity, often designing underground, bermed installations, such as the Brooklyn Children's Mu-

Allen Greenburg, *The Treaty Room of State, U.S. Department Suite*, Washington, D.C. Photo: Richard Creek

seum. Otherwise his exteriors are usually free-form, asymmetric shells which derive from the buildings' internal organization.

HARPER, ROBERT L.

Centerbrook Architects & Planners
(203) 767-0175
Box 409 Essex CT 06426

Born: 1939 **Studied:** Amherst College; Columbia University **Awards:** FAIA; Builder's Choice awards; New England AIA **Notable Works:** Williams College Museum of Art, Williamstown MA; Cold Spring Harbor Jones Laboratory, Long Island NY RESIDENTIAL 50%, INSTITUTIONAL/COMMERCIAL 50%

His architecture responds to the differing demands of users, sites and existing architecture. His plan for the expansion of the Williams College Museum of Art in Williamstown MA took into account multiple program requirements, varying access and security requirements for different users, all on a tiny, triangular plot adjacent to a 30-foot drop down a steep hillside. His addition orients itself to the existing museum, which is housed in a series of handsome rooms axially disposed around a columned rotunda.

An atrium, built on level ground south of the existing building, acts as an in-between space open to all building users. Museum galleries on the top floor and offices on the ground floor are easily closed off in evening hours, while classrooms are directly accessible from the outdoors at anytime. To the south and east of the atrium, the major additions are organized in two rectangular masses parallel to the slope of the hill, thus simplifying site work and foundations. A cantilevered structure lets the Art History floor be larger than the others as desired. New museum spaces on the top floor are organized around an axis which extends south from the original rotunda through a small gallery, across a long rectangular gallery, through the atrium on a bridge and finally into the octagonal end of the new main gallery. The shape of the gallery reminds visitors of the oldest part of the museum, while the expansive floor space, unbroken walls, and skylighted spaces offer all the amenities of a modern gallery. Brick and stucco exteriors harmonize the new with the spirit of the original building.

HARRIS, HARWELL HAMILTON

(Building Design)
122 Cox Avenue (919) 833-0624
Raleigh, North Carolina 27605

Born: 1903 **Studied:** Otis Art Institute, Los Angeles **Awards:** Fellow, AIA; Honor Award, AIA, Southern California Chapter, 1938; Richard Neutra Medal, 1982 **Notable Works:** Havens House, Berkeley, California; Entenza House, Santa Monica; Harris House, Raleigh, North Carolina COMMERCIAL/RETAIL: 45%, HOUSING: 15%, INDUSTRIAL: 10%, EDUCATION: 5%, MEDICAL: 5%, INTERIOR DESIGN: 5%, PLANNING: 10%

In many ways his work continues the earthy neo-stick style established a half-century earlier by fellow southern Californians Charles and Henry Greene and Berkeley architect Bernard Maybeck. But their influence has been filtered through his professional association with Richard Neutra, his passion for Asian sculpture, and his academic interest in Frank Lloyd Wright. From the Greenes he learned to build sensitively and delicately in wood, though stopping short of their exaltation of the material. From Neutra he learned to use modular design in humane ways, and by carrying them into wooden construction he produced distinctly Japanese interior effects in his houses. This Orientalism at home in the West, he realized, was a close gloss on Wright's contemporary work.

Parallels to Wright's late work are most dramatic in his 1951 Ralph Johnson House, which is probably still his best known work. For the sharply sloping site he designed a tri-level structure whose garage roof doubled as a terrace for the living room, which closely resembled Wright's expansive Usonian House. Its fundamental spatial formalism also followed Wright's lead, but the house's exposed timber frame and well-articulated roof structure were strictly original.

Robert C. Harper (with Charles Moore), *Williams College Museum of Art*. Photo: Norman McGrath

HARTMAN, CRAIG
(Building Design)
Skidmore, Ownings and Merrill
(202) 393-1400
1201 Pennsylvannia Ave. NW
Suite 600 Washington DC 20004

Studied: Ball State University **Notable Works:** Park Square, Albuquerque NM; Southwestern University's Academic Court and Library Addition, Georgetown TX

One of the younger design partners at SOM, his interest in urban architecture and large scale work was fostered by residencies at the Chicago office for seven years and at Houston for another five years. Now working in Washington DC, he remains adamant that style is not the overwhelming issue in architecture; rather, buildings should elaborate on where they are and on the facts that brought them into being. He advocates architecture that is evocative of its place, not in a historicist sense, but in its cultural sense and chosen materials.

At Southwestern University in Georgetown TX he spearheaded a reorganization master plan, creating a traditional academic court in the center of the campus. Articulating the southwest corner of the court is a library project, in which a new octagonal entrance pavilion, a new wing, an added third floor and a new sheathing of an earlier International Style addition in cream-colored Texas limestone, all contribute to reinterpreting campus underpinnings in basic form, not in imitation of details. His Albuquerque NM Park Square development also reflects his interest in public spaces. It organizes office, retail and parking areas around a series of outdoor courtyards and plazas, creating orderly, handsome "rooms" between the buildings.

HASBROUCK, WILBERT R.
(Historic Preservation)
Hasbrouck Petersen Associates
(312) 922-7211
711 S. Dearborn 2nd Floor Chicago IL 60605

Born: 1931 **Studied:** Iowa State College **Awards:** FAIA; Past President, Chicago Archi-

tectural Foundation; Chicago AIA; Third Annual Richard Nickel Award, Chicago Conference for Landmarks Preservation **Notable Works:** Restoration work on Dana Thomas House, Springfield IL, Rookery Building, Chicago; The Delaware Building, Chicago; John J. Glessner House Museum, Chicago HISTORIC PRESERVATION 100%

A leading Chicago preservationist, he was committed to full-time work on restoration long before Postmodernism made it fashionable. His passion for restoration work grows out of his conviction that memories are vital for people and culture. Memory is the cement that holds together the narratives of individuals, even as it ties each generation to the next. Though the nature of his work compels him to be a complete contextualist, he believes that good architecture, architecture "that makes an impact" the way Frank Lloyd Wright's Robie House impacted a generation of suburban dwellings, such architecture always dares to risk being somewhat out of stride, a little out of context.

His work has been marked by the discipline of restoring, not reconstructing, a great number of buildings, among them Wright's Dana Thomas House in Springfield IL and downtown Chicago's Manhattan Building. He focuses restorations on the period when a given building was most successful. From that period the building becomes a "trigger to the memory;" it may permit the building's viewers and users to experience something of the emotional impact felt by earlier generations.

HASSINGER, HERMAN
(Building Design)
Herman Hassinger Architects (609) 235-5760
282 Chester Ave. Moorestown NJ 08057

Born: 1929 **Studied:** University of Pennsylvania **Awards:** FAIA; Silver Medal Philadelphia AIA; New Jersey AIA **Notable Works:** First Lutheran Church, West Barnstable MA; Mermaid Hill, Block Island RI; Moorestown Emergency Services, Moorestown NJ HEALTH CARE 30%, RELIGIOUS 30%, INSTITUTIONAL 20%,

Harwell Hamilton Harris, *Entenza House*, 1937, Santa Monica, California. Photo: F. Dabbrich.

Harwell Hamilton Harris, *Weston Havens House*, Berkeley, California, 1941. Photo: Man Ray

RESIDENTIAL 5%

He seeks to design "appropriate architecture" which is right for its built context, its use, its users and its age. He favors simple forms with moderate to steeply pitched roofs whose elements are informally linked. Resolutely opposed to passing fads he calls 'starkitecture,' he looks for a visual richness of material and detail using traditional American design idioms.

His Moorestown Emergency Services firehouse in Moorestown NJ sensitively locates modern firefighting and emergency services in the middle of the 300-year-old town's Main Street. Neighborhood opposition had killed an earlier, more expensive modernization plan which would have razed three old houses on the site. His solution rehabilitates one of the houses, and attaches to it a new five-bay brick firehouse modeled after Frank Furness's nineteenth century train stations. A central tower housing the radio room and response center separates two emergency squad bays on one side of the tower from the three firefighting bays adjacent to the old house, where offices and crew space are located. The new structure is respectfully set back from the street, just touching the rear of the old one; its six-foot overhanging eaves minimize the visual impact of its garage doors. A strip of "grasscrete," concrete punctured with holes through which grass grows, bisects the wide driveway and reinforces the site's residential character. Skylights provide all necessary daytime illumination. Despite these details final costs were slightly lower than the national average for new firehouses of comparable size.

HAVEKOST, DANIEL J.

(Historic Preservation, Renovation, Building Design)
HWHL Associates, Inc. (303) 861-1121
707 Washington St Denver CO 80203

Born: 1936 **Studied:** University of Colorado
Awards: FAIA; Denver AIA; Colorado AIA
Notable Works: Encore Condominium Redevelopment, Denver CO; Mission Hills Baptist Church, Greenwood Village CO

COMMERCIAL/OFFICE 25%, RESIDENTIAL 40%, CHURCHES /THEATERS 30%

He believes that the best architecture is appropriate to its surroundings and reflects its community's history and values. His work aims to develop attractive spaces for human activity that use natural materials and straightforward methods while responding to its setting. Many completed projects involve infill design appropriate to surrounding architecture, and adaptive reuse of historically significant structures. He also focuses on religious architecture where musical acoustics, appropriate ecclesiastical statements and an environment conducive to worship are important.

His Encore Redevelopment restored a Denver national landmark, once a French Mediterranean-style mansion, to house the Mexican Consulate and offices and residences. Using its scale and materials in an adaptive reuse of the property, he built a 23-unit apartment building and underground parking for 45 cars, all interconnected in the basement and featuring a common loggia and overlooking patios. A repeated design of arched doorways, curved balconies and wrought-iron balustrades in the mansion was reused in the new wing, which also carried over its stucco and tile roofs.

For his religious architecture, acoustics figure heavily in his crafting of interiors. His major sanctuary addition to the Mission Hills Baptist Church in Greenwood Village CO incorporated continental seating—continuous rows without intermittent aisles—in a 90-degree fan shape. Large glue-laminated timber trusses spanning nearly 100 feet radiate over the chancel like spokes of a wheel. The wood surfaces mellow sounds and eliminate echoes, an important consideration for Baptist services so enlivened by music.

HEBALD-HEYMANN, MARGO

(Interior Architecture)
Margo Hebald-Heymann, AIA and Associates
(213) 829-2941
840 20th Street Santa Monica CA 90403

Born: 1941 **Studied:** Cornell University

Herman Hassinger, *Moorestown Emergency Services Building,* Moorestown, New Jersey. Project Architect: Gary Wagner. Photo: Lawrence S. Wilson

Norman Jaffe, *Gates of the Grove*, East Hampton, New York, 1988. Photo: Jeff Heatley.

College of Architecture and Planning; Universita di Roma, Italy **Awards:** Women in Design for Architecture, Women in Design International **Notable Works:** Terminal One at Los Angeles International Airport; Oxnard and Simi Valley Children's Dental Group, Oxnard, Simi Valley CA MEDICAL 85%, TRANSPORTATION 10%, RETAIL 5%

She believes that architecture is sculpture of the fourth dimension. We not only look at the three dimensions of a building, we experience it in space and time when we pass through it. She concentrates on circulation patterns in designing her interiors and often uses a combination of natural and artificial light to stress volume and shape and to create mood.

The Simi Valley Children's Dental Group in Simi Valley CA alleviates children's fear of dentists with a playful spaceship motif. Young patients enter the Pre-flight Check-in, a waiting room with a twenty-foot sky vault. Here they await the dentist while sitting on a semicircular modular unit where they can snuggle up to their parents. A large television screen shows educational videos. Next the child goes into the Time Warp Tunnel, a luminous arched corridor built with metallic slats which emphasize the curved ceiling. Another waiting room, the On-Deck Area, is stocked with video games. Above each patient chair in the operatory is a television monitor. Four clocks give the time at Nassau, on Mars, on the moon, and in Simi Valley. Many walls have vinyl coverings which give a polished, high-tech look. Rooms are laid out on angles which allow patients and doctors to circulate with a minimum of doubling back.

HEIKE, THOMAS A.
(Building Design, Exhibit Design, Facility Programming, Interior Architecture)
Heike Design Associates, Inc. (414) 786-0016
13255 W. Bluemound Road
Brookfield WI 53005

Born: 1946 **Studied:** University of Wisconsin at Milwaukee **Awards:** People's Choice Award, Wisconsin AIA; American Society of Interior Designers; *Building Management*

magazine Award of Excellence **Notable Works:** Experimental Aircraft Association Headquarters and Museum, Oshkosh, WI; Kohler Design Center, Kohler WI; Manitowoc Maritime Museum, Manitowoc WI COMMERCIAL 40%, INDUSTRIAL/CORPORATE 35%, EXHIBIT DESIGN 25%

He tries to create drama and spatial energy in his structures. Following the emphasis of his client, he aims to harmonize the aesthetics, cost and function of a project. He prefers to work with indigenous materials or those that derive from the context of the project.

In the two-story Experimental Aircraft Association Headquarters and Museum in Oshkosh WI the visitor enters a fifty-six-foot high glass main gallery. Three acrobatic airplanes hang from the ceiling in flight formation. The light-filled gallery contrasts with "black box" exhibit rooms—windowless areas that focus on historic aircraft displays. Museum rooms are compartmentalized to control the flow of people viewing the displays. This is an important feature of the Museum because so many of the 800,000 people who attend annual ten-day EAA fly-in conventions visit the museum at that time. The exterior of the steel-framed building is precast panels of exposed aggregate concrete.

His renovation of the Kohler Design Center in Kohler WI, which houses the Kohler art collection and displays the company's plumbing fixtures, gives a startling contrast between its 1920s Tudor exterior and its high tech interior, featuring an exposed steel truss ceiling and unistrut space frame. Glass block walls separate spa decks in the product display area. Water cascades down these glass walls illuminated by lights below, providing a soothing background sound as well as visual interest.

HEJDUK, JOHN
(Building Design, Exhibition Design)
John Hejduk Architect (212) 549-4089
5721 Huxley Avenue
Riverdale New York 10471

Born: 1929 **Studied:** Harvard University **Awards:** Fellow, AIA; Fellow, Royal Society of Arts; Duke Foundation Award, 1973 **Notable Works:** Foundation Building Restoration, Cooper Union, New York; Skinner Duplex Apartments, Austin, Texas; Hommel Apartment, New York

Although he has completed a handful of apartments, single family homes and architectural exhibitions in the last twenty years, his production has largely consisted of drawings and models. Consequently working outside the constraints of context, materials or client/user demands, his renderings are pure formal studies, undertaken to generate principles of form and space. In the 1950s he took up the spatial possibilities of frames and cubes. Later, inspired by the sharply geometric paintings of Mondrian, he undertook a study of diamonds and parallelograms, parsed out into successively smaller square grids. Recently he has moved into a more expansive phase, working with a variety of flat planes and curved masses in a range of neutral colors. His work has been criticized as over-idealized and irrelevant to the social forces shaping contemporary architecture. Design undertaken *en vacuo,* however, is a pointer and bridge toward our developing architectural vocabulary. Ultimately, posterity must judge the instructional and inspirational value of his contribution.

HEIMSATH, CLOVIS & MARYANN

(Building Design, Interior Architecture, Historic Preservation)
Clovis Heimsath Associates (409) 378-2592

Awards: Texas AIA **Notable Works:** Kagan-Rudy Chapel, Houston TX; St. Jerome Roman Catholic Church, Waco TX

To call the work of this husband and wife team historicist or revivalist is to miss the richness and serenity that their work inserts into a cityscape full of "business cathedrals."

Their Kagan-Rudy Chapel in Houston TX, located off an unremarkable highway, is a sanctuary filled with references to archaic architecture and Judaic culture. One enters through one of six arched portals flanked by bas-relief columns, each surmounted by a bronze medallion. Views through the chapel on each of three cross axes are interrupted by interior columns, six of which form a ring to support the central dome. Corbeled squinches— small arches of masonry—mediate up from the hexagonal drum to the circular base of the dome and alternate with six arched stained glass windows with Stars of David. The ceramic tile floor also has a Star of David pattern, with the interior columns positioned at the points of the internal hexagon. At the big star's eastern point, an "eternal flame" is embedded in the floor in front of a concrete screen with an affixed anodized bronze sculpture. This memorial to the Jewish dead is the chapel's sole Modernist or abstract design element. The rustic medallions at the portals depict the 12 tribes of Israel; the interior columns have ram's horn capitals; and squinches, nicely echoed on the exterior of the drum, support the dome. Handsome stained glass windows (designed by Maryann Heimsath) have an austere, archaic quality; the copper dome alludes to the Dome of the Rock in Jerusalem; and the spartan, tiered seating alludes to the small stepped synagogue cut into stone at Masada. The berming too is reminiscent of Masada.

Their St. Jerome Roman Church near Waco TX is remarkable for its exquisite decoration, unabashedly borrowed from the Italian Renaissance, especially Alberti's 15th century facade on the 13th century Santa Maria Novella in Florence. The famous icon appears in reduced scale above a striped arcade on the entry facade and is repeated in a gabled panel of brick and stained glass in the rear. The interior is richly decorated and suffused with colored light coming through stained glass windows, also designed by them.

HELFAND, MARGARET

(Building Design, Interior Architecture, Renovation)
Margaret Helfand Architects (212) 779-7260
32 E. 38 St. New York NY 10016

Born: 1947 **Studied:** Swarthmore College; University of California at Berkeley **Awards:** AIA; *Interiors* magazine annual award; *ID*

magazine annual award **Notable Works:** Jennifer Reed Showroom, New York City; Columbia University School of the Arts Painting and Sculpture facilities, New York City; proposed Rhode Island School of Design Museum Contemporary Art Wing, Providence RI INSTITUTIONAL 33%, RESIDENTIAL 33%, RETAIL 33%

Greatly influenced by the tenets of early twentieth century Modernism, her designs explore original ways to generate form, organize space and exploit material possibilities. Structural and functional requirements are freshly expressed in each project, often through irregular forms generated by specific program requirements.

Her personal office shares a room with her firm's conference area, a natural adaptation because she's present at all conferences. Her personal desk is an acute triangle cut out of the 8-foot conference table, installed on casters and nestled into a corner among her working effects. It rolls into the conference table to complete its rectangle. While working at her desk her conference table is a usable grand piano-shaped trapezoid. Desk and table surfaces are cantilevered on frames of thin bent steel plate which take strength and rigidity from their design curves. Work surfaces are supported on their cantilevered frames by thin sheets of corrugated precast cement, whose undulations are expressed especially along the diagonal cut. Her conference chairs too are expressions of simple, original material possibilities—each chair seat and back is a single flat steel sheet, bent 90 degrees and tilted back slightly with various design details. Disarmingly simple, the chairs are comfortable enough for prospective clients.

HELLMUTH, OBATA & KASSABAUM, INC (see Obata, Gyo; Hellmuth, George)

HELLMUTH, GEORGE FRANCIS
(Building Design, Cost Estimating)
Hellmuth, Obata and Kassabaum
(314) 421-2000
100 North Broadway St. Louis

Missouri 63102

Born: 1907 **Studied:** Washington University, St. Louis **Awards:** FAIA; Citation, *Engineering News--Record*, 1977 **Notable Works:** Dallas/ Fort Worth Airport; Married Student Housing, University of Alaska; National Air and Space Museum, Washington, D.C. COMMERCIAL/RETAIL: 50%, MEDICAL: 4%, INTERIOR DESIGN: 38%, PLANNING: 8%

Early in his career, he concluded that his skills as an organizer, motivator and administrator outstripped his considerable design abilities. As he worked in various offices for nearly a decade, he began to develop ideas for a more dynamic and efficient architectural practice. He noted that there are three broad phases to each commission: marketing/solicitation, design, and execution. He decided to assemble a firm of three principals, each with a special affinity and responsibility for one of these areas.

In 1949 he established the firm of Hellmuth, Yamasaki and Leinweber. Though dissolved after six years, its innovative structure had proven viable. His second partnership, with Gyo Obata as designer and George Kassabaum as construction supervisor, has become one of the most enduring and productive collaborations in the history of American architecture. In their 25 years of enlightened cooperation the firm has undertaken commissions in virtually every category of architectural endeavor, yet designs remain fresh, diverse and crisp.

HELPERN, DAVID PAUL
(Building Design, Construction Administration, Facility Programming, Historic Preservation, Interior Architecture, Renovation)

Helpern Architects (212) 505-2025
23 East 4th St. New York NY 10003

Born: 1938 **Studied:** Brown University; Harvard University Graduate School of Design **Awards:** Fifth Avenue Association; Builder's Institute of Westchester; New York City AIA/ Educational Facilities Laboratory design award **Notable Works:** 667 Madison Avenue, New

David Paul Helpern, *667 Madison Avenue*, New York City. Photo: Brian Rose

York City; Eastchester High School Gymnasium, Eastchester NY; General Theological Seminary rehabilitation master plan, Chelsea Square, New York City COMMERCIAL 50%, INSTITUTIONAL 50%

He has been called the "architect of the inevitable" for his commitment to discovering, in continuing collaboration with clients, needs that will define and make 'inevitable' his architectural spaces. Surrounding context too suggests forms and motifs at once historically sympathetic and contemporary.

His 667 Madison Avenue office tower at 61st St. is at the Midtown edge of Manhattan's Upper East Side historic district. The 25-story commercial building fronts Madison Avenue at the point where high-rise commerce meets low-rise residential elegance, and it turns appropriate faces and features to both worlds. The tower is sheathed in pale granite, with limestone detailing in the base that recalls the grand retail buildings of the 1920s and 1930s. Double-height display windows line the street facades, and arched display windows above them are highlighted by a continuous limestone ribbon passing through the granite. With a series of terraced setbacks beginning at the fifth floor, the tower makes a transition in scale from its historic neighbors to the north to the office buildings to the south. The lobby entrance is placed on 61st Street to make room for vital Madison Avenue retail space. A recessed, 41-foot high arcade gives access to a 23-foot-high limestone lobby with green marble floors and custom-designed chandeliers. Updated classical features such as these convey the formality and timelessness of traditional office towers. Tower windows feature another classical element used in a contemporary spirit. Half-round columns with granite bases and capitals are placed asymmetrically in the windows to give a dynamic rhythm to the facade.

HIBLER, ROBERT
(Building Design)
Boyd/Sobieray Associates (317) 849-7878
6810 N. Shadeland, Indianapolis IN 46220

Born: 1948 **Studied:** University of Cincinnati **Awards:** California Design Award, AIA; Indiana AIA Citation Award **Notable Works:** Sacramento Safety Center CA; Community Hospital North, Indianapolis IN

Clear, innovative and cost-effective solutions for complex medical facilities are his specialty in today's challenging medical environment. The solutions must be functional, yet friendly and comfortable for patients and visitors as well as staff. They must respond to the many rapid changes overtaking the practice of medicine, in financing and corporate structure no less than technology. These changes are reflected and harmonized in his medical architecture.

His Community Hospital North is molded by efficient triangular nursing stations that clearly define the circulation of visitors as well as staff. Courtyards and corridors too help to orient visitors, and feature soft, quiet details more characteristic of hotels.

HIGHTOWER, IRBY
(Building Design, Interior Architecture)
Alamo Architects (512) 227-2612
108 King William San Antonio TX 78204

Born: 1955 **Studied:** University of Texas at Austin **Awards:** Texas Award for the Preservation of Historic Architecture; Preservation award, San Antonio Conservation Society **Notable Works:** Fairmount Restaurant, San Antonio TX; Aztec Theater, San Antonio TX COMMERCIAL/RETAIL 75%, RESIDENTIAL 15% ,RENOVATION 10%

His architecture and that of his partners at Alamo Architects draws its inspiration from diverse sources: the Arts and Crafts movement, Texas vernacular, Frank Lloyd Wright and modern design.

In addition to restoring the Fairmount Hotel in San Antonio TX they designed its Fairmount Restaurant. Taking over the ground floor space originally used by a retail store, their contemporary design conforms with federal and state guidelines governing historic renovations. The restaurant bridges the hotel building and a newer addition. A bar section

David Paul Helpern, *667 Madison Avenue*, New York City.   Photo: Brian Rose

faces Alamo Street, looking out through a storefront shaded by an overhanging deck, which was common in earlier days. It screens the dining room which is wrapped around a large kitchen. A literal period look was avoided in favor of a generalized form. The finishes are in pale, understated colors.

HIMMEL BONNER ARCHITECTS (see Bonner, Darcy; Himmell, Scott)

HIMMEL, SCOTT D.

(Building Design, Interior Architecture)
Himmel Bonner Architects (312) 853-0222
205 West Wacker Drive Suite 305 Chicago IL 60606

Born: 1955 **Studied:** Tulane University **Awards:** Chicago AIA; Invited Lecturer, Emerging Voices Series, Architectural League of New York **Notable Works** (also see Darcy Bonner): Playboy Enterprises Corporate Headquarters, Chicago COMMERCIAL 35%, RESIDENTIAL 35%, RETAIL 20%

He and partner Darcy Bonner aren't among those who have abandoned the machine-age aesthetic. On the contrary, they like to use as much technology and electronics as possible. They believe that people still share "the excitement known by the architects of the twenties and the thirties—the excitement of the future." The warmth and richness of their work arises from bold and inventive use of materials on top of technologically sophisticated forms. They enjoy using natural and particularly "man-made" ingredients: marble, sandblasted glass, stainless steels and rubber.

Given a free hand in designing a warm and "not boring" environment for a highrise apartment in Chicago, they devised a series of visual events that unfold throughout the apartment. The elevator foyer, framed in hard surfaces of granite and pale opaque limestone, offers a precis of things to come. Matched heavy glass doors swing in intricately constructed arms of steel to seal the passage. Moving in, the aerodynamically inspired curves of the passageway are offset by a savvy warmth generated by the glossy automobile lacquer atop the apartment's millwork. The entertainment space, with a view of Lake Michigan, is framed by intersecting slabs of limestone which enclose the setting. These vertical surfaces project lines into the space that define three distinct zones, for video watching, conversation and dining. The private suite contains a sleeping area surrounded by a study, dressing area and bath. The bath includes a round exercise room enclosed by finely tooled metal doors and a green marble-clad shower. A raised platform extends through the sleeping area, past a retractable wall, to a private study beyond. Convex curved doors, which enclose the exercise room, complete the continuity of the space.

HINDS, GEORGE ALLEN

(Building Design, Urban Design)
Born: 1922 **Studied:** Yale University **Awards:** AIA Chicago Chapter **Notable Works:** Remodeling, University of Chicago; Renovation, 714 So. Dearborn St., Chicago; Renovation, Ginsburg Residence, Chicago; National College of Chiropractics Student Center, Lombard, IL

He studied in the late 1940s and early 1950s at Yale with such noted and innovative architects as Louis Kahn, Eero Saarinen and Sven Markelius. Early in his career he worked for a private architectural firm and for city planning commissions in Stockholm and Philadelphia. A project shortly after his relocation to Chicago presented a tricky problem: how to remodel and renovate several buildings on the University of Chicago's idiosyncratic neo-Gothic campus. His remodeling designs used modern materials while remaining faithful, or at least sympathetic, to the harmonious design of the campus's turn-of-the-century buildings, and to the greater ideal of the university in general. This is a problem that even his teacher, the great Saarinen, had trouble overcoming, as is evident in his somewhat less than successful design for the university's Center for Continuing Education.

Another design in Chicago's historic Hyde Park neighborhood—the Ginsburg residence—

posed similar problems. He maintained the house's external appearance, including the gabled roofs, but the interior design presents a rather sparse modernity, which lends greater decorative force to the original external features and to such interior elements as the iron grill-work of the stairway railing. The remodeling once again fuses the old with the new, a solution that reveals sensitivity to history but no fear of the modern. Part of his success is attributable to annual study trips he leads to Europe: there he sketches notable architectural sites, enhancing not only his sense of design and composition but also the appreciation of historical context.

HINTON, KEM GARDNER

(Building Design, Exhibition Design, Architectural Delineation, Facility Programming, Renovation)
Tuck Hinton Everton Architects
(615) 320-1810
1810 Hayes St. Nashville TN 37203

Born: 1954 **Studied:** University of Tennessee; University of Pennsylvania **Awards:** Tennessee AIA; Builder's Choice Grand Prize; Japan Architect Central Glass Competition First Prize **Notable Works:** Ragan Smith Murphy Rehabilitation, Nashville TN; Riverfront Apartments, Nashville TN; CNA Regional Headquarters, Nashville TN RESIDENTIAL 30%, OFFICE 25%, COMMERCIAL 20%

Each commission presents him with a hidden agenda, a "concealed constraint" which becomes the basis for his design solutions. Design restrictions possess strength; properly identified and exploited, they can be manipulated into the fabric of exciting places to live and work.

His Ragan Smith Murphy rehabilitation in Nashville TN is designed around a structurally sound but uninteresting shell. New interior spaces and divisions are arranged around existing column lines, emphasized by new skylights at circulation junctures. Outside, the former rhythm of windows and openings is extended into the front yard. In the main lobby, historic surveyor artifacts collected by

the owners are displayed in a horizontal case with a transparent top; one discovers the items only after walking around the articulated lobby. Three large murals are featured as the main artwork in the lobby, and synopsize the architectural solutions of the rehabilitation in two-dimensional renderings.

HOLABIRD & ROOT (see Horn, George; Solfisburg, Roy)

HOLL, STEVEN M.

(Building Design, Interior Design)
Steven Holl Architects (212) 989-0918
133 West 19th Top Floor
New York NY 10010

Born: 1947 **Studied:** University of Washington at Seattle; The Architectural Association in London **Awards:** AIA; New York AIA; *Progressive Architecture* citation **Notable Works:** Seaside Mixed Use Building, Seaside FL; Extension of the American Library, West Berlin INSTITUTIONAL 50%, COMMERCIAL 25%, RESIDENTIAL 25%

He derides Postmodernist architecture as over-decorative, and tweaks Modernists for ignoring the sensual elements of construction. Believing with the ancient Greeks that proportion determines the quality of a design, he takes a geometrical approach to his work, but balances the austerity of his plans by paying careful attention to details, especially in selecting materials. The Architectural League of New York picked him as an "emerging voice."

The inspiration for his Museum Tower apartment in New York City is the Cartesian coordinate system: he formed the rooms in the 1,500-square-foot shell by a series of planes positioned parallel or perpendicular to one another. These smooth plaster-covered planes correspond to the grid pattern of Manhattan's city streets. X-axis planes (north-south) are dark grey, Y-axis planes pale yellow. The vertical Z-axis is provided by the skyscrapers seen out the windows of the 42nd-story apartment, and by vertical design features in the lighting. Library shelving is built on a door with special hinges: it can swing open for display without spilling the books, or remain closed until needed.

HOLUB, MARTIN

(Building Design, Exhibition Design, Interior Architecture, Planning)
Martin Holub Architects & Planners
(212) 787-7644
116 West 72 St. Suite 16E
New York NY 10023

Born: 1938 **Studied:** Czech Technical University, Academy of Fine Arts, Prague, Czechoslovakia **Awards:** Gulf States AIA; Tennessee AIA **Notable Works:** Rokeby Condominium, Nashville TN; St. Pius X Parish Center, Old Tappan NJ COMMERCIAL 30%, RESIDENTIAL 30%, INSTITUTIONAL 15%, RELIGIOUS 15%, INDUSTRIAL 10%

He doesn't work in a preconceived style, believing that appropriate forms and materials emerge from analyzing the determining factors of a project. Once site, surroundings, program and budget have determined a project's plan, the plan generates forms and the forms suggest materials. Agreeing with Diana Vreeland's dictum that "elegance is refusal," he holds that the ideal design contains nothing unessential to solving client problems.

An example of this design-from-within approach is his Nashville TN Rokeby Condominium, which elegantly resolves a common but seldom visually expressed developer's quandary: how does one plan for the vagaries of market demand? His response was to design a flexible floor plan which permitted a wide range of apartment sizes to interlock differently on every floor. This allowed the condominium market itself to determine final apartment distribution: buyers were ordering apartments of their choice while the building went up, selecting from a stock of 23 apartment sizes rather than the usual two or three. Seemingly random exterior window patterns express the apartment layouts that were chosen on each floor. The building's final appearance has thus been determined by this unique solution to the client's problem, exemplifying the view of design as an honest response to the specific conditions of each project.

HOLZBOG, THOMAS JERALD

(Building Design, Interior Architecture)
Holzbog Matloob & Associates
(213) 854-3428
8797 Beverly Boulevard
Suite 220 Los Angeles CA 90048

Studied: Yale University; Harvard University **Awards:** AIA; American Society of Registered Architects **Notable Works:** West Los Angeles Chamber of Commerce, Los Angeles; Newton Lower Falls, Newton MA HOUSING 50%, COMMERCIAL 50%

He dedicates his practice to achieving design quality by giving imaginative and appropriate solutions that respond to peoples' real needs. Functional efficiency, durability and cost-effectiveness are primary concerns, yet his buildings strive for beauty, aiming to create an environment that attracts people to live in it. His architecture strikes a balance between the functional values of Modernism and the aestheticism of Postmodernism. His work ranges from interior design and space planning for single-family residences to high-rise developments, urban design and new town planning.

His Newton Lower Falls in Newton MA is a low-rise 60-unit condominium complex which combines wood-frame flats and duplexes. Staggered roof lines, deck and entryways lend architectural variety and individuality, while natural ledge-rock outcroppings no less than his pitched roofs hold to the low profile of its adjacent neighborhood. On a hill with good views of commercial streets and the river below, it's accessible by pedestrian links to a hilltop park above. The entry road is intentionally staggered to break up parking areas, which like the units themselves conform to site contours. The ten clusters of six units surround private courtyards, providing simultaneously a sense of privacy and community. Each dwelling has floor-through window exposures and eat-in kitchens. Courtyards serve as semi-private transitional areas and contain covered entryways.

Martin Holub, Architectural Design Consultant, (Design); Barber & McMurray, Architects, (Production). *Rokeby Apartments*, Nashville, Tennessee.

HOOD MILLER ASSOCIATES (see Hood, Bobbie Sue; Miller, L. Kirk)

HOOD, BOBBIE SUE

(Building Design, Facility Programming, Renovation)
Hood Miller Associates (415) 777-5775
60 Federal St. San Francisco CA 94107

Studied: Bryn Mawr College; Carnegie-Mellon University; University of California at Berkeley **Awards:** AIA; California AIA; *Builder* magazine's Project of the Year **Notable Works:** Russian Hill Terrace (1150 Lombard St.), San Francisco; 1055 Lombard St., San Francisco; Macondray Terrace, San Francisco RESIDENTIAL 75%, INSTITUTIONAL 15%, COMMERCIAL 10%

She specializes in building design for challenging sites and architectural programming for complex projects. Many of her designs are in difficult locations, such as steep hillsides or sites with tortuous approval processes.

Her three-unit Lombard Street condominium building, in the middle of San Francisco's famous winding block, had to meet 45 distinct deed restrictions and required 49 caissons to hold fast to its Russian Hill site. Neighbors insisted that a landmark palm tree and an old Italian pine be preserved on the tiny 38 x 78-foot lot; accustomed sight lines and views from nearby buildings also had to be preserved. Such restrictions, not uncommon in today's San Francisco, carve out difficult design 'envelopes' which define permissible shapes that must be rendered natural and contextually sympathetic by responsive design.

Lombard Street's traditional San Francisco bay windows are updated in her design with wide glass faces which are divided by a mullion grid for a measure of privacy where windows turn toward neighbors. The grid motif is repeated in a subtle relief pattern around the front door and windows, and also in wire-mesh balconies and staircase railings and in a trellised entry courtyard. Windows facing the most spectacular views don't have this mullion grid, but are topped at a uniform height by a clerestory band of fixed, mullioned glass which softly brings the grid motif inside the units. The preserved trees have a wild garden with overlooking patios and balconies, and upper windows open into their treetops. Bleached hardwood floors flow through open interiors, and eight-foot doorways admit generous light while making nine-foot ceilings seem taller. As part of the approval process she built a 1/4-inch scale model of the neighborhood that showed how the new condominiums would relate to existing buildings.

HOOVER, GEORGE

(Building Design)
Hoover Berg Desmond (303) 837-8811
1645 Grant Street Denver CO 80203

Born: 1935 **Studied:** Cornell University **Awards:** FAIA; AIA; Federal Design Achievement Award, National Endowment for the Arts **Notable Works:** Douglas County Administration Office Building, Castle Rock CO; Laboratory for Atmospheric and Space Physics, University of Colorado at Boulder; Park Central Office Building, Denver CO RESEARCH FACILITIES 20%, EDUCATIONAL 20%, CIVIC 20%, ADAPTIVE REUSE 10%, COMMERCIAL 10%, RELIGIOUS 20%

His work is diverse, from churches to civic buildings to educational institutions. It aims to be appropriate for its time, for its place and for those who will use it. It is unified in touching the spirit by responding to inner needs for order, continuity, intelligibility, connections to nature, and symbolic expression.

His award-winning Douglas County Administration Building at Castle Rock CO borrows from the surrounding Western vernacular yet asserts itself in contemporary terms. Ground-faced and split-faced masonry blocks echo the rough-hewn texture of nearby lowrise commercial buildings while scale and fenestration are reminiscent of an old courthouse which was destroyed by arson. The new building conveys civic dignity in its precise symmetry and its undersized square windows. Its formality is played off by ironic elements: playful lampposts adorn the front and rear entrances and a clock and flag decorate the front. Inside, the only walled-in office space is the commis-

Bobbie Sue Hood, *1055 Lombard Street,* San Francisco

sioners' hearing room. Stairs behind the front entrance lead to the skylit second floor.

HORN, GERALD
(Building Design)
Holabird & Root (312) 726-5960
300 W. Adams St. Chicago IL 60606
Born: 1934 **Awards:** FAIA; AIA National Honor Awards **Notable Works:** Kersten Physics Teaching Center, Chicago; American Bar Center, Northwestern University Law School, Chicago COMMERCIAL 25%, INSTITUTIONAL 25%, INDUSTRIAL 25% OFFICE 25%

He's a modernist who is nonetheless careful to avoid outdated modernist fashions. He observes new architectural trends and believes in pushing the technology of a building as far forward as possible. But he holds modern technology subservient to contextual concerns. Sensitivity to context and design character merge in what he terms "clarity of solution." Preferred materials include steel, glass and precast concrete.

His Kersten Physics Teaching Center at the University of Chicago illustrates his contextual sensitivity. The limestone facade which faces older campus buildings accords with their fervent neo-Gothic motifs. On the other side of the Center, facing into a modern science quadrangle, the building features a glass-walled atrium. 'Sacred/profane' symbolic oppositions are employed throughout the building design—he conceived its formal, conservative facade as 'sacred' and its playful modern side as 'profane.' The interior encourages students and faculty to linger and interact by means of a controlling single-spine circulation pattern punctuated by displays of scientific projects in open areas. Ascending the stairways symbolic changes of color, lighting and texture reinforce the imagery of the sacred pursuit of knowledge, and contrast with the—relatively—profane social atmosphere of the lower levels.

HOWARD, LUCIA
Ace Architects (415) 658-2543
Hieroglyph Building 5237 College Avenue
Oakland CA 94618
Studied: Wellesley College; University of California at Berkeley **Awards:** Interiors magazine "40 under 40" Honoree; Women in Design winner, Second Annual International Design Competition; Graham Foundation for Advance Studies in the Fine Arts **Notable Works** (also see David Weingarten): 2187 Shattuck Av., "Snake Building," Berkeley CA; Lakeside Delicatessen, Oakland CA; El Rancho Rio Building, Carmel Valley CA

She and partner David Weingarten believe that there is much untapped expressive potential in architecture. They view with regret the 'tasteful restraint' that weighs so heavily in the architectural legacy of this century and which, in their estimation, results in a nondescript environment which evokes little meaning. They are opposed to the abstract, proposing in its place a "literalness"; against the ideal they offer the concrete. Their houses aren't just houses; they are castles, ranches, fairy-tale cottages, Georgian townhouses, Spanish mansions. They prefer that their work arouse too many associations rather than too few, "even though they themselves won't have the luxury of reinterpreting their design." Pursuing such subjects results in an intense, visceral architecture that reflects our commodity culture.

A former bank turned mixed-use center in downtown Berkeley CA, their "Snake Building" has provoked much comment in its legendarily provokeable home city. Immense angular scrolls erupt from its corners and tilt over pedestrians; nylon awnings protrude above its storefronts in double chevrons; a squat pyramid flanked by four obelisks of wire mesh rears from its roof and glows red at night; sheet metal snakes coil over the parapet and stick out their forked tongues at Berkeley. The colors—cantaloupe, lemon and guava, flanked by brick buildings on either side—make the Snake Building look like a "spumoni confection."

JACOBSEN, HUGH NEWELL
(Building Design)
2529 P Street NW Washington D.C. 20007
Born: 1929 **Studied:** Yale University
Awards: Fellow, AIA; Architectural Record

Martin Holub Architects, *World-Wide Business Centers*, New York City.

Award, 1964-71, 1973, 1975-82 **Notable Works:** Smithsonian Arts and Industries Building, D.C.; Robert Porter House, Washington, D.C.; Brice House Restoration, Annapolis, Maryland

Good architecture, he often says, never shouts. Balance and contextual sensitivity characterize his work. He designs the spaces between buildings as deliberately as their interiors and shells, maintaining that the orderly development of communities must be planned before details like style can be addressed. Then he aims to create environments pleasant to the senses which equally address client needs. He concentrates on the user's experience as he moves through the crafted space: its appearance from varying distances and angles; the user's exposure to light at different times and angles; and how he perceives the warmth, hardness and scale of the structure's borders.

In his residential work he leans toward pavilion arrangements and the use of pyramid and prismatic volumes. But his restoration work, most significantly the Smithsonian Arts and Industries Building in Washington DC, is known for creating bright, simple spaces which seamlessly conceal ordinarily intrusive service technologies.

JAFFE, NORMAN
(Building Design)
Norman Jaffe AIA PC, Architects (516) 537-3359
P. O. Box 930 Bridgehampton NY 11932

Born: 1932 **Studied:** University of Illinois; University of California **Awards:** New York AIA; Long Island AIA; Interfaith Forum on Religion, Art and Architecture Merit Award **Notable Works:** Gates of the Grove Synagogue, East Hampton NY; 7 Hanover Square, New York City; Long Island Hassidic Academy, Lake Grove NY RELIGIOUS 70%, RESIDENTIAL 30%

His work brings out the qualities of natural materials which he assembles in a crafted, sculptural manner with particular attention to scale and detail. His designs fit gently into their surroundings, and often highlight the craft talents required for their realization.

His Gates of the Grove synagogue in East Hampton NY responds in an original and striking manner to the unique history of temple architecture. Until the nineteenth century European synagogues were unadorned private homes—they became distinctive only after civil freedoms were granted to worshipers. So the many revival styles of Jewish architecture have rather shallow roots, especially in view of the deep religious traditions which they celebrate. Further enriching the historical program with which his design began, the Gates of the Grove congregation was already meeting in a traditional Long Island shingled house on the site, to which his synagogue has been added. His design thus honors both sacred and secular traditions in an original way. The synagogue is wood, and partly shingled. Wooden temples were common in the central and eastern European homelands of many congregants' ancestors, and shingle architecture has long figured in the Long Island vernacular. The interior is a broad room supported by wide, squared wooden pillars set out from supporting walls. Rising to different heights to support a diversely angled sloping roof, the pillars angle back at 45 degrees before meeting ceiling supports. The resulting angles create ceiling bands for several rows of skylights. Below them, abstract Star of David and nature motifs play over the wooden surfaces. A New York AIA jury observed that "It uses a repetitive structural system much like Jacob's ladder; that is, one passes through gates, rungs on a ladder. . . toward the sacred arc. There is no rest; instead, one is on a journey whose motion the indirect light directs towards a great mystery."

JAHN, HELMUT
(Building Design)
Murphy/Jahn Associates (312) 427-7300
35 East Wacker Drive Chicago Illinois 60611

Born: 1940 **Studied:** Illinois Institute of Technology **Awards:** Distinguished Building Award, AIA, Chicago, 1984; Brunner Memorial Prize, 1982; *Progressive Architecture* Award, 1976, 1977, 1978 **Notable Works:**

Helmut Jahn, *State of Illinois Building*, 1985, Chicago.

Helmut Jahn, *State of Illinois Building* (interior), 1985, Chicago.

State of Illinois Building, Chicago; Board of Trade Annex, Chicago; One South Wacker Office Tower, Chicago COMMERCIAL/RETAIL: 55%, HOUSING: 2%, INDUSTRIAL: 5%, EDUCATION: 10%, MEDICAL: 10%, INTERIOR DESIGN: 5%, PLANNING: 13%

He began his career as a functionalist, apprenticing at Chicago's Miesian mainstay, C.F. Murphy and Associates. Like many architects of his generation he tired of the reductive, remote, "overplayed" Modernist credo. His strayings from the party line at first were subtle: a secondary neo-Georgian facade for the University of Illinois' Agriculture School in Champaign/Urbana IL; Deco accents and primary-color splashes for Chicago's Board of Trade high-rise annex. His imposing 1985 State of Illinois Building, however, was the first unambiguous signal of his arrival as major Postmodernist. Promoted as a prototype for the buildings of the next century, it has also been criticized as an exile from an alien land, marooned in an urban and historical context to which it bears no relation—its shape was loosely inspired by an earlier, destroyed federal building. Asymmetrical, ovoid, with his characteristic blue-glass banded curtain wall, the building drapes state offices around a huge glassed-in atrium. Its 75,000 square-feet of retail space, open rotunda and sunken, oval dining plaza have created the grand public meeting place he intended, but they also create unaccustomed noise and bustle which carries through open offices. Some have suggested he's succeeded too well in his goal of "opening up the government to the people."

JERDE, JON ADAMS
(Building Design, Construction
Administration)
Jerde Partnership (213) 413-0130
2789 Sunset Blvd Los Angeles CA 90026

Born: 1940 **Studied:** University of Southern California **Notable Works:** Horton Plaza, San Diego CA; Circle Center, Indianapolis IN; Los Angeles Summer Olympics, Los Angeles

COMMERCIAL, OFFICE, RETAIL 65%, PLANNING 30%

He's renowned for creating festive complexes which attract crowds with their vibrancy. His projects often combine diverse architectural styles in ways that admirers find stimulating, exuberant and fun, and critics call "assaultive." Since the late 1970s he's been in demand for rebuilding city centers.

The Horton Plaza, covering more than eleven acres of downtown San Diego CA, includes four large department stores, 150 shops, a 450-room hotel and parking for 2,400 cars. The multi-level walkways break from the city's grid pattern, beckoning shoppers to linger and wander. Graphic designer and colorist Deborah Sussman used a 49-color palette to tie together the profusion of bridges, arcades, balconies, and columns that make up its open air plaza. Upper levels give a fine view of the city and bay.

His design for Circle Center, a three-block shopping mall in downtown Indianapolis IN, has a circular traffic pattern inspired by nearby Monument Circle. Other features include a small atrium over the service entrance, underground parking, and hidden service drives. Containing an office tower, a hotel and department stores, the complex incorporates existing buildings into its design and connects them with a series of skywalks.

JOHANSEN, JOHN
(Building Design)
Johansen and Bhavnani (212) 533-8632
401 East 37th Street
New York New York 10016

Born: 1916 **Studied:** Harvard University **Awards:** FAIA; First Honor Award, AIA, Mid-Atlantic Chapter, 1968; Award of merit, Library Buildings, AIA, 1970 **Notable Works:** Kinetic House (project); Oklahoma Theater Center, Oklahoma City; Barna House, Bedford, New York COMMERCIAL/RETAIL: 50%, EDUCATION: 10%, PLANNING: 10%, CULTURAL: 30%

He uses a new conception of modularity, in

Helmut Jahn, *Northwestern Atrium Center*, Chicago.

ums, entranceways and passages— are designed in isolation and then forcibly assembled into a coherent whole. He finds that the process of shuffling parts and establishing interesting, effective connections among them adds poetry, spontaneity, and, occasionally, utility to his buildings. The fundamental question in his design process, he says, is how to make a responsive, practical structure which isn't predictable. A favorite ploy is to simultaneously solicit input from opposing groups of users. Recently his interests led to the design of his Kinetic House. This "house" consisted of a fixed central living area and a series of other living spaces and service systems capable of detaching and reconfiguring themselves around the main area, by traveling along a complex circuit of railroad track.

JOHNSON, PHILIP CORTELYOU
(Building Design)
John Burgee Architects with Philip Johnson
(212) 751-7440
885 3rd Avenue New York NY 10022

Born: 1906 **Studied:** Harvard University **Awards:** FAIA; Pritzker Architecture Prize, 1979; Fellow, American Academy of Arts and Letters **Notable Works:** AT&T Corporate Headquarters, New York; Philip Johnson House, New Canaan, Connecticut, Massachusetts; Seagram Building (with Mies van der Rohe)

After a half-century of seminal involvement in the American Modern movement he has radically shifted his stance but remains a fundamental tastemaker and spokesman for contemporary architecture. As a wealthy young man he recognized the power and elegance of the International Style which he saw emerging in Europe. In 1930 he commissioned Mies van der Rohe to design his New York City condominium. Subsequently he styled himself as the first large-scale importer and interpreter of European Modernism, organizing van der Rohe's and Le Corbusier's first visits to the United States and later serving as director of the Museum of Modern Art's Department of Architecture. Though an early and key propagandist for the Modern movement, he didn't convey the social ideology of equality for all

which was the heart of the European movement. Modernism in his presentations was a new style and nothing else. Yet in Europe it was a social stance for which its foremost practitioners were driven into exile, most often in the United States, where Johnson was instrumental in finding them prestigious employment.

He undertook his first major design, his own Glass House in New Caanan CT, after nearly 20 years of involvement in Modernism. The spare, open glass and steel cube derived from Mies' earlier Farnsworth House in overall form and tonality, but included a number of interesting and slightly subversive variations on linear functionalism. Glass House's dominating cylindrical fireplace, its asymmetrical floor plan and corner articulation all prefigured his eventual repudiation of the Puritanism of Modernist design.

By 1960 he was bored and disillusioned with Mies' rational, linear and homogeneous built environment. The future of architecture, he said, lay in chaos—out of chaos comes freedom, diversity and invention. His New York City AT&T building, topped with a thirty-foot curled pediment fashioned after the ornate crest of a Chippendale cabinet, was an instant totem for the swelling Postmodernist camp and an eloquent if not precisely elegant repudiation of his earlier approach to design.

JOHN BURGEE ARCHITECTS WITH PHILIP JOHNSON (see Burgee, John; Johnson, Philip)

JOHNSON, RALPH
(Building Design)
Perkins and Will (312) 977-1100
2 North Lasalle Street Chicago Il 60602

Born: 1948 **Studied:** Harvard University **Awards:** First prize, Biscayne West New Town Design Competion, Miami **Notable Works:** Ingalls Memorial Hospital, Harvey, Illinois; Solar Office, Peoria, Illinois

He began his career as an apprentice in the office of Stanley Tigerman, contributing to the firm's fanciful Boardwalk and (unbuilt) Parkplace high-rise designs. After leaving the shop of that iconoclast, he developed a his own set of highly idiosyncratic idioms in his mature commissions for Perkins and Will.

His unrealized 1981 design for a hotel/condominium/retail complex in Miami Beach's Art Deco Historic District, is the apotheosis of his nouveau-deco approach to high-rise design. The complex features a bifurcated ten-story base, notched to reveal the footings of a fifty-story tower which rises behind it. The base structure, which is swathed in primary colors and adjoins a sinuous, open pool and recreation area, is intended to echo the scale and tone of the 1920s resorts which surround it, while the tower signals the arrival of a new and more geometrically streamlined era of prosperity.

JONES, E. FAY

Fay Jones & Associates   (501) 443-4742
619 W. Dickson Fayetteville AR 72701

Born: 1921 **Studied:** University of Arkansas; Rice University **Awards:** FAIA; Fellow, American Academy of Rome; AIA **Notable Works:** Pinecote Pavilion, Crosby Arboretum Interpretive Center, Picayune MS; Thorncrown Chapel, Eureka Springs AR; Reed Residence, Hogeye AR   RESIDENTIAL 85%, RELIGIOUS 10%, COMMERCIAL 5%

A protege of Frank Lloyd Wright, he's well known for the skill and sensitivity that mark his work as that of a "native son of the earth." His work expresses the natural process of "organic unfolding, or blossoming," as he puts it, and encourages us to explore and meditate upon man's relationship with nature.

His arboretum design, part of a network of ten self-contained yet interrelated environmental systems in southern Mississippi, fulfills the mandate of its philanthropist clients: "To provide a natural habitat that allows scientist and layman to enjoy the rich diversity of the region's botanical heritage and to investigate the larger question of man's evolving relationship with the environment."

Pinecote Pavilion in Picayune MS is reticulated—its structural framework forms a unified network. Every element—columns, braces, connections—performs essential functions. Vertical members arise from the earth-toned brick pavement and spread out like trees to support the roof. Their repetition creates a rhythm; seen in perspective the receding crossed X-forms reinforce the roof's height. The geometric metal oculus joining the beams brings the composition into focus. The wood shingles of the roof "emulate and recall many of nature's surfaces—the bark of trees and the wings of birds." Surrounding it on three sides are pine trees, wild flowers and shrub undergrowth with water on the remaining side. This all-pine wood building seems to hover between earth, water and sky and captures, in its timeliness, the spirit of its place.

KALBAN, JEFFREY M.

(Building Design, Interior Architecture)
Kalban Architects/Designers (213) 208-5310
1145 Gayley Ave. Suite 305
Los Angeles CA 90024

Born: 1947 **Studied:** Ohio State University **Awards:** AIA **Notable Works:** Toyota Regional Offices, Irvine CA; Nonberg House, Pacific Palisades CA CORPORATE 45%, OFFICE & COMMERCIAL 30%, RESIDENTIAL 25%

Rooted in late Modernism, his aesthetic is influenced by Picasso's Cubist explorations of space perception. He plays off of the tension apparent in the best Modern art between rectilinear forms and sparingly juxtaposed curves.

His Pacific Palisades CA Nonberg House is a modified box form with a ribbon of curving glass and stucco running through it. Set in a splendid view lot which narrows toward sea views, he chose to respond as well to neighbors above and below the lot by turning the house perpendicular to the view, favoring the family's most important rooms with choice overlooks and southern exposure while using the mass of the house to create privacy from uphill neighbors. Challenged to design a family environment which could be both familiar and elegant, he thrust the formal living room in a curve out from the ground floor, and connected it to family rooms with a sweeping gallery space which swings through the rectilinear block of the

Helmut Jahn, *Northwestern Atrium Center* (drawing), 1987, Chicago. See page 135.
Project Architect: Rainer Schildknecht.

John M. Johansen, *Stage Center Theater*, Oklahoma City. Photo: Balthazar Korab

main house. A Renaissance-inspired double staircase is within the two-story area of the gallery. Upstairs his 'ribbon' wall blows across the straight mass of the downstairs wall, billowing out into large sitting and study areas in the master suite, then tucking in near the gallery stairs to create access to a deck over the downstairs dining room. The ribbon waves out again to create sea views for a child's bedroom beyond the deck, then surges farther out so that a second child's room can see past the first one, and look as well into uphill mountains. Finally the ribbon ends against a flat wall which defines a guest bedroom. As interior demands evolved during the design process this ribbon device proved very adaptable. The house is white from its stucco to its sloping roof tiles. Ground-floor and second-floor stucco is medium-textured, but upstairs the billowing ribbon wall stucco is smooth, punctuated with curving glass that expresses the rooms sheltered in its waves.

KALLMAN, McKINNELL & WOOD (see McKinnell, Noel; Kallmann, Gerhard)

KALLMANN, GERHARD MICHAEL
(Building Design)
Kallmann, McKinnell and Wood
(617) 482-5745
127 Tremont Street Boston MA 02108

Born: 1915 **Awards:** Fellow, AIA; Bard Award, City Club of New York, 1977; Bartlett Award, 1969 **Notable Works:** Portland City Hall, Boston; Dudley Street Library, Boston; School of Law, Columbia University, New York COMMERCIAL/RETAIL: 50%, EDUCATION: 20%, OTHER: 30%

His work with partner Noel Michael McKinnell continues in many senses Louis Kahn's compositional rigorism, though in its confrontation and contempt for aesthetic refinements it shows a strain of Le Corbusier's New Brutalism. Like the Rigorists, he believes that a building should be shaped primarily by anticipated patterns of movement through it. The arrangement of spaces and functions in his works is derived analytically from main paths of user traffic. In his 1968 design for a new Boston City Hall, the transport channel is the heart of the building and the foundation of its architectural order. Users move across an imposing institutional square; ascend a low, broad staircase; enter and pass through an austere yet powerfully expansive public room; and emerge to face the city's historic Faneuil Hall. To make the passage memorable he lofted the ceilings above the primary hallway, and installed skylights extending user experience to include the morning sun and evening stars. Piers and columns were placed along the intended path of travel to provide additional definition and to extend the usable floor spaces of private and semi-public areas.

KARST, GARY G.
(Building Design)
Horst, Terrill & Karst Architects, P.A.
(913) 266-5373
2900 MacVicar, Topeka KS 66611
Born: 1936 **Studied:** Kansas State University **Awards:** Kansas AIA award **Notable Works:** Durland Hall at Kansas State University, Manhattan KS; Medium Security Facility at Kansas State Penitentiary, Lansing KS EDUCATIONAL 40%, INSTITUTIONAL 40%, CIVIC 15%

His wide variety of government and commercial buildings are designed to withstand the environmental extremes of the Kansas plains. He works extensively in steel and concrete, emphasizing structural simplicity with purity of detail, and articulating spaces using sunlight and changes in volume.

His Kansas State University engineering complex was designed to reflect the high-tech orientation of the activities within while harmonizing with the traditional limestone-block campus that surrounds it. His solution uses columns of 16-foot square structural cut limestone with fluted faces, which support and separate 40-foot open faces of reflecting glass. The complex centers around an interior atrium which, like the curtain glass, contributes to winter heating.

KATSELAS, TASSO
(Building Design)

LTV Center
Dallas, Texas

Richard Keating, *LTV Center*, Dallas Photo: Aker/Burnette Studio, Houston

Tasso Katselas Architect (412) 681-7242
4951 Center Avenue
Pittsburgh Pennsylvania 15213

Born: 1927 **Studied:** Carnegie Mellon University **Awards:** *Progressive Architecture* Award, 1961; Architectural Award, Dow Corporation, 1964; House Award, 1974, *Architectural Record* **Notable Works:** St. Regis Housing for the Elderly, Pittsburgh; Platt House, Pittsburgh; American Institutes for Research, Washington, D.C.

In thirty years of practice he has never worked with a partner or collaborator. Though he employs a team of eight architects and engineers, he tries to maintain complete control over design matters. Good architecture, he feels, isn't temporary; this puts on the architect a responsibility too grave to delegate. Given his level of personal involvement sustained through years of practice, his legacy of commercial, industrial, educational, ecclesiastical and residential designs is the more remarkable.

Contemporary architecture, he argues, has come to be dominated by abstract and personal artistic statements. He decries this quest for novelty, and aims instead to address the technical, economic, political and social issues which ultimately shape man-made environments. His architecture is always a pragmatic exercise in applied geometry. He shuns arbitrarily decorative or self-consciously historical elements in his buildings. He is in no sense anti-aesthetic, but he believes that the lyrical qualities of a structure proceed naturally from a rational ordering of functional parts, and from an economical and contextually appropriate selection of materials.

KEATING, RICHARD

(Building Design, Planning)
Skidmore, Owings and Merrill
(213) 488-9700
725 S. Figueroa St. Los Angeles CA 90017

Born: 1944 **Studied:** University of California at Berkeley **Awards:** FAIA; *Progressive Architecture* design citations; Los Angeles AIA; Texas AIA; Award of Excellence, American

Institute of Steel Construction; Houston AIA
Notable Works: Texas Commerce Bank Tower, Dallas TX; LTV Center, Dallas TX; Columbia Savings Headquarters, Beverly Hills CA; Memphis Brooks Museum, Memphis TN; Aichi Corporate Headquarters, Tokyo

Despite several historicist/contextualist projects, including his Milwaukee Theatre District Plan inspired by the Flemish Renaissance-style Milwaukee City Hall and an addition to the Brooks Art Museum in Memphis TN, he considers himself a modernist. He says there's "a lot left in modernism as a word and as a design proposition that has gone untouched and needs more exploration." Projects in Houston and Los Angeles endeavor to entertain the diversity of the human spirit, moving away from strictly structural-expressionist motifs.

His collaboration with Edward C. Bassett in the Allied Bank Plaza of Houston TX resulted in a seventy-story tower of green reflective glass issuing from a base of polished black granite. Giant trusses housed in painted wood counterpoint massiveness with the illusion of immateriality as they support "skylobbies" for an adjacent elevator core. In the Columbia Savings headquarters in Beverly Hills CA, a Saarinenesque facade envelopes an interior with a central courtyard and a sculpture atrium, a "Piranesi in glass" replete with bridges and pools. Mechanical and service areas are located along the outer circumference, while access to the inner sanctum, housing a state-of-the-art kitchen, shooting gallery, gymnasium, art gallery and offices, is carefully controlled.

KECK, WILLIAM

(Building Design, Renovation, Solar)
George Fred Keck and William Keck, Architects (312) 288-5150
5551 S. University Ave. Chicago IL 60637

Born: 1908 **Studied:** University of Illinois; Bauhaus (Chicago) **Awards:** FAIA; Illinois Medal in Architecture (with George Keck), University of Illinois-Champaign; Distinctive Recognition as Pioneers in Passive Solar Architecture (with George Keck), American

Henry Klein (with Lowell Larsen and David Hall), *Skagit County Administration Building*, Mount Vernon, Washington, 1966. Photo: Dick Busher

Section of the International Solar Energy Society **Notable Works:** House of Tomorrow and Crystal House, Chicago World's Fair, 1933; Edward McCormick Blair House, Lake Bluff, IL; Sigmund Kunstadter House, Highland Park, IL **RESIDENTIAL 75%, COMMERCIAL 10%, INSTITUTIONAL 5%, INDUSTRIAL 10%**

Decades before it was fashionable he and his brother George Keck dedicated themselves to designing and building fuel-efficient and solar-heated houses. Believing that well-designed buildings stay as fresh as well-designed furniture, they designed their buildings with simple forms, often rectangular shapes with an accenting curved line. Three of their buildings are designated architectural landmarks. Their Edward McCormick Blair House in Lake Bluff IL, built in 1955, uses radiant heat from pipes under the floors and in selected ceilings and walls. The main body of the brick house curves along a 500-foot radius from a point in the meadow to the face of the house. The gently curved outside wall subtly changes the perspective inside the house. The living room of the brick house and many of the bedrooms face east toward Lake Michigan. On the south end is a two-story glass enclosure, double-paned for heat retention, which is a part of the living room on the first floor and part of the master bedroom on the second. Running on the sides of the windows are louvered ventilators which draw in the fresh air. A marble fireplace in the living room supplements the heat of the sun absorbed through the enclosure.

KELETI, PETER
(Building Design)
Peter Keleti Associates, Architects & Planners
(816) 561-1131
4310 Gilham Road Kansas City MO 64110

Born: 1925 **Studied:** Hungarian Technical University; Massachusetts Institute of Technology **Awards:** Arts in Architecture, Kansas City AIA; Kansas City AIA **Notable Works:** Longview Methodist Church, Kansas City MO; Student Union Building, Lincoln University, Jefferson City MO; Community Blood Center of Kansas City MO

He's a general practice architect and philosopher whose aesthetic concerns grow out of his practice. He is deeply conscious of the way in which the very particular form-language of architecture can release spiritual power in a way that no other art can. The expansion and contraction of a sequence of architectural spaces, the use of light, sensuous textures, horizontal and vertical tendencies, and elements such as windows and doors—all create accents, divisions and rhythms that crucially modulate the rate at which we experience and read a space.

The quality of architecture depends on "how many good ideas we are willing to give up in order to look for better ones," perhaps holding our own good ideas in reserve until a program suits them. Function is very important to him; he holds that "any object or architectural element which denies its function in its appearance, ceases to be an effective universal symbol of its possible uses." Function isn't narrowly defined; the meaning of any element or object depends on the roles it can play in various activities.

Using different architectural elements will define different action patterns. Great architecture arises from the ability to "pre-experience" the action patterns and emotional impact of buildings. Visualizing and feeling space, so that an architect kinetically feels his body moving through a hypothetical building, is essential to systematically projecting and articulating the emotional impact of buildings. As he says: "With the eyes of our mind, we [architects] have to be able to see spaces clearly enough to walk through them even before we have drawn them, and experience the pull of expanding spaces as modulated by light effects, and see and be aware of, in a tactile away, the textural treatments which can make enclosed space read in sensual terms." He is the author of *Action to Interaction: Values, Methods and Goals in Philosophy, Culture, and Education.*

KENISTON, STANLEY
(Building Design)

Keniston & Mosher Partners (619) 231-1312
666 State St. San Diego CA 92101

Born: 1948 **Studied:** University of California at Berkeley **Awards:** California AIA Presidential Citation; California AIA; San Diego AIA **Notable Works:** Julian CA Main Post Office; San Pasqual Battlefield State Historic Park Visitors Center, Escondido CA INSTITUTIONAL 55%, COMMERCIAL 15%, INDUSTRIAL 15%, ENERGY CONCEPTS CONSULTING 10%, RESIDENTIAL 5%

He believes that architecture must solve fundamental problems rather than complicating them. For this reason he builds energy efficient passive ventilation and comfort systems into all of his designs, simplifying the mechanics and expense of his buildings. He's worked to write into California energy codes flexible performance standards that can be followed in place of older prescriptive standards, to be used when prescriptive codes might inhibit innovation or impose counterproductive constraints. For example commercial users, even in winter, usually seek to dissipate excess heat, while private houses more often must retain as much heat as possible. The distinct challenges of heat gain and heat loss are difficult to separate in prescriptive codes; performance standards address each where appropriate.

His Escondido CA San Pasqual Battlefield State Historic Park Visitors Center is the earth-sheltered, low-impact focus of an important battlefield in the Mexican-American War. A repository for war mementos and an important historical monument, the Visitors Center had to respond to rigid site and program constraints without offending three user groups—Anglo- and Native-Americans and Hispanics—on a site where sensitivities are high. The Center is nestled into a ravine among large boulders, on a low base of pebbly split-face block suggestive of nearby geological banding. Above the base the wall design is inspired by deeply chiselled broken boulders, but rising from the deep cuts in the wall mass are air vents which open and close like nearby desert flowers, catching and conserving night air so that air-conditioning equipment is unnecessary. The Center is naturally lit and uses only occasionally a small backup heating system. In all the Center uses about a tenth of the energy that its program would seem to require. Earth covers the roof of the Center, and visitor walks wind above its site, where it blends uncontroversially into the valley floor.

KERBIS, GERTRUDE LEMPP
(Building Design)
Lempp Kerbis Architects (312) 664-0040
172 W. Burton Place Chicago IL 60610

Born: 1926 **Studied:** Harvard University **Notable Works:** United States Air Force Academy Dining Hall, Colorado Springs; Seven Continents Building, O'Hare International Airport, Chicago HOUSING 60%, EDUCATIONAL/INSTITUTIONAL 40%

She is a distinguished architectural educator (having served as professor at William Rainey Harper College, the University of Illinois at Chicago and Washington University in Saint Louis) as well as a fiercely innovative designer of large public spaces. She joined Skidmore, Owings and Merrill in 1954, where she remained until 1967, when she became disenchanted with the political intrigues of corporate architecture and established an independent practice. The success of her firm, Lempp Kerbis, in planning, renovation and new construction has been inspirational for younger female architects, and in 1974 she helped found Chicago Women in Architecture, a group which strives to expand professional opportunities for women.

Her best known commission is the Seven Continents Building at Chicago's O'Hare Airport, an enormous, tri-level, cylindrical restaurant. The structure's circular plan affords multiple views for patrons, and provides a refreshing counterpoint to the two elongated rectangular terminals which it separates.

KESSLER, WILLIAM
(Building Design)
William Kessler and Associates
(313) 963-5906
733 St. Antoine Detroit MI 48226

Born: 1924 **Studied:** Chicago Institute of Design; Harvard University **Awards:** FAIA; AIA; Detroit AIA Gold Medal; Michigan AIA Gold Medal; First Prize, Stuttgart Design Center **Notable Works:** Michigan Library and Historical Center, Lansing MI; Industrial Technology Institute, Ann Arbor MI; Center for Creative Studies, Detroit INSTITUTIONAL 75%, THEATERS 15%, RESIDENTIAL 10%

He believes in creating an architecture of our own times, an original architecture which truthfully reflects today's technologies and ways of living. Applying the highest appropriate technologies in inventive ways, his designs aim for the age-old goal of creating enriching and useful environments.

His Industrial Technology Institute in Ann Arbor MI is a research center for the factory of the future which is located in a gentle, wooded valley defined by a meandering stream. The Institute sits lightly along and over the streambed, low and sheltered in the valley amid wild grasses and hardwood trees. A wing of the Institute bridges the creek; the Institute's main approach is via another bridge. At once high-tech and in tune with its serene surroundings, the Institute makes a rich yet mutually flattering contrast between natural and machine-made materials and forms. Its stainless-steel and glass walls are strongly banded with black spandrel glass that stresses its low, spreading character. The main face is an articulated string of 64-foot modules. Into these round-cornered box forms labs and offices are distributed so that every activity has natural light. The pods are connected through narrower necks which contain lounges, conference rooms and stairs. The ensemble encourages rapports and informal contacts between different specialties and their often transient specialists by separating offices from labs; labs are bundled together in the center of the building. Labs are accessed only through the main lobby, a two-story space with filtered skylights whose effect is amplified by two bands of white neon running around the periphery of the room. The stainless steel motif of the exterior is carried into the lobby, which is further defined and enclosed by a border of brilliant blue carpet around a black ceramic tile floor. Lobby amenities, like the Institute's overall circulation program, slow down the passing specialists to put them in continuing informal contact.

KILEY, DANIEL URBAN
(Landscape Architecture)
Kiley/Walker (802) 425-2141 East Farm Charlotte Vermont 05445

Born: 1912 **Studied:** Harvard University **Awards:** Fellow, AIA; Residential Design Award, National Landscape Association, 1973; Collaborative Achievement in Architecture Award, 1972 **Notable Works:** Oakland Museum, Oakland, California; IBM Building, Rochester, Minnesota; Dulles Airport Terminal, Dallas, Texas

A pragmatist, he claims to derive a new set of investigations, forms and principles for each new problem he encounters in landscape design. His absorption with practical design began with his apprenticeship to Warren Manning, which he began immediately after graduating high school. At the Harvard School of Design he became indoctrinated in the modern movement, and flirted briefly with idea of creating designs as pure art and geometry. But he came to shun the abstraction and remoteness of academic architecture, and instead committed himself to making spaces which heighten public awareness of man's interdependence with his natural environment.

The industrial and technological revolutions, he has written, have alienated man from his agrarian roots. He wants to forestall oppressive urbanism and reintroduce man to the serenity of his natural world by making open and green space integral elements in the planning of high-rise construction.

KILLINGSWORTH, EDWARD ABEL
(Building Design)
Killingsworth, Strucker, Lindgren, Wilson and Associates (213) 427-7971
3833 Long Beach Boulevard
Long Beach California 90807

Born: 1917 **Studied:** University of Southern

Dan Kiley, *Oakland Museum*, Oakland, California. Photo: Chalmer Alexander

Tasso Katselas, *Allegheny Community College*, 1971.

California **Awards:** Fellow, AIA; First Prize, Bienal, San Paulo, 1961; California Governor's Award, 1966 **Notable Works:** Bali Hilton, Bali; Boca Beach Club, Boca Raton, Florida; Hyatt Regency Hotel, Grand Cypress, Florida

His first ambition was to be a painter and sculptor, and that original aestheticism is evident in his current work. His mature style began to crystallize in the early 1960s, when he undertook the design of a number of Case Study houses for *Arts and Architecture* magazine. He was searching, he recounts, for open spaces where the imagination could soar. His designs, freed from the usual financial and client constraints, included massive 17-foot high entrance doors, and multi-story atriums sheathed in glass plate. His work, he says, is not a search for novelty; he hopes to identify, adopt and exemplify what has been done well in the past. But he translates principles gleaned from historic traditions into today's technologies, informed by today's changing needs.

He's meticulous in observing and mimicking the character and scale of the environments in which he builds, and he argues that architects must learn to be better neighbors. In his commission for the Bali Hilton in Indonesia, for instance, he developed a broad design framework, then recruited eminent native craftspeople to fill in the large blanks in the plan, creating a piece of Balinese architecture which is only 'incidentally' a hotel. The hotel staff includes a number of sculptors and carvers who will continue to work through the next decade to develop traditional themes and link the hotel to the greater Balinese community.

KIM, TAI SOO
(Building Design, Facility Programming)
Tai Soo Kim Associates (203) 547-1970
285 Farmington Ave. Hartford CT 06105

Born: 1936 **Studied:** Engineering College of Seoul, National University, Korea; Yale University **Awards:** FAIA; AIA; Connecticut AIA **Notable Works:** Middlebury Elementary School, Middlebury CT; National Museum of Modern Art, Seoul, Korea; Building #427, Submarine Training Facility, Groton CT EDUCATIONAL 60%, INSTITUTIONAL 10%, RESIDENTIAL/HOUSING 10%, COMMERCIAL 20%

His work proceeds from a firm comprehension of the site, context and mission of a building. His upbringing and training in Korea enables him to combine strong features of Oriental architecture, such as "the wall as the definition of the beginning of man-made environment" with Western innovation. His designs evince a strong sense of one's approach to a structure and the experiences it contains.

His Middlebury CT Elementary School was conceived as a rectangular box broken in two, with a circulation spine connecting the halves. The building is then stepped back and wrapped with a bright red brick wall. Starting at one edge of the site of the school, one passes between two brick lampposts, approaching the building at an angle. The drive bends at a second gate, demarcated by two ancient oak trees. At the building's edge one passes through yet another gate which is framed by the wall's corner and another brick lamppost. The welcoming loggia behind the red wall, besides being a sheltered walkway, clearly defines the place for ritual comings and goings by schoolbus and car. Square windows and clerestories punctuate the spine and broad walls.

The picturesque route to his National Museum of Modern Art, at the foot of a mountain in Seoul's Grand Park, is approached by a series of offered discoveries and revelations. The predominant horizontal composition visible from the northern entry vantage point shifts to a vertical stack of concentric cylinders when seen from the west.

Arriving at the museum grounds, one crosses a footbridge and ascends a series of tree-lined sculpture terraces to the main entrance. While this approach borrows from the rusticated masonry platforms and gardens of Korean palaces and temples, the building itself is characterized by strong, abstract geometric curves and cylinders.

KIRBY, J. AUBREY
(Construction Administration, Building Design, Interior Architecture, Renovation)

Kirby Associates, Inc. (919) 723-6706
234 S. Broad St Winston-Salem NC 27101

Born: 1932 **Studied:** Oklahoma State University; North Carolina State University **Awards:** North Carolina Governor's Energy Achievement Award; Randolph E. Dumont Design Award **Notable Works:** Kingswood United Methodist Church, Rural Hall NC; Pine Hall House, Winston-Salem NC CIVIC 25%, COMMERCIAL 25%, OFFICE 25%, RELIGIOUS 25%

He looks for the one overriding design element that distinguishes each project, whether it be the religious mission of a church building or the economical function of a warehouse. It's in this element that designs succeed or fail. He finds further inspiration in the North Carolina countryside, whose barns, farms and even outhouses respond artlessly to program needs and site constraints.

His Kingswood United Methodist Church in Rural Hall NC is contemporary yet rural, designed to convey the spirit of worship without recourse to standard and more urban symbols like columns and pediments. The church's form comes from neighboring farms, with its religious mission conveyed in stained-glass windows lining the sides of the barnlike sanctuary, and clerestory glass running under the eaves. At the four corners of the church shedlike anterooms lean into the sanctuary, sheltering sacristy, stairs and cloak rooms. The church has a masonry base level supporting vernacular stained board and batten walls above.

His energy saving work features summer-shaded atria whose rising air is gathered and circulated back into rooms on their periphery.

KLEIN, HENRY
(Building Design)
The Henry Klein Partnership (206) 336-2155
205 Matheson Building
Mount Vernon WA 98273

Born: 1920 **Studied:** Cornell University **Awards:** FAIA; International Union of Bricklayers & Allied Craftsmen/AIA Louis Sullivan Award **Notable Works:** County Administration Building, Mount Vernon WA; Performing Arts Center and Residence Halls, Western Washington University, Bellingham WA EDUCATION 40%, MUNICIPAL 40%, RESIDENTIAL 20%

His work as a 'general practitioner' in a rural county might seem constraining, yet here he is freed from the mold of moment-to-moment fashion, and so enabled to do truer work. He takes inspiration for satisfying his clients' needs from the daily occurrences of life, "because it is the events of every day, the small, unconscious movements, the faint remembrances, the private looks and changing light, that are the very stuff that art is made of." Often clad in softly textured masonry, his buildings are rooted in their immediate environments and scaled to their surroundings and users.

His County Administration Building in Mount Vernon WA is located next to a classical courthouse on a 100-year flood plain. Though larger than its formal neighbor, his administration building is deferential: strong horizontal elements hold it low to the ground, and its complementary red brick walls contain precast concrete design elements that accord with the older building's terra cotta ornamentation. Many offices are accessed directly from second floor walks, minimizing the need for a high-visibility lobby that would compete with the courthouse next door. The flood-prone ground floor contains public meeting spaces and a high-traffic agricultural extension agency. By elevating the bulk of the office building, circulation through as well as to it is improved; an adjacent pedestrian street encourages walkers from downtown to take advantage of these amenities.

KNOWLES, BRIGITTE L. & JOHN CHRISTOPHER
(Building Design, Interior Architecture, Urban Design, Planning)
BJC/Knowles Architects and Planners
(215) 922-3859
419 South Third Street Philadelphia PA 19147

Studied: University of Pennsylvania; Harvard University; University of Pennsylvania

Awards: FAIA; Royal Institute of British Architects; AIA; First Place Entry, Center for Innovative Technology VA **Notable Works:** George D. Widener Indoor Sports Pavilion, Variety Club Camp for Handicapped Children, Worcester PA; P.A.B. Widener Memorial School pool addition, Philadelphia; Upsal School for the Blind, Germantown PA; Warwick University Housing, England; Aiken Residence, Philadelphia

Artists, teachers and consummate form-makers, their architecture draws inspiration from the late Louis Kahn. Their architecture, they have written, expresses their "desire to make space in the form of light. . . . Space is perceived as the residue of the mold, the building . . . material and craft create the molding surfaces, and light activates the spirit of the space." Seeing their architecture as "an essence of 'beginnings'," they continually re-investigate primary forms: the square, the circle and the triangle. Forms are layered with images from the past, transforming them into works "that hold inspiration from the universalness of the past . . . a coherence and remembrance . . . as it is evoked in the images and forms of the present."

Their early residential work sought to incorporate inherited vernacular forms such as the English thatched cottage, and they have a continuing interest in crafts traditions such as furniture-making. It is manifested in their adaptations and adoptions from the "machine-made aesthetic," for example in the crafting of steel into stairs, fireplace seats and decks. "The concerns for a utilitarian clarity of material and use is not a 'plain Jane' aesthetic but is instead an aesthetic of truth to material."

Their Widener School for Handicapped Children in Philadelphia, an example of their later work, is geometrically simple in plan and evocative in its use of primary forms. The eastern elevation has a triangular glass brick window. The triangular form serves three uses: it terminates an open axis, completes a stage set for a statue of the school's founder, and a gives a window of light to an enclosed pool. The triangular form is taken from the eastern light treatment of Christian churches, Lincoln Cathedral in particular. The image gives sacred memory to the founder. The pyramidal form suggests the unity of man with nature and symbolizes the founder's struggle to be one with handicapped children and their desire for acceptance in the world. The structure of self-supporting masonry is technologically truthful. Masonry bond beams structure its openings, and the glass-brick window supports itself. This technological truthfulness takes shape in three dimensions. The place of the founder, the place of light and the place of structure become one in the integrity of the building.

KNOWLES, EDWARD FRANK
(Building Design)
Edward F. Knowles Architect (212) 267-4459
130 West 56th Street New York NY 10019

Born: 1929 **Studied:** Pratt Institute **Awards:** Fellow, AIA; First Prize, Boston City Hall Competition, 1962 **Notable Works:** Boston City Hall; Filene Center for the Performing Arts, Vienna, Virginia; Lowell Nesbitt Studio, New York COMMERCIAL/RETAIL: 40%, HOUSING: 30%, INDUSTRIAL: 10%, INTERIOR DESIGN: 20%, PLANNING: 10%

He first came to critical attention for his contribution to the design of the monumental New Boston City Hall, with Gerhard Kallmann and Noel McKinnell. Subsequently he has been primarily known for his humane and often rustic designs for private residences and art institutions. Significant architecture, he now believes, must express the emotional states of its contributors as well as the pre-conditions of site, budget and function. So in his recent work he has abandoned academic approaches to design and instead proceeds piecemeal, attempting to 'feel out' the the emotional, aesthetic and practical textures of each project. His Filene Center for the Performing Arts in Wolf Trap Farm Park VA is a multi-story arts complex set amid a natural grassy amphitheater. Clear views of the main stage are offered both within the building and from the broad sloping front lawn. The structure's rough,

Keith Kolb, *Puget Sound Blood Center*, Seattle, Washington

Brigitte Knowles and John Christopher Knowles, *Widener Memorial School Pool Addition*, Philadelphia

unvarnished red cedar exterior evokes the long-weathered, gracefully sagging barns and water towers on the site's perimeter. Yet the smooth white paneling of the roof and the building's strong planes place it firmly in the the modernist tradition.

KOCH, ALBERT CARL

(Building Design, Urban Design)
Koch and Haible (617) 367-0378
54 Lewis Wharf Boston Massachusetts 02110

Born: 1912 **Studied:** Harvard University **Awards:** Fellow, AIA; Award of Merit, AIA/American Library Association, 1956; Boston Arts Festival Awards, 1963 **Notable Works:** Techbuilt House Prototype; Lewis Wharf, Boston; Acorn Prefabricated Housing

He aims that his buildings be consistent with constantly new technologies no less than with the universal human desire for open, accessible and comfortable spaces. He consults closely with commercial, industrial and governmental experts to produce cutting-edge designs, but he avoids novelty for its own sake.

He's a pioneer in the field of pre-fabricated housing. He began his practice as a designer of luxury homes, but he decided that he could make a stronger contribution acting as a liaison between the traditional industrial and architectural communities. He believed that the nation's urban housing crisis could be addressed by designing geometrically simplified, adaptable modular units crafted with modern factory production techniques. Throughout the 1950s he worked closely with the modular parts industry to make his series of Techbuilt Houses. Built on a simple rectilinear plan, the units included a series of plywood panels which could be moved for a wide variety of interior schemes. Later he conceded that in his haste to simplify, quantify and cheapen the construction process he had initially underestimated the importance of human scale and attractive aesthetics. In his recent work he has been primarily concerned with bringing humane values to high density, low cost housing.

KOENIG, PIERRE

(Building Design)

Pierre Koenig Architect (213) 826-1414
12221 Dorothy Street
Los Angeles California 90049

Born: 1925 **Studied:** University of Southern California **Awards:** Fellow, AIA; AIA/House and Home Award, 1957, 1960, 1962, 1963; Award, Bienal, San Paulo, 1957 **Notable Works:** Case Study House 21, for Arts and Architecture, Hollywood, California; Case Study House 22, Hollywood; Electronic Enclosures Building, El Segundo, California COMMERCIAL/RETAIL: 30%, HOUSING: 40%, INDUSTRIAL: 30%

His interest in mass-produced single-family housing began while he was a student. His first exposed steel and glass house, which featured a steel-frame sun deck which doubled as a roof for the first story, was completed as an extracurricular school project. The house, like all his subsequent residential designs, was meant to serve as a prototype for mass production. Among his most innovative designs are prototypes for desert and arctic conditions, which ironically both required combinations of steel and wood panels, glass plate, and steel frames. He has recently adapted a pair of Case Study Houses for *Arts and Architecture* magazine as models for the 28,000 acre Chemehuevi Indian Reservation in California. The second of the Case Study Houses was built on the lip of a canyon above Hollywood. He used a ten-foot cantilever to extend the living area over the precipice and create a stunning unobstructed view of the city.

KOFRANEK, JAN

(Building Design, Construction Administration)
Kofranek Architects (206) 623-5319
318 First Ave. So. Suite 200
Seattle WA 98104

Born: 1939 **Studied:** Czech National University of Prague **Awards:** Seattle AIA; AIA House of the Month Award **Notable Works:** Le Compte Residence, Edmonds WA; Wilcy Residence, Mercer Island WA; Bakos Residence, Portland OR COMMERCIAL 20%, RESIDENTIAL 55%, HOUSING/SMALL

Pierre Koenig, *Mandeville Canyon House*, 1969 (remodeled by architect in 1984), California

Pierre Koenig, *Case Study House #22*, Los Angeles

INDUSTRIAL 25%

Describing himself as a "modern classicist," he abides by the Modernist dictum that form follows function. He believes that the International Style rests on stable values that can only be temporarily overshadowed. They will reemerge as the verities they are. His work in the last ten years has concentrated on small office buildings and custom-designed single family residences which permit a greater exercise of ingenuity.

His sleek Modernist designs evade constricting box shapes with curves and slopes. His P-I Open House on Mercer Island WA has a box shape which is broken by a circular 'silo' section, where a section of roof overhang curves slightly outward from the roofline. From the corner entrance a sunken living room runs across the front of the house, with two interior walls giving it a triangular shape. The stairway from the front hall to the second floor, rising through the circular corner of the house, has a cutout semicircle in the ground-floor hall which matches the semi-circular shape of a landing half-way up. His Le Compte Residence in Edmonds WA is designed for a professional couple and features both formal and informal sides which are connected by an entranceway that doubles as an art gallery. The left side has a spacious kitchen with greenhouse windows and sliding glass doors that open to a patio, and a family room with skylight windows and wood-burning stove which is also separated from the kitchen by glass sliding doors. The right, formal side has the dining room and, separated from the living room by a fireplace, a combination study/guest room with maximum privacy.

KOHN PEDERSEN FOX ASSOCIATES
(see Louie, William; May, Arthur; Pedersen, William)

KOHN, EUGENE A.
(Building Design, Interior Architecture, Marketing)
Kohn Persen Fox Associates (212) 977-6500
111 West 57th Street New York NY 10019

Born: 1930 **Studied:** University of Pennsylvania **Awards:** FAIA; Royal Institute of Architects Flame of Truth Award **Notable Works:** Proctor & Gamble World Headquarters, Cincinnati; DG Bank, Frankfurt, West Germany; Four Seasons Hotel at Logan Square, Philadelphia COMMERCIAL HIGH-RISE 55%, COMMERCIAL LOW-RISE 30%

He's a contextualist guided by clear philosophical goals: he argues that urban commercial architecture, long dominated by bland functional design, has to attract the better architects away from traditional aesthetically oriented projects such as museums. Quality design must take into account the city's social reality, in which great numbers of people are concentrated and profoundly affected by their space. Sensitive to the quality and sense of space, architecture should appeal to the individual by appealing to the senses. Like great painting, great architecture should reward close and repeated observation, always unveiling new details.

Human scale is his prime concern. Technology and modernity sacrifice warmth and humanity, reinforcing alienation. The architect's moral mission should be to move beyond pure style in order to create socially conscious space where people feel welcome. He indentifies with postmodernism because the movement's emphasis on tops and bases brings the perceived scale of a building back to street-level — the human level. While he is critical of extreme, pastiche design, he uses postmodern historical references and rich detailing in his architecture.

Contextualism is his other dominant concern—it's a term his firm originally introduced. Contextualism is more than sensitivity to the surrounding buildings; it must express the history and spirit of the surrounding environment and more, it must add a "new thought"—a design solution oriented toward the future of modern architecture. A completed building represents a "beautiful balance" of forces: design, function, context, client creativity, and available funds. A building may also contextualize by its contrast with surrounding buildings. For example, a grace-

Kohn Pederson Fox, *333 Wacker Drive*, Chicago. Principal Architect: William Pederson Photo: Barbara Karant

ful, inviting building will provide relief from a context of starkly functional buildings in the modernist style. His 333 Wacker Drive in Chicago, co-designed with William Pedersen, is an office tower on a bend of the Chicago River whose curved skin of green-tinted glass reflects the green weather, providing counterpoint and respite from the surrounding black and gray. His One Logan Square building in Philadelphia exemplifies a more traditional contextualism. While modern in design, it harkens to the colonial style of neighboring buildings.

KOLB, KEITH R,
(Building Design, Programming, Preservation, Urban Design and Master Planning)
Kolb & Stansfield AIA Architects
(206) 622-0393
628 Skinner Building Seattle WA 98101

Born: 1922 **Studied:** Harvard University, University of Washington **Awards:** FAIA; AIA First Honor Award; J. F. Lincoln Arc Welding Foundation National Bronze Award **Notable Works:** Forks Branch, Seattle First National Bank, Forks, WA; Puget Sound Blood Center, Seattle MEDICAL 70%, INSTITUTIONAL 12%, EDUCATIONAL 10%, COMMERCIAL AND RESIDENTIAL 8%

Suspicious of specialization and the fads of the moment, he seeks to create environments in which the new is part of the old, and part of the future as well. Each of his buildings declare man's concern for his living, learning and working environment, clearly expressing the life and technology of a given time, place and culture. Expressing the rhythms of a given place and time in his hospital designs, he begins with an awareness that most patients come and go from hospitals very quickly, and are encouraged to do so. Doctors, nurses and technicians on the other hand spend their working lives inside his designs, so it is their needs and comforts, as well as their patients', which inform his designs.

His Forks Bank also shows this awareness both for how people live, and how they *want* to live. This branch bank in a small Washington coastal town reflects the love of the local environment which keeps people in the area. Though often cloudy, the pulsing play of sun and cloud above is lighter and more beguiling than in inland Seattle. This suggested an energy-efficient skylight and window system that lets the spell of the constantly changing sky pass through the work environment.

KOMMERS, PETER
(Building Design)
Peter Kommers, Architect (406) 586-3938
801 S. 6th Ave. Bozeman MT
Born: 1944 **Studied:** Montana State University; American Academy in Rome **Awards:** Rome Prize; Graham Foundation Fellowship 1987 **Notable Works:** Offices for Kommers, McLaughlin and Leavengood architectural firm, Bozeman MT INSTITUTIONAL 50%, OFFICE 50%

He defines architecture as "the act of making spaces;" his own work is an architecture of "inclusiveness." Many factors combine in a project: place, systems and materials, composition, and planning for human activity. Out of this complex interaction of elements he attempts to discover the ideal tension between 'rigor' and 'romance.' The evocative nature of the materials reveals the romantic underpinnings of his buildings, the soul which tells a story of human experience in narrative compositional features. So he prefers eloquent building materials, materials whose mass and thickness lends a three-dimensional quality.

His "People of the Morning Star" high school for the northern Cheyenne Indians in Lame Deer MT goes beyond the pure rationalization of modernism to a reverence for the Indians' rich traditions. Its low-lying linear forms hug the living earth, its solid walls are in rich earth colors. Whites, blues, blacks and reds—colors representing the guardians of the four quadrants of the circle of life—cover large beams which are superimposed over the building's structure. The interior contains an "elders' project," an open space where tribal elders interact with students and pass on their culture. This sacred space contrasts with the profane spaces of the classrooms.

KRUECK, RONALD ADRIAN
(Building Design)

Born: 1946 **Studied:** Illinois Institute of Technology **Awards:** AIA Chicago Chapter; American Institute of Steel Construction Architectural Award for Excellence **Notable Works:** McCormick Place landscaping, Chicago; Skokie Public Library, Skokie, IL; "Steel and Glass House" design

In association with his partner Keith Olsen, he creates solutions for a wide range of commercial and residential structures. His landscaping project while with C.F. Murphy Associates for Chicago's giant McCormick Place convention center and exhibition hall presented on one side of the structure walkways and bike paths in harmony with the park-like setting of Chicago's lake front, and on the other side overpasses, underpasses and entrance and exit ramps for Lake Shore Drive, an expressway that borders and serves the convention hall. The landscaping design is functional on the one hand, while on the other hand preserves a human dimension for the otherwise cold and imposing structure.

Recent work has ranged from suburban medical laboratories to showrooms in Chicago's massive Merchandise Mart and to remodeling of Victorian houses. In addition to building design, he is adept at developing decorative elements for interiors that complement the architectural design. For instance, the study for a wall painting for the "Steel and Glass House" offers geometric patterns of squares, rectangles and diagonal lines in sympathy with the structure's Post-Modern aesthetic.

KRUGER, KENNETH
(Building Design, Construction Technology)
Kruger Kruger Albenberg (617) 661-3812
2 Central Square Cambridge MA 02139

Born: 1928 **Studied:** Harvard University; Massachusetts Institute of Technology **Awards:** New Jersey AIA; Western Massachusetts AIA **Notable Works:** Lounsberry Hollow School, Vernon NJ; Camp Assembly Building, Stockbridge MA SPECIAL CONSULTATIONS 25%, GOVERNMENT 25%, RESIDENTIAL 25%, COMMERCIAL 10%, INDUSTRIAL 10%

A national director of the American Society of Home Inspectors, he is the only member who is both architect and engineer. His specialties come together in failure investigation and repair, peer review and expert witness services as well as in his practice of architecture. He finds that much successful architecture fails in its details, though not in its conceptions; an informed attention to visual and construction detail characterizes his own designs. He aims to stay true to the credo of his first architecture professor, the late Robert Woods Kennedy: "To the point, with the materials at hand, from the heart."

A typical building failure was the mysterious cracking of fiberglass-reinforced concrete panels which reface a Somerville MA bank. Though the panels had expansion joints, their built-in restraints turned out to be rigid, so that panels as small as 4 x 4 feet had no give and cracked. Flexible retainers solved the problem. In wood-frame renovation, he often uses plywood box girders to increase possible floor loads and span new openings cut into bearing walls. These girders are long, thin boxes faced with plywood which are set against or under walls and appropriately attached, for example with notching studs or steel strapping to structural members. Floors ordinarily support walls above, but walls with a section of box girder can be swung into supporting floors below—if the details are right.

KRUGER, KENNETH C.
(Building Design, Construction Administration)
Kruger, Bensen, Ziemer Architects
(805) 963-1726
30 W. Arrellaga Street
Santa Barbara CA 93101

Born: 1930 **Studied:** University of Southern California **Awards:** Santa Barbara AIA; Best Architect Engineer Award, American Military Engineers **Notable Works:** Raytheon Company, Goleta CA;   Archive Library, Santa Barbara Mission, Santa Barbara CA; Humanities Building, Alan Hancock College, Santa Maria CA   OFFICE 55%, RELIGIOUS 35%, RESIDENTIAL 10%

His approach allows materials which are unconcealed by paint or other opaque films to speak for themselves. His preferred building material is wood, finished with a transparent stain which highlights grain and special characteristics.

The Archive Library at Santa Barbara Mission, Santa Barbara CA is a completely modern building with controlled temperature and humidity to preserve its collection of manuscripts and rare books, some of which predate the founding of America. But it's almost impossible to distinguish the Library from original mission buildings, whose tiles and roof forms it closely imitates. Built of reinforced concrete and covered with stucco that matches the color and texture of existing exteriors, the Library nonetheless uses the latest earthquake-resistant technology. In research rooms, heavy nonstructural timber and handcrafted tile flooring continue the illusion.

The design of his wood frame and stucco Humanities Building at Alan Hancock College in Santa Maria CA uses a light shelf, a system of windows and a projecting shelf which blocks out direct sunlight but allows a diffused light to enter the room, so light but not heat may enter. Sensors turn on artificial lights when sunlight is insufficient.

KULSKI, JULIAN E.
(Building Design, Historic Preservation, Interiors, Landscaping)
Julian E. Kulski, FAIA, & Associates
(703) 687-3636
105 W. Federal St. Middlebury VA 22117

Born: 1929 **Studied:** Oxford School of Architecture, England; Yale School of Architecture **Awards:** FAIA; Book-of-the-Month Club author; Kosciuszko Foundation Prize **Notable Works:** Airlie Foundation Conference Center, Warrenton VA; own residence, Orlean VA; Boxwood, Middleburg VA RESIDEN-

TIAL 75%, INSTITUTIONAL 25%

Before settling full-time into his beloved Virginia hills he taught architecture for many years while practicing it the world over as a development architect for the World Bank. His large-scale projects, like his more recent country houses and restorations, show a concern for indigenous culture, tradition and materials, informed by site constraints. His hilltop homes in the Blue Ridge Mountains have rooflines matched to undulating mountain lines. But presented with sharper, larger mountains as in Yugoslavia, Greece, Afghanistan and Nepal, he cuts his buildings into the massed mountains rather than attempting to adorn them. In both cases local materials are used.

His current practice is grounded in the Virginia Blue Ridge foothills, where historic estates embody values that are central to his own work as well, integrating landscape, interior and way of life into a harmonious whole. His restorations are sensitive to classic sensibilities of proportion and simplicity achieved with a nature-based palette. His new buildings tend to shrink into their settings, giving the magnificent countryside emphatic pride of place. Some of his houses don't photograph easily— they are incomplete without their surroundings. "I am not sure I could design a house without the views we have here in Virginia," he says.

KUMP, ERNEST JOSEPH
(Building Design)
Ernest J. Kump, Consultants Schloss Matze
6230 Brixlegg Austria

Born: 1911 **Studied:** Harvard University **Awards:** Fellow, AIA; Member, Royal Institute of British Architects; Progressive Architecture Award, 1947, 1948, 1949, 1957, 1958, 1960 **Notable Works:** Foothill College, Los Altos Hills, California; DeAnza College, Cupertino, California; Reagan Presidential Library, Palo Alto, California

He argues for an "architecture without buildings" which recognizes that each structure is an element in a dynamic, interdependent system of crafted and natural spaces. He began his career as a stout structuralist, championing modular ideals in academia and exemplifying them in his professional practice. The first signal of his departure from the modernist/rationalist camp came with his romantic design for Foothill College in Los Altos Hills CA. His campus plan was hailed as a breakthrough in critical circles, for it solved the long-standing problem of creating a formal vocabulary for large-scale institutional buildings which echoed the relaxed, prosperous and earthy tenor of the San Francisco Bay area residential style. His critical innovation was the design of a wide-eaved, pitched redwood roof topped by a low, rectangular box. Adding the box enabled him to cover large floor areas with a pitched roof that was still low to ground, and so not overwhelming to neighboring buildings or budgets. Inside the boxes he concealed mechanical systems and so saved useable floorspace. After designing a prototypical building module he broke the campus into as many separate, similar-sized buildings as was functionally and financially practical. Then he dressed the buildings in uniform, rustic style to convey the image of a sprawling, affluent village.

KUNZ, KEN

(Building Design, Preservation, Interiors)
Sheiner Day Kunz Associates (602) 957-1077
Phoenix AZ 85008

Born: 1941 **Studied:** University of Cincinnati, University of Washington at Seattle **Awards:** AIA award for architectural excellence; Fisher Body craftsman's guild **Notable Works:** AIA office, Phoenix; Cincinnati Conservatory of Music RESIDENTIAL 50%, COMMERCIAL 25%, INSTITUTIONAL 25%

He aims to design buildings that look like "they've always been there," in an area with little awareness of architectural history. His 50-bed drug rehabilitation center in Chandler AZ recycles a Baptist church that served an old residential neighborhood. He wanted the new institution to blend into both its neighborhood

and region while conveying symbols of service and solidity. He plastered over the Baptist bricks in Southwestern stucco, and integrated the campus of new and recycled buildings with colonnades and arches.

His Bimson House in Paradise Valley AZ emphasizes its topographic context. The floors are of red Sodona granite mixed with reddish matrix, polished for a terrazzo effect. These surfaces are continued unpolished onto outdoor patios, where they meld into the rough granite desert floor surrounding the house. Interior walls rise in increasing complexity from this ground, first set on a horizontal band of modular granite-like blocks, then becoming plaster which is colored and mixed with the surrounding earth. Above that, at levels determined by exterior views and privacy needs, a band of glass—the ultimate manipulation of desert sand—continues up to the ceiling.

LANDES, ROBERT P.

(Building Design, Facility Programming)
BLGY Inc. (512) 451-8281
1600 W. 38th St. Austin TX 78731

Born: 1926 **Studied:** University of Texas at Austin **Awards** President AIA Chapter; NE Kiwanis Club Notable Work: Bowie High School, Austin TX EDUCATIONAL 50%, COMMERCIAL 25%, MEDICAL 25%

He designs functional and attractive buildings of reasonable cost and makes frequent use of contemporary styles and modern energy-efficient technology, including the use of computerized ventilation systems in combination with natural air circulation.

His Bowie High School in Austin TX is unique for its campus plan and highly efficient energy systems. A 400,000-square-foot complex, its cost per foot came out lower than that for typical single-structure high schools. Campus buildings are lined with covered walkways and surround a grassy recessed central court which serves for pep rallies and other outdoor functions. Low-lying building silhouettes create a neighborhood feel, belying the size of the complex. Students park in front of a grand entrance building which overviews all student activity. Four wings of classrooms radiate from a central library, forming a letter H. A partially exposed clerestory along one length maximizes natural light and air circulation while minimizing direct sunlight. Sloping metal panels, "light shells," reflect light back into classrooms. Assisted by the Public Utilities Commission, a water storage tank works with the computerized ventilation system to further increase energy efficiency.

LANDON, PETER

Landon Peter Architects Ltd. (312) 644-5456
70 W. Hubbard Chicago IL 60610

Studied: University of Kansas **Awards:** "Young Architects" Award **Notable Works:** Davis Residence, Union Pier MI; Martin/Savage Studio, Oak Park IL; The Monarchy Studio, Chicago

The vernacular architecture of the prairies is a strong influence on his work. But regardless of style he seeks an understated architecture, neither overblown nor obtuse. Whether renovating or designing in the Modern style, his work explores the themes of space and light. His Martin/Savage Studio in Oak Park IL is a simple volume inflected to particularize both the interior and surrounding exterior spaces. The inside is dominated by a two-story space. Incidental to the main space, stairs occupy an inflected corner and become central to the experience of the building. The exterior is sheathed in redwood panels set in a grid of galvanized metal beads.

His Monarchy Studio, a renovation of a third-floor loft space in Chicago, displays his characteristic configuration of spaces. The top floor contains the main living spaces, while a rooftop pavilion contains bedroom and bath. An existing grid of columns divides the space into three bays. The pavilion falls in the center bay. The outer edge of the pavilion's envelope carves a view of Chicago's Loop which is also visible through openings between the two floors, where stairs with a splayed base juxtapose against the curved opening above and the grid order below, and snap the divergent spaces into a tight focus.

LANE, JOHN

(Master Planning, Building Design, Interior Architecture)
Lane & Associates Architects (501) 782-4277
1318 North "B" P.O. Box 3929 Ft. Smith AR 72913

Born: 1938 **Studied:** University of Illinois **Awards:** Associate Research Fellow, Center for Suburban and Regional Studies, Towson State University, Listed in Who's Who in Interior Design **Notable Works:** Renovation of First National Bank, Tahleguh, OK COMMERCIAL 25%, RESIDENTIAL 25%, RELIGIOUS 25%

He takes a comprehensive, master-planning approach to architecture which involves building, furniture, and graphic design, site analysis, artistic consultation, and complete interior decorating. He believes that architecture must be people-oriented, which is to say built on a human scale, pleasantly appointed, with a minimum of glass and steel. Details are the key to such successful architecture. His recent work involves energy conservation studies and renovation and adaptive-use projects designed to maximize the use of existing facilities, so that expensive additive structures can be avoided while still in the planning stages.

His alterations to the First National Bank in Tahleguh OK is an example of such cost-saving renovation. The storefront of an adjacent building was gutted and the wall between the two buildings partially removed, freeing up a large space for a new commercial loan area. This extension maintains the bank's traditional decor, with similar oak panelling and fabric wall coverings, while adding some contemporary and functional design features such as lower ceilings for the office work area. The rock-finish facade of the extension is styled to appear to have been built at the same time as the original bank.

LANFORD, MICHAEL L.

(Building Design, Interior Architecture)
Alamo Architects (512) 227-2612
108 King William San Antonio TX 78204

Born: 1954 **Studied:** University of Texas at Austin **Awards:** Texas Award for the Preservation of Historic Architecture; Preservation award, San Antonio Conservation Society **Notable Works:** Alamo Heights Residence, San Antonio TX; renovation of Bookstop, Loma Theatre, San Diego CA Golden Residence, San Antonio TX COMMERCIAL/RETAIL 75%, RESIDENTIAL 15%, RENOVATION 10%

He and his partners object to being characterized with any architectural style, particularly the Postmodern one. They describe their work as a "collage of images pulled from historical and modern references, particularly Arts and Crafts...we don't exclude anything."

Sited on a floodplain, the ground floor of their Alamo Heights residence in San Antonio TX rises six feet above ground. Stone stairs go up to the front door on the second, top floor of the house while enclosing a palm court below. From the entry hall and living room, whose bay windows frame sweeping vistas, one passes through a glass-walled gallery to the dining room. A cupola rises twenty feet above the dining room. A sculpture of ornamental beams and glass rods makes the room more intimate. A private residence on a prominent lot, the house respects its neighbors with a cupola and deep eaves on the roof and limestone bands which diminish its height. On the opposite end of the palm court, a walkway to the kitchen door is sheltered by a stylized trellis. On the back side, spacious porches with posts and brackets in the Arts and Crafts style lead to a big yard.

LAPIDUS, MARVIN
(Building Design)
Marvin Lapidus Architect (305) 532-6837
3 Island Avenue Miami Beach Florida 33139

Born: 1902 **Studied:** Columbia University **Awards:** Fellow, AIA; Citation for Excellence in Community Architecture, AIA, 1965; Distinguished Service in the Arts Award, Brandeis University **Notable Works:** Fountainbleau Hotel, Miami Beach; Americana Hotel, Bal Harbor, Florida; Theater of Performing Arts, Miami Beach

He's "an architect by training," A. L. Freundlic once wrote, but "a mob psychologist through experience." His designs constantly waffle between the dictates of pure aesthetics and the demands of wide public appeal, to create "a joyful feeling of overabundance." In his famous designs for many of America's largest and poshest resorts, he evokes feelings of affluence, optimism and sensuality—achieved with equal doses of showmanship, technical wizardry, and sculptural sensitivity. His 1952 Fountainbleau Hotel in Miami Beach is perhaps the most cheerful, luxurious and reposed product of the city's long-time love affair with exotic escapist architecture. Its sweeping curve of white stone at once dominates and cradles the lush, neo-classical pool and plaza beneath its overhanging balconies. Indoors, its urbane and city-slick interiors bring a bit of Park Avenue to Miami Beach.

LAUTNER, JOHN
John Lautner Architect (213) 462-2373
(Building Design, Urban Design)
7046 Hollywood Boulevard Los Angeles California 90028

Born: 1911 **Studied:** Marquette University **Awards:** Fellow, AIA **Notable Works:** Arango House, Acapulco, Mexico; Zimmerman House, Studio City California; Malin House, Concannon House, Los Angeles COMMERCIAL/RETAIL: 10%, HOUSING: 80%, EDUCATION: 10%

In an architectural era marked by aggressively personal, idiosyncratic, and often fanciful statements, he stands out as one of the nation's most engaging and successful experimental designers. His dramatic, futuristic houses, perched on the highest crags above Los Angeles, take a unique vantage on the present possibilities and products below them. They are often compared to flying saucers and other alien visitors. His best-known work is Malin House, the prototype of his 'flying saucer' homes. Its enormous, disk-shaped shell is mounted atop a single concrete column which was initially criticized as counterfunctional and self-indulgent. But given the steepness and small size of the site, the column is a cost-effective alternative to the extensive bulldozing and retaining-wall construction that a conventional foundation would require.

LAWRENCE, BILLY A.
(Building Design, Interior Architecture)
Alamo Architects (512) 227-2612
108 King William San Antonio TX 78204

Born: 1955 **Studied:** University of Texas at Austin **Awards:** Texas Award for the Preservation of Historic Architecture; Preservation award, San Antonio Conservation Society **Notable Works:** Northwest Arkansas Mall renovation and Food Court, Fayetteville AR; Bookstop, New Orleans LA; Public Mass Site, San Antonio TX COMMERCIAL/RETAIL 75%, RESIDENTIAL 15%, RENOVATION 10%

Eclectic in design, he and his partners at Alamo Architects are more interested in the basis of building than in particular styles. They think of their work as a "found architecture." As students at the University of Texas at Austin in the 1970s, they were influenced by Paul Baker who stressed the "integration of abilities." This approach calls upon architects to invest in the design of a building the same investigation of world and self that an actor employs in portraying a character.

In their renovation of the Northwest Arkansas Mall in Fayetteville AR they took out a hung ceiling, painted over the exposed steel structure and installed variously arced-patterned skylights. At a lower level they hung scalloped banners alluding to trees. More references to the wooded countryside of Fayetteville are in similar banners draped around the columns of a newly created food court. Coordinated neon lights and perforated metal panels swirling overhead suggest a giant comet hurtling through the mall.

Their commission to create a public mass site for Pope John Paul II's visit to San Antonio in 1987 challenged them to create an altar that would make 300,000 attendees feel like wor-

shippers rather than spectators. Their colorful cut-out open air church had all the design considerations and utilities of an enclosed structure.

LAWTON AND UMEMURA ARCHITECTS (see Lawton, Herbert; Umemura, Robert)

LAWTON, HERBERT T.
(Building Design)
Lawton & Umemura Architects, AIA, Inc.
(808) 529-9700
No. 1 Capitol District Honolulu HI 96813

Born: 1930 **Studied:** University of Cincinnati **Awards:** AIA **Notable Works:** Hyatt Regency Waikoloa, Kona Coast, Hawaii; Jimmy Carter Presidential Library and Museum, Atlanta GA; Hyatt Regency Maui, Hawaii RESORT HOTELS 90%

With longtime partner Robert Umemura his practise has come to focus on resort design for the first great developer of mega-resort destinations, Chris Hemmeter. Hemmeter broke the mold of urban hotels for his sprawling destinations, which are shaped by the desires and fantasies of guests who seek the adventure and romance of waterfalls, tropical vines, dolphins and the like. The hugely successful resorts are designed to give brief visitors to the Hawaiian islands precisely what they want in undreamt-of abundance.

Lawton and Umemura came to work almost exclusively for Hemmeter, but as independent contractors they were reluctant to hire permanent staff for work that might disappear at any time. They eventually ironed out the uncertainties by selling their firm to Hemmeter. Lawton and Umemura have stayed on as principals in their unit of a larger Hemmeter corporation which now creates turnkey resort communities. The design group grew from 80 to 130 employees in the first years following the sale. This unusual evolution highlights the unique role of the architect, which Lawton finds comparable to that of orchestra conductor. Coordinating financing, programs and clients, contractors, consultants and constant

Herbert Lawton, *Hyatt Regency Waikoloa*, Hawaii. Project Architect: Robert Umemura Photo:
Angie Salbosa

Arthur Cotton Moore, *Canal Square*, Washington, D.C.

surprises into a harmonious whole—ideally one that bespeaks effortless composition—is an achievement of the consummate gadfly, requiring equal parts of delicacy and brute strength. Above all, Lawton points out what the invisible underpinnings of successful work make clear: that architecture is above all a people profession, and the challenge facing its highest practitioners is to orchestrate human and technical know-how into seamless works.

LEGGE, DIANE

(Building Design, Planning)
Skidmore, Owings and Merrill
(312) 641-5959
33 West Monroe Chicago IL 60603

Born: 1949 **Studied:** Wellesley College; Stanford University; Princeton University **Awards:** Chicago AIA Young Architects Award; Progressive Architecture; Chicago AIA **Notable Works:** Boston Globe Satellite Printing Facility, Billerica MA; Manufacturer's Hanover Tower, Wilmington DE; Quaker Tower, Chicago

She strives for a clarity of idea and a certain spareness in design, reducing to a minimum most aspects of a project in order to effectively contrast abundances in specific areas, such as lobbies. While she likes the richness of the past, she doesn't look far into history for ideas, preferring to draw from modernism's archives.

In her MD Bethesda Metro Development Project, a mixed-use complex mediating between office and residential blocks, her multi-faceted program allows for low-rise townhouses facing the residential area to escalate dramatically to an apartment building and ultimately to an office building. The complex takes in an oddly shaped site, whose curving plan and stepped-up elevations result in a central open area with both privacy and sunlight.

Large curves are also a unifying design component in her Boston Globe Satellite Printing Facility and her improvements to Globe offices. In a recent office building design, an asymmetrical lozenge-shaped plan gives way to a cross-braced cantilevered tower sheathed in curving green glass which cascades down to street-level storefronts. The variegated grid pattern of the curtain wall, resembling a shoji screen, provides a feeling of lightness while mirroring the constitution of the actual structure.

LEWIS, DAVID

(Urban Design)
UDA Architects (412) 765-1133
1133 Penn Avenue
Pittsburgh Pennsylvania 15222

Born: 1922 **Studied:** University of Cape Town, South Africa **Awards:** Fellow, AIA; Celebration of Architecture Award, AIA; Associate, Royal Society of Arts **Notable Works:** Liberty Center Site Plan, Pittsburgh; Master Plan, New Indiana University, Indianapolis; Rivertown Master Plan, Raritan, New Jersey COMMERCIAL/RETAIL: 40%, HOUSING: 15%, INDUSTRIAL: 5%, EDUCATION: 5%, PLANNING: 30%

His Urban Design Associates, founded in 1965, was one of the first private urban design firms in the United States. His work has ranged from individual buildings to comprehensive plans for entire urban environments. Recently much of his practice has involved retrofitting old buildings for new uses, including his 1984 plan for the revitalization of the Pittsburgh waterfront. He is widely known for the depth of his immersion in the political, economic and social affairs of the communities for which he undertakes designs, and for the user-feedback he solicits. Soon after moving to Pittsburgh PA to teach at Carnegie-Mellon University, he became a leading advocate for residents of the Hill District, a run-down, predominantly black area adjacent to the city's commercial district. As a a building consultant to the Pittsburgh Board of Education he became an active proponent of desegregation and drafted a series of proposals for school sites jointly accessible to affluent and low-income communities.

LEWIS, DONALD M.

(Building Design, Facility Programming, Renovation)

Dianne Legge, *Quaker Tower*, Chicago. Photo: Cable Studios

Lewis+Malm Architecture (207) 469-7440
P.O. Box 1459 Bucksport ME 04416

Born: 1947 **Studied:** Yale University; Massachusetts Institute of Technology **Awards:** Maine AIA; New England AIA adaptive reuse award **Notable Works:** St. Patrick's Parish Hall, Newcastle ME; Bucksport Health Center, Bucksport ME EDUCATION 60%, INSTITUTIONAL 20%, COMMERCIAL 10%, RESIDENTIAL 10%

He sees good design as a collage of functional details at every scale, from shelf width to site context. Building users are his best form-givers; he relies on beauty growing out of their experiences and needs. As architect, he sees himself as catalyst for this process of discovery, talking extensively with clients to learn about little activities that animate their buildings. His classrooms have wide windowsills because teachers need room to display things. And his schools often don't have hallways, which is where children most often get in trouble—instead he groups classrooms around common use areas that take less space than long corridors.   His St. Patrick's Parish Hall in Newcastle ME is attached to one of New England's oldest Catholic churches, in what is today a booming summer resort. The summer parish is much too large for its delicate eighteenth century church set in tall woods, but in winter the church is still sufficient for community needs. So his design includes an outdoor chapel among the woods to be used in months when good weather draws visitors. His new parish building is cut into a hillside rolling away from the church, and from a church vantage appears to be an associated outbuilding or carriage house subordinate to the old church. In fact the apparently small building is more of a subway station, leading to extensive parish activity spaces downstairs, out of sight of the church. Among the rooms is a meeting space large enough to accommodate the summer congregation on rainy days.

LEWIS, SIR GEORGE STEPHEN
(Building Design, Construction Administration, Historic Preservation)

George Stephen Lewis (617) 423-0744
101 Tremont Street Room 705
Boston MA 02108

Born: 1908 **Studied:** Boston Architectural Center; Harvard School of Architecture **Awards:** Great Silver Medal of Paris; Winston Churchill Medal of Wisdom; First Prize, Rhodes Traveling Fellow in Architecture; Honor Award, Massachusetts State Association of Architecture **Notable Works:** Chase Residence, Lexington MA; Suffolk County Courthouse, Boston MA RESIDENTIAL 50%, GOVERNMENTAL 40%, COMMERCIAL 10%

His buildings have a classical character but modern design and a fresh appearance, using materials that are energy- and cost-efficient. Aiming for an effect of dignity that commands attention in his commercial buildings, he uses modern materials. Residential buildings often use exterior fieldstone for a rustic country look.

His Suffolk County Courthouse was Boston's first modern high rise, with facing of granite and iron-speck brick, a granite look-alike. Incorporated into the design are irregularly formed sculptural planks on the front exterior and a sculptural work over the entrance. To emphasize the verticality of the building its window treatment is dark.

In the Chase residence in historic Lexington MA he used light-colored masonry with mostly horizontal metal windows to give a clean look to the building. The inside is as simple in character as possible, with an open social area created by not walling off the living and dining rooms.

LEWIS, ROGER K.
(Building and Exhibit Design, Interior Architecture, Architectural Journalism)
Roger K. Lewis, Architect (301) 454-3427
5034 1/2 Dana Place NW
Washington DC 20016

Born: 1941 **Studied:** Massachusetts Institute of Technology **Awards:** FAIA; Federal Design Achievement Award, National Endowment for the Arts; Baltimore AIA **Notable**

Works: Easter Shore Housing Project, Scattered Sites MD; Calvert Heights Housing Project, Chestertown MD; Baer Residence, Silver Spring MD HOUSING 70%, RESIDENTIAL 30%

He uses conventional materials and systems to create unconventional architectural forms. Undogmatic about design, he believes that architecture should reflect the circumstances of its genesis and the compositional will of its designer.

From the beginning of his practice he has been engaged with vital social issues such as low-income housing and haphazard urban growth. In the last few years, through books and his weekly "Shaping the City" column in *The Washington Post*, he has sought to explain to a wide public the intricacies of architectural practice and such matters as zoning, site characteristics and building facades.

His scattered-site infill and modestly scaled front-porch design strategies provide much-needed affordable housing for the elderly on Maryland's Eastern Shore. His standardized four-unit buildings are arranged around 'village greens' or 'country lanes'. Materials and details—brick, horizontal siding, pitched roofs—imitate regional architectural characteristics. The brick front porches, inserted between private and public spaces, promote informal socializing among residents.

LIDDLE, ALAN
(Building Design, Historic Preservation, Renovation)
The Architectural Offices of Alan Liddle
703 Pacific Avenue Tacoma WA 98402

Born: 1922 **Studied:** Eidgenoissche Technische Hochschule, Zurich Switzerland; University of Washington **Awards:** FAIA; Southwest Washington AIA; Northwest Regional AIA **Notable Works:** University of Washington Oceanography Building, Seattle; Liddle Mountain Cabin, near Mt. Rainier WA; McCarver Square, Tacoma WA RESIDENTIAL 75%, INSTITUTIONAL 25%

His contributions to design aren't innovative in the usual sense. He prefers to take a slower, more objective view of what's going on around him, and to interpret the modern movement in his own, more leisurely way.

His constant reevaluation and reassessment of historic architecture has convinced him that there are certain traditional fundamentals common to all substantial design. So he tries to restate in each of his buildings: the need for design transition between structure and ground and between structure and sky; the need for a building's purpose to be expressed in its materials and shape; the need to compromise the pure concept of a building deferentially to its neighbors; and, above all, the needs of his clients.

His work blends insight into his materials with his honest and appropriate uses of them. He takes a reserved view toward the cutting-edge materials and faddish shapes in favor of traditional approaches, using forms suggested by the potential of materials.

LOHAN, DIRK
(Building Design, Interior Architecture, Planning)
Lohan Associates, Inc. (312) 938-4455
225 N. Michigan Avenue Chicago IL 60601

Born: 1938 **Studied:** Technische Hochschule, Munich; Illinois Institute of Technology **Awards:** Chicago AIA; Chicago Building Congress Annual Merit Award; American Planning Association Development Honor Award; American Institute of Steel Construction Architectural Award **Notable Works:** TRW World Headquarters, Lyndhurst OH; McDonald's Corporate Campus, Oak Brook IL; Oceanarium, John G. Shedd Aquarium, Chicago; City Front Center, Chicago INSTITUTIONAL 50%, URBAN AND COMMERCIAL 50%

He seeks "to further develop and articulate the Modern style and humanize it, in an effort to find timeless architecture." Aware that Modernist design is often seen as a cold and impersonal architecture for architecture's sake alone, he uses a variety of materials, forms and details to make his buildings friendly and accessible to people. Often rich in open spaces, they make extensive use of natural light.

For the Oceanarium, an addition to the John G. Shedd Aquarium on Lake Michigan in Chicago, he designed a fan-shaped structure with the grace of its Beaux Arts original and a modern openness and sweep. The addition, requiring a two-acre landfill extension protected by a new sea wall, uses the original's Georgia marble where the old and new buildings join. The composition derives from classical colonnade, with columns now clad in aluminum. Steel trusses span the ceiling. A glass semicircular wall offers spectacular lake views, and pools containing whales, sea otters and other ocean mammals have a fiberglass rock outcrop made from moldings of rock formations on the animals' native Pacific coast.

His McDonald's Corporate Campus Headquarters in Oak Brook IL has a relaxed resort atmosphere and has become a model for other corporate headquarters complexes. Structures, including a 300-room hotel, a training center and offices, are low to the ground, never rising more than four stories. Built of Wisconsin lannon stone, brick, exposed concrete and glass, they are linked by walkways through a park-like setting with man-made lakes stocked with fish. Parking is hidden underground. Interiors have much wood detailing, on ceilings, panels and doors. Vibrant colors and sunlight from long linear skylights bring the warm resort atmosphere into building interiors.

LOUIE, WILLIAM C.

Kohn Pederson Fox Associates PC
(212) 977-6500
111 West 57 St., New York NY 10019

Awards: AIA **Notable Works:** Bond Building, Sydney, Australia; General Re, Stamford CO

He holds that buildings can't be designed in isolation. They must respond to the nature of their context. The goal in the creative process is to coalesce internal program demands with the contextual fabric to which a building is added. The density and quality of the built environment and nature's given amenities must be weighed to determine whether a project should participate in or keep a distance from its environment. So a building's architectural success should be measured in terms of how well it participates in and reinforces the attributes of its context, rather than how beautiful it may look in isolation.

His General Re in Stamford CT is an insular scheme because of its architecturally hostile surroundings. Its linear massing is in the form of a segmented curve which creates an environmentally protected precinct for users within. The Bond Building in Sydney, Australia uses its form to reinforce the complex street patterns and completes a much neglected urban square. Its various massing heights respond to adjacent building datums while its exterior texture and color bring to mind the quality and articulation of some of Sydney's landmark structures. Finally, the natural beauty of the surrounding harbor is reflected in its billowing curved glass facing the water. Each building component is given meaning by its context.

LOVETT, WENDELL H.

(Building Design, Interiors)
The Wendell Lovett Architects
(206) 329-2345
420 34th Ave. Seattle Washington 98122

Born: 1922 **Studied:** University of Washington; Massachusetts Institute of Technology **Awards:** FAIA; Second Prize, Progressive Architecture/US Junior Chamber of Commerce Competition; Decima Triennale de Milano **Notable Works:** Lovett Vacation House, Crane Island WA; Proctor Hous, Kirkland, WA RESIDENTIAL 100%

An evolved modernist, he believes that the basis for architectural form resides in the human psyche: the true language of architecture derives from human gestures—facial expressions, body posture and movement. His homes, like human heads and bodies, feature closed, tightly stretched and minimum surfaced backs, usually facing north. Conversely the fronts or 'faces' are open, expressive, and solar receptive. Because heavy winter weather in the

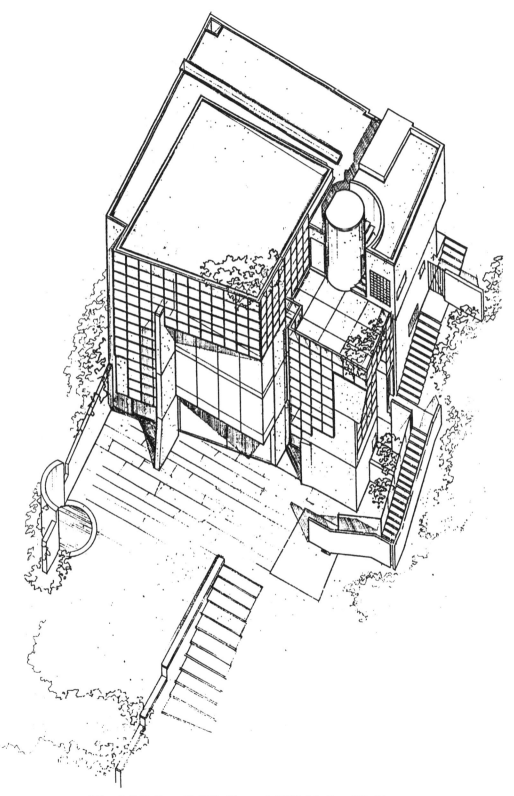

Wendell H. Lovett, *Villa Simonyi*, 1989, Medina, Washington.

Pacific Northwest tends to come from the south his houses often echo the shape of billed caps, high in back, long and low in front, catching the sun while ducking the weather. "What we're doing when we build houses," he says, "is building ourselves another skin." His goal is that our new 'skins' be psychically comfortable and adapted.

His Proctor House illustrates these features, the high blank back sloping down to a faceted, 'squinting' horizontal window band facing south. Southwest an overhang protects the bedroom window that looks out over a lake to the west. The effect is of a figure reclining along the road, an arm sheltering the eyes which focus on the lake in the distance. The house's parallelogram shape was suggested by its wide and shallow site.

LUMSDEN, ANTHONY

(Building Design, Urban Design)
DMJM Architects (213) 381-3663
3250 Wilshire Blvd. Los Angeles CA 90010

Born: 1928 **Studied:** University of Sydney, Australia **Awards:** Fellow, AIA; Eminent Conceptor Award, 1972; *House and Home* Award, 1970 **Notable Works:** Northlake Community College, Irving, Texas; Lockheed Weapons center, Rye Canyon, California; Continental City, Los Angeles **COMMERCIAL/RETAIL:** 13%, **HOUSING:** /INDUSTRIAL/EDUCATION 7%, PRIME ENGINEERING: 42%, OPERATIONS: 32%

From his studies of form and function in nature he concludes that an animal's makeup is usually determined by the external environment, not by its own internal organization. Carrying this over to architecture, the exterior structures of his buildings follow from immediate physical, functional and aesthetic demands of the outdoor environment, rather than from their arrangement of interior parts. He has applied this bifurcated design approach which separates structure from enclosure to a wide range of work, from vertical office complexes to rolling university campuses. His most acclaimed project of recent years is his 276 acre campus for Northlake Community College, in Irving TX. By designing cosmetically similar

silhouettes for a series of functionally and proportionally dissimilar structures, then arranging the buildings along a hillside like successively larger steps, he created the quaint veneer of a sleepy Japanese village. Large cantilevered and roof-mounted planters extend the Oriental idiom.

LUNDY, VICTOR ALFRED

(Building Design)
Taylor, Lundy HKS Architects 3000 Post Oak Boulevard Suite 1550 Houston Texas 77056

Born: 1923 **Studied:** Harvard University **Awards:** First Honor Award, 1965, Award of Merit, 1960, 1966, AIA **Notable Works:** United States Tax Court, Washington, D.C.; St. Paul's Lutheran Church, Sarasota, Florida; Church of the Resurrection East Harlem, New York

Although he strives for balance, repose and order in his work, he admits that his design process is an exercise in controlled turmoil. Seeking to make "perfect things," he approaches this end through a long, fitful process of trial and error. He begins simply with intuitions. The nonrational roots of his designs subtly distinguish them from the work of rote rationalists. His attention to pure form is mixed with an understated sense of drama and poetic fluidity.

Given the proper moment, he bends technology to create architectural accents that make his buildings memorable and addressable. His monolithic unfaceted United States Tax Court Building in Washington DC has a network of hidden steel cables which appear to levitate a 200 x 50-foot slab cantilevered above the structure's main entrance. He has also used structural cables to "energize" the silhouette of his otherwise stark concrete St. Paul's Lutheran Church in Sarasota FL.

LYNDON, DONLYN

(Building Design)
Lyndon Associates 948 Parker Street
Cambridge Massachusetts 02138

Born: 1936 **Studied:** Princeton University **Notable Works:** Condominium 1, Sea Ranch, California; Grass House, Hartland, Vermont;

Monte Vista Apartments, Monterey, California

He was an original member of MLTW—Moore, Turnbull, Lyndon and Whittaker—whose Sea Ranch CA projects of the 1960s were early counter-examples to the Modernist standard of a uniform, rigidly rational approach to architecture. While his partners have developed large private practices, he has concentrated on teaching and developing architectural theory. His 1974 book with Charles Moore, *The Place of the House,* has become a seminal text on "poetic" contextualism. In it he argues for a humane, anthropomorphic and addressable architecture which mirrors the pride, character, even irrationality of its users. The house, he argues, is most fundamentally a celebration of self.

The principles he has espoused in his academic work are embodied in his Pembroke Dormitory for Brown University in Providence RI. Working within tight financial constraints he crafted a shelter whose public and private surfaces vary continually, creating a sense of proprietary space for each inhabitant. His primary distinguishing device is the the rich and diverse use of color; strategically placed, highly-detailed doorway arches pro-

MACK, MARK
(Building Design)
MACK (415) 777-5305
246 First Street Suite 400
San Francisco CA 94109

Born: 1949 **Studied:** Academy of Fine Arts, Vienna, Austria **Awards:** Architectural Record planning and design award; Interiors Magazine "40 Under 40" citation; Sonoma League for Historic Preservation award **Notable Works:** San Francisco Design Center, San Francisco CA; Boise Museum of Art, Boise ID; J.P. Getty Center for the History of Art and the Humanities, Santa Monica CA RESIDENTIAL 50%, COMMERCIAL 20%, MIXED-USE DEVELOPMENT 20%, PUBLIC BUILDINGS 10%

He rejects postmodernism, which he believes ridicules and trivializes the architecture of the past. He espouses a primitivism that derives from Laugier's idea of the Primitive Hut; Laugier calls for an integrity of design that uses simple forms and hides nothing. Whatever materials are used, they should be not be disguised as anything else. Construction should be straightforward, and design should balance tradition and invention.

The San Francisco Design Center, located in the South of Market area, contains restaurants, a resource library and meeting rooms for professional design organization functions as well as a host of showrooms for contract furniture. Constructed with tilt-up concrete slabs, the 550-foot long building is punctured by a generous arrangement of windows. Corner pavilions and an entrance bay extend beyond the body of the main building. Parking is on the roof, hidden by a trellis rising up from the cornice. The interior of the center holds three levels of stores facing an interior walkway. Upper levels can be reached by skybridges and stairs.

MALHOTRA, AVINASH K.
(Building Design, Interior Architecture, Renovation)
Avinash K. Malhotra AIA (212) 808-0000
313 E. 45 St. New York NY 10017

Born: 1942 **Studied:** Columbia University; University of New Delhi **Awards:** New York City AIA **Notable Works:** The Archive, New York City; Bleeker Court, New York City; International Plaza, New York City HOUSING 60%, COMMERCIAL 30%, INTERIORS 10%

He specializes in innovative mixed-use and residential projects, often large-scale conversions and renovations which maintain historic street walls while transforming interior spaces. To provide light, air and a buffer against Manhattan's bustle he creates semi-public courtyards at the base of large open light courts which illuminate corridors as well as lobbies and provide a succession of increasingly private yet open spaces leading to each unit.

The Archive, his residential renovation in New York's Greenwich Village, was originally a Customs Service storage building which later became a post office. Declared government surplus property in 1976, the 10-story, 500,000-square-foot structure with its landmark-protected Romanesque Revival facade stood empty for 10 years. In converting it to 479 rental apartments he installed a 70 x 70-foot landscaped central courtyard over a skylit lobby. Elevators give onto the courtyard at every floor, providing orientation and light for interior corridors. Each apartment is loft or duplex, profiting from original 14-foot floor heights. On the roof 25 setback penthouses with gently raked copper roof lines are invisible from the street to a distance of 400 feet. Surrounding the penthouses, which are accessed from an outdoor rooftop promenade, open-air amenities are accessible to all tenants.

MANION, THOMAS

(Building Design, Renovation, Passive Solar and Earth-Sheltered Design)
Thomas Manion AIA Architect PC
(301) 229-7000
6412 79th St. Cabin John MD 20818

Born: 1944 **Studied:** Syracuse University **Awards:** Maryland AIA; Potomac Valley AIA **Notable Works:** Woman's National Democratic Club, Washington DC; Episcopal Center for Children Renovation, Washington DC; New Heights Restaurant, Washington DC HOUSING 80%, RETAIL 20%

He concentrates on adaptive reuse and contextual additions in older Washington/Baltimore communities. His renovations and additions use historic vocabularies in order to "expand the dialogue" between old and new, with the goal of making a given historic structure comfortably modern. Design features may be evolutions rather than imitations of original elements.

His Woman's National Democratic Club renovation updates a National Register building in Washington DC. The Arts and Crafts exterior and lower floors of the building are restored with the addition of handicap access, augmented plumbing and other modern facili-

ties. In the attic, a 27-foot-tall complex of turrets, gables and slants, he installed modern service and support offices which are accessed and lit through a new octagonal atrium. Its floor is an exact replica of the quarter-sawn octagonal design used in formal spaces below. Its high ceiling is broken up with colors, and molding follows the height of doors and transoms around the interior space.

MANKIN, HAVEN D.

(Building Design, Interior Architecture, Daylighting and Passive Solar Design, Construction Administration)
Baumeister Mankin Architects
(405) 525-8451

Born: 1950 **Studied:** University of Oklahoma **Awards:** Innovative Passive Solar Cooling Design Award **Notable Works:** 531 Couch Drive Building, Oklahoma City OK; Fashion Value Mall, Amarillo TX COMMERCIAL 50%, RETAIL 50%

He takes his inspiration from the 'organic' school of architecture. Only realizing the interdependence of all forms of nature allows the architect to leave his impress upon the built environment. He uses design elements that make his buildings "an integral part of the site and not merely a building sitting on the site." Like his associate Terry Baumeister, he too believes that the built environment—"spaces and negative spaces, the structure, color, landscaping, art, furnishings, sounds and even the smells"—must create a response that resonates to the "inner person".

Faced with the challenge of designing a discount mall that had a total budget of $35 per square foot including furniture and landscaping, he designed a monumental entry to remove any doubts about the entrance and, inside, recessed a center food court so that each storefront is in plain view.

A garden in the center of the building spills into planting areas down the wings, which are trimmed with three shades of tile pavers to further soften the commercial corridors. Steep vaulted ceilings down each wing recall a monumental vault, with one side in glass, in the central area.

Avinash K. Malhotra, *The Archive* (new court facades), New York City. Project Architects: Daniel Margulies and Vinod Devgan. Photo: Richard Saunderson

MARKSON, JEROME
(Building Design)
Jerome Markson Architects   161 Davenport Road   Ontario M5R 1J1 Canada

Born: 1929 **Studied:** University of Toronto **Awards:** Fellow, AIA; Design Award, Steel Company of Canada; Associate, Royal Canadian Academy of Arts **Notable Works:** True Davidson Home for the Aged, Toronto; Market Square Complex, Toronto; Munk Residence, Toronto

The greatest struggle in his practice, he says, has been to forget the rigid rules he was taught in his formal education. For years he had felt confined by the boxy forms of the International Style, by its automatic separation of man-made from natural materials and the economic pressure toward modular design. The only rules he now respects, he says, are those of nature—gravity still pulls down, water penetrates pores in surfaces, and so on. He belongs to a celebrated, ethnically diverse group of Toronto architects who entered practice in the early 1950s. But while Jack Klein, Irving Grossman and Henry Sears have become prominent in the academic community and their projects have become increasingly large and commercial, he is contemptuous of theoreticians and he has remained primarily interested in the problems of providing livable, low-cost housing for Canada. In his impeccably detailed public commissions, most notably the True Davidson Home for the Aged in Toronto, he has established an unmistakably Canadian architecture that makes subtle but sincere reference to the iconography of the nation's often overlooked vernacular styles.

MARSON, BERNARD A.
(Building Design, Historic Preservation, Interior Design)
Bernard A. Marson Architect (212) 755-9222 208 E. 58 St. New York NY 10022

Born: 1931 **Studied:** Cooper Union; New York University **Awards:** AIA First Honor award; New York AIA; Long Island AIA **Notable Works:** Montauk Manor, Montauk

NY; Union Headquarters and Medical Buildings, Islip and Babylon NY; High-Rise Apartment Building, New York City HOUSING 60%, COMMERCIAL AND OTHER 40%

He follows his training in looking for rational and therefore economic design, but he's inspired by Le Corbusier's admonition that one more wrinkle is necessary to "touch my heart." He looks for that added wrinkle in simple color or material combinations that result in unexpected beauty.

His Montauk Manor condominium hotel restoration builds from beautiful bones—an eclectic 1920s resort hotel combining Tudor, Moorish and Byzantine motifs which had fallen into disrepair. More than restoration was required. Earlier generations of vacationers looked forward to relaxing in the public eye; the vast public spaces they resorted to were sumptuously appointed, yet associated private rooms could be quite cramped and austere. Gut renovation was necessary to create modern apartments, yet fine public areas were preserved. The flagstone center arcade is reclaimed as a lobby and concourse with generous public seating under vaulted ceilings and original exposed beams. Other high- ceiling areas on the ground floor are converted to duplex apartments whose low dining areas below bedroom lofts lead to high, bright living rooms, where twelve-foot arched windows illuminate upper bedrooms as well as living areas. Seventy different apartment types were necessary to fit into the 140-unit renovation; many feature new cantilevered terraces which are stucco-finished to match the original exterior. New amenities have been integrated into the Manor complex, such as indoor and outdoor pools, saunas, shopping, recreation rooms and tennis courts. The renovation met Interior Department guidelines for historic preservation certification, thus qualifying it for tax credits.

MARTI, PAUL
(Building Design, Interior Architecture)
Paul Marti Associates Architects
(314) 822-0322

Bernard Marson, *FIrst Lady of the Valley Church*, 1980, New York City.   Photo: Guy Sussman

Bernard Marson, *Industrial Production Employees' Insurance Fund Union Headquarters and Medical Clinic*, 1970, Babylon, New York. Photo: Lou Reens

105 Minturn Oakland MO 63122

Born: 1929 **Studied:** Kansas State University; University of California at Berkeley **Awards:** American Plywood Association; AIA **Notable Works:** West Wing Renovation, St. Louis Art Museum, St. Louis MO; Schwach Residence, Town and Country MO INSTITUTIONAL 50%, HOUSING 50%

He believes that architectural success depends on the enthusiasm of the client no less than the skill of the architect. The client brings a 'backbone' of definite requirements that force the architect to search, study, and discover a solution; his framework of guidelines disciplines and generates thought, energy, and inspiration. Although he considers himself a regionalist, he works with the best ideas that the client has to offer and organizes his design around the owner's needs and living arrangements. He also emphasizes contemporary styles, believing that a building should be a product of the technological times in which it's produced.

His renovation of the West Wing of the St. Louis Art Museum carries forward the classical and Beaux Arts styles of the original building, designed by Cass Gilbert for the St. Louis World's Fair in the early 1900s. His renovation also takes into account an earlier renovation of the east wing over a decade ago. Aided by design consultant Charles Moore, he has sought to unify the new wing with the older structures by emphasizing beauty and classicism—particularly recapitulated Romanesque, Renaissance, and Greek motifs—over contemporary or modernist themes. The interior progression of spaces, in which visitors can take in several galleries in one glance, attests tp the building's classicism, as does a new grand staircase connecting the lower-level of decorative arts with the main-level of contemporary art. The upper-level ceiling has been opened up with skylights, providing a quiet, contemporary atmosphere complementing the building's classicism.

MASHBURN, JOE
Mashburn-Maffei Architects
Born: 1942 **Studied:** University of Houston; Texas A&M **Awards:** Texas AIA; Association of Collegiate Schools of Architecture **Notable Works:** Skiny House, College Station TX

He takes inspiration from Texas vernacular architecture and agrees with the fundamental strategy described as "Critical Regionalism" by Kenneth Frampton: "To mediate the impact of universal civilization with elements derived indirectly from the peculiarities of a particular place."

His own Mashburn House is unusual both in its shape and its materials, which derive from considerations of site, cost, and personal interest in particular building types and materials. His interest in the metal agricultural and light-industrial buildings common to Texas led to the corrugated galvanized steel siding used inside and out, and on the roof. From his interest in Texas vernacular architecture, and his desire to preserve all of the trees on the 6.3-acre site of wild bush while responding to its climate, a modified "dog trot" house emerged: major living spaces flank a central entry hall that runs through the house from front to rear, and the 186-foot-long building snakes around the site to avoid trees. "Like its ancestors," he explains, "this house allows economical zoning of heating, cooling, and ventilation systems to match our daily and seasonal patterns. The long east-west wings catch the southern breeze while shutting out excess sun. The house is elevated on concrete piers to allow drainage from subtropical storms."

Throughout he has chosen simple modular materials of economical, low-maintenance, and rural quality, which allowed speed and economy of construction by a very small crew. The 1800 square feet of the main living portions of the house are air conditioned, while the central "dog trot" hall is heated in winter by a wood stove.

MAUL, JAMES H.
(Building Design)
James H. Maul Associates, Inc.
(805) 772-8885
571 Embarcadero Morro Bay CA 93442

Bernard Marson, *Montauk Manor Condominiums* (historic renovation), 1986, Montauk, New York. Photo: Lou Reens

Bernard Marson, *Buonaguro-Swanson House* (exterior view from road), 1970, Monterey, Massachusetts. Photo: Lou Reens

Born: 1927 **Studied:** University of Southern California **Awards:** Presidential Citation from California AIA; AIA **Notable Works:** Covina Library, Covina CA; Prince of Peace Lutheran Church, CA; San Luis Obispo Air Terminal CA COMMERCIAL 40%, INSTITUTIONAL 30%, HOUSING 30%

He aims to make architecture that elicits a predetermined strong and positive emotional response in user/visitor and passerby alike. Both as practitioner and educator he hopes to foster natural humanistic design which begins with interior functions and grows outwardly. His design for the San Luis Obispo Air Terminal in CA was intended to express airplanes in flight through the use of interior and exterior curves a large cantilever over the main entry which also curves up dramatically. The looming quality of the single-story structure is heightened by its placement atop a 19-foot bank. The bank provides acoustic insulation for the structure as well as visual prominence, and ramps descend from the terminal to planes below. Sited at the end of a long valley stretching to the ocean, the terminal uses 15 to 25-knot breezes as natural air conditioning in a manner similar to Islamic architecture going back more than a thousand years. Large scoops on the side of the building allow air into a holding chamber which is activated manually by opening louvers on the facing side. All water is heated using solar collectors.

His design for the Agricultural Science Building at California Polytechnic University, also at San Luis Obispo CA, was generated by a Catch-22 situation: the program required greenhouses but the University had a policy forbidding appurtenances on roofs. His resolution incorporated greenhouses into the entire south side of the three-story building through the use of six flying buttresses connected with glass. Offices and labs were situated facing the remaining directions with entrances on all three sides.

MAY, ARTHUR
(Building Design)
Kohn Pedersen Fox Associates PC
(212) 977-6500
111 West 57 St. New York NY 10019

Born: 1940 **Studied:** Rensselaer Polytechnic Institute **Awards:** AIA Arnold W. Brunner Memorial Prize; Distinguished Design Award, New York AIA **Notable Works:** 180 E. 70th St, New York City; Hyatt Regency Hotel, Greenwich CT COMMERCIAL 100%

His firm, Kohn Pedersen Fox, displays a unified design philosophy. They are Postmodernists with an important qualification: they eschew the superficial tendency of Postmodernists to use historical elements and motifs ironically and humorously. He believes that Postmodernism has three genuine components: decoration, contextualism, and history. Rather than as an isolated, fashionable movement, Postmodernism should be seen in historical relation to Modernism and classicism; elements of all three movements may play a role in his architecture. What is important to him is that historical precedents be respected: "the thousands of years of dealing with all the problems of making buildings: the problem of entering a building, framing a door, a set of steps, making a portico, an entry vestibule, etc.:" He has been influenced by Alvar Aalto and Frank Lloyd Wright, and the great American classicists Mckim, Mead and White.

He likes to contrast architecture to painting, and he's tempted to compare his firm's work with the breakthroughs associated with Picasso and Braque. But he notes crucial differences between the two genres. He faults Modernism in architecture for being too openly subservient to and derivative of Modernist painters. Unlike painting, architecture is concerned with problems of human scale. For example, an architect must find a way of breaking down the expanse of a building's walls, so that it doesn't appear overly forbidding from the street; in order to do this, he will exploit the orienting possibilities of columns, moldings, string courses, and cornices. Moreover, a building must concern itself with its context, its juxtaposition among a cluster of buildings and nature. Contextualism strives to establish a language or dialogue of coherently formed spaces. Such problems and concerns are unique to architecture, and are generally irrelevant to painting.

MAYNE, THOM
Morphosis (213) 453-2247
2113 Stiner Av. Los Angeles CA 90025

Born: 1944 **Studied:** Harvard University **Awards:** AIA; "40 under 40" Honoree, *Interiors* magazine; California AIA; *Progressive Architecture* magazine awards **Notable Works** (also see Michael Rotondi): Sixth Street Residence, Santa Monica CA; Kate Mantilini Restaurant, Beverly Hills CA; Prototype Hamburger Stand, Los Angeles CA; Comprehensive Cancer Center, Los Angeles CA

For him and partner Michael Rotondi, relevant architecture must express the"terrible beauty " of industrial reality, the risk and tension of unsettled urban life and the ruined quality of decaying matter. Their work is simultaneously functional and funky, orderly and dissonant, straight forward and hedonistic, contextual yet resisting assimilation.

Of their design for the Sixth Street Residence in Los Angeles, they write: "The work is made up of spaces and objects whose original purpose has been lost due to obsolescence and over-investment brought about by a constant recycling. The invention and importation of ten pieces brings to the site—and has the capacity to embody in built form—an imagined prehistory of a place, a contemporary archaeology - past and future - and its subsequent transmission over time. The house explores the ground between these found objects and building. The ten pieces—dead machinery or dead tech—present ideas of decay . . . leading towards a distopian architecture. Discrete pieces manipulated independently, simultaneously separated and associated through a geometric order, describe a vision of a world which is neither fragment nor whole. Beauty and ugliness blur."

McCUE, GERALD MALLON
(Building Design)
Department of Architecture and Urban Design Gund Hall Harvard University Cambridge Massachusetts 02138

Born: 1928 **Studied:** University of California, Berkley **Awards:** Fellow, AIA; Architectural Record Award, 1973; Print Magazine Award, 1978 **Notable Works:** IBM Santa Teresa Computer Programming Center, San Jose, California; Ames Research Center, Moffet Field, California; Epstein House, Orinda, California

In his practice as well as his teaching at the Harvard Graduate School of Design he has worked to refine and extend the theory and techniques of Modernism. He has aspired to identify, adapt and deploy the most advanced materials and construction technologies, and to craft buildings whose forms echo and accentuate their advanced structural features. In his early designs, most notably the Ames Research rocket testing Center in Moffett Field CA, he worked directly from the "homogeneous" prototypes of Mies van der Rohe and Le Corbusier, whose interior surfaces, structural supports and exterior membranes are as cosmetically similar as possible to each another, thus unifying structure and finish.

In later projects, for example his 1976 IBM Santa Teresa Computer Programming Center in San Jose CA, he developed new "heterogeneous" prototypes whose facades, supports and interior surfaces are crafted from materials selected for durability and affordability rather than superficial similarity. He believes that to do otherwise and cease to reflect evolving technologies and user concerns would violate the spirit no less than the canons of Modernism. His designs are contemporary reinterpretations of its continuing wisdom.

McCURRY, MARGARET I.
(Building Design, Facility Programming, Interior Architecture, Renovation)
Tigerman, Fugman, McCurry (312) 644-5880
444 North Wells Chicago IL 60610

Born: 1942 **Studied:** Vassar College; Harvard University **Awards:** AIA; *Interiors* magazine Big I award; Builder's Magazine *Builder's Choice* Award; Chicago AIA Interior Architecture Award **Notable Works:** Van Straaten Gallery, Chicago IL; McCurry/ Tigerman residence, Lakeside MI; Juvenile Protective Association Headquarters, Chicago IL RESIDENTIAL 40%, INSTITUTIONAL 10%, COMMERCIAL, OFFICE AND RETAIL 50%

Though an enthusiast of American vernacular architecture, she doesn't impose one style on every project. She enjoys taking different approaches for different projects.

Her interest in American vernacular forms and materials is evident in the cottage she built with her husband in Lakeside MI. Built of corrugated steel and topped in one portion with a grain silo roof, the house makes fresh use of materials found in Michigan industrial farm buildings. The house has a rectangular layout; an adjoining circular building is designed to suggest a barn and silo, or basilica and baptistery. The interior has the serenity of a church nave, with light coming in from upper-story windows.

In the Juvenile Protection Association Headquarters in Chicago she uses natural light to create a tranquil environment. A large skylight is installed towards the rear of the building, with a ring of offices with French doors underneath it. Wall sconces rather than fluorescent lighting are placed on either side of the office doors to provide light on overcast days. Another skylight illuminates a latticed gazebo where children can play while waiting to see counselors.

McGLONE, BOBBY MICHAEL
(Building Design, Historic Preservation)
Alamo Architects (512) 227-2612
108 King William San Antonio TX 78204

Born: 1955 **Studied:** University of Texas at Austin **Awards:** Texas AIA **Notable Works** (with Irby Hightower, Michael Lanford, Billy Lawrence): The Fairmont Hotel Restoration, San Antonio TX COMMERCIAL/RETAIL 75%, RESIDENTIAL 15%, RENOVATION 10%

His firm's first major project was to relocate and restore the Fairmount Hotel in San Antonio TX, then design an addition to it. They were first hired by a local conservation society to document the building in drawings and photographs prior to its demolition. They then worked with a local developer to move and restore the building for use as a luxury hotel. At the time of its move the 2200-ton building was, according to the Guinness Book of World Records, the heaviest building ever moved in one piece on pneumatic wheels.

On its new site the building was chemically cleaned and its original porches rebuilt, based upon old photographs. An addition repeats the rhythm of small and large bays in the original structure, but differs from it in form and detail.

The main floor contains a lobby in the addition and a bar/restaurant in the original building, with stairs in the joint between them. On the upper floors, the tiny original guest rooms and their scarcity of bathrooms required a major rearrangement of spaces. New bathrooms were inserted into the original corridors, while an old light well was floored over to become the new corridor. The stepped form of the addition created several private terraces accessible from guest rooms.

McHARG, IAN LENNOX
(Urban Design, Landscape Architecture)
Ian McHarg Architect (215) 898-6591
5 Broad Street
Philadelphia Pennsylvania 19103

Born: 1920 **Studied:** Harvard University **Awards:** Fellow, AIA; Fellow, American Society of Landscape Architects; Fellow, Royal Institute of British Architects **Notable Works:** Inner Harbor Plan, Baltimore; Ecological Study for Minneapolis; Plan for Center Los Angeles COMMERCIAL/RETAIL: 20%, HOUSING: 5%, INDUSTRIAL: 8%, EDUCATION: 8%, LANDSCAPE ARCHITECTURE: 12%, WATERFRONT DEVELOPMENT: 17%

The primary consequence of man's struggle to build economical and comfortable communities of dwellings, he has written in his landmark ecological treatise, *Design With Nature* has been the creation of increasing (noxious) legions on the surface of a fragile planet. He describes human attempts to adapt and extend the (holistic) living environment as hopelessly "low brow" and anthropocentric. As man's technical knowledge and abilities have increased, he points out, so to has his potential to damage and pervert. The ecological dangers of large scale development necessitates costly and painstaking attention to siting.

He has developed a rigorous, mechanistic approach to assessing the ecological feasibility of large-scale construction. He is particularly adept at identifying potential drainage, pollution, and erosion hazards; and he is also deeply concerned with preserving historically and aesthetically significant features of the built environment. Much of his recent practise involves consulting with major urban planning organizations to develop broad guidelines to future development.

McKINNELL, NOEL
(Building Design)
Kallmann, McKinnell & Wood   Boston MA
Born: 1935 **Studied:** Columbia **Awards:** 1984 AIA Firm of the Year; AIA Honor Award (with Gerhard Kallmann) **Notable Works:** Boston City Hall, Boston MA; American Academy of Arts and Sciences, Cambridge, MA; Boston Five Cents Savings Bank, Boston, MA (all with Kallman)

Working with partner Gerhard M. Kallmann—so closely that they often cannot remember who added what to the preliminary sketches of projects—he has created aggressive and powerful structures that transform and use traditional elements of architecture. In an *AIA Journal* poll asking critics and architects to list the most significant buildings in American history, their Boston City Hall came in at sixth place.

If the Boston City Hall, with its division of base, shaft, and entablature, looks back to classical architecture, their rustic Cambridge MA headquarters for the American Academy of Arts and Sciences is inspired by the arts and crafts movement. The hilltop villa has spreading copper roofs which pull its two stories low

to its wooded site. Brick-piered arcades and stained wood trim bring inside and out into continuing rapport, and public spaces for academy fellows are all accommodated on the airy ground floor, while office and support work is done upstairs.

MEIER, HENRY G.
(Building Design, Construction Administration, Landscape Architecture)
Henry G. Meier, Architect   (317) 253)1604
6101 N. College Ave. Indianapolis IN 46220

Born: 1929 **Studied:** University of Cincinnati **Awards:** FAIA; Edward J. Pierre Award, Indiana AIA **Notable Works:** Hoosier Village Chapel, Zionsville IN; Community Health Care Center, Indianapolis IN; Tipton County Jail, Tipton IN   RELIGIOUS 40%, COMMERCIAL 30%, OTHER 30%

He strives to create intimate spaces in major buildings. At his Indianapolis IN Community Health Care complex, instead of one large and costly community room he built small alcoves on every floor for card playing and other activities. Each of the four buildings on the forty acre complex overlook the lake; more than half of the rooms have a lake view. Parking and green space separate the four units, which are further differentiated by their individual shades of red brick and light wood trim. A vine pattern, derived from nearby Pennsylvania Dutch barn emblems, ornaments one of the buildings.

In his Tipton IN County Jail he uses Indiana limestone to match existing structures. Working with the constraints that govern the housing of prisoners, he creates a jailer's area, actually a hub where one person can control prisoners while in contact with deputies and clerical staff. Jail cells, the check-in area, and the office and garage form radial spokes off this hub.

MEIER, RICHARD ALAN
(Building Design)
Richard Meier and Partners (212) 967-6060
136 East 57th Street
New York New York 10022

Born: 1935 **Studied:** Columbia University **Awards:** Fellow, AIA; Award of Merit, Concrete Industry Board, 1974; Bard Award, City Club of New York, 1977; Firm Award, AIA, 1984 **Notable Works:** Smith House, Darien, Connecticut; Douglas House, Harbor Springs, Michigan; High Museum of Art, Atlanta, Georgia COMMERCIAL/RETAIL: 20%, HOUSING: 15%, INTERIOR DESIGN: 5%, EDUCATION: 15%, PLANNING: 10%, OTHER: 35%

Architecture, he believes, is a wholly artificial, rational and inorganic activity. In his view, the alteration or destruction of nature is the invariable consequence of any construction. He shuns the pursuit of naturalism in his commissions; any material that has been refined and reformed by human agency, he argues, is already inherently unnatural.

To highlight the contrasts between his made buildings and the found, natural environment, he sheathes them in white paint. This accentuates the artificial sharpness of their faceting, and so creates the greatest possible counterpoint to more amorphous and texturally diverse geological and biological forms.

To distinguish the horizontal plane from the vertical, he generally selects lightly-stained wood flooring as a foil to his prim white walls and window banks. In his residential commissions, — like the Smith House, in Darien, Connecticut and the Douglas House, in Harbor Springs, Michigan —he has extended the flooring through a glass wall to form exterior deck areas, which give the effect of ramps only recently declared off-limits to pedestrian traffic.

MENDERS, CLAUDE EMANUEL
(Building Design, Historic Preservation, Renovation, Interior Architecture)
Claude Emanuel Menders Architect Inc.
(617) 227-1477
59 Commercial Wharf Boston MA 02110

Born: 1944 **Studied:** Carnegie-Mellon University **Awards:** Lighting Design Award of Merit, Illuminating Engineering Society of North America **Notable Works:** Temple Beth David, Westwood MA; East Commercial Wharf Development, Boston MA; 95 Commercial Wharf, Boston COMMERCIAL 50%, PRIVATE RESIDENCE 50%

He believes that "the art in architecture is achieved when a balance of volumes and spaces, and proportions and forms, is met in a visual harmony." He tends to use simple basic forms for his structures upon which he places a "hierarchy of visual symbols." His interior designs often use stratagems and materials which achieve the greatest architectural effect for little expense: wood trim, moldings and interesting window patterns. He likes to use indirect lighting to create a mood of comfort. His buildings often include imaginative woodwork, juxtaposing two types of wood for their color effects, and he enjoys using slate and granite as compliments of the wood.

The Temple Beth David in Westwood MA is a one-story wood frame building with a partial second story. Clapboard, asphalt shingles and vertical siding make up the exterior. The interior is plasterboard with oak trim and walnut. A clerestory lets in sunlight from three sides, while additional artificial lighting is indirect.

MERCI, WILLIAM PAUL
(Building Design)
Kessler, Merci and Associates, Inc.
(312) 775-4242
6225 W. Touhy Ave., Chicago IL 60648

Born: 1931 **Studied:** Northwestern University; Illinois Institute of Technology **Awards:** Athletic Business Merit Award, Illinois Association of School Boards **Notable Works:** Western Montana Sports Medicine & Fitness Center, Missoula MT; George Halas Jr. Sports Center, Loyola University of Chicago ATHLETIC AND RECREATION 60%, INSTITUTIONAL 20%, RELIGIOUS 10%, HOUSING 10%

He innovates new solutions to design problems in the constantly evolving field of recreation, sports and physical fitness facilities. For example, his George Halas Jr. Sports Center at Loyola University is clad in stainless steel cones embedded in precast concrete panels, which solves two problems commonly found in concrete structures: They weather in extreme temperatures and consequently suffer from water penetration. His solution not only protects the concrete from weather and water, it permits edge-to-edge internal insulation with no need for a thermal bridge, for greater efficiency and facility flexibility. His active program research and long-term post-construction analysis are reflected in the adventurous and responsive nature of his designs.

MEREDITH, W. DEAN
(Building Design)
SGPA/Architecture and Planning
(619) 297-0131
1565 Hotel Circle South San Diego CA 92108

Born: 1949 **Studied:** Arizona State University **Awards:** Building Industry Association of Southern California; California Coastal Commission **Notable Works:** Chart House Restaurant, Montara & Dana Point CA; Oak Communications Headquarters, Carlsbad CA

His projects evolve from a synthesis of project-specific issues. He approaches the creative process as a constant interaction between the physical realities of a building and the theories and ideas of architecture. His design process is an intense orchestration of the architectural generators of form, including site, program, context and cost issues. Building upon these, he integrates a careful balance of art, ornamentation, order and rhythm, assimilating the undefinable magic of an idea. The final synthesis moves beyond building expressionism, moving creative interpretation into the realm of art, magic and fantasy. He explains this with a Carl Jung quotation: "Without this playing with fantasy, no creative work has yet come to birth. The debt we owe to the play of the imagination is incalculable."

His work includes the design of the award-winning Chart House restaurants in Montara and Dana Point CA. At Montara, the restaurant is nestled among cliffs overlooking a spectacular 180-degree oceanfront view where the sand, ocean, and sandstone cliffs offer inspiration. The building takes on a sculptured, swept-back form, mirroring the natural cliffs and windswept silhouettes of Monterey cypress trees nearby.

MEUS, DANIEL L.
(Building Design, Facility Programming, Interior Architecture, Renovation)
Graham/Meus Architects (617) 267-9399
224 Clarendon St. Boston MA 02116

Born: 1942 **Studied:** University of Detroit **Awards:** New England AIA; Massachusetts Commonwealth design award **Notable Works:** Back Bay Racket Club; Arbour Hospital; House on New England Coast, MA HEALTH CARE 50%, HEALTH CLUBS 15% HOUSING 10% INTERIORS 5%

He suspects that many architects begin their design process with intuitions and then invent theories to explain them. He prefers to begin very practically with client needs and desires, with what he calls "situation and site." The situation—client needs—creates its own appropriate architecture.

His New England Coast House is a large home for a single man. The mass of the more than 6000-square-foot project is broken up by assigning functions to three different buildings which lie in loose rapport with each other while addressing the sea. Built on beachfront dunes, a fieldstone plinth several feet high acts as a platform for the ensemble of buildings, which lie in a U-shape facing and embracing the ocean. The middle house is an intimate year-round home; on one side a guest/caretaker's house also contains an exercise room and indoor-outdoor pool, and on the other side another guest house contains a large summer living room which serves the whole complex when visitors are abundant. Each house sits informally on the stone plinth, and here and there a house wall projects into the dune vegetation which surrounds the edge of the plinth. Further pulling the house into rapport with surrounding nature, the sea-facing plinth wall is serpentine rather than flat, giving an eroded and natural appearance. An interior wall continues out toward the sea with lintels and columns which frame on a protected patio the huge blue and green planes of water and sky intersecting. A compositional foreground, the wall also screens the view of a house down the beach.

MILLER, J. ARTHUR
(Computer Design, Construction Administration, Building Design, Renovation)
J. Arthur Miller AIA & Associates
(619) 756-5603
Box 8937 Rancho Santa Fe CA 92067

Born: 1933 **Studied:** Amherst College; Massachusetts Institute of Technology **Awards:** AIA; Michigan Governor's Award for Excellence in Architecture **Notable Works:** Miller House, Milford MI; Doctor's Mall, Bradenton FL OFFICE 50%, COMMERCIAL 25%, HOUSING 25%

Striving for "simple buildings made beautiful with light", he views architecture as 3-dimensional painting using space and light as media. The art is in solving complex problems with elegant clarity, creating architecture that is "inhabited" and encourages free-flowing movement of people through space. In order to control costs as well as oversee his designs' fulfillment, he is frequently the builder of projects he has designed.

His single-family residence in San Diego CA employs passive solar heating and was designed to elaborate on a sense of both shelter and space. Oriented to allow for rhythmic variations of shade and illumination both inside and out, its contemporary styling incorporates interior surprises where sunlight pops in unexpectedly. A pastel color scheme and the lack of applied ornament place the home in the vernacular of the Southwest.

MILLER, L. KIRK
(Construction Administration, Project Development)
Hood Miller Associates (415) 777-5775
60 Federal St. San Francisco CA 94107

Born: 1942 **Studied:** University of Alberta, Canada; Universite Laval, Canada; University of California at Berkeley **Awards:** AIA; California AIA; *Builder* magazine's Project of the Year **Notable Works:** Russian Hill Terrace, San Francisco; 1055 Lombard St., San Francisco; Macondray Terrace, San Francisco HOUSING 75%, INSTITUTIONAL 15%, COMMERCIAL 10%

With his partner Bobbie Sue Hood he handles the business, real-estate development and approvals side of a practice that thrives on design and construction challenges. Often a project owner and developer as well as architect, he advocates that architects take up again the 'Master Builder' responsibilities formerly characteristic of their profession. He points out that while architects' income declines, their legal responsibilities and liabilities are declining too: by actively reducing the legal liabilities of architects, AIA policy is passing over to engineers, environmental consultants and planners oversight responsibilities which used to be in the informal domain of architects. He prefers to stay in control of design and construction, noting that the inexact science of architecture often yields better results by adapting to design, construction and site surprises as they arise.

The firm's Lombard Street condominiums design in San Francisco was made possible by financial as well as architectural ingenuity. Its vacant lot was part of a larger Russian Hill package owned by a bankrupt investor. The property was repossessed by a troubled investor which was eager to cooperate in making the investment productive. Thus it was possible to assemble easements that comfortably nestled the condominiums into their site—he shifted a rear neighbor's emergency access to gain five feet of crucial width and street frontage, and built parking and a stairway on land which he bought from the developer's adjoining properties. As adjoining developer, meanwhile, he was able to insert riders into new deeds of sale which specifically assented to his Lombard Street plan, thus reducing the welter of easements and agreements that new buildings in San Francisco must negotiate.

MITCHELL/GIURGOLA ARCHITECTS
(see Giurgola, Romaldo and Mitchell, Ehrman)

MITCHELL, EHRMAN BURKMAN JR.
(Building Design, Planning)
Mitchell/Giurgola Architects
170 West 97th Street New York
New York 10025

Born: 1959 **Studied:** University of Rome **Awards:** Fellow, AIA; Fist Honor Award, 1977, Pennsylvania Society of Architects; Design Award, *Urban Design*, 1978 **Notable Works:** Liberty Pavilion, Philadelphia; Mitchell House, Lafayette Hill, Pennsylvania; Parliament House, Canberra, Australia COMMERCIAL/RETAIL: 40%, INTERIOR DESIGN: 5%, EDUCATION: 20%, OTHER: 35%

He and his longtime partner, Romaldo Giurgola, attempt to craft structures which reflect the wide variety of life in their communities. His buildings express a continuity with architectural tradition and movement toward the future. His designs emerge from a synthesis of the implicit and explicit needs of users and technological constraints, but he never loses sight of the broader contexts of his work. The unmistakeable timelessness and solidarity in his institutional commisions is perhaps best seen in his 1975 Pavilion for Philadelphia's Liberty Bell, which creates the effect of an enormous, ahistorical display case, offering an engaging counter to the colonial meeting house and monolithic skyscraper which rise behind it.

MOCK, JOHN R.
(Construction Administration, Building Design, Interior Architecture, Renovation)
Hendrick & Mock Architects (619) 280-6282
3901 Adams Avenue San Diego CA 92116

Born: 1934 **Studied:** University of Detroit **Awards:** Exceptional Merit Citation, San Diego AIA; Fellow, Society of American Registered Architects; Mr. Masonry for 1974, Masonry Contractors Association of San Diego and Imperial Counties **Notable Works:** Hanalei Hotel, San Diego CA; Good Shepherd Catholic Church, San Diego CA INSTITUTIONAL 33%, RELIGIOUS 33%, HOTELS 33%.

As comfortable designing hotels as churches, he considers his firm neither a trendsetter nor a trendfollower. His primary concern is how well a building functions and serves client needs.

He specializes in masonry design, and his eight-story Hanalei Hotel in San Diego was California's first load-bearing masonry building taller than three stories. For this hotel he developed a system of rapid construction, using masonry bearing walls and cast-in-place or precast floors, which was later adapted by the U.S. Navy and Army, and a great many American hotels of fewer than twelve stories. The 207-room Hanalei Hotel was built in 120 days.

Its exterior is a concrete gridlock broken by projecting balconies. Glass elevators overlook courtyard filled with fountains and Polynesian artifacts. On the patio side of the building, waterfalls cascade from the second floor. A restaurant across the courtyard features walls with volcanic stone veneer and a long shallow pool built with weirs to simulate a flowing stream.

MOCKBEE, SAMUEL
(Building Design, Construction Administration)
Mockbee-Coker-Howarth Architects
(601) 353-9409
414 North Street Jackson MS 39202

Born: 1944 **Studied:** Auburn University **Awards:** Progressive Architecture First Award; Mississippi AIA **Notable Works:** Christ Church, Clinton MS; Presbyterian Church, Rankin County MS; Herring Residence, Tensas Bluff LA COMMERCIAL 40%, HOUSING 30%, INSTITUTIONAL 20%

Judges have commented on the pristine quality of his designs and the elegance he evokes even with limited budgets. His buildings often take design cues from surrounding architecture.

His design for a Fire Station in Canton MS gives the aluminum-clad prefab structure a bit of style and wit. The living quarter's entrance is set off by pink pillars that hold up a double-peaked sign resembling a fireman's helmet. A painted metal trellis connects the pillars to the building. The living quarters, housing eight men, are separated from the lounge area by a kitchen, bath and storage area. The garage portion of the building is a drive-through bay with a white brick interior that holds two trucks.

Three houses designed for low-income families in Madison County MS had to be inexpensive and easy to construct because both labor and materials were donated. The buildings feature gabled windows and steeply pitched roofs, true to the vernacular of the area. Exteriors use board and batten siding, galvanized corrugated metal and roll composition roofing.

MOORE RUBLE YUDELL ARCHITECTS (see Moore, Charles Willard and Rotondi, Michael)

MOORE, ARTHUR COTTON
(Building Design, Urban Design)
Arthur Cotton Moore Associates (202) 337-9081
1214 28th Street N.W. Washington D.C. 20007

Born: 1935 **Studied:** Princeton University **Awards:** Fellow, AIA; Grand Award, National Assocation of Homemakers; First Honor Award, AIA, North Virginia Chapter; Owens Corning Energy Award, 1976 **Notable Works:** Washington Harbor Project, D.C.; Canal Square project, Washington, D.C.; Rockefeller Housing Development, Washington, D.C. COMMERCIAL/RETAIL: 75%, HOUSING: 14%, EDUCATION: 1%, OTHER: 10%

As architectural critic for the *Washingtonian* and the *Washington Post* he was one of the nation's earliest and most vociferous critics of knock-it-down urban renewal. In the last two decades his firm has moved beyond the traditional design realm, undertaking major development projects which he hopes will contribute to the greater Washington DC area.

He has been a leader in elaborating strategies for adaptive re-use, and is sensitive and resourceful in incorporating architectural fragments and historic allusions into new buildings. His 1965 Canal Square project, in Washington's then troubled Georgetown area, was one of the nation's earliest and most extensive urban recycling efforts. He grafted a sumptuously renovated nineteenth century brick warehouse to 75,000 square feet of new retail and commercial space sheathed in a consonant weathered brickface, producing produce a highly functional yet contextually sensitive enclosure.

MOORE, CHARLES WILLARD
(Building Design)
Moore Ruble Yudell Architects
(213) 829-9923
1063 Gayley Los Angeles California 90024

Born: 1899 **Studied:** Cornell University **Awards:** Fellow, AIA; Knight Commander, Republic of Italy, 1965 **Notable Works:** Sea Ranch Condo, Sea Ranch, CA; Faculty Club, University of California at Santa Barbara COMMERCIAL/RETAIL: 20%, HOUSING: 50%, INTERIOR DESIGN: 10%, EDUCATION: 10%, PLANNING: 10%

He is an accomplished and erudite spokesman for a group of 'dissident' architects that includes Donlyn Lyndon and William Turnbull. Under the firm name of MLTW—Moore, Turnbull, Lyndon and Whittaker—he has produced diverse designs which he offers as counter-examples to the Modernist standard of uniform, analytic and narrowly rational architecture. He believes that individual buildings should grow from personal needs, aspirations and symbols, as well as from the constraints of site and environment. His architecture makes room for whimsy, mythology, historicism and even neurosis. When he has undertaken commissions for institutions, he has attempted to isolate quirks in the collective psychology of their members and make them design motifs, producing an unusually representative and revealing architecture. In his design for the Faculty Club at the University of California at Santa Barbara, for instance, he

Charles W. Moore (with Robert L. Harper), *Williams College Museum of Art*

adorned the building's main space with mock-heraldic reliefs to gently lampoon the faculty's unspoken desire for continuity with the traditions of East Coast and Continental academia.

MORGAN, HARRY S.

(Design, Construction Administration, Facility Programming, Interior Architecture, Specifications)
Harry S. Morgan and Associates
(312) 724-6285
1701 E. Lake Avenue Glenview IL 60025

Born: 1914 **Studied:** Iowa State University **Awards:** AIA; Long Island AIA; Illinois/Indiana Masonry Council Award. **Notable Works:** Cedar Creek Plant, Long Island NY; O'Hare Pollution Control, Chicago IL; Ravenswood Hospital Medical Center, Chicago IL INDUSTRIAL 50%, INSTITUTIONAL AND MEDICAL 50%

Wary of architectural trends, he concerns himself with how a design will age over time. His projects match building details to their larger environments, placing wide, sun-blocking eaves on California buildings and avoiding needless projections which would collect dirt and snow on buildings in the Midwest.

Many of the features of his Chicago Ravenswood Hospital, such as its human scale and low ceilings, are designed to sooth anxious patients. Large windows give patient rooms a sense of openness, and partitions in double rooms are arranged so that each bed has a view out the window. The hospital's dining rooms resemble intimate restaurants rather than institutional cafeterias: chandeliers and wall sconces reduce the need for recessed lighting, and dividing walls create more intimate alcoves. For the hospital exterior he developed a special blend of red/brown brick which reacts subtly with changing sunlight. The blend is now sold nationwide as the Ravenswood Blend.

His Cedar Creek Waste Treatment Plant on Long Island is designed to fit unobtrusively into its surrounding neighborhood, using a large roof line that gives the plant the appearance of a resort and silencing the roar of the engine rooms with a honeycomb lined with sound-absorbing material.

MORGAN, JOHN C. JR.

(Building Design)
Freeman and Morgan Architects
(804) 282-9700
7110 Forest Ave. Suite 201
Richmond VA 23226

Born: 1939 **Studied:** Virginia Polytechnic Institute & State University; Virginia Commonwealth University **Awards:** AIA Test of Time Award **Notable Works:** Dreelin Office Building, Richmond VA; Forest Financial Building, Richmond VA COMMERCIAL 80%, MEDICAL 20%

He identifies with Postmodernism with reservations; he compromises between Postmodern richness of detail and emphasis on human scale, and sensitivity to the tastes of his clientele, who don't respond to extremism or faddishness. Central Virginia is conservative, and the ageless quality of his work is popular. Owner needs, cost-effectiveness, and energy-efficiency are his primary concerns, as well his aim of integrating his architecture into the local community.

His Dreelin Office Building in Richmond VA is a two-story structure with one broadly curved corner. The brick and glass surface is balanced with Postmodern sawtooth and marble design elements. Butt-glazed glass, bronze-tinted with eight percent light transmission, runs around the building's surface in horizontal bands that alternate with black contrasting bands. A colonnade of brick columns around the first story is visible inside and out. The columns lend a traditional, classical feeling which nonetheless has a Postmodern edge. The building anchors its surrounding suburban office park whose other buildings, some by him, some by others, maintain the same style. His Forest Financial Building, also in Richmond VA, is constructed in a similar conservative style, except that its horizontal lines create a predominantly conservative and classical solidity, with Postmodern elements kept to a minimum. The reddish brown bricks are shaped with S figures which form elegant

Charles W. Moore (with William Turnbull, Jr.), *Sea Ranch Condominium*, California

William Morgan, *Westinghouse World Headquarters,* Orlando, Florida.

shadow lines that are heightened by a Colonial style of bricklaying.

MORGAN, WILLIAM
(Building Design, Landscape Architecture)
William Morgan Architects (904) 356-4195
220 East Forsyth Street
Jacksonville Florida 32202

Born: 1930 **Studied:** Harvard University
Awards: Fellow, AIA; Design Award, Progressive Architecture, 1975; Graham Foundation Grant, 1973 **Notable Works:** Dunehouse Apartments, Atlantic Beach, Florida; Trident Submarine Base Headquarters, Kings Bay, Georgia; Riverfront Esplanade, Norfolk, Virginia COMMERCIAL/RETAIL: 65%, HOUSING: 5%, INTERIOR DESIGN: 5%, EDUCATION: 5%, PLANNING: 5%

After completing a ten-year inquiry into the evolution of prehistoric architecture in North America and Micronesia, his work changed dramatically.

In the early 1960s he designed a series of luxury houses which showed a boxy, Miesian face to the outside world but featured airy, two-story central atriums with integral balconies and unexpectedly intimate and earthy fireplace nooks. After his immersion in the organic forms of ancient vernacular architecture he took up a series of commissions through which he hoped to prove that architecture could be an extension of traditional landscaping.

One of his most striking designs, the 1975 Dunehouse Apartments in Atlantic Beach FL, is a multi-unit duplex built into the slope of a natural sand dune. The structure so closely follows the natural contours of the dune and the adjacent shoreline that its presence is only betrayed by a pair of small oval patios and a modest entrance way.

MORIYAMA, RAYMOND
(Building Design)
Raymond Moriyama Architects and Planners
32 Davenport Road
Toronto Ontario M5R 1H3 Canada

Born: 1929 **Studied:** McGill University

Awards: Fellow, AIA; Massey Medal, 1961; Canadian Architects Yearbook Award, 1968
Notable Works: Metropolitan Toronto Library; Place St. Charles, New Orleans; City Centre Plan, North York, Ontario

In the last decade he has emerged as Canada's most prolific and resourceful institutional architect. His formal vocabulary is rigorously modern but his agile alternations between planar and curvilinear geometries lend a grace that distinguishes him from most structuralists. His affinity for natural light and open, sweeping spaces provides a counterpoint to the self evidently "made", often prefabricated materials he typically employs.

His 1977 design for the Metropolitan Toronto Library exemplifies his intricate but relaxed approach to creating public meeting and work places. Four balcony levels circle the library's main level, which houses the card catalog and other primary resources. Banners of varying lengths hang from the ceiling and are positioned so that they abut the exhibits and collections which they advertise. Ferns are placed on the balcony railings, so that their leaves trail over their white side-walls, lending a quaint, organic quality to a potentially overwhelming urban center.

MOSES, IRVING BYRON
(Building Design)
Moses Associates (312) 670-6710
225 W. Ohio St. Chicago IL 60610

Born: 1925 **Studied:** University of Illinois
Awards: AIA **Notable Works:** Oppenheim Residence, Highland Park IL; Bnei Ruven Temple, Chicago COMMERCIAL 50%, HOUSING 20%, INDUSTRIAL 10%

He has designed more than 2000 structures to serve scores of applications. His Bnei Ruven Temple in Chicago is built around a central dome, supported at the center by a column incorporated into the worship altar. In the brick column is a niche in which the torahs are held, on a turntable which makes them all readily accessible. The doors of the niche are also brick in a metal frame.

He has diverse sources for design, from

external beam-ends in the adobe manner, which he uses in residential and office contexts, to the classical pyramid form, in a proposed 500-room hotel-resort complex in Florida.

MOSS, ERIC OWEN
(Building Design)
Born: 1943 **Studied:** Harvard University **Awards:** AIA; *Progressive Architecture* magazine awards **Notable Works:** Petal House, Los Angeles CA; 708 House, Pacific Palisades CA; Escondido Civic Center, Escondido CA; Costa Mesa Office Building, Costa Mesa CA COMMERCIAL/INSTITUTIONAL 75%, HOUSING 25%

He's a gadfly whose works assay critical discourses on the modern condition. Whether seeming to comment on urban realities or mixing highbrow genres with lowbrow, his architecture is playful, inventive, and heedless of propriety. He wants to make the viewer feel that "somebody just punched a hole in their sky." His willful discordances aim to do more than just snap the viewer into attention: "Architecture is in a fundamental sense a manifestation of the content of the time in which it is produced. It can communicate certain things about the nature of the time; about the way people live, or the way people might live; or about what people aspire to, or what they should aspire to. It raises questions: 'What's a building?' 'What's a house?' 'How do people live?' "

His design for his own 708 House in Pacific Palisades CA features a menu of provoking devices, such as 'flying buttresses' which frame the entrance. Identically shaped, one is of wood and plaster, and painted blue; the other is of perforated 20-gauge steel painted green and set in a hardwood frame. He calls the north facade of a freestanding 'flying wall' "Swiss Cheese." It's made of two layers of half-inch plywood, the first blue and the second white with holes eight inches in diameter. With its gabled profile it is configured as a sort of Little Bo-Peep's House.

His work has been characterized as "an assemblage of discordant parts into an artful non-sequitor." He denounces historicism as "rancid" and modernism as "emotionally dead." His own work he conceives as a way of keeping architecture alive by making us ask questions.

MOUNT, JAMES
(Building Design, Teaching)
James W. Mount Architect (404) 261-6319
74 Park Circle NE Atlanta GA 30305

Born: 1937 **Studied:** Auburn University; Louis Kahn Studio, University of Pennsylvania **Awards:** Atlanta AIA; Georgia AIA

No dogmatist, his work is free-spirited and playfully combines simple geometric forms with such materials as are favored by deconstructionists—plywood faced in kraft paper and galvanized metal, for example. His award-winning beach cottage, situated on a narrow strip of Florida land between Choctawhatchee Bay and the Gulf of Mexico in a region of great beauty, has a local reputation for its unusual features. Most of the houses on the beach, owing to its punishing environment of blistering sun, high winds and tides, and corrosive salt, are inexpensive, simple, weathered wood-frame affairs raised on pilings which require little maintenance. His house uses a wide palette based on the white beach sand and its color-changes, from rosy pink at dawn to yellow pink at dusk. This, and a pyramid on the roof, announce the house emphatically.

Sited in the thick undergrowth of a scrub grove, the house has a direct visual axis from a parking area to its entrance on the inland elevation. An enclosed ramp, concealing storage and well pumps and serving as an impromptu playground, blocks direct access to the house. Circulation moves around it, through a series of layered partitions. A series of squares on the east-west axis form the plan of the house. Three overlapping squares, comprising the dining, kitchen and living rooms form the center. They are flanked by two bedrooms stacked on top of each other on the eastern side, and a screen porch on the western end composed of an open square inscribing a corrugated metal cylinder. An interior staircase connecting the two bedrooms is marked on the exterior by the rooftop pyramid.

MUCHOW, WILLIAM CHARLES
(Building Design)
W.C.Muchow and Partners (303) 295-1805
1725 Blake Street Denver Colorado 80202

Born: 1922 **Studied:** Cranbrook Academy of Arts **Awards:** Award of Honor, AIA, 1963; First Design Award, *Progressive Architecture*, 1971; First Honor Award, AIA/U.S. Office of Education **Notable Works:** Blue Cross/Blue Shield Building, Denver, Colorado; First Methodist Church, Laramie, Wyoming; Currigan Exhibition Hall, Denver COMMERCIAL/RETAIL: 30%, HOUSING: 5%, INTERIOR DESIGN: 5%, EDUCATION: 30%, OTHER: 30%

He has developed an international reputation while working almost exclusively in the environs of Denver CO. Though much of his work is in striking mountain sites his designs are remarkably cosmopolitan, and he has shunned the self-conscious Rocky Mountain rural style. He is interested in creating "honest" buildings, whose exterior envelopes follow directly from the logical ordering of internal parts. His exterior forms are often similar, mirroring the regularity of his interior schemes.

Always rigorous in deriving forms from logistical constraints, his designs solutions can be quite original. When zoning and blue-sky restrictions defeated his plans for a conventional office tower for Denver Blue Cross/Blue Shield, he turned the skyscraper onto its side and set it on the roof of a parking substructure.

MURPHY/JAHN ASSOCIATES (see Jahn, Helmut and Pran, Peter)

MYERS, BARTON
(Planning, Building Design)
Barton Myers Associates 322 King Street West Ontario M5V 1J4 Canada

Born: 1934 **Studied:** University of Pennsylvania **Awards:** Habitation Space International Award, 1978; Stelco Design Award, 1978; Record Interior Award, 1981, 1982 **Notable Works:** Center for Performing Arts, Portland, Oregon; Hasbro Corporate Headquarters, Providence, Rhode Island; IBM Westlake Park Master Plan, Dallas, Texas COMMERCIAL/RETAIL: 30%, HOUSING: 5%, INTERIOR DESIGN: 5%, PLANNING: 40%, OTHER INSTITUTIONAL: 20%

Since his emigration to Canada from the United States in 1968 he has been a polemical critic of contemporary North American urban design. His designs arise from his vision of a multi-centered city consisting of robustly linked, semi-self-sufficient, low-rise neighborhoods. Arguing academically for reconfiguring vast urban expanses, in his professional designs he works piecemeal towards his ideals. The majority of his commissions involve infill building, adaptive re-use or non-destructive extension. He attempts to create accessible common social space as integral elements or additions to all his projects. Generally his large buildings have relatively unarticulated, flat exterior envelopes. He approaches the construction of interior spaces by designing a grand room, conforming to the borders of the outer membrane, then parsing that space into "rooms within rooms." Formally he favors planes and orthogonal geometries. He reserves curves and cylinder forms for major entry portals and plazas. His buildings include off-the-shelf materials, found contemporary objects, and historical elements from classical and vernacular structures. Conventional materials define overt structure, and 'custom' materials are juxtaposed to create drama and variety.

NAGLE, JAMES L.
(Building Design, Historical Preservation)
Nagle Hartray and Associates (312) 266-2800
230 East Ohio Street Chicago IL 60602

Born: 1937 **Studied:** Stanford University **Awards:** Henry Adams Award, AIA; Fulbright Traveling Fellowship **Notable Works:** City Houses, Chicago; Cook Residence, Minneapolis; Oaks Housing Remodelling, Oak Park, Illinois

He is a humanist who has not forgotten the pragmatic necessity for immersion in the intricacies of new materials and techniques. All of his projects — which range from minor institutional remodelings to full-scale commercial and residential high-rises—betray the cool eye and steady hand of a builder, as well as the sublime vision of a sculptor and veteran civic planner. His current projects include the design of a dormitory complex for Illinois' Northwestern University and the renovation of the University of Chicago's School of Business, but his clean, functional approach is best seen in his recent commercial mid-rise on Chicago's Lake Shore Drive. Its strong rectilinear symmetry, simple masonry construction, atrium core and bay windows strongly recall the solid, utilitarian efforts of the first Chicago School.

NEAL, JAMES A.

(Building Design, Construction Administration)
Neal-Prince & Partners Architects Incorporated (803) 235-0405
110 W. North Street Greenville SC 29601

Born: 1935 **Studied:** Clemson University **Awards:** Energy Design Award, South Carolina AIA; South Carolina AIA **Notable Works:** Lander College Housing, Greenwood SC; The Perone Residence, Greenville SC; Don C. Wall Residence, Greer SC HOUSING 20%, COMMERCIAL 30%, INSTITUTIONAL 20%, RELIGIOUS 15%

He takes pride in designing workable, efficient buildings and holds that architecture is successful only when it fulfills basic human needs. Taking advantage of a sloping, wooded site, his student housing at Lander College in Greenwood SC employs three-story dormitory buildings whose uphill units have lower level entries joined to downhill units with mid-level entries. They are joined by wooden decks. First floors are masonry, and the upper two floors are wood-framed with applied fir plywood siding. Their rustic character fits into the surrounding residential neighborhood. His Perone Residence in Greenville is also three-story with load-bearing masonry at the lower level and wood frame floors above, in this case trimmed in cedar siding and shakes. Major living spaces are oriented towards a panoramic view of the Blue Ridge foothills. A faceted cylindrical form accommodates at once a bar at pool level, the dining space at mid level, and a lounge adjacent to the master bedroom at the upper level.

NEIGHBORS, GLENN ALLEN

Kerns Group Architects, P.C. (202) 393-2800
666 11th St., Washington DC 20001

Born: 1960 **Studied:** University of Maryland **Awards:** American Wood Council **Notable Works:** Montessori Country School, Darnestown MD; Blessed Sacrament Catholic Community, Alexandria VA; St. Anne's Episcopal Church, Reston VA RELIGIOUS/INSTITUTIONAL 60%, HOUSING 20%, COMMERCIAL/RETAIL 20%

He values unpretentious sensitivity and simplicity. Working with tight budgets, he feels, has taught him "the importance of clarity, of getting to the point in solving problems elegantly and distinctively....Design, after all, is the attempt to control disorder."

His Montessori Country School in Darnestown MD was designed to be a stimulating environment for its pupils while meeting a $30 per square foot budget. For simplicity, and to complement the rolling, treeless pastureland on which the 3600-square-foot building is sited, the spaces—two classrooms, an office, and bathrooms to serve an adjacent pool—were organized into a rectangle that nestles into the hill and follows its slope. To show young children how the building's parts are interrelated, its components and systems were exposed.

The structure is simple, with 36-foot-long truss joists spanning the space. Materials too are basic—exposed concrete block, stained plywood, and inexpensive aluminum windows. Because of the tight budget, every part of the building had to be functional, so each part has a double function whenever possible: a rhythmic overhang, for example, provides a decorative cap, while its three-foot depth on the south side conserves energy. Only the entrance has obviously applied decoration. It's whimsical to suit its young users, and distinctive enough to give importance to its function.

NELSON, GEORGE
(Building Design, Exhibition Design, Furniture Design)
George Nelson Associates
257 Park Avenue South
New York New York 10010

Born: 1908 **Studied:** Yale University
Awards: Fellow, AIA; Medal of Honor, New York AIA, 1979; Elsie de Wolfe Award, American Society of Interior Designers, 1975 **Notable Works:** Storagewall Storage System; Design, Industrial Design USA traveling exhibition; Rosenthal Studio, New York

Although his formal training is in architecture he has become one of American's most respected industrial and graphic designers. He is also an accomplished journalist, a world renowned exhibition designer and a key researcher in urban design.

After completing his undergraduate training at Yale he wrote for a number of architectural journals and served as associate editor of *Architectural Forum.* In that period and quite on his own he developed several flexible prefabricated architectural component systems. His Storagewall system, a multi-unit storage matrix and room divider, earned him a staff position with Herman Miller Incorporated, a small Wisconsin furniture manufacturer. After a short tenure at Herman Miller he recruited another brilliant designer, Charles Eames, and the pair established a climate of innovation and interdisciplinary freedom which attracted talented industrial designers from across the country. Within a decade Herman Miller had become one of America's most respected and imitated manufacturers. His projects characteristically blur distinctions between industrial, interior, and architectural design. Often he creates complete room environments, crafted from components that are both furniture and architecture, form and content. By the late 1950s his talent for creating total environments had been widely recognized, and he was commissioned to design a succession of artistic and architectural exhibitions. In his design for the American National Exhibition in Moscow he used enormous, parachute-shaped, transparent bubbles—they gave maximum visibility— to form the roof and main display area.

NEREIM, ANDERS
(Building Design, Interior Architecture, Renovation)
Anders Nereim Architects (312) 275-1119
4546 N. Leavett Ave. Chicago IL 60625

Born: 1947 **Studied:** University of Chicago; University of Illinois **Awards:** "Young Architects," Chicago AIA; Editor, Inland Architect **Notable Works:** Morgenstern House, Highland Park IL; Ruskin Street Residence, Seaside FL; Inter-Faith Chapel, University of Chicago Medical Center, Chicago HOUSING 50%, INSTITUTIONAL 25%, COMMERCIAL 25%

Though trained as a Modernist, he is very sympathetic to historic structures and believes in working in empathy with the environment. He considers ornamentation and decorative details as integral parts of his designs. Without the "lucidity and completeness of decorative elements," a building becomes "an incomplete sentence." His work seeks to enunciate "complete thoughts."

His award-winning Carigan Residence in Chicago, designed with former partner Stuart Cohen, is a tiny, 18-ft. wide townhouse rebuilt to create the ambience of a great mansion. The interior was gutted and reconfigured. All trim, woodwork, cabinets and built-in architecture was custom designed. High ceilings and manipulated details such as a 2-foot high chair rail give the house its grand scale. Its new open plan features slots of space on either side of the dining room piers and a narrow top lit two-story space at its center. Visually the plan expands the house vertically and horizontally.

NETSCH, WALTER ANDREW JR.
(Building Design, Landscape Architecture)
1700 North Hudson Street Chicago 60614

Born: 1920 **Studied:** M.I.T **Awards:** Fel-

Robert S. Newman, *Colgate University Library*

low, AIA; R.S. Reynolds Award, 1964; AIA Library Award, 1978 **Notable Works:** Miami University Art Museum; Joseph Regenstein Library, University of Chicago; University of Illinois at Chicago Circle

In his three decades with Skidmore, Owings and Merrill he has been responsible for the design of many of Chicago's largest and most visible institutional structures. In the mid 1960s he began to develop an architectural method based on his embryonic "field theory," for which his own townhouse served as prototype. It involved a novel, densely connected ordering of volumes completely without corridors. This spatial integration and elimination of gaps was also extended vertically, with upper levels spiraling around and down a central core. He first applied the theory on a large scale in his Community Social Center for Grinnell College in Grinnell IA. But his vision didn't attract attention or critical endorsement until the first phase of construction at his University of Illinois at Chicago Circle—this was his famous "concrete campus" which he spent more than five years planning. The school's Architecture and Arts Building is a pure extension of his field theory. The basic formal unit is the octagon. Cells abut, overlap, and abridge each other, but with a conspicuous absence of formal passageways or transport vestibules.

NEWMAN, HERBERT S.

(Building Design, Interior Architecture, Planning)
Herbert S Newman Associates AIA P.C.
(203) 772-1990
300 York Street New Haven CT 06511

Born: 1934 **Studied:** Brown University; Yale University **Awards:** FAIA; AIA **Notable Works:** Dana Addition, Case Library, Cogate University, Hamilton NY; Kariotis Hall, Northeastern Univeristy, Boston MA; School of Management, Yale University, New Haven CT

His scheme for a law school expansion at Northeastern University's Kariotis Hall In Boston took account of the random plan of its dull neo-classical buildings and focused them by imaginatively designing and placing the new structure among them. Lying at the confluence of several major roads and visual axes, and acting as a bridge between uninteresting buildings to the east and a nineteenth century warehouse, he gave Kariotis Hall a half-circular plan that pulls it away from an adjacent building to avoid blocking light and ventilation and simultaneously emphasize the entrance to a newly landscaped plaza to the north. Ashlar concrete coping, strong horizontal banding and a bold overhanging cornice relate the building to the old warehouse. The facade steps down to the north and increases in transparency to modulate transition from building to plaza.

His renovation and expansion design for Colgate University's Case Library in Hamilton NY breathed new life into an architectural anomaly. A plain boxy structure with yellow porcelain enamelled wall panels, it was ill at ease with the campus's traditional grey stone gables and slate roofs. Borrowing from two Victorian landmarks, he gave his addition a polychromatic stone-and-brick facade and modulated it with rhythmic banding, a simple roof line, and repeated modular bays. Cylindrical brick-stain towers form visual links between the two library segments and minimize the contrast of old and new stonework. Stairways anchor the long axis of the reading room, and a progression of spaces from public to private is formed by adopting the parti of a lofty skylighted wall with alcoves and galleries. Moving ceiling louvers, closing to conserve heat on winter nights or shield from summer glare, permit sunlight to dance inside.

NIBLACK, RICHARD C.

(Building Design, Facility Programming, Renovation)
SGPA/Architecture and Planning
(619) 297-0131
1565 Hotel Circle South San Diego CA 92108

Born: 1929 **Studied:** University of Southern California; University of California at Los Angeles **Awards:** AIA; Alaska AIA; American Institute of Steel Construction **Notable**

Works: Arco Alaska, Anchorage AK; CBS Television City, Los Angeles; Interstate Bank Corporate Headquarters, Los Angeles; Johnson Space Center, Houston TX   OFFICE 40%, MIXED-USE 30%, INDUSTRIAL 20%, RETAIL 10%

Site and location, programmatic issues, cost problems—and the lack of knowing future uses—all have a significant influence on his approach to building design. He prefers to use structure and functional form rather than arbitrary architectural decoration to make a meaningful statement. But in addition to their functional attributes, he wants the design qualities of his buildings to be appreciated as they exhibit themselves in detailing.

His Arco Alaska building, the tallest in Anchorage AK, is a press-steel design that relates architecturally to four adjacent 9-story buildings yet presents a somewhat more slick, flush look. The strip banding of windows and spandrels is rendered on thermal-insulating glass and aluminum panels in compatible colors. The core of the building, which with its cut corners looks like two triangles joined together, lies on a 45-degree angle and yields "extra" private triangular offices.

OBATA, GYO
(Building Design)
Hellmuth, Obata & Kassabaum, Inc.
(314) 421-2000
1831 Chestnut St. St. Louis MO 63103

Born: 1923 **Studied:** Washington University; Cranbrook Academy of Art **Awards:** General Services Administration Honor Award; Urban Land Institute Award; Society of American Registered Architects Distinguished Building Award; 25 Year Award, Construction Products Manufacturer's Council **Notable Works:** St. Louis Union Station, St. Louis; Levi's Plaza, San Francisco; National Air and Space Museum, Washington DC; The Galleria, Dallas TX   CORPORATE 25%, COMMERCIAL/OFFICE 20%, PUBLIC AND INSTITUTIONAL 15%, RESEARCH FACILITIES 10%, HEALTH CARE FACILITIES 5%

He designs from the inside out, influenced by the micro-to-macro approach of Eliel Saarinen and aiming to enhance the lives of the people who work and live in his designs. He frequently emphasizes natural lighting, using glass to form atriums and skylights and then stressing the interplay between strong architectural forms and light. His instructor Eliel Saarinen used to say, "First you design a chair, then you design a room, then you design a house, then you design a street, then you design a city. You always ask, 'what's the next relationship?' " By this standard the ultimate test of a building is how it relates to its users and surroundings. He approaches each project without preconceptions beyond serving client needs.

His National Air and Space Museum on the Mall in Washington DC is the world's most popular museum, having received more than 100 million visitors since its opening in 1976. Impressive without overwhelming either its neighbors or its exhibits, it features huge display bays, glass fronts and skylights which open the museum to the Mall. Inside, suspended aircraft are seen against the natural backdrop of open sky. *Smithsonian* magazine said of it, "Thirty years in the planning, four years in the building, the National Air and Space Museum can possibly be called the finest building of its kind ever erected. It is pretty safe to call it unique. And there is no quibble with calling it extraordinary."

OLSEN, KEITH RODNEY
Address Krueck and Olsen Architects
(312) 787-0056
18-20 East Pearson Street Chicago IL 60611

Born: 1947 **Studied:** Illinois Institute of Technology **Awards:** Honor Award, AIA Chicago Chapter; American Institute of Steel Construction Architectural Award **Notable Works:** "Steel and Glass House"; Louisville Regional Health Center; Illinois Beach State Park Interpretive Center; Hewitt Associates General Offices

In association with his partner Ronald Krueck, he works on an eclectic range of commercial, institutional and residential projects, from suburban medical testing laboratories to furniture showrooms in Chicago's sprawling Merchandise Mart to general offices. Early in his career he worked on the McCormick Place Guest and Reception Center, which melds with the convention center's overall design that emphasizes long lines and exposed girders and beams reminiscent of Mies and the international school. Recent residential projects reveal an ease with diverse styles and materials—on the one hand remodeling the Kerrigan Residence, a Chicago Victorian townhouse, and on the other designing the award-winning "Steel and Glass House," a proposal with a Post-Modern flair incorporating those materials.

OWEN, CHRISTOPHER H. L.

(Building Design, Interior Architecture, Renovation)
Christopher H.L. Owen, A.I.A.
(212) 421-3441
330 E. 59th St. New York NY 10022

Born: 1937 **Studied:** University of Virginia; Columbia University **Awards:** AIA; *Architectural Record* awards of excellence; First Prize, Institute of Business Designers and *Interior Design* Magazine **Notable Works:** Owen Residence, Block Island RI; Globtik Tankers USA offices, New York City; Loomis Residence, Stockbridge MA COMMERCIAL 33%, OFFICE 33%, HOUSING 33%

Influenced by early Modern masters such as Mies and Le Corbusier, his designs use a less restricted vocabulary to achieve comparable formal and timeless effects.

His Stockbridge MA Loomis residence issues from conflicting program requirements: its professor owner wanted a small winter home for weekend use and a summer home large enough for constant use and frequent visitors. The resulting design features a two-bedroom guest wing on one side of a central living area and a wraparound summer living room on the other side which is easily sealed off to serve as a winter heat buffer. Spread along a winding river bluff among thick woods, the single-level home comfortably shrinks to 60 per cent of its total floor area for winter use.

It makes the most of a difficult rock ledge on the building site by dropping the summer living room floor two feet down from year-round areas, thus admitting dramatic river views winter and summer through the glassed-in or open lower level. All windows are fitted with insulating shades which are recessed into the ceiling when not in use. Hollow planes stretching out from the house at two corners create frames for views from the master bedroom and living room, at the same time seeming to anchor the house in its natural setting.

PADUKOW, SERGEY

(Historic Renovation, Preservation)
(201) 341-0565
610 Main Street Toms River NJ 08753

Born: 1922 **Studied:** Technical University, Karlsruhe, West Germany; Unnra University, Munich, West Germany **Awards:** AIA; New Jersey AIA **Notable Works:** St. Andrew Methodist Church, Toms River NJ; St. Michael's Cathedral, Sitka, AK; St. Paul Methodist Church, Bricktown NJ CHURCHES 100%

He's a traditionalist who uses contemporary materials to build and renovate churches. His contemporary churches set elements of historical design in a modern structural framework, so that he may gold-leaf fiberglass domes and cupolas, or build shaped, laminated arches. His churches tend to have steel frames to reduce fire damage and to avoid high-cost fire insurance, and he applies maintenance-free and earthquake-resistant technology where necessary. He has built more than 50 churches.

His St. Michael's Cathedral in Sitka AK is a complete reconstruction of a 19th century Russian Orthodox church that burned down in 1967. He worked entirely from 1200 photographs and slides and a knowledge of overall dimensions. The structures uses Sitka spruce logs with steel reinforcements. Originally ships' sails covered the inner walls and ceiling for lack of other material; now a fire-retardant canvas is used which imitates the seams and patterned saggings of the original. To reconstruct its open bell tower and steeple, brown

Christopher H. L. Owen, *Loomis Residence* (deck and detail of East facade showing "outrigger" beams), 1980. Structural/Foundation Engineer: Paul Gossen. Mechanical/Electrical Engineer: R.J. Aloisi. Job Captain: David Murphy. Interior Consultant: Sylvia Owen. Contractor: Berkshire Engineering and Construction. Photo: Norman McGrath

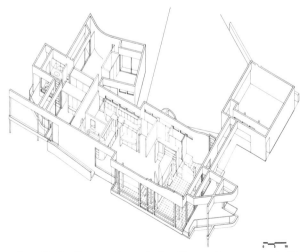

Christopher H. L. Owen, *Loomis Residence* (Axonometric Drawing).

painted steel and pipe replace the original logs, though the tower stairs are still made of wood. The onion dome is layered with copper. There is a new basement addition used as a community center for local native Indians who are the great majority of the Orthodox community in Alaska. His St. Andrew Methodist Church on the other hand recreates the Tudor style common in New Jersey. Heavy timber forms the frame and crossbeams, but the beams and laminates provide a modern feeling of strength and precision.

PANNICCIA, MARIO
Pannicia Architects (203) 374-0363
4270 Main Street Bridgeport CT 06606

Born: 1948 **Studied:** University of Miami; Cooper Union **Awards:** former President, Bridgeport AIA; Connecticut AIA **Notable Works:** Highway Theatre, Stratford CT; Bethany Church Renovation, Bridgeport CT; Oyster Landing Condominiums, Stratford CT COMMERCIAL 40%, HOUSING 40%, INSTITUTIONAL 15%

His designs integrate building with site. He tries to project nature into his buildings and prefers to use indigenous building materials. Spaces in his buildings are varied and accentuate major functions with different heights. Large window openings open most internal spaces to natural day lighting. While the entries are generally classical in approach with moderate use of ornamentation, his restoration projects meld classical and modern forms.

His renovation of a church into an office space in Bridgeport CT drew upon historical church design elements such as flying buttresses, reminiscent of Notre Dame. He also added a greenhouse. His conversion of a formerly blighted "Highway Theatre" in Stratford CT into office space involved more drastic departures, principally in the use of glass. Dark green used in the glass and the metal roof introduce a country feeling into the cityscape without hiding modern surfaces.

PARKIN, JOHN CRESTWELL
(Building Design)
Parkin Partnership 55 University Avenue
Toronto Ontario M5J 2H7 Canada

Born: 1922 **Studied:** University of Manitoba, Winnipeg **Awards:** Fellow, AIA; Fellow, Royal institute of British Architects; First Prize, national Gallery of Canada Competition **Notable Works:** Aeroquay Terminal Complex for Toronto International Airport; Marathon Realty Headquarters, Toronto

Ironically, he was once best known for the confusion surrounding his name and that of his long-time partner, John Burnett Parkin, to whom he is not related. In all his work he seeks clarity of form and structure, and simplicity of materials and construction. Creating elegantly functional plans, he believes, is architectural art. He's committed to "trusting" his materials, which is to say avoiding arbitrary material changes within formal units, and to identifying and exploiting their most natural, dramatic applications.

A frequent theme in his work has been the juxtaposition of steel and concrete. In his Aeroquay Terminal Complex for Toronto International Airport a large circular ring sheathed in steel surrounds a central concrete rectangle. In the Aeroquay Terminal, as in many of his larger public designs, he invites automobile traffic into the building—a very sensible concession to Canada's often punishing climate.

PASANELLA, GIOVANNI
(Building Design, Urban Design)
Pasanella + Klein 330 West 42nd Street New York New York 10036

Born: 1931 **Studied:** Yale University **Awards:** Architectural Record Award, 1968, 1970, 1974; Residential Award, AIA **Notable Works:** Twin Parks East and West Developments, Bronx, New York; Fieldhouse, State University of New York at Fredonia; Elementary School P205, New York

He came to prominence in 1967 as a founding member of the landmark Urban Design Group of the New York Planning Commission, created by mayor John Lindsay. Though he has done major designs for educational, correctional, industrial and commercial institutions, he continues to be known for the low- and

Bernard A. Marson (with Alexander Edelman, consultant), *High Rise Apartments, 402 East 64 Street*, New York City, 1988. Photo: Peter Mauss/ESTO

Ronald Peters, *La Cueva High School,* Albuquerque, New Mexico, 1986. Principal-In-Charge: Bill Waters. Project Designer: Ronald L. Peters. Project Architects: Carol Meincke, Tyler Mason. Photographer: Kint Giddings.

Frederick Phillips, *Private Residence*, Lake Forest, Illinois.
Photo: Howard Kaplan

James William Ritter, *Private Residence*, Maclean, Virginia.

William Ryan, *Zion Lutheran Church* (model).

Maxwell Starkman, *The Filmcorp Center*, Culver City, California, 1987.

Maxwell Starkman, *Westwood Place,* Los Angeles, California, 1988.

David Paul Helpern, *667 Madison Avenue* (interior view), New York City.

Maxwell Starkman, *Meridian Condominiums,* San Diego, California, 1988.

Maxwell Starkman, *Shoreline Square,* Long Beach, California, 1988.

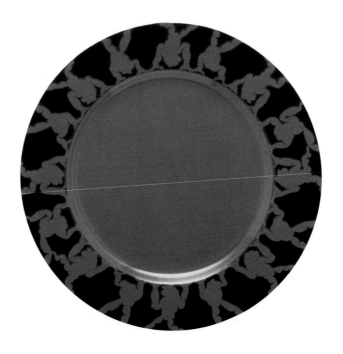

Stanley Tigerman, *Pompei Plate*, 1985.

Robert Umemura, *Hyatt Regency Waikoloa*, 1988.   Project Designer: Herbert T. Lawton.

Dean F. Unger, *Yolo County Administration Center*, 1986.

Francisco Urrutia, *Barbara Sinatra Children's Center*. Photo: Arthur Coleman.

Paul Whitehead, *Greentree Commons,* 1986. Project Architect: Jeffrey Kline Landscape Architect: Joseph Hajnas.

middle-income housing projects he designed in conjunction with New York State urban development agencies until the early 1980s. His most remarkable urban housing innovations were his effective prototypes for the tight, irregular sites that characterized the last wave of urban renewal. In his 1974 Twin Parks East Project in the Bronx he designed a novel and perhaps exasperating elevator system whose stops were limited to every other floor. The result was a 60 percent savings in public corridor space which allowed him to achieve a density of 135 units per acre, while providing integral day-care, parking, educational, and geriatric nursing facilities.

PASCO, H. MERRILL, JR.
(Building Design, Resort Planning and Design)
Archipelagos (803) 681-8521
P.O.Box 4820 Hilton Head SC

Born: 1942 **Studied:** Yale University Awards: Urban Land Institute Excellence in Community Planning; South Carolina AIA **Notable Works:** Sea Pines Plantation & Center; Windmill Harbour Club, Hilton Head SC COMMERCIAL 60%, HOUSING 40%

While distinctly pragmatic, his approach to architectural design is original in its development of structured site relationships and its use of program elements to choreograph environs. Much of his work involves resort planning and design in locations where the natural environment is especially striking and as a result especially delicate. He aims for a balance between economic and environmental requirements, enabling people to use the land without disturbing its essential qualities.

His Sea Pines Plantation and Sea Pines Center in Hilton Head SC is a benchmark of comprehensively planned resort and retirement communities. Integrated into a lush natural environment, the Plantation is a 6,000 acre private community started by Charles Fraser. The site of golf and tennis tournaments, hotels and retirement and pre-retirement dwellings, it predominantly features unobtrusive colonial structures situated around golf courses, marshes and lagoons. Careful spacing and homogeneous design allows lush vegetation indigenous to the coastal area to provide privacy and tranquility. Residential units are limited to one and 1/2 stories, insuring easy mobility for older residents and low-impact design for all. Built of cypress and other local woods with some stucco accents, the homes have low sweeping roofs that provide a cool, shady transition during the hot and humid summer months. Local Savannah brick is recycled for use in retaining walls, walkways and other landscaping features, heightening the development's sense of the Old South.

PEABODY, DAVID
(Building Design, Preservation)
David Peabody Associates (601) 445-2180
Box 70C, Natchez MS 39120

Born: 1948 **Studied:** Yale University **Awards:** AIA; New Hampshire AIA **Notable Works:** Historic Natchez Storefront Foundation Storefront Restoration Program, Natchez MS; Ecola Guest House INSTITUTIONAL 50% HOUSING 50%

He practices in a small city where the general population isn't particularly savvy about trends and fashions. He believes therefore that he best serves his clients by non-obtrusively building upon what he is given to work with. Disavowing "look-at-me" architecture, he designs buildings that are easily understandable. Strongly sensitive to tradition, he believes in firmly rooting architecture to particular sites and communities. Ralph Emerson, Frank Lloyd Wright and the poet Wendell Berry have particularly influenced him.

In the extraordinarily rich built context of Natchez, he converted an old outbuilding into a guesthouse in such a manner that additions are indistinguishable from older elements. In the same spirit of relatively self-effacing architecture he is presently "putting back together," by the use of attenuated additives, the master plan for the Metaikir Park County Day School.

PEDERSEN, WILLIAM

(Building Design)
Kohn Pedersen Fox Associates PC
(212) 977-6500
111 West 57th St. New York NY 10019

Born: 1938 **Studied:** University of Minnesota; Massachusetts Institute of Technology **Awards:** Rome Prize in Architecture; AIA **Notable Works:** 333 Wacker Drive, Chicago; 225 Wacker Drive, Chicago; Proctor & Gamble Headquarters, Cincinnati OH COMMERCIAL 100%

As chief design architect at Kohn Pedersen Fox, he takes prime credit for many of the firm's award-winning projects. His buildings achieve contextual solutions by "explaining" the geography of their site. But 'contextualizing' a building doesn't consist simply in blending it into surrounding structures; the building might instead strike a stylistic counterpoint to its environment to provide aesthetic relief. His firm's design philosophy sets the scale of his buildings to the street and emphasize human and social elements.

His 333 Wacker Drive is an office highrise sited at a dramatic bend of the Chicago River. It faces away from the downtown Loop and toward the expanse of the city. Matching the river's bend, the outward face of the building is broadly and strikingly curved; its green-tinted glass sheet reflects the setting sun as well as the green of the river in a contextual play of color. The side of the building facing the Loop is a broad plane which extends above the opposite side's curve, as though intersecting it, while the base, several stories of horizontal marble and granite bands, adjusts the bold expanse of the building to the scale of the street. Its granite carries on a dialogue with the massive stone Merchandise Mart which faces the building across the river.

His Cincinnati OH Proctor and Gamble headquarters is an 800,000-square-foot addition to their 1960s headquarters which was designed by Skidmore, Owings and Merrill. The addition, joined to the original structure by a covered bridge which jointly forms an L-shape, stands at the edge of Cincinnati and symbolizes at once the city's termination and, from the building's front, its gateway. The addition's limestone surface carries on the limestone and white marble elegance of the original. Its principle design feature is two octagonal towers which, together with the 'void' between them, create the symbolic gateway.

I.M. PEI AND PARTNER (see Cobb, Henry; Freed, James; Pei, I.M.)

PEI, IEOH MING
(Building Design, Master Planning)
I.M. Pei & Partners (212) 751-3122
600 Madison Ave. New York NY 10022

Born: 1917 **Studied:** Massachusetts Institute of Technology; Harvard Graduate School of Design **Awards:** FAIA; Pritzker Architectural Prize; AIA Gold Medal; Chevalier de la Legion d'Honneur, France; American Academy and Institute of Arts and Letters' Brunner Memorial Prize **Notable Works:** Le Grand Louvre, Paris; Bank of China, Honk Kong; Fragrant Hill Hotel, Beijing, China; East Building, National Gallery of Art, Washington DC

Since completing his National Center for Atmospheric Research in Boulder CO in 1967, and even more after his 1978 East Wing for the National Gallery of Art in Washington DC, he has been known for his monumental yet essentially simple stereometric forms. Recently these forms have expressed their underlying architectural complexity, most famously in the three eccentric glass pyramids—admitting light to a new underground visitors center—which he places in the grand courtyard of France's most famous and historic museum, the Louvre.

His Bank of China tower in Hong Kong responds to challenging program requirements quite apart from its freeway-tangled, hilly site. He was to create a strong architectural presence for the mainland state bank just a few blocks from the enormously expensive new headquarters of the Hongkong and Shanghai Bank, with a slender fraction of their building-budget. The largest building outside of North America, his tower is designed to withstand Honk Kong harbor's typhoon winds which are

William E. Pedersen, *Proctor and Gamble Building*, 1986, Cincinnati, Ohio.

twice the velocity of New York winds, and which create shear forces four times more powerful than those anticipated in the earthquake codes of Los Angeles. Yet the composite structural geometry of his design, created for this building, actually reduces by half the structural steel required for the 1034-foot structure.

At ground level it is a square-sided bundle of triangular prisms whose borders convey stress and weight to deep-set caissons. As it rises, one stack of pyramids after another ends under elevated atriums, leaving three, then two, then a single stack of interlocked pyramids which continue to rise. Its structural steel members come together at corners and joints in large reinforced concrete blocks; these blocks are of various sizes to absorb and respond to different angles and degrees of stress. Steel and concrete interact in other ways: many structural steel members were installed hollow, then filled with extruded concrete. Weight and shear are conveyed down exterior walls through the distinctive triangular cross-bracing, and down a fifth column in the center of the building, where the bundled pyramids come together. This column goes from the apex to the 25th floor, where its weight is conveyed down stuctural members— again, the outer edges of pyramids—to exterior walls, and thence to bedrock. This opens lower-floor interiors for a 17-floor atrium where the Bank's public business is transacted.

PELLI, CESAR
(Building Design)
Cesar Pelli and Associates 1056 Chapel Street (203) 777-2515
New Haven Connecticut 06510

Born: 1926 **Studied:** University of Illinois, Champaign/Urbana **Awards:** First Prize, United Nations City Competition, 1969; Brunner Prize, National Institute of Arts and Letters; Design Award, *Progressive Architecture*, 1966 **Notable Works:** World Financial Center, new York; Northwest Center, Minneapolis; Pacific Design Center, Los Angeles COMMERCIAL/RETAIL: 60%, HOUSING: 5%, INTERIOR DESIGN: 5%, EDUCATION: 10%, PLANNING: 5%, OTHER: 15%

Architecture, he believes, is the soundest of the arts, for it is deeply and inseparably rooted in practical reality. He immerses himself in the fine details of a project, to find and maintain design direction. He argues that looking for opportunities within the framework of a well-considered problem is the methodological obverse of functionalism, which looks for a single, linear solution in each new set of architectural considerations.   He is committed to an architecture which "celebrates life." Rejecting the massive inorganic forms and materials of Modernism, he wants his buildings to be light, changeable and humane. In his early work he showed a fascination with transparency, crafting large, sculptural forms in glass and steel. In his mature work, most notably The World Financial Center near New York City's Battery Park, he has sheathed his skyscrapers in thin curtain walls to achieve a sometimes disconcerting effect of lightness and freedom of form. The Financial Towers sympathetically bridge the old landmarks of the Manhattan skyline with the new. Their pointed tops recall the Chrysler Building, the RCA and the Empire State Building, but their vertical sweep and simple massing associate them firmly with the towers of the World Trade Center which they adjoin.

PEREIRA, WILLIAM LEONARD
(Building Design)
William L. Pereira Associates (213) 933-8341
5657 Wilshire Blvd. Los Angeles CA

Born: 1909 **Studied:** University of Illinois, Urbana **Awards:** Fellow, AIA; Honor Award, AIA, Southern California Chapter, 1963; Fellow, Academy of Motion Picture Arts and Sciences **Notable Works:** Transamerica Building, San Francisco; Marine Land of the Pacific, Palos Verde, California; Citicorp Building, San Francisco COMMERCIAL/RETAIL: 50%, HOUSING: 5%, INTERIOR DESIGN: 5%, EDUCATION: 5%, PLANNING: 10%, MEDICAL: 10%

Although born and educated in the Midwest he

Cesar Pelli, *World Financial Center*, New York City. Photo: Timothy Hursley

I.M. Pei, *Bank of China/Hong Kong Branch* (Model), Hong Kong, 1988.

Cesar Pelli, *World Financial Center* (seen from the Hudson River), New York City. Photo: Erich Hartman

has contributed heavily to the development of a distinct style for large-scale commercial architecture on the West Coast. A major goal has been to give digestible and immediately recognizable silhouettes to each of his buildings. His pyramid-like Transamerica Building has become a national symbol for the Transamerica corporation, and a landmark of Eiffel Tower-like stature on the San Francisco skyline. His forms derive from the Modernist ethos, but his commitment to distinguishing them is more suggestive of the Beaux-Arts tradition. He also designs large projects that spread masses of people horizontally, with great sensitivity to crowd dynamics. His Marineland of the Pacific in Palos Verdes CA and his Los Angeles International Airport are sensitive to the human scale and comfortably master automotive and pedestrian traffic logistics.

PERKINS AND WILL (see Brubaker, Charles William; Johnson, Ralph; Perkins, Lawrence Bradford)

PERKINS, LAWRENCE BRADFORD
(Building Design)
Perkins and Will Architects (312) 977-1100
2 North Lasalle Street Chicago Illinois 60602

Born: 1907 **Studied:** Cornell University **Awards:** Fellow, AIA; 25 Year Award, AIA, 1971; Dean of Architecture Award, American Society of Interior Designers **Notable Works:** Crow Island Elementary School, Winnetka, Illinois; First National Bank Building, Chicago (with C.F. Murphy and Associates); Chapel, Ithaca College, Ithaca, New York COMMERCIAL/RETAIL: 40%, HOUSING: 10%, INTERIOR DESIGN: 25%, EDUCATION: 10%, PLANNING: 5%

He maintains that designing consistently successful architecture requires input from a variety of informed voices. After more than fifty years of practice his firm, Perkins and Will, has become one of the nation's largest, but he has upheld his original commitment to providing his associates with an unrestrictive and egalitarian design environment. His first and still most famous commission was the Crow Island Elementary School for the Winnetka IL school district. Working in concert with Eliel and Eero Saarinen, he developed a new prototype for small-scale educational installations. His design traded the long, flat rectangles of traditional elementary school buildings for a series of functionally autonomous wings radiating from a central common area of comparable size. Each of the school's classrooms overlook a meticulously landscaped courtyard, and each is fitted with integral restroom and drinking facilities. Every detail of the building, including its custom-designed furnishings, was tailored to the petite, human scale of its primary users, schoolchildren. Though the majority of his firm's work is still in educational and institutional low-rises, his 60-story First National Bank Building (with C.F. Murphy Associates), which features curving granite walls and a large sunken plaza with fountain, has received wide critical and virtually universal public acclaim.

PERKINS, LAWRENCE BRADFORD, JR.
(Building Design, Interior Architecture, Renovation)
Perkins Geddis Eastman (212) 889-1720
437 Fifth Ave. New York NY 10016

Born: 1943 **Studied:** Cornell University, Stanford University **Awards:** AIA **Notable Works:** Canterbury Green, Stamford CT; St. George Seaport, Staten Island NY; Montefiore Home, Beachwood OH INSTITUTIONAL AND HEALTH CARE 30%, OFFICE AND MIXED USE 30%, HOUSING AND MIXED USE 25%

He puts particular emphasis on designing buildings that are pleasant to be in, working with widely accepted colors and materials. True to the modernist ethic of telling a building's internal program in its external design, he is also contextually sensitive and often works with traditional idioms—wood and stone, pitched roofs—in according with neighboring forms and landscapes. Careful landscape design integrated into the building plan also characterizes his work. His Stamford CT Canterbury Green is a large mixed-use downtown building that shares its site, and so its colors and forms, with a granite and redstone collegiate-gothic church. Built in precast grey concrete block and rose granite, Canterbury Green climbs by a series of setbacks from six to thirteen stories, the setbacks topped by pitched roofs in stainless steel. The ground floor features an arched cloister that circles a new one-acre urban park, which makes an ensemble of the two buildings it lies between. The park is landscaped into different zones. Bordering the busy street is a fountain whose plaza provides both acoustic separation and a breakout area for worshipers after service. The central green is open for concerts and art shows, and closer to Canterbury Green the landscaping is thicker, with a restaurant and benches available for lunch-hour relaxation.

PETERS, RONALD L.

(Building Design, Project Management)
BPLW Architects and Engineers, Inc.
(505) 881-2759
2400 Louisiana Blvd. Albuquerque NM 87110

Born: 1946 **Studied:** Texas Technological University, University of New Mexico **Awards:** AIA; New Mexico AIA; American Corrections Association **Notable Works:** La Cueva High School, Albuquerque NM; Albuquerque International Airport, NM COMMERCIAL 50%, CIVIC 20%, INSTITUTIONAL 20%, OFFICE 10%

His goal is to design buildings that won't be dated. Sensitive to detail, his designs evince appreciation of material and color, and a concern for appropriateness in the Southwestern landscape. Users, however, are his strongest influence—when he asked what building most excited them, Albuquerque high school students answered unequivocally that their Parnassus was a local shopping mall. His La Cueva High School understands and accepts their feelings, with a view to providing them with a dynamic learning environment. Laid out around an open mall which spills into special function areas—snack bar, gymnasium,

cafeteria, and a sunken, open amphitheater with glass-block wall wrapped around it that serves as a focal point—the airy design also results in extraordinary energy-saving opportunities. Even in winter a roomful of students must be cooled more often than heated; his computerized air control system uses the central mall as a mixing box which can be heated with warm air vented from full classrooms. During swing periods a water evaporative cooler, rather than more energy-intensive refrigeration, provides all necessary cooling. The mall is defined by a red steel space frame which extends outside to help form the school's main entrance. The complex is sited with reference to views through clerestory windows of the surrounding Sandia Mountains and Rio Grande valley.

PFEIFFER, NORMAN

(Building Design)
Hardy Holaman Pfeiffer Associates
(212) 677-6030
257 Park Avenue South NY NY 10010

His firm has been characterized as "the designated off-the-wall architect for the respectable middle." Their work features exposed and colorfully painted ducts and pipes, open, multilayered floors and design motifs unabashedly derived from the qualities of their often inexpensive materials. They aim to make the practice of architecture more inclusive by this catholic acknowledgment of the richness in materials and articles that people are already familiar with, though perhaps from other contexts. They were early and eager apostles of adaptive reuse of older structures, especially downtown train stations which they often converted to artistic purposes.

Their St. Louis Art Museum project in St. Louis MO began with a master plan for bringing a much-beset Beaux-Arts palace back to its original intentions while simultaneously guiding it into the next century. Public access was updated and a new wing added which harmonized with the older structure, while the old galleries were restored to their original logic of a grand central hall upon which horizontal axes giving onto smaller galleries converge.

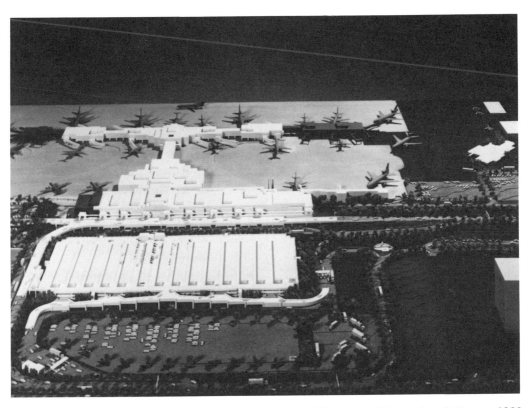

Ronald L. Peters, Project Manager, Principle-in-Charge, *Albuquerque International Airport, 1989.*
Design Consultants: TRA Airport Consultants, Seattle, Washington, Principal-In-Charge: Ted McCagg.
Project Team (BPLW): Jack R. Alley, Jack Cook, Wally Mitchell, Charlie M. Ortero. Project Team
(TRA): Nabil Jammal, Jim Suehiro, Gerry Ginader. Model Maker: Tom Saunders. Photo: Jerry Goffe.

PFISTER, PETER JOHN

(Building Design, Interior Architecture, Solar and Energy Conservation and Design)
Pfister Architects (612) 349-6006
212 Third Ave. North #302
Minneapolis MN 55401

Born: 1949 **Studied:** University of Wisconsin at Milwaukee School of Architecture **Awards:** Minnesota AIA; American Solar Energy Society; Department of Housing and Urban Development passive solar design award **Notable Works:** Twining Photography Studio, Minneapolis MN; Land O' Lakes Corporate Offices, Arden Hills MN; Bristol Apartments, Bloomington MN HOUSING 40%, OFFICE 35%, COMMERCIAL 25%

He enjoys unique problems, which he and his design team address with unusual detail inside and out. Working with client thoughts and needs he prefers carefully to plan such details as exterior lighting and landscaping and interior color treatments, so that technical and design solutions work comfortably together. He often includes strong vertical spaces both for their visual interest and their daylighting and passive solar uses. Strong colors too often characterize his designs.

His Minneapolis Twining Photography Studio is a warehouse-district rehab which makes the most of loft ceilings, high windows and open space. Necessarily closed spaces such as the darkroom and bath are sealed bubbles rather than floor-to-ceiling rooms: the studio's focal point is the darkroom, a peaked-roof, warm grey island whose 10 x 10-foot mass separates more private areas such as office and conference spaces within the open loft. The shooting area is funnel-shaped rather than square, in accordance with a stationary camera's true sight lines. This cone motif is carried through lesser space divisions. A client lounge area and associated kitchen is elevated three steps above the studio floor, which keeps visitors at hand but not underfoot while shoots are under way.

PHELPS, BARTON

(Building Design, Historic Preservation)

Barton Phelps, Architect (213) 934-8615
5514 Wilshire Blvd. Los Angeles CA 90077

Born: 1946 **Studied:** Williams College; Yale University **Awards:** AIA Honor for Collaborative Design, Games of the XXIIIrd Olympiad, Los Angeles; Los Angeles AIA; National Endowment for the Arts Individual Design Advancement Grant **Notable Works:** Arroyo House, Los Angeles; Canyon House, Los Angeles; Pershing Square Design (Finalist), Los Angeles INSTITUTIONAL 50%, HOUSING 50%

Having moved from the east coast to the studios of Frank Gehry in the early 1970s, his historicist and structuralist design origins have evolved toward more fragmented forms in Southern California. Responding to local design influences from Schindler and the mature Wright—and to ranch houses and ubiquitous Spanish Colonial styling as well—he notes that well-known eastern building typologies have given way in Los Angeles building design to an associative approach which alludes more naturally to contemporary art than to nearby architecture. He aims to balance his orderly training with the idioms of this new landscape.

His Arroyo House in Los Angeles is a transitional design in his discovery of appropriate fragmented forms. Conceived as two pavilions connected by a closed stair and trapezoidal courtyard, site restrictions required that one pavilion sit five feet higher than the other and at an angle to it. One pavilion becomes a pivoting tower, turning away at an angle from the other broad, low pavilion. Both pavilions are of wood and stucco, but the tower is topped with gable and parapets in the Spanish manner while its low neighbor features low overhanging eaves reminiscent of Wright. These features aren't prominent in front, however, where the two pavilions blend together through a curving stucco wall.

His Los Angeles Canyon House continues this evolution. Sited in a dropping-off canyon, the front of the Canyon House resembles a flat ranch house, but in back it becomes a three-story assembly of varied window bays that suggest a city overlooking the canyon.

PHILLIPS, FREDERICK

(Design, Interiors, Renovation) Frederick Phillips and Associates (312) 922-0092
53 W. Jackson Blvd. Chicago IL 60604

Born:1946 **Studied:** University of Pennsylvania **Awards:** AIA Distinguished Building Awards **Notable Works:** Logan Square Townhouse, Chicago; Willow Street Houses, Chicago; Pinewood Farm, Lake Forest IL COMMERCIAL 50%, HOUSING 50%

His designs aim to simplify and reduce programmatic requirements, in order to make minimal and direct statements of a building's purpose. But the buildings often make symbolic, even spiritual statements as well. He has drawn inspiration from the simplicity of Shaker designs, and from archetypal American forms. A Chicago house under construction consists of an ordinary concrete block box, to which he's attached a tower reminiscent of Great Lakes lighthouses. At Pinewood Farm in Lake Forest IL he echoes the simple gable and cylindrical forms seen in surrounding farms and silos.

Natural light too is an important design element for him, finding that it can work unconsciously to heighten a structure's appeal. In fact his Willow Street Houses in Chicago, two row houses on a long, narrow lot, are separated by a white tubular steel frame outlining a third gabled house between them. Within this frame, set back 3 feet, are floor-to-ceiling windows otherwise out of context in the Willow Street neighborhood.

PITTAS, MICHAEL

(Building Design, City Planning)
Studied: Cooper Union; Princeton University

The director of the National Endowment for the Arts Design Arts Program from 1978 to 1984, his incentives and initiatives contributed to a historic shift in public attitudes toward our common historical environment. He advocated creative reuse of older buildings and wide-open design competitions for important public commissions. The most famous result of his NEA tenure is the Vietnam Veterans Memorial on the Mall in Washington DC. The open competition he directed received 1450 entries, and was won by a second-year architecture student from Yale University, Maya Ling Yin. Her black granite slabs, cutting into the Mall lawn and covered with names of American war dead, virtually overnight became one of the capital city's most popular yet most personal attractions.

POLSHEK, JAMES STEWART

(Building Design)
James Stewart Polshek and Partners
(212) 807-7171
320 West 13th Street New York
New York 10014

Born: 1930 **Studied:** Yale University **Awards:** Fellow, AIA; Honor Award, AIA, 1972 **Notable Works:** 500 Park Avenue, New York; Service Group, State University of New York at Old Westbury; Albany New York State Bar Center COMMERCIAL/ RETAIL: 50%, HOUSING: 5%, INTERIOR DESIGN: 15%, EDUCATION: 10%, PLANNING: 15%

A visiting Japanese industrialist was so impressed with Polshek's first design, a small house in Stony Point NY, that he recruited him to design his company's $30 million Tokyo research complex. From his experience in Japan he developed an interest in the formal geometry of Oriental vernacular architecture. On his return to the United States he began to experiment with twin-axis symmetries and 3-part systems of formal organization. The latter became something of a trademark, emerging in a trio of L-shaped structures in his Service Group for the State University of New York at Old Westbury; in the 3-part main facade of his unbuilt Weselyan University Student Center; and his Albany, New York Bar Center divided into three sections. He's known for his interest in architectural contextualism and historic preservation. He consistently refuses commission for show places and "one-offs." Architecture that doesn't consciously serve a broad social purpose, he argues, is "inconsequential."

After taking time off to serve as dean of Columbia University's Graduate School of Architecture and Planning, he has re-emerged as one of the nation's preeminent high- rise designers. His 1980 office tower at 500 Park Avenue, a sympathetic redevelopment of Skidmore, Owing and Merrill's elegant Pepsi Cola Pavilion at Park and East 59th Street, is perhaps his most mature, controlled and impressive work to date.

POPE, JANET CAMPBELL
(Building Design, Rendering)
Campbell Pope and Associates, Inc.
(404) 233-6847
Suite 1035 3400 Peachtree Road
Atlanta GA 30326

Born: 1953 **Studied:** Georgia Tech **Awards** AIA; CSI **Notable Works:** The Toy School, Inc., Atlanta GA COMMERCIAL 35%, INDUSTRIAL 25%, PRIVATE HOUSING 25%

She has chosen to build up a solid, reliable practice through referrals rather than through currying the time-consuming and sometimes fickle market. Trained as a behaviorist, she listens attentively to clients and uses her psychological sensitivity to help establish client needs. She aims not to impose architectural styles and forms, but to help clients sell their own projects effectively. Originally a commercial artist, she also has a keen sense of color.

Her Atlanta Toy School is a shopping center that sells high quality toys, books, and children's educational materials. It includes classrooms for related educational activity. The plate glass window in front reveals a striking view, of educational toys displayed on white podiums inside, with a wicker fence enclosing a garden area which attracts children's interest. Classrooms in the heart of the store are visible through plate- glass windows set at 45 degrees, and can also be seen from the display area; this constant sightline into classrooms is designed to quiet possible concern over adult/child activities. Visitors to the store are encouraged to linger and relax on platforms that line interior sides while their children use a small library and bookshelf area, stocked with children's classics. Postmodern schemes of simple shapes, forms and references catch children's eyes. An elliptical arch rises above the curved sales counter. An upper blue band lines the white walls. Tones of gray, light blue, and pink predominate, and create a soft and comfortable yet subtle atmosphere.

PORTMAN, JOHN CALVIN JR.
(Building Design)
John Portman and Associates (404) 522-8811
225 Peachtree Street, N.E. Suite 201
Atlanta Georgia 30303

Born: 1924 **Studied:** M.I.T. **Awards:** Medal for Innovation in Hotel Desin, AIA; Silver Medal, AIA, Georgia Chapter **Notable Works:** Peachtree Center, Atlanta; Renaissance Center, Detroit; Four Embarcadero Center, San Francisco COMMERCIAL/RETAIL: 85%, HOUSING: 10%, EDUCATION: 5%

For the last decade his elegant glass open atrium towers have been the de facto standard for America's urban luxury hotels. Offering an appealing mix of finance and finesse, his hotels have become a new kind of city showplace which attracts casual sightseers as often as bona fide guests.

His firm provides comprehensive design services for each project he undertakes, and he is as skilled in the fiscal management of large-scale developments as he is in their technical conception and execution. Although he worked almost exclusively in Georgia for the first half of his career, his designs for the Marriott and Hyatt Regency hotel chains are now found in most of the nation's major metropolises.

His best known individual design is downtown Detroit's 1978 Renaissance Center. His mirrored glass towers had already been recognized as signs of commercial and civic prosperity, and his selection as principal architect for the huge five-building complex was symbolic of the community's hopes for a better future. The glittering cluster of rectangular office towers, orbiting around a central cylin-

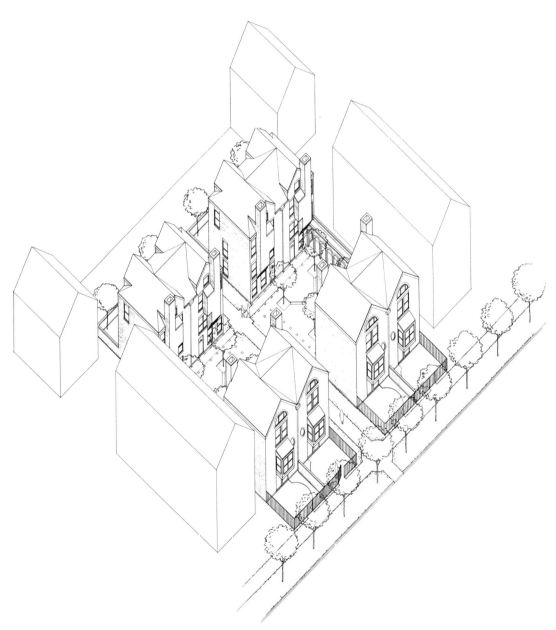

Frederick Phillips (with Leim T. Lee), *Howe Street Houses*, Chicago

drical hotel core, was indeed instrumental in focusing national attention on Detroit's continuing economic rebirth.

POTOKAR, RICHARD A. M.
(Building Design, Interior Architecture)
Richard A. M. Potokar, Incorporated
(312) 442-5575
77 Herrick Road   Riverside IL 60546

Born: 1951 **Studied:** University of Illinois at Chicago **Awards:** Chicago AIA Interior Architecture Award;   Townhouse Competition, Graham Foundation; Chicago Bar Association Young Architect Award **Notable Works:** South Central Bell Telephone Headquarters, Nashville TN;   Meridian Business Campus, Aurora IL   COMMERCIAL 50%, INDUSTRIAL 25%, MEDICAL 25%.

He calls himself a New Modernist/Rationalist, concerned with balancing regional setting and specific site with a given building's function. He enjoys working with precast concrete, which doesn't limit the size of a project and enables him to custom design building exteriors.

In his Mercy Memorial Medical Center in St. Joseph MI he lightens the precast concrete structure with large areas of glass cutting into it. The playful interior of the pediatric floor tries to "bring the house into the hospital" by using traditional home shapes and materials instead of institutional fixtures wherever possible. Patients walking in the corridor see the rooms as a village of houses: each room has a mailbox and number on its door, and room fronts have applied facades which give the appearance of a pitched roof. Instead of fluorescent lights, incandescent lighting from wall sconces light the floor. His North Shore Medical Center in Evanston IL is adjacent to a hospital but in a residential neighborhood It's designed to resemble an apartment building more than an institution. A parking structure is concealed by a brick facade with punched openings, and motorists park on the level of their doctor's office and enter it through a central atrium that penetrates the entire building.

POZZI, LOMBARD JOHN
(Historic Preservation, Renovation, Building Design, Infill Design)
Lombard John , Architect (401) 253-7979
1226 Hope Street/P.O. Box 711
Bristol RI 02809

Born: 1945 **Studied:** Rensselaer Polytechnic Institute; Columbia University   **Awards:** Rhode Island AIA Excellence in Restoration **Notable Works:** Roger Williams Park: Casino, Bandstand, Betsey Williams Cottage, Lovers' Retreat Bridge and Rose Garden Gazebo, Providence RI;   George Hail Free Library, Warren RI;   Dame Farm Historical Museum, Johnston RI. HOUSING 20%, RESTORATION 40%, ADAPTIVE REUSE 40%.

A solo practitioner who enjoys the diversity of working on a wide variety of projects, he is as at home with renovations as with original designs.   His restorations save as much as possible of existing structures, and often work in new materials and materials salvaged from other buildings marked for demolition.

In downtown Bristol RI's new Peaberry Building he used design elements from one of the two earlier buildings on the site which had been destroyed by fire, and drew from another Greek Revival building as well. Pilasters set off each of the seven front bays, creating a Greek Revival formal appearance. Windows are replicas of the previous building's fenestration, and use surviving exterior blinds from the 1840s. The interior combines a commercial first floor which can be adapted for one to three businesses with a residential second floor. Concrete plank floors provide noise insulation for residents while providing fire protection. The apartments have two-panel Greek Revival doors, either salvaged originals from another town or fine replicas.

PRAN, PETER C.
(Building Design, Historical Preservation)
Nagle Hartray and Associates (312) 266-2800
230 East Ohio Street Chicago IL 60602

Born: 1935   **Studied:** Illinois Institute of Technology   **Notable Works:** Methodist Hospital Family Center, Gary, Indiana; Mar-

John C. Portman, Jr., *Atlanta Marriott Marquis* (atrium), Alanta, Georgia. Photo: Jaime Ardiles-Arce

ian College, Fond du Lac, Wisconsin; KRPL radio building, Moscow, Iowa

In 1963, he undertook a pilgrimage from his native Denmark to work under Mies van der Rohe in Chicago. After nearly a decade of work in the lockstep Modernist tradition (under Mies and under Myron Goldsmith at Skidmore, Owings and Merrill), his designs began to take on a distinctly Post-Modern tone. His pervasive use of primary color and gentle exterior curves suggest parallels with the recent designs of Michael Graves and Robert A. M. Stern, but his buildings are much truer to their Art Deco inspirations. Their extensive window detailing and relatively restrained massing recall the classic work of Graham, Anderson, Probst and White in the late twenties and early thirties.

PRATT, JAMES REECE
(Building Design, Exhibition Design)
Pratt, Box, Henderson Partners (214) 526-6609
3526 Cedar Springs Dallas Texas 75219

Born: 1924 **Studied:** Harvard University
Awards: Burlington Award for Interiors, 1975; Fellow, AIA **Notable Works:** Brookhaven College, Farmers Branch, Texas; Quadrangle Shopping Center, Dallas; Great Hall, Apparel Mart, Dallas COMMERCIAL/RETAIL:25%, HOUSING: 15%, INTERIOR DESIGN: 30%

Practicing in Texas before the era of effective climate control, he learned to control the interaction of natural and crafted environments, and to use natural forces to produce subtle psychological states. Sunshine and wind are as present in his work as brick, wood and glass. Introducing a new structure to an area of existing development, he notes, inevitably creates new spaces between buildings. For 30 years he's studied the unplanned interstices between buildings, in an effort to use them better and more consciously in his own work. He aims to make neighboring buildings more useful with each of his own designs. He has few stylistic patterns beyond contextual appropriateness and a meticulous attention to detail. In his largest works, Brookhaven College in Farmers

Branch TX and the Great Hall of the Dallas TX Apparel Center, he takes special care to articulate potentially overwhelming spaces into smaller, more addressable sub-units. This hierarchical ordering of spaces also allows for multiple simultaneous uses.

PREDOCK, ANTOINE
(Building Design, Construction Administration)
Antoine Predock Architect (505) 843-7390
300 12th Street NW Albuquerque NM 87102

Born: 1936 **Studied:** Columbia University
Awards: FAIA; AIA; *Progressive Architecture* competition citation **Notable Works:** Fuller House, Scottsdale AZ; The Beach, Albuquerque NM; New Mexico Heart Clinic, Albuquerque NM CULTURAL/INSTITUTIONAL 90%, HOUSING 10%

New Mexico's geography and history inspire his work. His buildings draw inspiration from ancient Pueblo architecture and often reflect the shapes of the terrain surrounding Albuquerque.

His New Mexico Heart Clinic in Albuquerque NM turns toward the interstate a wall of earth-colored concrete block which insulates the clinic from traffic noise. The wall slopes down on both sides, recalling the slopes of the mountains in the distance. Square glass windows and a heart-shaped opening add interest to the facade. The entrance-side of the wood-frame clinic with its cubic massing suggests the arrangement of a pueblo village.

In the interior sunlight enters through heart-shaped windows which illuminate the stairs. Small rectangular rooms surround a pair of rotundas, inspired by Indian kivas or ceremonial chambers. One of these kivas serves as a joint workroom where the eight physicians can meet for a coffee-klatsch while checking the results of tests.

PRINCE, BART
(Building Design, Construction Administration)
Bart Prince, Architect
3501 Monte Vista NE Albuquerque NM 87106

Born: 1947 **Studied:** Arizona State University

His influences include the work of Frank Lloyd Wright and Bruce Goff (whom he worked for after taking his degree, and whose work he has supervised) as well as the architecture and landscape of New Mexico. Rather than adhering to a form of Southwestern adobe contextualism, he creates buildings that express the personalities of his clients.

His own residence in Albuquerque NM resembles a beached Jules Verne submarine or a space ship on blocks. Its basic design unit is the circle, much as Wright's later work explores the circle as architectural form. The three-level building has an oblong upper floor supported by four structural cylinders. The walls of the upper level are convex. Circular staircases connect the floors and spiral ramps form the entrances.

The design uses several energy efficient climate controls. Solar collectors provide heat for the bedrooms. The northern side of the building is partially submerged into an earth berm. Steel rods spike out from the top level, creating a frame for a fabric sun shield. This prickly appearance isn't continued inside, where gray carpeting covers floors and walls. Light filters in through translucent acrylic panels.

PRUS, VICTOR
(Building Design, Monument Design)
Victor Prus and Associates 1420 Sherbrooke Street West Suite 301
Montreal Quebec H3g 1k5 Canada

Born: 1917 **Studied:** Technical University, Warsaw **Awards:** Fellow, AIA; Massey Medal for Architecture **Notable Works:** Metro Bonaventure Terminus Complex, Montreal; Royal Canadian Air Force Memorial Complex, Ontario; Palais de Congres, Montreal

He believes that an autonomous "language of architecture" is a contradiction in terms, because architecture is an ambient and subjective experience. He has often said that his work models an "architecture of conditions," which is to say that its features are conditioned by function, physical context, and historic milieu. As practical responses to external conditions, his designs don't derive from any immutable program or aesthetic vocabulary. As a result his designs are often agglomerations of heterogeneous parts. In the case of his Montreal Congres Centre, he designed a structure with two radically dissimilar elevations, to match the textures of two disparate sectors of Montreal which it divides. In his Grand Theatre de Quebec City the formal disjunction is between the building's prim, self-effacing facade and its highly articulated deluxe interior.

RAILLA, JOSEPH J.
(Construction Administration, Design, Real Estate Development)
Joseph J. Railla Architect (818) 893-4167
16921 Parthenia #201 Sepulveda CA 91343

Born: 1934 **Studied:** University of Southern California **Awards:** Featured in *Architectural Record Houses*; design award, San Fernando Valley AIA **Notable Works:** Park Regency Office Building, Sepulveda CA; Railla Office Building, Sepulveda CA; Browder residence, Burbank CA OFFICE 50%, HOUSING 30%, RETAIL 20%

As developer, contractor and owner as well as architect of speculative developments, he sees himself in the master builder tradition and takes pride in setting and executing the qualities that each of his specialties brings to a finished building. Wearing his many hats he balances the dense and sometimes conflicting demands of southern California's many code requirements, while designing with and for the sensitivities of a local resident.

His Park Regency is a 25,000 square foot speculative office building which draws its tenants locally. Its three floors are separately sculpted from the building mass, creating diverse yet easily adaptable floor plans appropriate for small as well as larger users. The second floor cantilevers over the main entrance to provide shelter from the San Fernando Valley sun, creating a well-used meeting place adjacent to the circular stair enclosure inside. Natural light penetrates offices through windows in partition walls, and the third floor stairway tower gives out on a rooftop terrace popular for relaxing as well as code-contingent smoking.

RAMSAY, JOHN ERVING
(Building Design, Planning)
Ramsay Associates Inc. (704) 633-3121
P. O. Box 1285 Salisbury NC 28144

Born: 1915 **Studied:** Yale University; University of North Carolina at Chapel Hill **Awards:** FAIA; North Carolina AIA **Notable Works:** College Community Center, Catawba College, Salisbury NC; Fairfield Chair Display Center, Lenorr NC COMMERCIAL 33%, PRIVATE RESIDENTIAL 33%, RELIGIOUS 33%

He strikes a balance between traditional creative and aesthetic styles and the functional housing needs of man. While architecture should stimulate thought and represent peoples' social aspirations, it should also be practical and free of "the bondage of system, style and habit, of class opinions and family traditions, of nostalgia and emotion."

His Salisbury NC Catawba College Community Center combines three spaces and functions: a main 1500-seat theater, a small 33-seat theater, and an entr'acte assembly area. The main house is unusual for its sideways-running aisles. The little theater lies off to one end of the main stage, and the theaters share backstage facilities. The main house lobby feeds into the assembly area so that intermission crowds can relax in a freer, more leisurely space. Called the "crystal cage," the assembly area is enclosed by three large glass exposures supported by wooden mullions, and it expresses the design intent of the Center as a whole, to create a compelling artificial environment for the artifices of the stage. His Fairfield Chair Display Center in Lenorr NC solved a construction site problem. The developer wanted the complete display area on one level, but the site was on the edge of a hill. His solution was to build a four-module structure joined by a central core, resembling a Greek cross in shape. Two of the modules are raised

to accommodate the slope, but the interiors of all four modules can be taken in at one glance from the central core.

RAPSON, RALPH
(Building Design)
Ralph Rapson and Associates 1503 Washington Avenue South
Minneapolis Minnesota 55454

Born: 1914 **Studied:** University of Michigan, Cranbrook Academy **Awards:** FAIA, American Collegiate Schools of Architecture/AIA Topaz Medallion, First Gold Medal of Minnesota AIA **Notable Works:** Tyrone Guthrie Theater, Minneapolis; US Embassy, Stockholm, Sweden; Cedar Square West, Minneapolis INSTITUTIONAL 50%, HOUSING 25%, URBAN DESIGN 15%

He sees architecture as physical and social science, however imprecise, as well as art. Therefore significant design is a complete integration of many apparently isolated or conflicting factors. Using human values as well as technological systems and materials, he aims to respect the ecologies of time and place— and symbolism—in which his designs will be used.

His Tyrone Guthrie Theater in Minneapolis is conceived as an exploded cube: the theater 'box' is framed, yet open and inviting, designed for informal promenading and people-watching as well as watching theater. Through exterior glass and screen walls the inner theater is clearly visible. A dramatic staircase connects balcony and orchestra patrons, and the upper tier of the lobby is hung away from the theater wall, providing many sight lines between the two levels of theatergoers.

Inside the theater too, his design breaks down what Guthrie perceived as the second-class citizenship of balcony patrons. One side of the asymmetrical house seating features steeply raked balcony seats that flow down to the stage. This section—of very popular seats—then sweeps around and above orchestra seating in the rest of the house, fulfilling as well Guthrie's desire for an intimate actor-audience relationship, with seats as close as pos-

Ralph Rapson, *Tyrone Guthrie Theater*, Minneapolis, Minnesota.

Joseph Railla, *Park Regency Office Building,* Sepulveda, California.

sible to the stage. The 200-degree seating layout around an open stage features bright, confetti-like seat covers in many colors, giving the theater a fantastical air even before its house lights fade.

RAUCH, JOHN
(Building Design, Planning)
Venturi, Rauch and Scott Brown
(215) 487-0400
4236 Main Street Philadelphia PA 19127

Born: 1930 **Studied:** University of Pennsylvania **Awards:** Honor Award, Department of Housing and Urban Development, 1980; Merit Award, Pennsylvania AIA 1983; *Interiors* award, 1983 **Notable Works** (with Robert Venturi): Social Science Center, State University of New York at Purchase, 1970; Summer Residence, Tuckers Town, Bermuda, 1975; Fire Station #4, Columbus, Indiana, 1966

For more than two decades he has worked in the long shadows of his evangelistic and vocal partners Robert Venturi and (more recently) Denise Scott Brown. In reality, however, his expert construction and client management—and his terse, incisive design critiques—have been integral to the firm's success and notoriety.

While Venturi and Scott Brown have devoted much of their attention to exegeses on the philosophy and rationality of architecture, he has remained most concerned with its practical application. He has become an energetic proponent of excellence in architectural education, and he serves as trustee of the Foundation for Architectural Education. He is also a widely-read and respected architectural critic.

REESLUND, GEOFFREY B.
(Building Design, Construction Administration, Renovation)
SGPA/Architecture and Planning
(619) 297-0131
1565 Hotel Circle South San Diego CA 92108

Born: 1950 **Studied:** University of Southern California **Awards:** Building Industry Association **Notable Works:** Rancho Penasquitos Towne Center, Rancho Penasquitos CA RETAIL 70%, MIXED-USE 20%, COMMERCIAL 10%,

He has worked on more than 150 retail shopping centers in California and across the West. He believes that retail architecture should be responsive to, and evolve quickly with, marketplace trends. He integrates signage, parking layouts, landscaping, and individual tenant themes with retail merchandising. Site planning minimizes conflicts between vehicular and pedestrian traffic. Hardscape, landscape and pedestrian amenities play a vital role in reducing building mass. He strives for timeless design, not over-decorated boxes, but adds signage and lighting to make the center attractive at night. He believes that being responsive is being responsible, which overrides any desire to create self-serving design.

Contextual design is important in his work. The design theme for his award-winning Rancho Penasquitos Towne Center CA is located on the site of a former Mexican rancho, and was developed within its historic context. Its use of arched colonnades, bell-towers, clock-tower elements, Mexican-tile pavers, and pedestrian piazzas with fountains continue its community heritage.

RENO, AUGUST
(Building Design, Interior Architecture, Historic Preservation)
Gibson & Reno Architects (303) 925-5968
418 E. Cooper Aspen CO 81611

Born: 1952 **Studied:** University of Illinois at Chicago **Awards:** Colorado West AIA; Colorado AIA **Notable Works:** Ruby Park Transit Center, Aspen CO; Wilkinson Library, Telluride CO INSTITUTIONAL 30%, HOUSING 30%, OTHER 40%

Working as an individual performer in a team context with partner David Gibson, he feels architecture is at once the art of blending forms and materials, the science of making them sturdy and durable, and the challenge of leadership to see a project successfully completed.

His design for the Kanozan Resort in Japan exemplifies the "Aspen" idea of man and nature coming together, uniting body, mind and soul in interaction with site. Located on a promontory overlooking Tokyo Bay, the resort is comprised of detached single-family residences, townhouses and condominiums sited in the mountains. Of the five major ridgetops on the 25,000 acre site, four are given to housing with the highest reserved for the town center. Hosting an indoor/outdoor amphitheater, performing arts center, and athletic facilities as well as offices and small-scale commercial outlets, the center is on a grid which provides axial views of Tokyo, Tokyo Bay and Mt. Fuji. The two- and three-story homes are designed on a human scale with dormers and varied fenestration, in order to provide respite from the boxlike concentration of the city.

His Wilkinson Library in Telluride CO on the other hand is an unassuming structure that skillfully adapts the vernacular forms, materials and color of its setting.

RILEY, JEFFERSON B.
Centerbrook Architects & Planners
(203) 767-0175
Box 409 Essex CT 06426

Born: 1945 **Studied:** Lawrence University; Yale University **Awards:** Builder's Choice award; Connecticut AIA; National Endowment for the Arts design award **Notable Works:** Colby College Student Center, Waterville ME; Elliott House, Ligonier PA HOUSING 50%, INSTITUTIONAL/COMMERCIAL 50%

A Postmodernist, he believes that at last an architecture is being created that tries to be "part of the whole life of the world ... Postmodernism is, in part, a product of the mass communications revolution." He feels that when it is finely executed, Postmodernist architecture can be "sociable, receptive and inclusive," but carried to an excess it can appear to be just a "fake."

His design for the Colby College Center in Waterville MA bridges a path between two halves of the campus, and becomes a "gateway" linking the two sides physically and symbolically. Approaching from the north side of the Center, which is faced in red brick

to match surrounding other campus buildings, one passes through the gateway into a south-facing terrace. White clapboard walls spread to shield this enclave from prevailing north winds and to collect the sun's warmth. From here one enters the main lobby. Off the main lobby is a multi-purpose room, ringed with balconies set behind freestanding facades which give a sense of intimate space suited to small groups. In fact the room can accommodate up to 800 people. The lobby-wide stairs ascend to a bridge which leads to the pub. Nearby is a lounge with fireplace and windows that overlook the main lobby. Along the bridge is a quiet, sun-filled lounge looking down on the path below. In the pub, banquettes step down from the second to the main floor and form a bowl for small-scale performances. From this level an outdoor terrace affords views from under the spreading branches of a grove of maple trees to distant hills. Steps lead further down to the lower pub lounge whose octagonal shape centers around a fireplace and mirrors a post office lounge. The two sun-filled lounges flank the highly trafficked campus path, delightful overlooks to the gateway that joins the campus together.

RITTER, JAMES W.
(Building Design)
James William Ritter Architect
(703) 548-4405
705 King St. Alexandria VA 22314

Born: 1942 **Studied:** Virginia Polytechnic Institute **Awards:** First Award, Masonry Institute; Grand Award, Innovations in Housing Competition; Virginia AIA; Northern Virginia AIA **Notable Works:** LeCompte Studio, Loudoun County VA; Quantico Post Office, Quantico VA COMMERCIAL 25%, OFFICE 25%, HOUSING 25%, RETAIL 25%

He's searching for an American architecture that reflects our culture and times. He doesn't identify with style labels, and looks to create an architecture of ideas rather than appearances. His Quantico Post Office was commissioned to be a simple box, which is nonetheless enlivened with design features. Using 8-inch bricks as the basic construction element, non-loadbearing walls are punctuated with 8-inch "transparent bricks," actually glass block. The building's steel frame rests on precast concrete bearing blocks which are clearly expressed on the exterior. An important program requirement for rural post offices is to accommodate all the impromptu meetings that take place while patrons come and go—he gives pedestrians a landscaped and paved area through the parking lot for such chance meetings. Inside, the exposed ceiling ductwork visible in the public area sweeps on into the work area over the heads of patrons, conveying the larger scale and function of the greater building.

His LeCompte Studio is a working and living space for the creation of clerestory windows for the National Cathedral in Washington, D.C. The artist requested a "beautiful barn;" the result is a curved roof supported by bowstring trusses that on the higher side of its sloping site comes down to the ground. Sheathed in metal with walls of vertical siding, the structure uses the technology of rural Virginia barns while taking a more cathedral-like form, with a high centerspace flanked by aisles, in which a whole clerestory window at a time may be mounted and viewed before installation in Washington.

ROBERTSON, JACQUELIN
(Building Design, Urban design)
211 East 70th Street
New York New York 10021

Born: 1933 **Studied:** Yale University **Awards:** Albert S. Bard Award, City Club of New York, 1970; Parks Council Award, New York, 1971; Design Award, *Progressive Architecture*, 1977 **Notable Works:** Louis Camu House, Alsost, Belgium; West Midtown Master Plan, Manhattan, New York; Museum of Modern Art Tower Expansion (with Cesar Pelli), New York

He argues that architects who hope to meaningfully affect the built environment must become participants in government. Although he has earned a national reputation for a trio of early single-family homes, he's known primarily as an urban planner, developer and activist.

He began the public phase of his career as director of the office of Midtown Planning, a division of the famous Urban Design group of former New York mayor John Lindsay. His first responsibility was to produce a series of detailed development plans for Manhattan's largest commercial district. Though they proved, like many another urban master plans, interesting but ineffectual, the zoning incentives he designed were an effective strategic tool. By offering zoning variances and tax concessions to developers, city planning officials were able to exert influence on the appearance and street-level impact of new construction and renovation. He particularly encouraged providing street-level amenities at a time when glass elevator lobbies often displaced small commerce. He also gave abatements for preserving the city's fragmented but rich architectural heritage.

After nearly a decade in public planning he took a position as vice-president of Arlen Realty, a development firm with which he had worked closely during his tenure as zoning administrator. Despite moving to the private sector he has remained a determinedly public man and activist.

ROCHE, BONNIE
Bonnie Roche and Associates, Inc.
(212) 582-3067
154 W. 57th St. Studio 839
New York NY 10019

Born: 1946 **Studied:** Architectural Association, London; Yale University; Massachusetts Institute of Technology **Awards:** "Young Architects" award; Progressive Architecture award **Notable Works:** Apartment Renovation, New York City; Picasso Apartment, New York City; Soft Shell, New York City

Her interest in dance has given her a passion for a "sense of theatricality" in architecture. She explains her choice of profession by her interest "in movement and space, and in the sense of dramatic illusion....Set design is a

Jefferson Riley, *Colby College Student Center*, Waterville, Maine. Photo: Norman McGrath

Kevin Roche, *Union Carbide Corporation Headquarters*

very strong influence, and I like to use very real materials in unorthodox ways."

In her renovation of a 4000-square-foot New York City apartment, she concentrated her efforts on the kitchen and office, which total about 1000 square feet. While carrying through the proportions and axial formality of the entry, living, and dining rooms into the kitchen and office, her design's understated, rather hard-edged feel contrasts with the ornate decorative approach her client took in the more public areas of the apartment. Her materials—stainless steel for the door frame and work table, polyester lacquer for kitchen cabinets and room divider, and backpainted glass for the door, counter backsplashes, light cove, and work table top—are clean, yet full of depth and richness. Her etched-out squares in the glass door create a sense of transparency without sacrificing privacy, and the cove lighting evokes a sense of space beyond the literal plane of the wall; with the backsplashes, they make the cabinets appear to float. The work table's glass top is counter height, but its stainless steel supports are standard table height, thereby mediating between function and tradition.

ROCHE, EAMONN KEVIN
(Building Design)
Kevin Roche John Dinkeloo and Associates
(203) 777-7251
20 Davis Street Hamden Connecticut 06517

Born: 1922 **Studied:** Illinois Institute of Technology **Awards:** Academician, National Institute of Arts and Letters; Total Design Award, American Institute of Industrial Design; Member, Royal Institute of British Architects **Notable Works:** Ford Foundation Headquarters (with John Dinkeloo), New York; Air Force Museum, Wight-Patterson, Ohio; Union Carbide Headquarters, New York

He and partner John Dinkeloo comprise one of the most prolific and consistently innovative design teams of the postwar era. In the last two decades he has completed almost forty major commissions, many of which have attracted international attention. His work is in the Modernist mainstream, glassy and elegant. Postmodernists have complained that his buildings are abstractions, wholly crafted objects with no historic ties and few concessions to their immediate surroundings. He's above all an architect of imposing buildings for educational, corporate and governmental institutions, and for architectural gravity and 'bigness' his work seldom disappoints. Though his 1963 Ford Foundation Headquarters in New York City is only 12 stories, its integral greenhouse atrium rises nine stories on the building's primary elevation and covers a third of an acre. His Knights of Columbus building in New Haven CT also is a relatively modest 23 stories. Yet its siting against smaller, older and more horizontal buildings at the city's edge, and its muscular and distinctly industrial massing scheme, produce an effect of great size and power.

ROCKWOOD, DAVID
(Building Design)
David Rockwood Architect & Associates
(503) 274-2051

Born: 1955 **Studied:** University of Oregon; Princeton University **Notable Works:** Rockwood Residence, Portland OR

Influenced by the work of Terragini and Eisenman, the dialectic and interplay between opposing ideas triggers his imagination. He says: "I'm interested in how you could begin to set up initial concepts and then posit concepts that are different from the first, presenting both simultaneously to allow the possibility of understanding these differences."

His Rockwood Residence in Portland OR overlooks the Columbia River. The house is structured by two interrelated concepts. It is based on a vertical and horizontal grid of 11 x 6 feet, with submodules dividing the overall grid. Precast concrete sandwich panels are used in floor, roof, and wall construction, teamed with a system of steel tube wall and roof frames. Wall panels are ten inches thick, comprised of an inner bearing rigid urethane insulation and an outer layer of pumice concrete. Welded wire girders bind the outer

Kevin Roche, *Ford Foundation Headquarters*, New York City

panels together, and floor and roof panels are also 10 inches thick.

Spatially and visually, the notions of three-dimensional grid and the volumes produced by that grid are reinforced in the house. But the house is not something abstract. He adds, "the house still has signs of closure, through the layers, even though it may be eroded to some extent, as an approach. Some symmetry and axial relationships are still set up in many of the rooms. I continue to see validity in those notions, and to change them without a solid philosophical reason would be simply reactionary."

ROGERS, ARCHIBALD COLEMAN
(Urban Design)
RTKL Associates   (301) 528-8600
400 East Pratt Street
Baltimore Maryland 21202

Born: 1917 **Studied:** Princeton University **Awards:** President, AIA, 1974; Member, Maryland Arts Council; Chairman, Israeli-American Symposium **Notable Works:** Plan for Downtown Cincinnati; Plan for Downtown Jacksonville, FL; Fountain Square, Cincinnati   COMMERCIAL/RETAIL: 40%, HOUSING: 2%, MEDICAL: 25%, INTERIOR DESIGN: 10%

He is the founder and former principal of one of the nation's leading urban design firms. His most lasting contribution to urban design was a four-point method for collaborating effectively with public administrators and decision makers, which he refined while formulating his master plan for the city of Cincinnati OH in 1966.

The first stage in a successful planning collaboration, he maintains, is a consensus definition of the problem to be addressed. The second stage is a search for and analysis of possible solutions and sub-solutions. The third stage is the selection of the most promising alternatives; the fourth and final stage involves identifying, endorsing and implementing the remedies which have been selected. Although this framework now seems obvious and intuitive, its effect was galvaniz-

ing. The unambiguous agenda greatly simplified the machinations of Cincinnati's planning board and city council, and facilitated construction of a number of useful public spaces, including his own firm's exemplary Fountain Square. Subsequently his formalism has been adopted by urban designers and planning authorities across the country.

ROSE, PETER
(Building Design)
1315 de Maisonneuve West
Montreal Quebec Canada

Born: 1943 **Studied:** Yale University **Awards:** Design Award, *Progressive Architecture*, 1978; Design Award, Ordre des Architectes du Quebec, 1978; Post Prize, McGill University, 1978 **Notable Works:** Badley House, North Hatley, Quebec; Marosi House, North Hatley, Quebec; Pavilion 70, St. Sauveur, Quebec

His expansive, rustic Quebec houses owe much to the new Vernacularism of Robert Venturi and Charles Moore, with whom he studied at Yale. From Venturi he learned the impact of carefully chosen false fronts, and the movement and quiet drama of abrupt but calculated scale changes. From Moore he learned to create an imposing, grounding sense of place with broad chimneys and wide, sweeping roofs. But his work has avoided the exaggerated quality of the ordinary which has plagued so many of Venturi's imitators. It has matured and evolved to an extent that his must now be regarded as an autonomous voice which has remained consonant with those of his mentors. The massive chimneys of his Bradley House in North Hatley, Quebec, for instance, owe a debt to Moore, but they are also evoke the stately seventeenth and eighteenth century homes of Quebec City's French quarter. His roofs, too, owe as much to the sprawling forts and rail-side hotels of nineteenth century Canada as they do to Moore's seminal Sea Ranch CA. Their steep pitches are, in fact, an eminently practical adaptation to Canada's snowfalls.

Paul Rudolph, *Corporate Headquarters, Burroughs Wellcome & Co.*, Research Triangle Park, North Carolina. Photo: Joseph W. Molitor

Paul Rudolph, *Yale University Art and Architecture Building*, New Haven, Connecticut.

ROTONDI, MICHAEL
Morphosis (213) 453-2247
2113 Stiner Av. Los Angeles CA 90025

Born: 1949 **Studied:** Southern California Institute of Architecture **Awards:** AIA; *Progressive Architecture* magazine awards, "40 under 40" Honoree, *Interiors* magazine; California AIA **Notable Works** (also see Thom Mayne): Lawrence House, Hermosa Beach CA; Crawford Residence, Montecito CA; Bergren Residence, Venice CA

The work of Morphosis, his partnership firm with Thom Mayne, is complex and contradictory, seeking to create collisions and paradoxes that echo the larger contradictions that they see around them. Their work doesn't insist on the invariability or permanence of society's characteristics and values. They have written, "Architecture is a form of communication. It aims to reach and affect the emotional life of its viewer. What is important is that the language remains conceptual and open in nature...it is the ability to absorb the idiosyncratic which, in the end, gives the work its energy, immediacy and life. Our work attempts to formulate an inclusive architecture, something which is simultaneously a part of its context, its immediate world, while isolated, detached, disquieting, critical and untrustful of the world 'as it exists'; one is at home in the world without ever feeling complacent."

Their Lawrence House in Hermosa Beach CA is in a neighborhood of single-family houses and small apartment buildings. Their design collides the two building types by recalling an earlier house that stood on the site, and diagonally slicing through it a large apartment-style box. A monumental semi-cylindrical vestibule rises through three floors in the interior. Openings in this circulation wall frame views of rooms set in axis. Landings in the twin stairs flanking the vestibule offer varied vistas. The sense of exploration they offer inverts the service character of the stairway, which in this use takes up two thirds of the square footage of the building. The asphalt-shingled, gable roofed house is weathering a patchy blue-gray as the corrosive sea works upon it. Elsewhere, building elements are re-prioritized: the unimportant becomes essential and the essential peripheral. Spaces erode and interpenetrate and are carried through with a blank abstraction, a late Modern aesthetic and frequently something more; the machine has become both creator and destroyer. Of a prototype hamburger stand they designed, inspired by Duchamp and replete with wheels and weights, they write, "This project rejects the notion of architecture asoptimization of advanced technology. It is androgynous; it has no interest in 'good taste;' there is comic relief."

RTKL ASSOSIATES (see Blessing, Charles; Rogers, Archibald Coleman)

RUDOLPH, PAUL MARVIN
(Building Design)
Paul Rudolph Architect (212) 765-1450
54 West 57th Street New York NY 10019

Born: 1918 **Studied:** Harvard University **Awards:** Fellow, AIA; Fellow, American Society of Interior Designers; Member, National Institute of Arts and Letters **Notable Works:** Healy Guest House, Sarasota, Florida; Yale Art and Architecture Building, New Haven, Connecticut; Bristol-Myers Research Laboratory, Bridgeport, Connecticut COMMERCIAL/RETAIL: 40%, HOUSING: 10%, OTHER INSTITUIONAL: 30%

He is one of the most prolific and revered figures of the Modern movement, having completed more than 160 commissions in almost every imaginable category of architectural endeavor. His early work was marked by an almost mechanical precision—a direct consequence of his graduate studies with Walter Gropius at Harvard. His 1949 Healy House in Sarasota FL was treated as a single pavilion and parsed into severe functional sub-spaces. Less than a decade later, however, his work had grown much more expressive, plastic and sculptural. He began to build functional buildings with the visual impact for which he is famed. In 1958 he became chairman of the Yale School of architecture, and

Wiliam H. Ryan, *East Central High School* (drawing), Tulsa County, Oklahoma, 1960. Structural Engineer: Al Solnok. Electrical and Mechanical Engineer: John Penafeatha.

Wiliam H. Ryan, *East Central High School*, Tulsa County, Oklahoma, 1960. Structural Engineer: Al Solnok. Electrical and Mechanical Engineer: John Penafeatha.

shortly later he designed the University's new Art and Architecture Building. Influenced by Frank Lloyd Wright and Louis Kahn, most of all the designed evinced affinities with Le Corbusier. The upper floors extend dramatically from massive concrete corner piers, with long thin windows set so deeply that street-level viewers might mistake the floors for enormous roof supports. Lower-floors ceilings are more than twice the conventional height, and painting lofts and other utility levels are suspended in mid-room from the corner supports. To increase exposures of the primary windows, enclosed balconies extend around the multi-level rooms, adding to the structure's total of more than thirty vertical levels.

RYAN, WILLIAM HENRY
(Construction Administration, Building Design, Interiors)
Ryan and Associates (918) 479-5678
P.O. Box 217 Rose OK 74364-0217

Born: 1924 **Studied:** University of Oklahoma **Awards:** *Nation's Schools* magazine and National Council of Schoolhouse Construction School of the Month Award **Notable Works:** East Central High School, Tulsa OK; Immanuel Lutheran Church, Broken Arrow OK EDUCATIONAL 60%, MEDICAL 20%, HOUSING 10%, PLANNING 5%

His projects begin with their vacant sites, where he often camps and sits in all conditions, looking for the best faces and strongest constraints of each site. His attention to natural surroundings leads to a bias towards natural and durable construction materials. A concern with proportion and rhythm characterizes his designs.

His East Central High School is a curvilinear pod design capped by articulated dentels that grow larger as the roofs they terminate go higher, pulling the complex into a single harmonious scale. As a staccato counterpoint to the mass of his curving walls, he uses the campus pod motif as a design element in, for example, the ornamental screen that overhangs the four main entrances which nestle between the pods. This treatment of macro

shapes on a 'microscopic' scale can also be seen in the arches of his dentels and awnings. The broad convex lens of the school's open wall was designed to bounce back air traffic noise as well as Great Plains winds, in consideration of the heavily used flight paths directly above. All exterior walls incorporate chase walls containing mechanical and ductwork, creating a four-foot wall mass that insulates against outside noise.

SAFDIE, MOSHE
(Building Design)
(617) 491-3921
100 Properzi Way Somerville MA 02143

Born: 1938 **Studied:** McGill University **Awards:** New York Medal of Honor, AIA, 1980; Rechter Prize, Association of Architects and Planners of Israel; Gold Star Award, Philadelphia College of Art, 1970 **Notable Works:** Habitat, Montreal; National Gallery of Canada, Ottawa; Habitat Elahieh, Tehran, Iran

A quarter-century after completion his epic Montreal Habitat remains one of the most controversial buildings of the modern era. The highly experimental group housing prototype was plagued by cost overruns, minor misfunctions and general ungainliness, but it was a landmark in the history of residential architecture which may point toward developments of the next century. Habitat was the world's first pre-fabricated mid-rise complex at anything like its scale. The fundamental units were finished multi-room concrete-shell apartments. One hundred and fifty eight units—too few to justify the initial expense of prefabrication—were stacked into an elongated 12-story faceted mound. A system of setbacks created multiple unobstructed exposures, while each unit's roof provided a private terrace and garden for units above.

Although much of the criticism of Habitat centered on its ahistorical appearance, the cubistic concrete structure is quite reminiscent of the larger apartments of Le Corbusier. More apt and stinging criticisms of its expense were partially answered in his duplication of the Habitat project in Puerto Rico, where costs were held low enough that it qualified as low

Moshe Safdie, *Habitat,* Montreal, 1967.

Moshe Safdie, *Toronto Ballet Opera House* (model). Photo: Steve Rosenthal

middle-income housing.

SALZMAN, ARTHUR G.
(Construction Administration, Specifications)
Lohan Associates (312) 938-4455
225 N. Michigan Avenue Chicago IL 60601

Born: 1929 **Studied:** University of Illinois; Illinois Institute of Technology **Awards:** American Institute of Steel Construction **Notable Works:** TRW World Headquarters, Lyndhurst OH; McDonald's Office Campus, Oak Brook IL; IBM Research Development Campus, Endicott NY

He believes that architectural practice consists of one part inspiration and nine parts perspiration. It is technical expertise that turns dream into reality. His expertise is much in evidence in his specifications for TRW's Lyndhurst OH headquarters. The company is involved in high technology aerospace, computer and energy business and manufacturing. Sited on a plateau in a rolling, wooded Cleveland suburb, it is approached by curving drives through woods, small valleys and meadows. Four slightly offset terraced office pavilions radiate from a skylit central atrium, which reduces the apparent size of the building. Colors and materials emphasize the technological sophistication of the company and its wooded environment. Set on a base and substructure of Ohio sandstone, the building is framed in steel clad in dark anodized aluminium. Nonstructural elements, such as window frames and sun screens, are expressed in bronze-colored anodized aluminium. Exterior glass walls are recessed behind the structure for shade. Circulation elements—fire stairs projecting outside, and elevator cores inside—are surfaced in green marble. Entrance pavers and atrium pavers are brown granite. Inside, a moveable system of custom partitions, which create low-walled workstations around the perimeter and glass-fronted enclosed offices near the four service cores, permit personnel throughout the building to see the surrounding parklands.

SAMUELS, DANNY
(Building Design)
Taft Architects (713) 522-2988
807 Peden St. Houston TX 77006

Studied: Rice University **Awards:** AIA; Interiors magazine "40 under 40" Honoree, Texas AIA **Notable Works** (also see John Casbarian & Robert Timme): YWCA Masterson Branch, Houston TX; Corpus Christi City Hall, Corpus Christi TX; Commonwealth Townhouses, Houston TX

The work of his firm, the Taft Architects, is notable for its provocative and pleasing use of historical motifs in an eclectic manner. They amplify or distort classical motifs to make architecture that is simultaneously modest, friendly and symbolic, which is to say readable.

A "strong and fresh image" desired for a new administrative facility and downtown branch by the YWCA in Houston TX resulted in a Modernist plan overlaid with abstracted and distorted motifs drawn from the public symbolism of colonial Texas. The two main entrances are surmounted by blown-up, flat-arch shapes reminiscent of Spanish Mission architecture. The women's entrance is a Mexican Serliana arch with stepped edges, while office workers enter through a 'cathedral' door under a similarly proportioned round window at the other end of the building. Inside, industrial textures and features are highlighted—overhead doors, sodium vapor lights, return air gulles—with resurgent Bauhaus sympathies. Color and material are fragmented in layers, reminding of the semantic distinctions marked by the entrances. Terra cotta tile unifies the base around the building and climbs up the front facade around entrances, giving a ceremonial weight to the wall and marking it as the public facade. In back the terra cotta merges with similar colored brown paint which marks the office area. Cream stucco with a scored grid and grey stucco with blue tile stripes further fragment and lighten the heavy wall. Handicapped access to all areas is provided by ramps and bridges between structures which also function as galleries for viewing activities. In sum, the building is both dignified and "user-friendly."

Frank Schlesinger, *League of Cities Building*, Washington, D.C.   Photo: Lawrence S. Williams

SASAKI, HIDEO
(Landscape Architecture)
Sasaki Associates 64 Pleasant street Watertown Massachusetts 02172

Born: 1919 **Studied:** University of Illinois, Urbana **Awards:** Fellow, American Institute of Landscape Architects; First Honor Award, United States Bureau of Higher Education; Allied Professions Medal, AIA, 1973 **Notable Works:** Greenacre Park, New York; National Arboretum Master Plan, Washington, D.C.; Foothill College, Los Altos Hills, California

After wartime internment in West Coast concentration camps for Americans of Japanese descent, he was permitted to move inland to Illinois, where he resumed his architectural education. After nearly a decade of teaching in the Midwest, he became chairman of Harvard University's department of landscape architecture.

In Massachusetts he established a multi-disciplinary design firm which relied heavily on the creative contributions of his students and colleagues. Today Sasaki Associates employs over three hundred planners, architects, engineers and landscape architects. Despite the size of his practice he remains committed to a creative "cross- pollination" with the academic community. His most recent commissions reveal a mature and conservative approach to the modeling of exterior space. In his most successful projects he seamlessly mixes ethnic vernacular styles, creating an powerful sense of grounding and serenity. His Greenacre Park in New York City simultaneously evokes the solid repose of a weather-beaten Mexican plaza, with high terra-cotta arches and rough suspended beams, and the elegance of Japanese gardens, with long, low wooden overhangs and short, bristly shrubs.

SAUER, LOUIS
(Building Design)
Louis Sauer Architect (303) 499-0715
6367 Clearview Road Boulder Colorado

Born: 1928 **Studied:** Illinois Institute of Technology **Awards:** Fellow, AIA; *Architectural Record* Award, 1967; Design Fellow-

ship, National Endowment for the Arts **Notable Works:** Cincinnati Plaza, Cincinnati, Ohio; Newmarket Retail Development, Philadelphia

He believes that architecture is primarily a cultural activity, by which a people can heighten its self-awareness. His approach to design is restrained and conservative, but not derivative or plain. He is expert in contextual accommodation, designing structures that blend seamlessly with extant designs while adding quiet character of their own. His numerous multi-unit townhouse complexes near Philadelphia's Society Hill use subtle variants on local silhouettes to blend in among rows of distinguished colonial and neo-colonial homes.

When camouflage fails, he is not above outright concealment. After community activists in Philadelphia derailed several plans to develop a retail mall along the Delaware River, he designed a complex to which they could not possibly object. His glass and steel Newmarket mall—accented with exposed electrical and ventilation conduits painted in primary colors—was concealed on three sides by smartly renovated apartment houses. The mall's only exposed side innocuously faced the waterfront. Newmarket is also notable for its novel merchandise display scheme. Shops are designed so that the majority of their interior rack and counter area is visible through the mall's glass facade, making conventional window displays unnecessary.

SCHLESINGER, FRANK
(Building Design)
732 17th Street NW
Washington D.C. 20006

Born: 1925 **Studied:** Harvard University **Awards:** Fellow, AIA; *Architectural Record* Award, 1960, 1974; Distinguished Designer Fellowship, National Endowment for the Arts **Notable Works:** 1301 Pennsylvania Avenue, Washington, D.C.; Rochester Waterfront Crossroads Plaza, Rochester, NY COMMERCIAL/RETAIL: 90%, HOUSING: 10%

He argues that Modernism is not dead. Instead, the artificial homogeneity of the last era has given way to a more informed and equally

Der Scutt, *Trump Tower*, New York City. Photo: Norman McGrath

valid diversity of approaches and techniques. A distinguished teacher, he has simultaneously directed a professional practice which has garnered more than 30 design awards in the last quarter century.

In 1977 he became associated with the Pennsylvania Avenue Development Corporation, a government agency charged with refurbishing and developing the blocks adjacent to the White House in Washington DC. His unimposing curtain-walled mid-rise at 1301 Pennsylvania Avenue, completed in 1981, was the first office building in what looks like a major pulse of expansion. His 1984 National Place, a mixed-use complex funded by Marriott Corporation and the Quadrangle Development Corporation and designed in collaboration with Mitchell/Giurgola, was the only entry in a national competition which proposed to preserve the landmark National Theater.

SCHROEDER, KENNETH
(Building Design)

Born: 1943 **Studied:** University of Illinois **Awards:** AIA Chicago Chapter **Notable Works:** Wilson House, Evanston, IL; Renovation, Morganthaler Linotype Building, Chicago; Donohue Diner; Thonet Showroom, Merchandise Mart, Chicago

His striking design for the remodeling of the Morganthaler Linotype building in Chicago—being renovated, like many old structures on the border of downtown and warehouse districts, into residential lofts—retains the building exterior's early 20th-century flavor and harmonizes with the surrounding environment, while creating an interior, with its columns and open spaces, which some have likened to the work of Post-Modern architect Charles Moore. In a bold design stroke, he has left standing the framework of a old diner adjoining the Linotype building, further lending a sense of context and history.

Another residential concept he has developed is that of the "aedicula house," in which a centralized hall serves as the axis on which other rooms pivot. This concept is played out in the brick and frame residence he designed in Oak Brook, Illinois in 1978, and also in his own home, which features the concept. He has been expanding his theories of residential design in multi-unit dwellings in addition to individual residences.

SCHWEIKER, (ROBERT) PAUL
(Building Design)
Rural Route #3 High Tor Sedona Arizona 86336

Born: 1903 **Studied:** Yale University **Awards:** Merit Citation, AIA, 1962; *Progressive Architecture* Award, 1956, 1957 1960; Ford Foundation Research Grant, 1962 **Notable Works:** Chicago Hall Center, Vassar College, Poughkeepsie, New York; Unitarian Church, Evanston, Illinois; Trinity United Presbyterian Church, East Liverpool, Ohio

Like Le Corbusier he makes unified, homogeneous buildings whose outer shells differ little from their interior spaces. Walls are solid, three-dimensional slabs that do not change front to back, nor indeed outside to inside. He prefers durable materials with a natural richness of texture: wood, copper, concrete, brick, stone, tile and occasionally glass. He shuns finishes and garnishes, and alters surfaces only when he is forced to by severe climates. He wants his designs to accentuate the natural qualities of their materials and transparently reveal their structural stresses and solutions. At times his frankness with materials echoes the unyielding, massive work of the New Brutalists. For his Unitarian Church in Evanston IL he designed a vaulted concrete and glass envelope which seems at once to suggest God's grandeur and His severe authority. The weight of the church's unfaceted, inward-sloping concrete sidewalls is punctuated only by a series of slit-like rectangular portals. Concrete fins rise diagonally from the sidewalls to reinforce a system of bulky concrete roof supports. Two solid glass end-walls, however, provide dramatic counterpoint to the mass of the mainframe and suffuse the church with light.

SCOTT BROWN, DENISE
(Urban Design, Building Design)
Venturi, Rauch, Scott Brown (215) 487-0400
4236 Main Street Philadelphia Pennsylvania

Der Scutt, *The Corinthian*, New York City. Photo: Peter Mauss/ESTO

19127

Born:1931 **Studied:** University of Pennslyvania **Awards:** Adaptive Re-use Award, AIA, Philadelphia Chapter, 1976; *Progressive Architecture* Award, 1980, 1981, 1982; Historic Preservation Award, 1980 **Notable Works:** Republic Square District Plan, Austin, Texas; New Building, Seattle Art Museum; Master Plan, California City, California COMMERCIAL/RETAIL: 15%, HOUSING: 20%, INTERIOR DESIGN: 5%, EDUCATION: 30%, PLANNING: 21%

As a long-time associate of Robert Venturi and John Rauch she has a deep appreciation for American commercial vernacular architecture. Like Venturi she champions an eclectic architecture which makes frequent references to the familiar and "comforting" forms of the American roadside. But she's a sociologist as much as an architect or public planner, and she believes that careful arrangements and interpretations of conventional forms can create an effective language for communicating social mores and concerns. She argues in her book *Learning From Las Vegas*, which she co-wrote with Venturi and Steven Izenour, that architectural enclaves are robust snapshots of the gestalt of peoples and their eras. Her recent work, which reflects the influence of her firm's formal studies of Levittown and Las Vegas, has been criticized as banal and socially irrelevant. She responds that these charges have been leveled by affectedly upper middle class architects who have been raised instinctively to abhor lower middle class aspirations and tastes.

SCUTT, DER

(Building Design)
Der Scutt Architect (212) 725-2300
244 Fifth Avenue New York
New York 10001

Born: 1934 **Studied:** Yale University **Awards:** Fellow, Illuminating Engineering Society; *Architectural Record* Award of Excellence, 1970, 1974, 1975; E.F. Gruth Award, 1970 **Notable Works:** Trump Tower, New York; Continental Center Corporate Head-quarters, New York; West Houston Street Hotel, New York COMMERCIAL/RETAIL: 25%, HOUSING: 30%, INTERIOR DESIGN: 15%

When he began his practise he pledged to involve himself only with monumental, important projects. He didn't establish his own practice for nearly two decades, but in the intervening years he apprenticed to some of the Modern movement's greatest masters: Philip Johnson, Vincent Kling, Edward Durell Stone, Paul Rudolph and Ely Kahn.

In 1981 he emerged as a mature, commanding talent. His first solo commissions reflected an obvious delight in inspiring and motivating the occupants of his buildings with bold, opulent spaces—sometimes stretching the limits of budget and decorum in the process. Early designs had revealed a deep interest in the aesthetic and practical psychological effects of lighting. Lighting is a key factor in worker efficiency and user enjoyment in any space, he believes, and lighting sources should be completely integrated with architectural form. His particular fondness for the steel and glass skyscraper comes from its unique ability to capture natural light—even in Manhattan's concrete canyons. The rippling, striated, mirrored-glass facade of his 58-story Trump Tower in New York City is at once an eloquent repudiation of the "raw," unmodeled envelopes of neighboring Brutalist towers, and an impassioned effort to catch and capture the transforming rays of the sun.

SELIGMANN, WERNER

(Building Design)
Werner Seligmann and Associates
(607) 753-7526
9 Homer Avenue Cortland New York 13045

Born: 1930 **Studied:** Cornell University **Notable Works:** Olean Central Fire Station, Olean, New York; Beth David Synagogue, Binghamton, New York; Urban Development Corporation Housing, Ithaca, New York

His work extends from the seminal Modernism of Wright and Le Corbusier. His first commission, the concrete-block Beth David Synagogue in Binghamton NY, borrowed its

Werner Seligmann (with Michael Dennis), *Willard* (State Hospital)*Administration Building*, 1972, Willard, New York. Structural Engineer: Donald Greenberg. Mechanical Engineer: Galston & Galston

massing scheme directly from Wright's Oak Park IL Unity Temple. The symmetry and interior plan of the design also leaned heavily on Wright precedents, with some contemporary updates, but the obtuse lines of the structure's main stairway and the intricate sculptural detail of its chapel were early signs of a new and productive line of thought.

In his well known 235-unit Urban Development Corporation Housing project in Ithaca NY a decade later, he showed how he took in the cubist paradigms of Le Corbusier in synthesis with the technically progressive ideas of Switzerland's Atelier 5 group. The broad strokes of his design were clearly taken from Atelier 5's 1961 Halen Estate project, but a limited budget forced him to make several challenging, provoking improvisations. Halen's landscaped terraces he replaced with compact enclosed atriums. Its central, richly landscaped plaza gave way to a strongly repetitive geometric system of pedestrian causeways, which increased the development's sense of regularity and holism without detracting from the individuality of each unit.

SGPA/ARCHITECTURE AND PLANNING (see Meredith, Dean; Niblack, Richard; Reeslund, Geoffrey)

SHAW, PATRICK
(Building Design)

Born: 1933 **Studied:** Harvard University **Notable Works:** Lafayette Square Project, Washington, D.C.; Executive Plaza Office Buildings, Oak Brook, IL; Campus Center and Residence Hall, Loyola University, Chicago; Mid-Continental Plaza Office Building, Chicago; Dearborn Street Railroad Station Renovation, Chicago

The task of renovating Chicago's Dearborn Street Railroad Station was an ambitious but problematic one. The structure is an impressive melding of influences and elements—an Italianate clock tower, red-brick facing, large ground-floor windows with rounded tops reminiscent of Louis Sullivan and of the early Prairie school. But the station, like many noble railroad terminals in Chicago and other cities, is no longer used for trains, reflecting the sad, slow decline of inter-city rail travel in the U.S. In renovating such a structure, his design breathes new life into an old but still noble building. He preserves the exterior and adds new office buildings that feature the same red-brick facing of the old building. The interior features an atrium and multi-level walkways conecting the original structure with the addition. The older terminal section is intended for banks and other small shops. Thus he creates a mixed-use structure solidly anchoring Chicago's unique, historical Printer's Row neighborhood.

SIMON, MARK
Centerbrook Architects & Planners
(203) 767-0175
Box 409 Essex CT 06426

Born: 1946 **Studied:** Brandeis University; Yale University **Awards:** "40 under 40" Honoree, *Interiors* magazine; Invited lecturer for "Emerging Voices," New York Architectural League; Long Island AIA Gold Award **Notable Works:** East Hampton Library/Multipurpose Center, East Hampton NY; Lenz Winery CT HOUSING 50%, INSTITUTIONAL/COMMERCIAL 50%

His work and that of his partners is distinguished for its consideration and regard for its users. A notable example of articulating the aspirations of users is his East Hampton CT Community Center in a small Connecticut mill town. Desiring a coordinated facility to house a senior center, library and day care, architects and citizens worked together to "write an essay in folk architecture." Committees and workshops focused on the site and user needs. "Dream drawings" were solicited for architectural images; the attitudes and visions expressed in these became the essence of the built design.

Laid out on a east-west axis, the building opens to light from the south and avoids the cold with long roofs. The smallest component, the Senior Center, is closest to the road and scaled to match residential neighbors. The day

Werner Seligmann (with Bruce Coleman), *Urban Development Corporation Housing*, Ithaca, New York, 1972. Structural Engineer: Donald Greenberg. Mechanical Engineer: Galston & Galston

Mark Simon, *East Hampton Library/ Community Center*, East Hampton, New York. Photo: Steve Rosenthal

care center and library are behind it in a stepped plan which gives all parts equal recognition from the street. The building was designed as a steel-framed barn—space under the sloping roof is used for mechanical attics because a high water table preventing digging a basement. Ceilings rise and fall as needed, making grand spaces where appropriate, as in the library entry and reading room, and the seniors' main hall. Other places are more cozy—a senior fireplace niche, a day care cove and children's library.

The building harmonizes with its village surroundings. Users and architects stenciled bell patterns at entries and at the library, recalling the town's heritage as "Belltown," the original home of American bell manufacturing. The Center's chimney, ventilator and bell tower serve as civic markers, while windows and dormers give a friendly cadence to the building's substantial mass. A long porch, anchored at the street by the bell tower entry, ties the complex together.

SIMONDS, JOHN ORMSBEE
(Landscape Architecture, Planning)
The Loft (412) 734-0220
17 Penhurst Road Pittsburgh Pennsylvania 15202

Born: 1913 **Studied:** Harvard University **Awards:** Fellow, American Society of Landscape Architects; Fellow, Royal Academy of Design, London; Honor Award in housing, civic design, parks and recreation and environmental design, American Society of Landscape Architects **Notable Works:** Development Plan for six community parks, Collier County, Florida; Riverfront, Louisville, Kentucky; Master Plan for New Community of Pelican Bay, Florida

He tries to make his outdoor spaces both functional and expressive. He has pursued this ambition in projects as straightforward as a community pre-school playlot and as complex as the design of a new suburban community. His greatest contribution, he believes, has been to initiate and administer collaborations among large groups of engineers, architects, planners and scientists. Since so many of his firm's more than 500 commissions in its half-century of operation have involved large casts of characters, it is difficult to characterize his individual design contribution. But his expertise in geology, hydrology, environmental biology and ecology, physiography and—perhaps most important—human relations, has informed all the projects undertaken in his name. In his 1983 book, *Landscape Architecture, A Manual of Site Planning and Design,* he argued that designers must plan sequences of experiences rather than spaces, attractions or borders. His extensive study of the gardens of the Far East has convinced him that form must derive transparently from an engaging, vital series of stimuli.

SITE INC. (see Wines, James)

SKELTON, DOUGLAS
(Design, Construction, Preservation)
Douglas Skelton AIA Architect
(503) 773-7781
26 Hawthorne Ave. Medford OR 97504

Born: 1939 **Studied:** University of Oregon School of Architecture **Awards:** American School and University 1987 portfolio of outstanding school and university buildings **Notable Works:** South Medford High School, Medford OR; Eagle Point High School, Eagle Point OR EDUCATION 60%, OFFICE 15%, HOUSING 15%, RETAIL 10%

His philosophy is that good design can be translated into a successful facility within a modest budget. His work is designed to be compatible with its neighbors, and to satisfy program needs while being attractive and enjoyable to those who use its spaces. Sensitive both to history and to current attitudes, it is designed with an eye to the future. He believes that the success of a design solution can often be measured by the attitudes of its users.

His South Medford High added to and renovated a 50-year-old facility located in a historic neighborhood. The original exterior was restored and its features emphasized with shaded painting. His addition duplicated the

Skidmore, Owings & Merrill, *Houston Skyline* (including *Allied Bank Plaza, Interfirst Plaza, San Felipe Plaza and One and Two Shell Plaza*. Photo: Aker/Burnette Studio, Houston

scale and proportion of the original building's stucco and pressed concrete ornamentation, while inexpensively adding new walls of harmonious textured and sandblasted concrete. He takes pride that a year after his project's completion the school was selected one of the top 10 in the nation by the National Teachers Organization.

SKIDMORE, OWINGS & MERRILL (see
DeStefano, Donald; Gonzalez, Joseph; Graham, Bruce; Hartman, Craig; Keating, Richard; Legge, Diane; Netsch, Walter; Smith, Adrian; Stoker, Donald)

SMITH, ADRIAN
(Building Design, Planning) Skidmore, Owings and Merrill (312) 641-5959
33 West Monroe Chicago IL 60603

Born: 1944 **Studied:** University of Illinois at Chicago **Awards:** AIA; The Waterfront Center Excellence in Waterfront Design award; *Progressive Architecture* design citation **Notable Works:** Rowes Wharf, Boston; 225 West Washington, Chicago; AT&T Building, Chicago; Capital Square, Des Moines IA

Influenced more by human issues than engineering principles in his overall design work, he has a reputation as a modern neo-classical architect. Respectful of the work of previous generations of architects, he attempts to knit together materials, color, compositional elements, scaling devices, geographical and cultural influences and attitudes towards proportion inherent in the character of the cities in which his projects are situated.

His AT&T building design in Chicago is stylistically reminiscent of the finely detailed skyscrapers of the 1920s, in the heyday of Chicago architecture, but technologically it is firmly situated within the 1980s and 1990s generation of Saarinen-style skyscrapers. Double-glazed tinted glass reaches floor to ceiling and a granite skin with multiple finishes and colors contains state-of-the-art mechanical systems such as constant air volume air conditioning, complete cellular floor electrified decks, automatic window washing

systems and clear interior spans of 40 to 50 feet. His mixed-use, exuberantly detailed Rowes Wharf project in Boston is designed around a large scale central rotunda which serves as a passageway for residential and office "fingers". Clad in articulated precast panels, the fingers erode as they reach toward the harbor. Contrasting with the fingers is a domed octagonal terminal which receives ferry passengers with the celebratory bombast of nineteenth century pavilions.

SMITH, WHITNEY ROLAND
(Building Design, Planning)
Whitney Roland Smith Architect
(213) 682-3877
1517 Fair Oaks Avenue
South Pasadena California 91030

Born: 1911 **Studied:** U.C.L.A. **Awards:** Fellow, AIA; Los Angeles Beautiful Award, 1958; Homes for Better Living Award, 1962 **Notable Works:** Neighborhood Church, Pasadena, California; Linda Vista Shopping Center, San Diego; Westbridge School, Pasadena COMMERCIAL/RETAIL: 20%, HOUSING: 10%, PLANNING: 70%

Although he had just a brief internship in the office of California's 'poet of wood' Harwell Hamilton Harris, his experience with him had a remarkable effect on his subsequent work. In 1942 he designed the Linda Vista Shopping Center, which was remarkable in incorporating a small central green—an oddity amidst the unabashed urbanism of other area developments. During the building and renewal boom that followed World War II he designed a number of rustic wooden post-and- beam projects in the Los Angeles area, including the planar Mutual Housing Association Community and the loosely constructed, gangly Griffin Park Girl's Camp.

In 1946 he began a fruitful collaboration with Wayne R. Williams. In his residential commissions of this period he typically used panel-post construction techniques with infills of sheet-wood or glass. To combat California's summer sun he sometimes incorporated large sliding doors and cooler natural materials such

Adrian Smith, *AT&T Corporate Center* (Model), Chicago. Photo: Hedrich-Blessing

as adobe and conventional brick. More often the southern-facing entranceways to his houses were covered by small lath greenhouses, planted and groomed by renowned landscape architect Garrett Eckbo.

SOLERI, PAOLO
(Building Design, Planning, Landscape Architecture)
The Cosanti Foundation   6433 Doubletree Road Scottsdale Arizona 85253

Born: 1919 **Studied:** Turin Polytechnic, Turin, Italy **Awards:** Gold Medal, World Biennale of Architecture, Sofia, Bulgaria, 1981; Silver Medal, Academie d'Architecture, Paris, 1984; Design Award, *Progressive Architecture*, 1979 **Notable Works:** Arcosanti (in progress), Cordes Junction, Arizona; Earth House, Scottsdale, Arizona; Deconcini House, Phoenix, Arizona

Like an Old Testament prophet he has spent the last 20 years in the desert, waiting for his grand vision to become reality. In 1970 he began work on Arcosanti, a 25-story, 13-acre urban "arcology" set on 860 beautiful acres 70 miles north of Phoenix AZ. An arcology is a highly integrated three-dimensional complex, which he considers the solution to the problems of present-day cities. The best alternatives to conventional, loosely planned urban developments, arcologies reinforce interdependence and interpenetration between individuals and their collective resources and critical community services. Beyond economical and logistical practicality, he believes, arcologies will provide a rich social framework which can improve the quality of man's physical, psychic and aesthetic well-being.

Arcosanti, at the intersection of two of Arizona's most important highways, will eventually accommodate 5000 people, though the project may be as much as 20 years from completion. Greenhouses fitted with advanced-design solar panels will provide food, electrical power and heating/refrigeration for the entire community. Integral waste disposal systems and eliminating most automotive and industrial pollution will simplify routine maintenance and cleaning for the mammoth cast-concrete installation. A complex of theaters now under construction will provide a source of income.

SOLFISBURG, ROY J. III
(Building Design, Programming)
Holabird & Root (312) 726-5960
300 W. Adams St. Chicago IL 60606:

Born: 1943 **Studied:** Williams College; University of Pennsylvania **Awards:** FAIA **Notable Works:** Saenger Theatre, Pensacola FL; Villa Tondo, Captiva Island FL; Casa Chameleon, Sanibel Island FL INSTITUTIONAL 33%, MEDICAL 33%, OFFICE 33%

He unites boldly articulated geometric volumes with strongly colored feature elements, yet his buildings yield 'softening' characteristics which acknowledge the human dimension: he feels that buildings should be fun. His colors articulate spatial functions: subtle pastels cover broadly used feature elements, while bright colors reveal finely used elements— recessed joints for example might be bright red. In short, he perfects and highlights his projects' structural and circulation systems and balances conservative and contemporary styles, innovative designs and human touches.

His Saenger Theatre is a remodeling of a vaudeville house which dates from the 1920s. He plays with the formal Moorish flourishes of the exterior facade, "jazzing up" its wide circular marquee and tall arched windows with neon lights. But interior restoration is true to the original Spanish church-style stage house— his renovation of its exuberant baroque detailing is calculated to satisfy contemporary flashy tastes.

His Northwestern Sports and Aquatics Center exemplifies his delicate balance between geometrical and human elements. Its circulation patterns are adapted to the large spaces of the gymnasiums and pools. Exterior walls are load-bearing and reveal tall supporting columns inside and out, yet the columns seem melded into the walls' surfaces, as though covered with skin.

Adrian Smith, *225 West Washington*, Chicago. Photo: Hedrich-Blessing

SORIANO, RALPH SIMON
(Building Design)
Ralph Soriano Architect
21 Main Street Belvedere
Tiburon California 94920

Born: 1930 **Studied:** U.C.L.A. **Awards:** *House and Home* Award, 1960; Pan American Congress Award, 1951; *Architectural Record* Award, 1956 **Notable Works:** Lipetz House, Los Angeles; Case Study House for *Arts and Architecture*, Pacific Palisades, California; World Peace Center, Alcatraz Island (project)

He is a leader of the California Modernist movement who has continued the traditions of his one-time mentor, Richard Neutra. His first commissions after leaving Neutra's office, a series of Los Angeles luxury residences, were in familiar patterns, but evinced a more classical, restrained handling of form and materials. These early homes combined the stark white cubes of the Bauhaus and Le Corbusier with the ineffably American balloon frame house, which he accentuated by exposing and glazing his vertical studs. In 1948 he contributed to *Arts and Architecture* magazine's famous series of Los Angeles Case Study Homes, and the design marked a major change in his stylistic and material preferences. His house was framed by thin, round columns of steel. Its dark fascia covering, punctuated with a pattern of light infills and accentuated by lush hanging plants and integral landscaping, reconciled the hard-edged urbanism of the East Coast with the airy openness of southern California. Subsequent houses refined his technique of using light, natural materials to soften the edges of his eminently functional steel frames, producing comfortable and diffuse light.

SPECK, LAWRENCE W.
(Building Design)

His work as a teacher and a writer of architecture informs his work, which often subtly transforms regional or classic architecture. The layouts of many of his structures surprise with portions angling off to form private spaces and alcoves.

His Matthews Ranch House in Burnet TX uses the materials and forms of the regional vernacular—limestone and cedar, pitch roof and porches—but arranges them in novel ways. Rather than a linear pattern, house units are arranged in a hook shape which protects and secludes the yard it encloses. A carport is connected to the the the tripartite living quarters by a curving stone wall topped with a turret (containing a children's playhouse) which wittily plays off of the fortlike arrangement. Interior room placement allows for privacy: the parents' room is separated from the childrens' rooms by a large living room—the focus of the house. His generous proportion of porch space to housing space (1800 square feet of porch space around the 2000-square-foot house) makes the porches an integral extension of the house and no mere ornament, thus blurring where the house ends and the outdoors begins.

SPECTOR, PAT L.
(Building Design, Facility Programming, Interior Architecture)
Sverdrup Corporation (314) 436-7600
801 North Eleventh St. Louis MO 63101

Born: 1944 **Studied:** Washington University; University of Washington **Awards:** AIA; Top Honor Award, Producer's Council Triennial; Walter Taylor Award, AIA/AASA **Notable Works:** Riverfront Office Complex, St. Louis MO; Business/Technology Complex, Webster University COMMERCIAL 30%, HIGH-RISE 30%, HOUSING 30%

His designs are versatile and respond to the dynamic nature of the needs of his clients, their environment, and their contextual issues. For the Union Electric Company in St. Louis he responded to a need for "understated elegance" by designing a corporate headquarters addition that features Missouri red granite, green-tinted glass, and a jewel-like glass-enclosed atrium of four stories. To complement its environment (wetlands that were to be preserved) and produce a powerful corporate image for the headquarters building in St. Louis's Riverport Office Complex, he combined a sunset red granite facade with complementary accent bands of flamed granite and green reflective glass windows, capped with a green sloped roof. Other projects reflecting his sensitivity to client needs include Webster University's Business/Technology Complex, which received notable press for its historic sensitivity; the U.S. Unified Space Command Headquarters at Peterson Air Force Base in Colorado which received the Air Force's Award for Design Excellence; and a unique, highly visible pedestrian bridge at Barnes Hospital in St. Louis, which established a new entrance to the hospital.

STARKMAN, MAXWELL
(Building Design)
Maxwell Starkman Associates
(213) 278-6400
9420 Wilshire Blvd. Beverly Hills CA 90212

Born: 1922 **Studied:** University of Manitoba, Canada **Awards:** AIA; Society of American Registered Architects design awards **Notable Works:** Meridian Condominiums, San Diego CA; Mirabella Condominium, Los Angeles; Shoreline Square, Long Beach CA HIGHRISE HOUSING 20%, HOTELS 20%, OFFICE 10%, SHOPPING CENTERS 10%, MIXED-USE AND OTHER 30%

He was a pioneer California market for what he calls "architecture of investment:" speculative projects initiated by developers rather than end-users. His unique background gave him skills for addressing developers' special needs—for rigid cost controls and quality design, for flexible responses to shifting markets and opportunities, and for 'fast-track' construction and design techniques that he innovated even before the phrase existed. Starting with mass housing and master planning, his firm evolved into a broadly based practice with a staff of more than 180 personnel, designing large projects of all kinds.

His wartime career in the Royal Canadian Engineers gave him firm footing in analyzing difficult or flatly impossible program demands, then arranging the necessary teamwork for solving them. Emigrating to Los Angeles after the war, he worked in the offices of Richard

Neutra for several years before starting his own firm. His office and projects have grown with southern California, in an evolving partnership with the many specialists and consultants required to bring increasingly complex projects into being. In 1988 two executive employees acquired his practice to form Starkman + Vidal + Christensen.

His 27-story Ticor Office Building in Los Angeles, completed in the 1960s, shows his approach to cost-effective quality—the building had to go through the design, bidding and government approvals process and into construction in less than six months, before a client tax deadline expired. It features a custom curtain wall of thin, stamped and formed sheet metal with a Kynar finish which is sprayed in back with automobile undercoating to keep it from having a hollow ring in high winds. At ground level a thicker gauge steel is used for solid effect.

STEPHENS, THOMAS
(Building Design)
Smith & Stephens, Architects, Inc.
(312) 629-3500
17W601 14th St. Oak Brook Terrace IL 60181

Born: 1931 **Studied:** University of Illinois **Notable Works:** Grant Square Complex, Hinsdale IL; Mid-American Federal Savings Corporate Headquarters, Clarendon Hills IL; Oakbrook Hyatt Hotel, Oakbrook IL COMMERCIAL 33%, INDUSTRIAL 33%, HOTELS 33%

A general-practice architect, he emphatically holds that the client's needs and wants are primary, and he doesn't believe in awards. While all projects must follow regional environments and locales, it is clients, in his opinion, not award committees, who must create programs, and judge them. In his experience most clients know exactly what they want, and need guidance in such matters as cost constraints and realism. His standard is that one should be able to live with a building forever.

His Grant Square Complex in Hinsdale IL was severely constrained by zoning, traffic flow challenges, and a strong existing sense of neighborhood identity. The owners wanted to upgrade an existing colonial-style mall in order to increase the space of the office and food facilities, and build as well a 38,000-square-foot medical center on adjacent land. His resulting renovation and addition heightens the colonial flavor. An original one-story office facility was enlarged with a second story now trimmed with cupolas, dupolas, and high columns which accentuate its existing reddish-brown brick and white trim finish. Projecting bay windows with copper canopies are added to the new story, and cedar shingles replace the original asphalt roof. Maintaining the traditional style of the complex did not prevent the incorporation of modern amenities such as revolving doors.

STERBA, JOSEPH
(Building Design, Specifications)
The Sterba Partnership (201) 790-4200
79 Union Building, Totawa NJ 07512

Born: 1948 **Studied:** Pennsylvania State University **Awards:** New Jersey AIA **Notable Works:** Bergen County Day School for the Multiple Handicapped, Parnus NJ COMMERCIAL 65%, PRIVATE HOUSING 25%

He believes that good design is functional with minimal ornamentation, and he is uninterested in terminology like modernism and postmodernism. Simply put, his architecture aims to balance modern materials and techniques with classical design elements. His use of natural light to punctuate spaces and enliven interiors brings an integrated theme to both entrances and central spaces in his designs. The strongly articulated geometry of his facades scales the mass of his buildings down to elements related to human proportions. Typically his geometric patterns are based on multiples of like forms. His preferred materials are metal and aluminum panels, regular masonry, and insulated wall systems.

His Bergen County Day School in Parnus NJ exemplifies his geometric approach. Clusters of six classrooms forming a cruciform join at the corners in a diagonal row from a bird's eye view, and appear at ground level as overlapping geometric blocks that step upward along the diagonal spine. The architectural integrity of the school arises out of the sawtooth effect of the interlocking clusters and the unifying diagonal spine, which also acts as a corridor through the series of clusters. High clerestories alternate with lower roofs to lend architectural variety and humanity that contrasts with the formal geometry.

STERN, ROBERT A.M.
(Building Design)
Robert A.M. Stern Architects (212) 246-1980
200 West 72nd Street
New York New York 10023

Born: 1939 **Studied:** Yale University **Awards:** Fellow, AIA; National Honor Award, AIA, 1980, 1985; Award of Merit, *Housing*, 1977 **Notable Works:** Point West Place Office Building, Framingham, Massachusetts; Cohn House, Martha's Vineyard, Massachusetts

A widely influential critic, author and teacher, he has only recently devoted his primary energies to design. He remains an articulate spokesman for the Grays, a group of Postmodern architects and academics who believe that architecture is at base a communicating art, that ornamentation isn't an affront to otherwise functional designs, and that referring to the history of architecture and deferring to surrounding structures both can strengthen designs. His buildings share a pronounced historicism and a disdain for revealing structural elements. But his small scale residential works and his larger commercial commissions strongly diverge. His homes, like many of those of Robert Venturi, draw closely from the American Shingle Style. But he works much closer to the vernacular than Venturi, outfitting his New England cottages with large front gables, open staircases, solid traditional window frames—the full array of opulent Shingle Style embellishments.

His corporate commissions, most notably his Point West Place in Framingham MA, share much with the recent institutional work of Michael Graves and to a lesser extent Philip

Johnson. Point West Place is a modified horizontal glass box, accented with bright ribbons of primary color and accessed through a large arching concrete-block portico. A small, stylized concrete-block facade dominates the center of the primary elevation, behind the portico, evoking the grand entrances of early twentieth century rail stations and municipal buildings.

STERN, WILLIAM F.

(Building Design, Interior Architecture, Planning, Renovation)
William F. Stern & Associates
(713) 527-0186
4902 Travis Houston TX 77002

Born: 1947 **Studied:** Harvard University **Awards:** Houston AIA; Texas AIA **Notable Works:** Colquitt Townhouses, Houston TX; Albans Townhouses, Houston TX; Orton Condominiums, Houston TX HOUSING 80%, COMMERCIAL 20%

His work is fastidious in every detail—in how his trim meets cabinetry, in the precision of molding, in the granite lips that overhang counter edges. He says, "the design process begins with the table, expands to the space around it, and goes on from there . . . a lot of architecture is about making rooms." Informed by neighborhoods and places, backyards and bungalows, his work transforms contextual materials and imagery into contemporary cultural expressions.

His classically composed Modernist designs provide individuality without compromising the residential neighborhoods of Houston that have escaped that metropolis's uncontrolled growth. Within modest means he carries on a dialogue between formal and informal elements, between social and private space.

A tight ground-floor area for his Colquitt Townhouse dictated a small entry from which the visitor is either beckoned to a concave niche that gestures towards an enlarged space, or else to a staircase that invites ascent to the major living spaces on the second floor. A quality of formality, conveyed by symmetry in the living room, is juxtaposed with informal,

rambling elements in the dining and kitchen areas. Indigenous cottage forms, such as flat gable ends, add density and urbanity to the street facade. A change in texture and scale in the wood siding creates a rusticated base which emphasizes privacy and provides continuity.

STIENE, FRANK J.

(Building Design, Interior Architecture)
Frank J. Stiene Group P.A. (201) 447-5514
555 Route 17 South Ridgewood NJ 07450

Born: 1939 **Studied:** University of Cincinnati Awards: New ersey AIA; Good Neighbor Award, New Jersey Chamber of Commerce **Notable Works:** Mercedes Benz of North America Corporate Headquarters NJ; Siemens Medical Systems, Inc., Piscataway NJ OFFICE 75%, COMMERCIAL 20%, INDUSTRIAL 5%

A modernist who feels that buildings should function as unobtrusive backdrops for their occupants, he also aims to make structures as recognizable in the interior as on the exterior.

His 1972 headquarters for Mercedes Benz of North America was the first building in the United States to incorporate 'office landscaping' into its design. A concept originated in the late 1950s by the West German Quick Borner Team, office landscaping establishes an organization's needs as guidelines for the architect. In the Mercedes Benz headquarters this resulted in several innovative design features, such as an open office concept that uses screens and varying ceiling heights to delineate space, and placing electrical and phone outlets below floor level to allow for maximum flexibility in future redesigns.

Using a trapezoid made of three truncated triangles as design motif, the glass and steel structure is built with an eye toward future expansion by providing for additional truncated triangles. Acoustic baffles house indirect lights, and all furniture was custom-designed using the trapezoidal motif.

STINSON, NOLAN

(Construction Administration, Cost Estimating, Building Design)

8029 Clayton Road, St. Louis, MO 63177
(314) 725-0444

Born: 1922 **Studied:** Washington University
Awards: President, St. Louis AIA **Notable Works:** National Council of State Garden Clubs, St. Louis MO; St. Paul's Cathedral, Peoria IL COMMERCIAL 50%, INSTITUTIONAL 50%

In his diverse practice his first priorities are functional simplicity and sensitivity to site and client needs. He uses natural materials such as lumber, granite, and brick which have traditionally been used in the St. Louis area, and orients his buildings to make the best use of their environment, providing natural solutions to site problems. Buildings face the path of the sun to maximize natural lighting, and absorb prevailing winds to encourage natural ventilation. He often collaborates with artists to reveal a building's functional relationship to its natural setting.

His National Council of State Garden Clubs in St. Louis orients a building and sculptured wall around the internationally famous Shaws Garden, a tourist attraction. The 300-foot long William Tabbott sculptured wall runs parallel to the street, intersecting the building in T-fashion. At the street-side joint sits a plaza, fountain and reflecting pool; the fountain directs water through the wall. The building itself is a one-story structure set in the garden terrain, but on the garden side it forms two stories of large-paned glass and aluminum, allowing both natural lighting and a full view of the garden. The side of the sculptured wall facing the garden features engraved granite inserts detailing various state membership groups.

His A.S. Aloe Corporation in St. Louis has an original ventilation design which takes in air through the loading areas, and by means of large fans set in sculptural patterns, circulates the air through the building.

STOCKWELL, SHERWOOD

Bull Volkman Stockwell (415) 781-1526
Musto Plaza 350 Pacific Avenue
San Francisco CA 94111

Born: 1926 **Studied:** Massachusetts Institute of Technology **Awards:** FAIA; AIA; Cedar Shingle Bureau/AIA award; "Transformations in Architecture" Exhibition, Museum of Modern Art New York City **Notable Works:** Marin County Regional Library, Fairfax CA; Venetian Gardens, Stockton CA; Master Plan for Stanford Shopping Center, Palo Alto CA COMMERCIAL 35%, RESORT 35%, HOUSING 15%

The task that he and his co-principals at Bull Volkman Stockwell have taken on isn't just to design good, timeless architecture, but "to create buildings that relate sympathetically to each other and to the surrounding environment." In addition to their warm and inviting architecture, he and his firm have become distinguished for their site and community planning. He has twice received grants from the National Endowment for the Arts, to study alpine town planning in Europe and urban town spaces in Great Britain.

A composite community complex, his Venetian Gardens in Stockton CA is in the quadrant form typical of a small city. His shopping plaza at the crossroads of two major parkways serves as project's focal point. From the plaza a public walkway bordering a scenic canal leads to community open spaces and a recreation building. Building densities decrease and open spaces increase as one moves outward. Though auto access is possible, primary internal circulation routes are for pedestrians and bicyclists. Many waterways and pools provide both visual delight and a cool sense in a valley known for its blistering summers.

STOKER, DONALD F.

(Computer Design)
Skidmore, Owings & Merrill (312) 641-5959
33 West Monroe Street Chicago IL 60603
Born: 1946 **Studied:** University of Illinois; University of Chicago Business School **Awards:** AIA Roundtable on Computers **Notable Works:** Three First National, Chicago; 60 State Street, Boston MA COMMERCIAL 33%, INDUSTRIAL 33%, OFFICE 33%

Hugh Stubbins, *Citicorp Center*, New York City. Photo: Edward Jacoby

An architect by training, he develops CAD (Computer-Aided Design) computer systems for architects, which are used throughout the architectural planning and design process. His purpose is to integrate evolving computer technology into building design, so that architects can more effectively find solutions to architectural problems. His computer programs will "describe" buildings that don't yet exist, based on optimum estimates of energy efficiency, stress loads, occupancy, and so forth. His programs also improve building maintenance, by enabling owners to "view" through computer descriptions a building's potential operations. His work isn't concerned with specific architectural projects, but rather with the evolving architectural fields of engineering, space planning, interior design, and management.

STUBBINS, HUGH ASHER JR.
(Building Design)
The Stubbins Associates (617) 491-6450
1033 Massachusetts Avenue Cambridge Massachusetts 02138

Born: 1912 **Studied:** Harvard University **Awards:** Fellow, AIA; AIA New York Chapter Award, 1978; Award of Excellence, *Urban Design*, 1978 **Notable Works:** Citicorp Center, New York City; Federal Reserve Plaza, Boston; Crerar Library, The University of Chicago COMMERCIAL/RETAIL: 55%, HOUSING: 10%, INTERIOR DESIGN: 25%, EDUCATION: 5%, PLANNING: 5%

His buildings achieve a rare balance between utility and drama. A consummate designer, he's also a gifted programmer and planner of usable, stimulating environments. He holds that contemporary society is accurately reflected in its forms and proportions. His buildings reflect society's needs and solutions as well as our prevailing aesthetic idioms. His 1978 Citicorp Center with Emory Roth and Sons in New York City was a landmark achievement in mixed-use high-rise design. The Center transformed the public perception of one of the world's busiest commercial districts. Formerly the area had been virtually deserted at night. He lifted the 46-story tower, topped with a steeply angled, unfenestrated concrete crown, 126 feet in the air atop massive stilts in order to provide ground space for a multi-story atrium which houses public performance spaces, 'outdoor' cafes, snack shops, financial service centers and rows of diverse boutiques. The Center, along with several of its new neighbors, has become an all-hours magnet for shoppers, diners and tourists.

SUMMERS, GENE
(Building Design)
Ridgway Ltd.
610 Newport Center Drive #1800
Newport Beach CA 92660

Born: 1928 **Studied:** Illinois Institute of Technology **Awards:** FAIA **Notable Works:** McCormick Place Convention Center, Chicago; National Gallery of Berlin; Kemper Arena, Kansas City

His recent works are elegant and persuasive refutations of Postmodern criticisms of Miesian functionalism. In his hands, the clean, hard surfaces of glass and steel create a sense of propriety, solidity and grandeur, instead of mere austerity.

After a sixteen-year stint at van der Rohe's Chicago office—where he worked on such seminal projects as New York's Seagram Building and Chicago's Federal Center—he accepted a position as partner in charge of design at C.F. Murphy and Associates. There he undertook a series of mammoth public commissions, including McCormick Place, Chicago's huge convention and entertainment center. His flat-roofed jet-black steel and glass box houses the City's largest theater auditorium and three rehearsal theaters, as well as a 300,00 square foot exhibition space which has proven superbly responsive to a huge variety of spatial and functional demands.

SUSSNA, ROBERT
(Computer Design, Construction Administration, Building Design, Facility Programming, Interior Architecture, Renovation)
Sussna Design Office, P.A. (609) 924-6611
53 State Rd. Princeton NJ 08540

Born: 1939 **Studied:** Cornell University **Awards:** New Jersey AIA **Notable Works:** Home, Hunterton County NJ; Dining Hall, Trenton State University, Trenton NJ COR-PORATE 40%, INSTITUTIONAL 40%, MEDICAL 10%, COMMERCIAL 10%, HOUSING 10%

His designs are airy and uncluttered in the modernist idiom and playfully use materials in unexpected ways, such as his Hunterdon County NJ Home's glass-block wall on an otherwise wood frame house, which also features oak caps on aluminum-finished balustrades. Often working with transitional decks and terraces that mediate between indoors and out, he attentively responds to the immediate natural environment in his siting and program analysis.

His Hunterton County NJ home is slipped into a hillside forest of tall old trees where it lies perpendicular to the hill, thus minimizing impact as well as addressing the house to its strongest views. Though not large, the long and narrow home takes mass from its dramatic siting. Its glass-block front wall set at a slight angle to the home visually guides visitors around its corner toward the front door, and provides translucent light to the colorful two-floor gallery which connects the rooms inside.

TAFT ARCHITECTS (see Casbarian, John; Samuels, Danny; Timme, Robert)

TAKASHINA, MAKOTO
(Building Design, Urban Design)
Makoto Takashina & Associates
(415) 453-4090
425 Mission Ave. San Rafael CA 94901

Born: 1946 **Studied:** University of Tokyo; University of California at Berkeley **Awards:** Todos Santos Plaza International Competition, Concord CA **Notable Works:** Todos Santos Plaza, Concord CA; Villa with Ocean View, Half Moon Bay CA

Already a practicing architect in Japan before coming to the United States, his bicultural affinities set him apart from the design traditions of both countries. His work is bolder than most Japanese architecture, yet more sensuous and attentive to details than the American norm. His work is characterized by American-style clear and logical organization of spaces, yet his sense of the progression of spaces, of the continuously evolving human experience of architecture, recalls the elaborate arrangement of spaces in traditional Japanese gardens and buildings.

In his Villa with Ocean View in Half Moon Bay CA the visitor is led through a hallway to an atrium at the center of the house. With its lofty ceiling and skylights overlooking the sea the atrium room has a spiritual quality appropriate for both tranquil meditation and lively social gathering. Sited with a strong attraction to the ocean, the house is approached from the landward side. Visitors pass through an entry, then a skylit hallway, before the two-story great room overlooking the Pacific comes into view. The master bedroom is behind a gallery on a jutting mezzanine which gives out on the central windows; through the windows an exterior trim motif of ceramic tile and stucco continues in the trim of a courtyard fountain which stands between the house and the sea. Each room, and each vantage, thus experiences the water and the sea on ever changing terms.

TANAKA, TED TOKIO
(Building Design, Interior Architecture, Renovation, Furniture Design)
Ted T. Tanaka, Architect (213) 392-8521
41 Market St. Venice CA 90291

Born: 1942 **Studied:** Arizona State University **Awards:** California AIA; City of Beverly Hills **Notable Works:** Mineries Condominium, Venice CA; Ellman Apartments, Venice CA COMMERCIAL 50%, HOUSING 50%

His architectural goal is to contribute beauty to the environment while satisfying client needs. But beauty exists in rapport with the less beautiful that surrounds it; his designs reflect careful attention to the aesthetic needs of specific places. In Los Angeles a sometimes chaotic and ugly built environment suggests serene, simple and gentle designs. In his

Kusatsu, Japan ski resort the tranquility and beauty of the mountains permits stronger colors and more complex designs.

In his own Venice CA house he began with a 45 x 135-foot lot in an undramatic neighborhood. The house has few exterior windows but looks inward to a central courtyard which is planted in the Japanese manner. The property line too is planted, with bamboo trees for gentle privacy. The ceiling is punctured with twelve 4 x 4-foot skylights which fit into the house's grid frame, and in the living, dining and kitchen areas rises to 20 feet. White walls highlight his furniture designs, and in the living room a wall relief of his own design uses drywall and aluminum channels to form patterns reminiscent of Mondrian.

TAPLEY, CHARLES
(Building Design)
Charles Tapley Assoc. Inc. (713) 522-2776
1729 Sunset Blvd. Houston TX 77005

Studied: William Marsh Rice University **Awards:** FAIA; AIA **Notable Works:** Bethany Lutheran Church, Englewood CO; St. Rita Catholic Church, Dallas TX; Live Oaks Recreational Retreat, Rockport TX INSTITUTIONAL 50%, HOUSING 15%, COMMERCIAL 10%

His works are remarkable for their directness and use of basic shapes in a surprising but never showy manner. His buildings often draw upon vernacular forms and use light to define spaces.

The Saint Rita Catholic Church in Dallas TX is located on a campus surrounded by office buildings, adjacent to a tollway. To offset this less than pastoral setting he built the church facing the buildings with a plaza before it. The red brick church, with its low roof line, has a quiet solidity. Triangular stained glass windows and a crowning spire give it an upward sweep. The belltower, a high rectangular structure raised on squat columns, repeats the central gable's angles in the pitch of its roof. The church interior uses load-bearing masonry which sets off beams of exposed timber. Wooden pews wrap around the altar, making

the thousand-seat church more intimate.

Covenant Presbyterian Church on the western edge of Houston TX has an exterior of wood siding painted autumn sky-blue. The windows—narrow rectangles on the first floor, small portholes under the roof and thin gabled windows above—have been kept small to let in light without overheating the building. The interior, unembellished but for its golden oak floor, has an understated grace.

THIRY, PAUL
(Building Design, Exhibition Design, Planning)
Thiry Architects (206) 682-4483
800 Columbia Street Seattle
Washington 98104

Born: 1904 **Studied:** University of Washington, Seattle **Awards:** First Honor Medal, AIA, Seattle, 1984; Fellow, AIA; Academician, National Academy of Design **Notable Works:** Seattle Center Coliseum,; Libby Dam, Montana; Christ the King Church, Seattle

He's known for his pioneering work in prefabrication and his seminal Pacific Northwest-style public buildings and exhibition spaces. But his greatest renown is as a polemicist and evangelist for responsible building, renovation and urban expansion. America's obsession with 'progress,' he believes, has led to an often irrational urge to build and to build quickly. Too quickly; he argues that man's physical life can only be improved through architecture, which provides his environment.

For many years he served on the National Capital Planning Commission, routinely jetting between Washington State and Washington DC. His greatest victory as a preservationist was in 1966 when he staged a filibuster at the AIA national convention to table a resolution in favor of remodeling the West Front Wall of the Capitol Building. He also assisted the Army Corps of Engineers, a highly unusual client for a conservationist, in designing Montana's Libby Dam. His restraining wall worked as efficiently and cost-effectively as traditional designs with much less damage to site surroundings.

THOM, RONALD JAMES
(Building Design)
The Thom Partnership 47 Colborne Street Suite 101 Toronto Ontario m5e 1e3 Canada

Born: 1923 **Studied:** Vancouver School of Art **Awards:** Design Award, Canadian Institute of Architects, 1970; Merit Award, Canadian National Design Council, 1971; Fellow, Royal Architectural Institute of Canada **Notable Works:** Champlain College, Peterborough, Ontario; Massey College, University of Toronto; Metropolitan Toronto Zoo

He considers his responsibility as an architect to be acknowledging and encouraging the cohesion of the social fabric, and so combatting unplanned urban disorder. New buildings, he argues, must be designed with a view to the new degree of integration, overlap and interdependence in traditional "functions of living."

He's known for his meticulous attention to material selection, siting and accessory design—fixtures, doors, wastebaskets, table-settings, and furniture often elicit comparisons to Frank Lloyd Wright, but his work is more practical, less theory-laden than Wright's. His primary obligation is to the immediate needs of his clients and their tenants, and he doesn't concern himself with creating prototypes or principles for universal application. His first institutional commission, Massey College at the University of Toronto, set the tone for much of his later work. The main quadrangle turns its back to a nearby major intersection, reducing classroom and pedestrian annoyance. The main classroom space is broken into a number of house-sized brick buildings to maintain human scale. These 'houses,' further reduced by his trademark cubical recessions and setbacks, are grouped into a quiet shaded square.

THOMPSON, BENJAMIN
(Building Design, Interior Architecture, Master Planning)
Benjamin Thompson & Associates, Inc. (617) 876-4300

One Story Street Cambridge MA 02138

Born: 1918 **Studied:** Yale University School of Architecture **Awards:** FAIA; AIA Firm of the Year; International Union of Bricklayers and Allied Craftsmen Louis Sullivan Award **Notable Works:** Union Station renovation, Washington DC; South Street Seaport, New York City; Ordway Music Theatre, St. Paul MN COMMERCIAL AND RETAIL 50%, CULTURAL 20%, INSTITUTIONAL 15%, OFFICE 15%

As a gifted advocate no less than an inspired prophet, he's played a pivotal role in America's rediscovery and reinvention of its central cities. His early ideas for the "City of Man," integrating an architecture of joy and sensitivity into modern urban life, were first realized in Boston's Faneuil Hall Marketplace with developer James W. Rouse. He has since been commissioned across North America and western Europe to provide downtown destinations, social places and homes for a generation raised without urban idioms or experiences. Reacting to criticism that such marketplaces are sanitized city-Disneylands, the *Boston Globe's* Robert Campbell calls them "an impersonation of a kind of urban life that no longer exists, . . . a halfway house for people from the car culture who are trying to love cities again." His projects are awake to social as well as architectural history, creating safe places for spontaneity while turning a visionary's eye to what Thompson has called "the vast middle class slum created by business and bureaucratic indifference and sustained by public insensitivity."

Whether recycling historic waterfront buildings, as in Boston, New York, Dublin and London, or building new, vernacular-sensitive consumer gardens at water's edge as in Baltimore, Miami and Jacksonville FL, he uses human-scale detailing and merchandising, especially of diverse fast food, to create an unfolding sense of intimacy and excitement which is sympathetic with and open to the surrounding urban environment. His regard for urban vitality is no less apparent in other building types, for example his New York

University Law School city campus complex, the Performing Arts Center in Fort Lauderdale FL, and the acclaimed Ordway Music Theatre that has brought new life to downtown St. Paul MN.

TIGERMAN, FUGMAN, McCURRY (see McCurry, Margaret; Tigerman, Stanley)

TIGERMAN, STANLEY
(Building Design)
Tigerman, Fugman, McCurry Architects
(312) 644 5880
444 North Wells Street 2c
Chicago Illinois 60610

Born: 1930 **Studied:** Yale University **Awards:** Award of Merit, AIA, 1970; *Progressive Architecture* Award, 1980; Masonry Institute Award, 1982 **Notable Works:** Hard Rock Cafe, Chicago; Illinois Regional Library for the Blind and Physically Handicapped, Chicago; "Animal Crackers" (Blender House), Highland Park, Illinois   COMMERCIAL/RETAIL: 12%, HOUSING: 8%, INTERIOR DESIGN: 80%

His work is perhaps an architectural analog to the Pop Art of the 1960s and early 1970s. He's best known for a group of fancifully and often self-descriptively titled projects: Kosher Kitchen of a Suburban Jewish-American Princess, Hot Dog House and Zipper Townhouses are among his residential oeuvre. He shocks as often as he amuses; his Daisy House is in the shape of a human phallus, and his proposed Catholic cathedral included a series of confessional boxes which resembled the stalls of a public men's room.

For all his whimsy and irreverence, his career has been far from frivolous. In the early 1970s he brought new energy and finesse to Chicago's public housing pool with his largely vernacular designs for indigent and low-income low-rises. Later he addressed third-world poverty in a series of Bangladesh development efforts. Even in the heyday of Miesian minimalism his eclectic architecture won favor as well as comment. His recent work is moving toward large, simplified neo-classical spaces, solid yet theatrical. The low, boxy

facade of his Chicago Hard Rock Cafe, for example, is broken by a huge palladian window/doorway and capped with a central domed rotunda.

TIMME, ROBERT
(Building Design)
Taft Architects (713) 522-2988
807 Peden St. Houston TX 77006

Studied: Rice University **Awards:** AIA; *Interiors* magazine "40 under 40" Honoree; Texas AIA **Notable Works** (also see John Casbarian & Danny Samuels): Grove Court Condominiums, Houston TX; Fat Franks Restaurant, Houston TX; Talbot House, Nevis, West Indies

His work is a collaborative effort with the other principals of Taft Architects. Their common discovery of a native Texan vernacular has tempered their earlier belief in self-sustaining abstract ordering systems, and led them to reinterpret older types. Their work doesn't refer directly to history, but rather has to do with continuity of issues and appropriateness of attitudes.

An example of the continuity and tradition in context is their award-winning Talbot House, sited halfway up Nevis Peak on the island of Nevis, overlooking the Caribbean Sea. The house employs a Palladian organizational system adapted from British colonial architecture on the island. Four two-story structures of locally cut stone define a central pavilion. In place of a central dome there is a pyramidal ceiling oriented to the four horizons. The motif is taken up by four corner pavilions and emphasized by cross-bracing that also points to the four views, while allowing for cross ventilation in all spaces. A major concern was the relationship of private spaces for individuals in the corner structures to the central living space where the whole family congregates. A sense of family structure is imparted by channeling people through the family space before they enter private areas. Bright, traditional colors are used: complementary red-orange for the roofs and blue-green for window trim and exterior wood; lighter cream colors for the

Hugh Stubbins, *Berlin Congress Hall*, West Germany.

Benjamin Thompson (with Jane Thompson), *Fulton Market, South Street Seaport,* New York City, 1983. Associates-in-Charge: Bruno D'Agostino and Philip Loheed. Project Architect: John Shank. Photo: Steve Rosenthal

stone structures and darker ones for the central pavilions. Patterned floral bands are hand-stenciled along the ceilings of each room.

TOD WILLIAMS, BILLIE TSIEN AND ASSOCIATES (see Tsien, Billie; Williams, Tod)

TORRE, SUSANA
(Building Design, Renovation)
Torre Beeler and Associates (212) 334-3625
270 Lafayette Street New York NY 10012

Born: 1944 **Studied:** Columbia University **Awards:** NEA Individual Fellowship in Architecture; NEA Grant in Architecture and Environmental Arts **Notable Works:** Fire Station #5, Columbus IN; Schermerhorn Hall renovation, Columbia University, New York City

Her buildings often reconcile apparent contrasts, such as public spaces with private spaces, open areas with closed, and vernacular styles with innovative shapes. When renovating she looks not to the style of the original building but to its underlying rhythm and proportion.

Fire Station #5 in Columbus IN is a symmetrical structure of concrete-block walls covered with beige brick and exposed, gray-painted steel frames. Two cylinders of the same radius serve as foils to the building's U-shape. One cylinder, alongside the building, is used to hang hoses to dry. The other cylinder, in the opening of the U, houses stairs which wrap around the fireman's pole.

For her renovation of a portion of Schermerhorn Hall on the Columbia campus in New York City, she found in the original 1896 plans a pattern of overlapping grids. Her floor and ceiling patterns reinforce the original design scheme. The original lobby and stairs had been destroyed by an earlier renovation. She created a lobby and marble-clad staircase leading to the mezzanine level, opening up what had been a closed-in vestibule. Globes of light held by columns and brass rails restore some of the grandeur of the original structure.

TSIEN, BILLIE
Tod Williams, Billie Tsien and Associates Architects (212) 582-2385

222 Central Park South New York NY

Born: 1949 **Studied:** Brown University; University of California at Los Angeles **Awards:** "40 under 40" Honoree, *Interiors* magazine; Design Arts Program Grant, National Endowment for the Arts **Notable Works:** Spiegel pool house NY; Whitney Museum of American Art, New York City

Spartan and rigorous, her work is in a Postmodern vein, enthused by bold uses of industrial materials and imaginative detailing. Working in artistic liaison with fellow principal Tod Williams, they highlighted the downtown Whitney Museum's inconspicuous location by positioning a 20-foot high marker column at the base of an escalator. The classic boxy plan of the building is tempered by detail gestures. On entering, one crosses an aluminum-plate threshold that leads into a cantilevered balcony which overlooks the entire gallery. Traffic then descends a slightly splayed stair to arrive at an aluminum-clad information desk with its own cantilevered projection.

Their Spiegel pool house was designed to accommodate a mural of three pyramids by a New York painter. The pool house is entered through a small Oriental courtyard. Water from a round pool on a raised platform flows into a lap pool, faced in granite. The mural is on a stuccoed wall on one side of the pool. In contrast, aluminum-gridded windows are on another wall, which abuts a stainless-steel one. Colors used—browns, purple, lush blue, rich aqua mire for the pool itself—are somber and in counterpoint to the crystalline glass. At night, lights embedded in the sides of the pool illuminate the painting with an eerie glow.

TUCK HINTON EVERTON ARCHITECTS (see Everton, Gary; Hinton, Kem Gardner; Tuck, Seab A. III)

TUCK, SEAB A. III
(Building Design, Architectural Delineation, Facility Programming, Renovation)
Tuck Hinton Everton Architects
(615) 320-1810
1810 Hayes St. Nashville TN 37203

William Turnbull, Jr., *The American Club,* 1987, Hong Kong

Born: 1952 **Studied:** Auburn University **Awards:** Tennessee AIA; Builder's Choice Grand Prize; Gulf States AIA **Notable Works:** Riverfront Apartments, Nashville TN; Mandrell Residence, Nashville TN; Skyhigh Residence, Monteagle TN RESIDENTIAL 30%, OFFICE 25%, COMMERCIAL 20%

He says that "each program is an organization of various functions (room, circulation, entry), while each building is an assembly of various parts (roof, wall, structure). Our projects typically separate these functions and parts, and exhibit them in a manner that may manipulate the sequence of entry, exhibit a sense of organization, or many times allude to a historical reference."

His Riverfront Apartments, a housing complex on the site of a long industrial shed which formerly housed an ironworks, capitalizes on river views and begins the renaissance of an abandoned light industrial area near downtown Nashville TN. The shed, which over the years had grown bay by bay, was stripped of its rusted metal siding, cleaned, and retained as a covered shelter for housing units. Its original ironwork was sandblasted and painted, and ventilation fans and sash units were left in place. Transformers from the site are also refinished, and are stationed like sentinels at the ends of the complex. Textured block screen walls and stairs are offset by metal grillwork symbolic of the products once made in the shed. Projecting catwalk bridges—access elements for earlier overhead cranes—are salvaged as well. The apartments project out from the shed, addressing the river directly. At the north end a cluster of courtyard units focuses on a 180-foot chimney, a remnant from a city incinerator which abuts a river bridge. The composition creates a portal for the new residential community.

TUCKER, JAMES F.

(Construction Administration, Design, Interior Architecture, Renovation)
James F. Tucker, AIA, Architect
(703) 347-3451
15 S. Fifth St. Warrenton VA 22186

Born: 1946 **Studied:** Virginia Polytechnic Institute **Awards:** Awards of Honor, Northern Virginia AIA **Notable Works:** Tenant House, Washington VA; Springfield Farm Guest House, Middleburg VA RELIGIOUS 35%, HOUSING 25%, COMMERCIAL 20%, CIVIC 20%

His designs begin with basic, inexpensive materials appropriate to his rural setting. His low-maintenance and economical structures use form rather than material to achieve design effects, and tend to stress beauty of proportion rather than refinement.

His Springfield Farm Guest House is a renovated stone outbuilding, actually an old icehouse cut into a farm hillside. The farm is laced with "slave walls," fences of local stone, and the Guest House adjoins old stone stock pens which had been covered in wood. His restoration concentrates on peacefully integrating the dilapidated building back into its surroundings: The stone walls of the ground floor, still flecked with old peeling whitewash, are left to age as they are, while the upper story is renovated in the local stuccoed-wood style to match its nearby farmhouse. Adjoining stock pen walls are stripped down to stone, reconnecting them to the farm fabric, and the lower walls are pierced carefully to let in light. Throughout he uses a restrained palette and indigenous materials—tin roof, stone, stucco—to hold the new old building in its gentle landscape.

TURNBULL, WILLIAM JR.

(Building Design, Planning)
William Turnbull Architects (415) 986-3642
Pier 1-1/2 The Embarcadero
San Francisco California 94111

Born: 1935 **Studied:** Princeton University **Awards:** Award of Honor, AIA, East Bay, 1983; Design Award, American Wood Council, 1984; Fellow, AIA **Notable Works:** Johnson House, Sea Ranch, California; Embarcadero Center Theater, San Francisco; Corte Madero Plan, Corte Madero, California COMMERCIAL/RETAIL: 10%, HOUSING: 55%, INTERIOR DESIGN: 10%, PLAN-

Herbert Umemura, *Hyatt Regency Waikoloa* (interior), 1988, Hawaii.

NING: 20%

He, like his associates, Donlyn Lyndon and Charles Moore, believes that his buildings must provide more than just shelter for some specific set of activities. He tries to make buildings which celebrate the individual, and give voice to very human aspirations — and even foibles — in an increasingly mechanistic age. Like many California architects, he also emphasizes the need to look to the site for design resources and constraints: to take what the land can give and respect what it will not give.

His buildings, he says, begin with a conceptual idea, an insight into a client's explicit and unspoken desires. His 1975 Zimmerman House arose from two very different concepts. The husband, Mr. Zimmerman wanted an open, airy house, built from a loose agglomeration of large, sunny rooms. Mrs. Zimmerman, however, pined for wide, shady porches of her New England childhood. The two ideas seemed incommensurable, for a conventional porch would cut off much of Mr. Zimmerman's prized sunlight. His novel design solution was to treat the entire house as a gazebo — or as he called it, a "grand porch" — covered with a translucent fiberglass roof, and framed with a 1x 4 system of latticework to filter the light entering the insulated 'interior' area.

TURNER, ROBERT
(Building Design, Planning)
Skidmore, Owings and Merril 441-930-9711
Devonshire House 9th Flr Mayfair Place, London WIX-F11 England

Born: 1947 **Studied:** Virginia Polytechnic Institute **Awards:** American Institute of Steel Construction award **Notable Works:** Canary Wharf, London; Morrow Dam Powerhouse, MI; Southwest Crossing, Eden Prairie MN

Considering "design by nature" to be inefficient, he goes over and over projects, working through inevitable mistakes to devise a vocabulary that will intrinsically express the unique qualities of a given program. In his master plan and infrastructure of London's three billion dollar Canary Wharf, he plans for

traffic circulation patterns on two street levels for an anticipated 8,000 cars a day, and provides garage and service access below grade while permitting general traffic around the circus at grade. With SOM partner Adrian Smith he designed Southwest Crossing in suburban Eden Prairie MN with an idea of heightening an illusion of thickness on exterior walls. Windows are surrounded with precast panels that provide extra articulation in a manner similar to limestone surrounds. An atrium continues the scheme of graceful articulation with dramatically stepped back side walls and an elegant main staircase.

UMEMURA, ROBERT K.
(Building Design)
Lawton & Umemura Architects, AIA, Inc.
(808) 529-9700
No. 1 Capitol District Honolulu HI 96813

Born: 1941 **Studied:** University of Hawaii **Awards:** AIA **Notable Works:** Hyatt Regency Waikoloa, Kona Coast, Hawaii; Jimmy Carter Presidential Library and Museum, Atlanta GA; Hyatt Regency Maui, Hawaii RESORT HOTELS 90%

Resort visitors usually hope to experience fantasies rather than outstanding architecture. So the resort designs he and partner Herbert Lawton create for developer Chris Hemmeter aim above all to give tourists the experiences they have saved and longed for; architecture is one component of an experience which also uses breathtaking landscaping, wildlife and art.

His Hyatt Regency Waikoloa on the west coast of the Big Island of Hawaii is designed as a series of experiences that continually excite wonder. The resort airport is located on an enormous black lava field, and the 20-minute drive across it to the resort entrance is an exercise in suspended expectation. Then the resort gates and a winding, increasingly landscaped drive to a porte-cochere gradually raise interest, which is again suspended by a low-roofed entrance and low-key front desk at the door. But from here visitors can glimpse boats passing through the hotel lobby; suddenly the

Dean Unger, *Davis Science Center*, Davis, California. Photo: Angie Salbosa

Francisco J. Urrutia, *Urrutia Professional Building.* Photo: Arthur Coleman

roof soars to 65 feet. Below it a 75-foot wide stairway spills down to a lagoon in which dolphins and swimmers play. Trellises hung with huge vines soar above the stairs. The three towers of the 1244-room resort are connected by a covered museum walkway which is lined with art, display niches containing artifacts from across the Pacific Basin, and large display rooms. Tired visitors also have the choice of riding one of 14 boats or two trams which also pass through the lobby to the towers. A man-made lagoon, waterfalls, dolphins and tropical menagerie have emphatic pride of place in this design, which is fully open to sea, sky and lagoon on its monumental side—not even storm winds could blow through the lobby unless it were open on both sides. So there are practical reasons too for the gentle, low-key beginnings to this carefully unforgettable resort experience.

UNGER, DEAN F.
(Building Design)
Dean F. Unger AIA Inc. (916) 443-5747
700 Alhambra Blvd. Sacramento CA 95816

Born: 1928 **Studied:** University of California at Berkeley **Awards:** FAIA **Notable Works:** Yolo County Administration Building, Woodland CA; Alkalai Flat Family Housing COMMERCIAL 50%, INSTITUTIONAL 50%

His work reflects the diverse architectural and natural history of northern California and his own predilection for warm and inviting materials and forms. Bernard Maybeck and Green and Green are strong influences, having created the best of the built heritage into which he integrates his designs. His Yolo County Administration Center highlights as well an awareness of natural and cultural diversity, exemplified in a cost-effective way. The Center is built around a below-grade, energy efficient atrium with walls of adobe-like slumpstone (an extruded concrete block). The three-story Center thus gives striking internal effects without dominating its surrounding neighbors. Douglas fir timbers and tile floors warm the interior space, which features platform stairs

and an adjacent glass elevator which both mount to a glass clerestory which helps to light the interior.

Atrium space is used for exhibits, receptions and musical events as well as access to county meetings of all kinds. The Supervisor's Chambers feature segregated access to and from the atrium, which has become a separate focus of animation day and night.

URRUTIA, FRANCISCO J.
(Construction Administration, Design) Urrutia Architects (619) 341-2555
73550 Alessandro Dr. Suite 1
Palm Desert CA 92260

Born: 1945 **Studied:** California State Polytechnic University; University of Florence, Italy **Awards:** Pacific Coast Builders Conference Home of the Year Award; Modern Healthcare/AIA Citation Award **Notable Works:** Barbara Sinatra Children's Center, Rancho Mirage CA; Vintage Club Patio Homes, Indian Wells CA HOUSING 65%, MEDICAL 25%, COMMERCIAL 10%

His desert environment creates unique program requirements. Indigenous materials here last much longer than customary ones, and the unique cooling requirements of the desert can pit him against the statewide California Title 24 Energy Conservation Act, which addresses the common problem of heat loss rather than the desert problem of heat *gain*. Working around its sometimes inappropriate system he designs total living environments, integrating inside and out through the flow of materials, sight lines and light. Landscaping and interior design are reciprocal specialties in this approach to total design.

His interest in appropriate desert design is apparent in his Rancho Mirage model post office which integrates both natural and cultural geographies in energy-efficient ways. Payback studies indicated that a completely photo-voltaic facility wouldn't be cost-effective. But between the hours of 10 A.M. and 3 P.M., when the summer sun creates peak demands for expensive cooling electricity, the facility cools itself entirely with photo-voltaic energy. Water is cooled almost to freezing with nighttime energy when electricity is cheaper, and stored in a large buried water tank. The cooling water water is circulated through the building during the day with photovoltaic power. The $250,000 cost of the system that generates and stores this energy is repaid by rebates and power savings over five years.

VALERIO, JOSEPH
(Building Design)

His Arbour Park in Tempe AZ illustrates how good design can compensate for awkward sites and provide flare and drama—Arbour Park is easily distinguished from neighboring medium-priced rental apartment complexes. Nine three-story buildings form three triangles on the thin rectangular lot. The hypotenuses of these triangles create its street facade, which is broken by circular entry courts whose form derives from the curved end walls of the buildings. The buildings, wood frame with reinforced masonry and concrete foundations, radiate from these entry courts. Parking spaces are set outside the triangles and out of view. From balconies or terraces, residents overlook one of the triangular courts which have as their focus either a swimming pool or volleyball court. Additional recreational facilities include a weight room, tennis and racquetball courts, a track, a fitness trail, and a party hall.

VECSEI, EVA
(Building Design, Planning)
Vecsei Architects 1405 Bishop Street Montreal Quebec H3G 2E4 Canada

Born: 1935 **Studied:** University of Technical Sciences, Budapest **Awards:** Massey Architecture Award; Award of Excellence, *The Canadian Architect*, Toronto, 1983 **Notable Works:** Place Bonadventure, Montreal; La Cité, Montreal; City Centre Master Plan, Karachi, Pakistan (with John Schrieber)

She played key design roles in two of the world's largest and most ambitious mixed-use complexes, Montreal's 1960 Place Bonaventure and 1977 La Cité. Her designs arise, she says, in response to the need for a more stimulating Modernism. Mies van der Rohe, she has written, taught the elegance and beauty of simplicity, and the thrift of modules and repetitions. But without a greater accent on the senses these are empty virtues. Her buildings have forsaken the flat, uniform envelopes of the International Style for massing schemes that communicate the identities and functions of their parts, and leave room for restrained ornament. La Cité incorporates three 30-story residential towers, a 500-room luxury hotel, a 25-story office tower, and a two-level, 200,000-square-foot retail area. The residential buildings, with 1350 units, are sculpted, stepped-back 'half-pyramids' which are interconnected by the commercial substructure. The landscaped roofs of the retail section are divided into a number of public and semi-private spaces.

VENTURI, RAUCH AND SCOTT BROWN (see Rauch, John; Scott Brown, Denise; Venturi, Robert; Wallace, David)

VENTURI, ROBERT
(Building Design, Planning)
Venturi, Rauch and Scott Brown
4236 Main Street Philadelphia 19127

Born: 1925 **Studied:** Princeton University **Awards:** FAIA; Design Award, *Progressive Architecture*; 1967; Honor Award and Medal, National AIA **Notable Works:** Guild House, Philadelphia; Vanna Venturi House, Philadelphia; Wu Hall, Princeton University, Princeton, New Jersey

He is one of the nation's most vehement and incisive polemicists for architectural pluralism and pragmatic realism, and one of the most energetic and imitated builders of the post-war epoch. His landmark text *Complexity and Contradiction in Architecture* (1967) laid firm intellectual ground for a move past the idealized, exclusivist credo of American functionalism, and toward an eclectic, unfussy 'architecture that works'.

"Main street," he has written, "is almost night." There is more to be learned from the chaotic, often rococo building legacy of the baby boom, he argues in *Learning From Las Vegas*, than the stark, cool towers of the International School; "Less," he says, "is a bore." The 'ordinary' structures that middle class America has built for itself, he believes are vastly more functional than the majority of academic modernist efforts, in that they attend to creative comforts without embarrassment or pretension.

Surprisingly, he rejects the conscious historicism of the post-modern camp, and works toward an architecture that will embody the functionalistic rigour of modernism, while dispensing with its hidden minimalistic agenda. His 1960 Guild House, an apartment complex for the elderly, for instance, he worked analytically from the real needs and concerns of the housebound occupants. The polite symmetry of the main facade is sacrificed to ungainly rows of large, industrial window units to draw the sun and facilitate street watching. At the buildings too is a huge, segmented, semi-circular window which lights a commodities television lounge. The central importance of this 'coarse' entertainment is humorously underscored by an enormous gold-plated antenna which performs a purely symbolic ceremonial function at the crest of the building's roof.

VINCI, JOHN

(Historical Preservation, Building Design, Exhibition Design)
John Vinci Inc. (312) 733-7744
1147 West Ohio Chicago Il 60622

Born: 1937 **Studied:** Illinois Institute of Technology **Notable Works:** Auditorium Building Restoration, Chicago; Chicago Stock Exchange Trading Room Reconstruction, Chicago RESTORATION 50%, COMMERCIAL 20%, OTHER 30%

Since the mid-sixties he has been known as one of America's most sensitive and prolific restorationists. His first experience in historical preservation/restoration came during his very brief apprenticeship at Skidmore, Owings and Merrill, when he became involved in efforts to preserve the original ornamentation

of Adler and Sullivan's Garrick Theater (Chicago). Shortly later he undertook a number of important beaux-arts restorations, including Richard Schmidt's Madlener House (now the Graham Foundation Building). Since founding his own practice in 1977, he has reworked such landmark buildings as Frank Lloyd Wright's Heller, Tomek and Millard Houses; and Adler and Sullivan's Auditorium Theater, Charnley Residence and Carson Pirie Scott and Company retail headquarters

He has also been a frequent designer of exhibition installations for Chicago's Art Institute (whose Burnham Gallery he renovated in 1979). He currently serves on the Landmarks Preservation Board of the Chicago Historical and Architectural Landmarks Commission.

WALLACE, DAVID A.

(Building Design, Urban Design,Planning)
Wallace Roberts and Todd (215) 732-5215
1737 Chestnut Street Philadelphia
Pennsylvania

Born: 1917 **Studied:** Harvard University **Awards:** Design Award, *Progressive Architecture*, 1973; Fellow, AIA; Member, Board of Governors, American Institute of Planners **Notable Works:** Charles Center Master Plan, Baltimore; Liberty State Park Master Plan, Jersey City, New Jersey; Mission Bay Master Plan, San Francisco COMMERCIAL/RETAIL: 20%, HOUSING: 5%, INSTITUTIONAL: 8%, LANDSCAPE ARCHITECTURE: 12%: 10%, PLANNING: 30%, WATERFRONT DESIGN: 17%

As supervising planner for the Chicago Housing Authority and director of planning for the Philadelphia Redevelopment Authority in the early 1950s, he received an education by fire in the intricacies and irrationalities of American urban government. Joining the Planning Department of the University of Pennsylvania in 1961, he began to elaborate the comprehensive planning approach with which the school has become widely identified.

This approach, which he field tested through his firm, centers on the application of "scientific rigor" to the usually amorphous urban design process. A broad-based project begins with environmental analysis, often supplemented by detailed sociographic and demographic studies. Effective planning, he argues, requires predicting collective human behavior as well as can possibly be done. Though quantitative methods are notoriously unreliable in predicting human psychology and behavior, his projects evince a powerful command of crowd dynamics. His Inner Harbor Plan for Baltimore MD, which he began in 1964 and whose influence continues, is a model for effectively converting decrepit maritime areas into multi-use public park land.

WARNECKE, JOHN CARL
(Building Design, Planning)
John Carl Warnecke and Associates
(415) 397-4200
417 Montgomery Street San Francisco
California 94104

Born: 1919 **Studied:** Harvard University **Awards:** FAIA; Brunner Prize, National Institutes of Arts and Letters; Member, National Commission on the Fine Arts **Notable Works:** Hawaii State Capitol, Honolulu (with Belt, Lemmon and Lo); United States Court of Claims Building, Washington, D.C.; George Washington University, Washington, D.C. COMMERCIAL/RETAIL: 35%, HOUSING: 16%, INTERIOR DESIGN: 4%, EDUCATION: 25%, PLANNING: 5%, MEDICAL: 10%

His work is a curious blend of Beaux-Arts neoclassicism, Bauhaus Modernism and Far Eastern exoticism. He completed his graduate studies under Walter Gropius at Harvard, but his apprenticeship at his father's 'old-school' firm of Miller and Warnecke may have had a stronger influence. He has emerged as a charismatic, virtuoustic artisan, capable both of sensitive, contextually conscious design and renovation, and of architectural exhibitionism. His friendship with John F. Kennedy led to a number of sensitive commissions for the renovation of historic government buildings such as the Federal National Mortgage Association and the construction of other capital-area projects. In this period he established himself as a committed, persistent and accomplished preservationist. At the same time he completed several controversial public commissions with heavy Oriental overtones. His unbuilt design for the American Embassy in Thailand, whose pagoda-like roof and stilt foundation drew heavily from the Thai vernacular, first brought him critical attention. His 1969 Hawaii State Capitol went even farther outside the stylistic mainstream, replacing the traditional capitol dome with a volcano-shaped cone. It is his Mabel Elementary School, in Columbus IN where his Far Eastern motifs were most controversial. Columbus residents complain that the schoolhouse, touted as a historic gloss on Columbus's stately Victorian residences, looks more like a Japanese bordello than a Midwestern house.

WARNER, WILLIAM D.
(Design, Urban Design and Planning)
William D. Warner, Architects and Planners, Ltd. (401) 295-8851
Locust Valley Farm, Exeter RI 02822

Born: 1929 **Studied:** Massachusetts Institute of Technology **Awards:** FAIA; First Place, NEA Eugene O'Neill Provincetown Theatre Competition, MA; National AIA award jurist **Notable Works:** Bancroft School, Andover MA; New Pierce School, Brookline MA; Providence Waterfront Study, RI INSTITUTIONAL 33%, HOUSING 33%, URBAN DESIGN AND PLANNING 33%

He is an original regionalist, taking inspiration from familiar New England forms and materials and adapting them to precise program requirements. His buildings are often reminiscent of New England barns or brick mills which might be punctuated with lighthouse-like towers, dormer windows, porches and public clocks. Materials are usually local: load-bearing masonry, brick and exposed timber.

His open-space Bancroft School draws its inspiration from a wider source: the world of children. It resembles a child's house built of blocks, and aims to draw children into easy intimacy with it. It's conceived as a collection of blocks connected by an overlaying roof, so outdoor masonry walls continue through the doorways, flow around the corridor corners and back outside. Wide overhanging eaves shelter the front doors where children wait for buses; the children often sit in circles of block arches made, as in children's architecture, by setting one arch block atop another upside-down one. Kindergarten rooms feature low-gabled alcoves that teachers must stoop to enter, creating a safe place for children to play house. The school is conceived as three houses grouped around an open resource center which is split level, giving access to open classrooms up and down its stairs. These wide stairs giving access to classrooms become amphitheater seating for the classrooms themselves, which are lined up in connecting U shapes. At the corners are classroom towers containing specialty rooms—shop, art room, even a science-class greenhouse. All structural, mechanical and electrical elements of the school are geometrically organized, color coded and left exposed.

WEBER, HANNO

(Building Design, Urban Design)
Hanno Weber and Associates (312) 922-5589
417 South Dearborn Street Chicago IL 60605

Born: 1937 **Studied:** Princeton University **Awards:** Chicago AIA; First Place, West Palm Beach Waterfront Design Competition; First Place, Municipal Government Center, Leesburg VA **Notable Works:** Altamira Terrace, Highland Park FL; Market Square Adaptive Reuse, Lake Forest IL INSTITUTION 45%, COMMERCIAL 45%, HOUSING 10%

His buildings are 'good neighbors,' influenced by context and climate but not mimicking surrounding structures. They tend to merge into their surroundings. Altamira Terrace, a retirement housing development and golf club in Highland Park FL, takes its cue from pre-existing vernacular Florida resort buildings, employing stucco and tile roofs and incorporating a courtyard. But new units are larger than the old ones, built in the twenties. New windows use the same proportions as pre-existing windows, with different designs and arrangements. Stucco walls, well underneath the roof in the original structures, are now extended beyond the roof and topped with parapets.

His plan for the Leesburg VA Municipal Government Center calls for structures in keeping with the town's colonial history which have all the modern amenities. A 400-car precast garage is hidden by other structures and surrounded by arcades. In the Town Hall all the features in public view, such as large wooden baseboards and profiled molding around door frames, fits in with colonial styles. Out of the public eye are current materials and construction such as acoustical tiles, air conditioning and suspended indirect light fixtures.

WEESE, BENJAMIN

(Building Design, Urban Design)

Born: 1929 **Studied:** Harvard University **Awards:** NEA Grant **Notable Works:** Kenwood Gardens Townhouse, Chicago; Master Plans for the Lincoln Park Zoo, Chicago; Drake University, Des Moines; Cornell College, Mt. Vernon, IA; Illinois Wesleyan University Chapel, Bloomington, Illinois

He has developed a number of forceful architectural concepts, chief among them the idea of "minimum perimeter," exemplified by the Lake Village East project. By developing a uniform design that approaches a full circle, he creates a successful, even striking, structure, while still making economical and efficient use of construction materials and space. He is adept at university design—both buildings and overall layout—especially at rural universities, such as Cornell College and Illinois Wesleyan. His design for a Methodist chapel at Illinois Wesleyan consciously imitates the unadorned, Puritan style of the small-town New England church and meeting hall, down to the use of very basic materials. The arched entrance is echoed by smaller windows that run along the sides of the building. The bell tower fittingly caps the design.

William D. Warner, *Bancroft Elementary School,* Andover, Massachusetts. Photo: Randolph Lagenbach

Paul Whitehead, *Board Room for the Hawthorne Group*

A strong proponent of the preservation of older buildings, he developed a manual for the National Trust for Historic Preservation and received a grant to from the National Endowment for the Arts to examine the problems and possibilities in preserving historic buildings.

WEESE, CYNTHIA
(Building Design)

Born: 1940 **Studied:** Washington University **Awards:** Distinguished Building Award, Chicago AIA **Notable Works:** South Shore National Bank, Chicago; Cornell College Science Building, Mt. Vernon, IA; Kuntz Residence, Wayne, IL; Chestnut Place Apartments, Chicago; Apartments, 100 Chestnut St., Chicago

The towering sister apartment buildings on Chestnut Street in Chicago for which she has served as project architect play off of each other in designs whose overall forms are similar but whose details diverge in important ways. The Chestnut Place building is perhaps the more visually striking of the two, with its dramatic staggered bay windows and Postmodern top. But the building, like many modern apartment designs, is imposing and impersonal at street level, with its commercial-use first floor shops and windowless parking garage. In fact, the limited window space overall is a slightly unsettling feature, although the bays do allow each residence a "corner view." The sister structure at 100 West Chestnut recapitulates many of the earlier building's features, such as the red-brick facing and small windows. The bays, however, are cut at a more severe angle—ninety degrees. But the ground floor is occupied by the building's offices, whose windows are at waist level with pedestrians. The gray parking garage is set off behind the building by a red brick medical center. These features, plus the improved landscaping, give the building a more residential, more human feel than its sister. Overall, the use of red brick is sympathetic with the older two- and three-story residential and commercial structures on Chestnut and with the Moody Bible Institute buildings at LaSalle Street that anchor the several blocks, creating a nice red-brick residential neighborhood.

Her expertise in residential buildings can be seen in other designs as well, such as the award-winning Kuntz Residence, with its centralized common areas, cone-roofed bays and long lines in the Prairie School tradition.

WEESE, HARRY MOHR
(Building Design, Planning)
Harry Weese and Associates (312) 467-7030 10 West Hubbard Street Chicago Illinois 60610

Born: 1915 **Studied:** M.I.T. **Awards:** FAIA; Merit Award, American Society of Landscape Architects, 1981; Merit Award, AIA, D.C. Chapter, 1983 **Notable Works:** Hawaii State Capitol, Honolulu (with Belt, Lemmon and Lo); United States Court of Claims Building, Washington, D.C.; George Washington University, Washington, D.C. COMMERCIAL/RETAIL: 30%, HOUSING: 7%, INTERIOR DESIGN: 5%, EDUCATION: 5%, TRANSPORTATION: 40%

Although he has often argued that the main responsibility of architecture is innovation, his own work is typified by a thorough, perfectionist attention to design details. His success derives from his willingness to suspend all technical and aesthetic preconceptions and approach each design problem freshly.

His 1967 renovation of Louis Sullivan and Dankmar Adler's landmark Auditorium Theater in his native Chicago launched a long and distinguished career as a preservationist. His gift for designing and reworking dignified, substantial public buildings led to his appointment as chief architect for Washington DC's rail transit system. The fundamental challenge of that commission, he felt, was to establish a uniform and quickly identifiable style for the system's wide variety of terminals. This style would extend beyond mere cosmetics to include the commuter's entire sequence of experiences. His ingenious solution was to design a set of functional station sub-units which individual designers could shuffle as needed, and so create custom yet cost-effective terminals.

WEINGARTEN, DAVID

Ace Architects (415) 658-2543
Hieroglyph Building 5237 College Avenue
Oakland CA 94618

Studied: Yale University; University of California at Berkeley **Awards:** Interiors magazine "40 under 40" Honoree; First Prize, Japan Architect International Shinkenchiku Residential Design Competition; First Prize, Architectural League "Site, Scale and Spectacle" Competition **Notable Works** (also see Lucia Howard): Country, Pier 39, San Francisco CA; Brick Row Book Shop, San Francisco CA; Figaro Cafe, Oakland CA

Considered renegade by their former professors, he and co-principal Lucia Howard seek to revive through their architecture the conventional and public nature of symbolism. To this end they deliberately conflate categories of good taste and bad, logic and unreason, decent and indecent, hoping thereby to commend attention to the buildings that we look at and inhabit. They wish to make architecture representational, and believe that the archetype can be teased out of the ordinary. In their forthcoming book, *The Shock of Recognition*, they write, "We prefer architecture more as costume than as theater. . . .It is in their specificity, literalness and appropriateness that costumes are effective. . . .Our aim is to make buildings intimately suited to the client. . .Towards this aim, ours is a literal, as opposed to abstract architecture. It is an architecture comprised of the recognizable, and relying on the familiar. It is an architecture of remembered forms, experiences, thoughts and feelings. Our buildings are fashioned from these costumes stitched together. Within these resides the potential for the shock of recognition."

Their Figaro Ice Cream Parlor in Oakland CA features a Mexican arch motif, repeated inside and multiplied by mirrors, as are interior obelisks. The overworked design is in their estimation only a restatement of the commercial vernacular. To bring out the "sensually potent essences of everyday artifacts and experiences" they use techniques of "simplification, exaggeration and incantation." A landscape of archetypes—obelisks, Palladian walls, the Italian flag, white chairs and tables—simplification and exaggeration—endlessly repeated by mirrors, the effect is to conjure a landscape which encourages the metamorphosis of espresso and gelati into idea and sensation.

WEINSTEIN, RICHARD S.

(Planning, Building Design)
Richard S. Weinstein Associates 200 Park Avenue Suite 3024 New York NY 10017

Born: 1932 **Studied:** Columbia University **Awards:** Member, Architectural League of New York; Member, Visiting Committee, Harvard Graduate School of Design **Notable Works:** Twin Parks Urban Renewal Plan, Bronx, New York; Master Plan for Park Central, Dallas, Texas; Plan for Floyd Bennett Field, Gateway National Recreation Area, New York

Modern architecture, he believes, has been increasingly shaped by the effect of institutions. So, if they would function effectively, architects must be well versed in the economic, political and legal processes.

In 1967 he suspended a successful career in building design to join New York Mayor John Lindsay's Urban Design group. While serving as Director of Development for Lower Manhattan he created a system of development districts in which the allocation of zoning variances was used to encourage builders and owners to coordinate long-term efforts with city planners and to plan for more architecturally homogeneous and culturally diverse projects. Lower Manhattan was broken into four zoning areas—Lincoln Square, Manhattan Waterfront, Greenwich Street and the Theater District—with distinctly different long-term incremental planning agendas.

In private practice he has helped many cities establish similar voluntary zoning districts and conventions, although it's still too early to assess the effectiveness of his segmented development approach in New York. He has become a major advocate for public/private-sector collaboration—what he calls "venture philanthropy." He has recently established a non-profit corporation, New Sources of Funding, to help cultural institutions to capitalize on overlooked air rights and other hidden real-estate assets.

WERNER, WILLIAM ARNO
(Interior Architecture, Building Design, Research Facility Design)
Werner & Sullivan (415) 986-3311
207 Powell Street 800   San Francisco CA 94102

Born: 1937 **Studied:** Yale School of Architecture **Awards:** Northern California Design; Dupont Antron Design Award; *Progressive Architecture* design award **Notable Works:** Jessie Street Substation, San Francisco; Touche Ross & Company, Oakland CA COMMERCIAL 50%, OFFICE 40%, RETAIL 10%

His belief that all good architecture stems from a unique relationship between architect, client, site and project results in many designs highly responsive to their surroundings.

His recent Alameda Credit Union in Alameda CA translates the gentle scale and proportions of the small Victorian maritime community into a contemporary office/commercial structure by eliminating much design bric-a-brac and exposing the "muscle" beneath. Although retaining detailed door and window trim in response to the surrounding turn-of-the-century buildings, and adding some ceramic tile inserts on moulding, the two-story building displays its modernity in its energy-efficiency and its drive-thru gate which bisects the ground floor leading to a rear parking lot.

Typical of his interior design work is the US Postal Service's Rincon Finance Station in San Francisco. Programmed as a replacement for the adjacent historic post office which was sold to developers, it is situated on the ground floor of twin 25-story office towers. It's designed to look like a building tucked within a building. Artificial stucco walls, ornate lighting, a coiffured ceiling and stone floors patterned in an art deco style pay tribute to the heritage of the station, and an adjoining room houses a small philatelic museum.

WEST, DERALD M.
(Building Design, Interior Architecture, Renovation)
Design Center Architects (414) 248-8391
645 Main Street Lake Geneva WI   53147

Born: 1918 **Studied:** University of Wisconsin at Milwaukee; Illinois Institute of Technology **Awards:** Greater Chicago AIA **Notable Works:** First National Bank, Lake Geneva WI; Emerald Green, Warrenville IL COMMERCIAL 25%, OFFICE 25%, HOUSING 25%, RETAIL 25%

He is a contemporary designer attuned both to regional and modern styles. His architectural philosophy is rooted in the International style, particularly the modernism of Mies van der Rohe. But he expects a designer's ingenuity to express a building's personality independent of any tradition. A good building can be identified as outstanding only if its owner continues to be satisfied with it years after it's built.

His Lake Geneva WI First National Bank expresses security with traditional bank symbols—arched concrete nave, thick walls, and natural stone elements. A large stone-faced vault of richly veined granite surrounds the round stainless steel vault door, which is the first thing seen by bank visitors. The exterior of copper-capped stone walls and recessed bronze-tinted windows similarly conveys stability and security. Emerald Green, his multi-family housing project in Warrenville IL is also sensitive to client needs. A four-unit condominium set on a quadrant plan, the units combine to form a single structure, yet each unit visibly and functionally is unique, designed to meet individual owner requirements. For example one unit is built entirely at grade, for a client with difficulty walking up steps. The units have a sense of isolation and independence, down to their separate garages.

WHITEHEAD, PAUL ALLEN
(Building Design)
Williams Trebilcock Whitehead, Architects
(412) 321-0550
Timber Court Pittsburgh PA 15212

Paul Whitehead, *Greentree Commons*, 1986 Project Architect: Jeffrey Kline Landscape Architect: Joseph Hajnas

Terrance R. Williams, *1 Wall Street Court* (side view with torcheres), New York City, 1989. Senior Associate: Ronald J. Zeytoonian. Design Team: Kevin Perry, Paul Drago, Christine Mahoney, Frank Gonzalez, Frank De Leon. Interior Design: Donghia Contract Inc. Construction Manager: Tishman Construction Corporation. Structural Engineer: Superstructures. Mechanical and Electrical Engineer: Cosentini Associates. Lighting Consultant: Cline Bettridge Bernstein Lighting Design Inc. Owner: London & Leeds of New York. Photo: James R. Morse

Born: 1932 **Studied:** University of Pittsburgh; Carnegie-Mellon University **Awards:** AIA; Building Owners and Managers Building of the Year; Masonry Institute design award **Notable Works:** Greentree Commons, Greentree PA; Commercial College of Allegheny County, Pittsburgh OFFICE 40%, INSTITUTIONAL 30%, COMMERCIAL 20%, HOUSING 10%

He sees architecture as an art whose expressions shouldn't be blatant; rather, architecture should aim to be a virtually unapparent extension of nature. He uses scale and proportion, light and shadow, and the innate nature of his materials to set his designs, with the end in view of expressing human qualities—honesty, integrity, intelligence—while cultivating spiritual sensitivities. It's his conviction that aesthetic awareness can be raised using very common elements, if arrayed in their purity with an overall sense of harmony and balance.

His Greentree Commons in Greentree PA is built on a challenging site amidst a bustling commercial area. Extensive landscaping and grading created a natural environment that the Commons could open to. Enlivened with a fountain and reflecting pools, the surrounding gardens fill the large windows of the Commons, whose overhangs look without obstruction into greenery while reducing window glare on the floor below. The exterior is of wood, glass and earth-tone brick and features stained redwood banding beneath soft sloping roofs.

WIENS, CLIFFORD DONALD
(Building Design)
2139 Albert Street, Regina Saskatchewan
S4P 2V1 Canada

Born: 1926 **Studied:** Rhode Island School of Design **Awards:** First Award, AIA, 1975; Massey Medal, 1967; Fellow, Royal Architectural Institute of Canada **Notable Works:** St. Mark's Candle Shop, Saskatchewan; Silton Chapel, Saskatchewan; Visitor Information Center, Fleming, Saskatchewan

He believes that his first obligation is to respect and elaborate his client's explicit needs,

but he's also painfully aware that in real-world projects the client's expressed desires are often far from consistent. He has learned by necessity to communicate to clients the evolving possibilities of his designs at key junctures.

The great majority of his residential, industrial and institutional commissions have been on Canada's Saskatchewan plains. Often his floor plans use perfect squares and circles. Primarily he designs symmetrical buildings which echo the vast horizontal prairie. Although a meticulous functionalist, he's frank in his aim to create structures with strong visual impact. He frequently sinks the bases of his larger buildings deeply into the ground to highlight their wide, sweeping roof planes, and to give a sense of solidity and continuity with the land. Other times, as with his 1969 Silton Chapel, he creates a 'floating,' isolated roof assemblage to accentuate the horizontal plane dominating the building's vertical elevation.

WIERZBOWSKI, STEPHEN
(Building Design)
Born: 1953 **Studied:** Carnegie-Mellon University **Awards:** Honorable Mention, 1978 Townhouse Competition, Chicago **Notable Works:** "The Seven Veils of Architecture"

He studied under Rodolfo Machado and Jorge Silvetti at Carnegie-Mellon University, two proponents of developing architectural design and philosophy through the use of imagery. This approach is obvious in his drawings, which probe the conflict between practicality and architectural theory. The resulting images not only make new architectural discoveries and establish unique pragmatic solutions, but stand on their own as works of artistic, not simply architectural, merit. Indeed, his drawings have been exhibited at fine-art galleries in Chicago in addition to winning design awards.

His entry in the Townhouse Competition exemplifies the imagistic, theoretical approach to design. Entitled "The Seven Veils of Architecture," the drawing is an examination of the progress of architectural styles: layers of style are built one upon the other and culminate in a

Terrance R. Williams, *1 Wall Street Court*, New York City, 1989. Photo: James R. Morse

Postmodern facade that recapitulates—or rehashes—elements from all the previous styles. The design adroitly addresses the essence of the Postmodern aesthetic, and perhaps the contradictions or drawbacks inherent therein: is it a culmination and synthesis of architectural styles, or merely a vacuous facade that incorporates but does not truly comprehend the past from which it borrows so freely?

WILLIAMS, TERRANCE R.
(Building Design, Urban Design,
Historic Preservation, Interior Architecture)
The Williams Group (212) 807-9500
30 W. 22nd St. New York NY 10010

Born: 1938 **Studied:** University of Oregon; Cornell University **Awards:** FAIA; California Governor's Award of Merit; AISI Award of Excellence; *Progressive Architecture* citation and awards **Notable Works:** Brooklyn Museum Master Plan, Brooklyn, New York City; Royal Reception Center, Jubai, SA; One Wall Street Court Restoration, New York City COMMERCIAL 33%, INSTITUTIONAL 33%, RESIDENTIAL 33%

A firm believer in architecture as evolutionary process, he endeavors to extrude classic plan types into three dimensions using contemporary forms and materials in an "appropriate postmodernism". Although previously identified with award winning urban design projects such as the Lower Manhattan Waterfront Plan and Shahestan Pahlavi in Iran, his present focus is primarily on the expansion and adaptive reuse of historic buildings such as his conversion of a Victorian police warehouse to luxury apartments in the West Village of New York City. His redesign of the nine-story, 24-unit complex was undertaken after the previous owner altered its Victorian facade to the irritation of neighbors and left the building structurally unsound. Renovation plans included neighborhood meetings to establish a vocabulary of desirable nineteenth century industrial building components, and resulted in a return to the original axiality of the facade and sympathetic redesign of the cornice.

His New York City renovation of One Wall Street Court, a classic Beaux Arts building previously known as the Cocoa Exchange, drew on unusual materials in the interpretive restoration of its richly detailed limestone and granite base, glazed terra cotta insert patterns and gilded medallions. When the owners specified that these features be emphasized and illuminated, he added a colonnade of torcheres.

Varying in height from 12 to 17 feet, the steel torcheres are painted with metallic bronze paint and conceal lights in their colossal capitals.

WILLIAMS, TOD
Tod Williams, Billie Tsien and Associates Architects (212) 582-2385
222 Central Park South New York NY 10019

Born: 1943 **Studied:** Princeton University; Cambridge University **Awards:** National Endowment for the Arts grant; AIA; "40 under 40" *Interiors* magazine honoree **Notable Works:** Eisenberg Residence, Hampton Bays NY; Feinberg Hall, Woodrow Wilson College, Princeton University, Princeton NJ

His architecture has the uncompromising rigor of late Modernism. By pursuing the logic of tectonics and the Kahnian qualities of space, his buildings impress without benefit of the accoutrements mined by Postmodernists.

His Feinberg Hall, a dormitory at Princeton University in New Jersey, is poised as a portal linking the upper and lower campuses. The building addresses its neighbors somewhat gingerly. Hinged on the east, the building pivots to align with a set of dormitories. Its formal front has a stepped bluestone-paved forecourt on the southern quadrangle. By standing free of nearby dormitories, the rotation opens the building to develop more freely, mindful of its neighbors and yet rooted in its own ethos. Its actual front door is off a stair passage on a ridge to the west.

The building is allied to the neo-gothic old campus in its load-bearing masonry structure, whose design further asserts its similar qualities of density and permanence. Its vertically

James Wines, *Allsteel Furniture Showroom*, Long Island City, 1987, New York.

composed fenestration, the lift of false pediments on the east and west faces and the exaggerated pitch of the standing seam copper roof also acknowledge the example of older buildings. Deep interior sills invert to notches that emphasize the load-bearing thickness of the walls; elsewhere exaggerated lintels stress the weight of the masonry.

The most interesting feature turned out to be an unexpected late addition in the back, required by the demand for a second staircase and elevator for the handicapped. The elevator is detached from the building and clad in a brick-shielded fire stair, which is tied back to the building by its landings that double as dormitory porches. The offset shaft with its transparent face and butterfly canopy give the building a unique presence on the north quadrangle.

WILSON, DONALD P.
(Building Design, Interior Architecture, Renovation)
Wilson Architects, Inc. (314) 725-7530
8025 Forsyth St. Louis MO 63105

Born: 1940 **Studied:** Colgate University; Washington University **Awards:** St. Louis AIA; Central States Regional AIA **Notable Works:** Interpretive Museum at Mastodon State Park; Hazelwood Community Center; Continental Baking Corporation Headquarters, St. Louis   OFFICE 75%, GOVERNMENT 25%

Seeing his role as primarily interpretive, he approaches projects as opportunities for give and take between client and architect, balancing cost control and long-range value. Sensitive to environmental issues, site influences and careful material use and detailing, he views architecture as an extension of and response to a given site, which requires a gestation period for properly identifying the needs of a project before the drawing stage begins.

He conceived the Interpretive Museum at Mastodon State Park as a total sensory experience of the Pleistocene era, using the materials and landscape of the stony site as an extension of the building. Originally sited to overlook a valley filled with 1970s tract homes, he shifted the building's orientation to provide views of the park and landscaped parking lot. The building winds down a hill, blending into its site. The interior exhibition space takes advantage of this descent with its design sensation of traveling into the earth where remnants of the prehistoric past are found. Materials such as local wood and locally quarried fieldstone also relate the modern-day museum to its geological antecedents.

His St. Louis Continental Baking Corporation Headquarters is also site-sensitive, designed to be noticed from a nearby highway as well as serving as a dramatic focal point for neighboring buildings. The circulation plan of the 5-story structure is set at a diagonal, with stair towers marking the 45-degree plan in both interior and exterior massings.

WINES, JAMES
(Building Design)
SITE Inc.   (212) 254-8300
65 Bleeker Street New York NY 10012

Born: 1932 **Studied:** Syracuse University **Awards:** Rome Prize, American Academy in Rome, 1956; Ford Foundation Grant, 1964; Graham Foundation Grant, 1974 **Notable Works:** Indeterminate Facade, Best Products Showroom, Houston, Texas; Peeling Facade, Best Products Store, Richmond, Virginia (with Cynthia Eardley); Perpetual Savings and Loan Association, Rapid City, South Dakota

A ferociously creative, whimsical and iconoclastic builder and critic, he's responsible for inventing and popularizing Duck Design Theory and de-architecture. His approach is a radical and extravagant response to functionalism and minimalism. He thinks that the ideas that buildings can express through their structure and function are trivial. His buildings instead express the social and cultural scenes outside their walls. Inverting the Modernist credo, he builds from the outside in. His own credo is "form follows fantasy." His architecture, he has noted, is primarily artistic rather than practical. But he holds that standard architectural design is art enslaved to expedi-

James Wines, *Allsteel Arecheology*, Long Island City, 1986, New York.

James Wines, *Intermediate Facade Showroom - Best Products*, 1975, Houston, Texas

ency. The materials and technologies of traditional engineering and architecture are "throw-aways" in his work; they are convenient means to the end of artistic and socio/political expression. His best known works are his facade designs for the retail stores of the Best Products Company. To lampoon the boxiness and mock-functionality of Best's Houston TX showroom, an archetypal 1970s "mall monster," his false front appears to be in collapse, indeed cataclysm, showering bricks and mortar onto the awning above unwary shoppers.

WOLD, ROBERT L.
(Building Design, Facility Programming, Historic Preservation, Renovation)
Robert Lee Wold & Associates, Inc. (616) 456-9944
Front, NW Suite 300 Grand Rapids MI 49504

Born: 1931 **Studied:** University of Illinois **Awards:** FAIA; Michigan AIA Gold Medal; American School and University design award **Notable Works:** Grand Valley State University Downtown Campus, Grand Rapids MI; Campau Parking Facility, Grand Rapids MI INSTITUTIONAL 30%, COMMERCIAL 20%, OFFICE 20%, OTHER 30%

His projects begin with a plan for their entire area, in which he works out design characters appropriate for both the intended use and users, and their surrounding neighborhood. His Midwestern practice leads him to use masonry extensively for its long-term durability against winter and summer climate extremes. His Grand Valley State University Downtown Campus is mostly for upper-level students, many of them coming from the business district across the Grand River from campus. He incorporated an abandoned interurban railroad bridge into his pedestrian access plan, recycling it as a footbridge joining plazas on either side. The 11-story campus tower orients all student-break and circulation areas to the striking river views of downtown, with the added advantage of creating predictable circulation patterns for students seeking classrooms. Also containing a conference center and local public television studios, the tower concentrates high volume activities and classrooms

on lower floors and locates smaller technical and advanced classes on upper floors. The elevator column serving the upper floors is thus much smaller.

WOLF, HARRY CHARLES
Ellerbe Becket (213- 207) 8000
2501 Colorado Place Santa Monica CA 90404

Born: 1938 **Studied:** Georgia Tech; Massachusetts Institute of Technology **Awards:** FAIA; AIA; New York AIA; South Atlantic AIA; Exhibit, Deutsches Architektur museum, Frankfurt, Germany **Notable Works:** NCNB National Bank Headquarters, Tampa FL; Mecklenburg Country Courthouse, Charlotte NC; U.S.Embassy, Abu Dabai, United Arab Emirates; North Carolina National Bank, ParkRoad Branch & Beatties Road Branch, Charlotte NC

He has been praised by critic Kenneth Frampton for his "architecture of understatement—an architecture above all of tectonic rigor, subtle surface enrichment and discrete plastic energy," and for his "exceptional ability as a public architect in a privatized age." Against the blandishments of historicism and other Postmodern experiments, his work pursues in singular, determined fashion the "enduring qualites of beauty, order and clarity" by means of rigorous geometry.

His design for the North Carolina National Bank headquarters in Tampa FL consists of a 33-story cylindrical tower with two adjacent six-story cubic halls. The height of the tower is five times its 78-foot radius; the 78-foot dimension occurs again in the framing of the two adjoining cubic halls. This key dimension is a multiple of the 13-foot module that is both the floor-to-floor height and, using the ratios of the Fibonacci series $(1,2,3,5,8,13, \ldots)$, the basis of a modular plaid that underlies much of the design. The number play extends to the tower which is punctuated throughout its perimeter and length by 5-foot recessed windows separated by 3-foot piers horizontally and 2-foot downward-slanting sills vertically.

The repetitive squares of the space-frame, structural-cage form of the two adjoining halls are countered by two big circular openings which face the tower. The main source of light to these halls is the glazing to the north and south. The geometry of both the structures is highlighted by finely crafted materials. Creamy French limestone clads the thick pre-cast units of the tower walls, above a base of a more textured Texas stone for the tower. Texas shell limestone sits in the painted steel grids of the banking pavilion. Tempering this constructional logic is an influence from Islamic architecture, partly derived from his work in the Middle east and manifested here in an adjacent garden where bands of stone and pre-cast concrete interweave with water troughs and greenery.

WOLFF, DARRELL B.

(Building design, Interior Architecture, Landscape Architecture)
Baxter, Hodell, Donnelly, Preston, Architects
(513) 271-1634
3500 Red Bank Road Cincinnati OH 45227

Born: 1939 **Studied:** University of Cincinnati; University of Washington **Awards:** Ohio AIA; Cincinnati AIA; Citation for Outstanding Architectural Design, American Association of School Administrators **Notable Works:** Fountain Square Performing Arts Pavilion, Cincinnati OH; U.S. Shoe Corporation Corporate Headquarters, Cincinnati OH; Sycamore High School, Cincinnati OH COMMERCIAL 20%, INSTITUTIONAL 20%, OFFICE 25%, RESEARCH FACILITIES 33%

His designs rise out of the needs and images of clients, with specific client demands suggesting overall concepts. Working from those concepts he aims to create designs that surprise and delight.

For the Merrill-Dow Pharmaceutical Research facility in Redding OH executives wanted a light-filled building whose every laboratory enjoyed window views. Rather than a long narrow building he designed a compact, less expensive brick structure flooded with light from an atrium made of partially reflective glass. Open and closed meeting rooms surround the atrium. For impromptu discussions and brainstorming he has put seats in the hallways, on raised platforms and balconies. The main staircase handrail extends past the steps and forms the back of a tubular metal frame and metal mesh seating area. Hood ducts which carry off noxious fumes from labs aren't hidden, but rather exposed and painted primary colors to create striking designs against the grey walls.

WOMACK, JOHN CALVIN

(Building Design, Interior Architecture, Landscape Architecture)
John Calvin Womack Architect
(501) 521-5067
240 North Block Ave. Fayetteville AR 72701
Born: 1950 **Studied:** University of Arkansas Awards: Outstanding Young Men of America; Who's Who in the Southwest **Notable Works:** John M. Walker House, Fayetteville AR COMMERCIAL 75%, RESIDENTIAL 25%

Influenced by Fay Jones and Frank Lloyd Wright, he places himself in the organic tradition. His architecture represents a concerted effort to create a unified, harmonious entity, achieved through close acknowledgement of site, materials, and client purpose. He believes in fleshing out a structure's inherent style while emphasizing appropriateness, function, and detail. He stresses the importance of nature, and frequently employs Arkansas field stone and cypress and oak native to the region.

His John Walker House sits on a Fayetteville AR hillside, blending into the landscape and giving a feeling of quietness requested by the client. A lower level contains a game room "grotto" which is recessed into the hillside. The main level is much larger, extending outward in four wings with a living room, sleeping quarters and kitchen, and an overhanging balcony forty feet above the ground. A small loft is above this level. Horizontally set fieldstones give exterior walls a natural rough-hewn look, as do cypress beams and red cedar shakes on the roof. Interior matches exterior in color schemes and textures. Flagstone segments cover the floors in randomly shaped patterns, with beige carpets, gypsum board wall surfaces and oak wood cabinets complementing the stone. The architect himself designed the wooden chandelier, oak office, desk and coffee tables.

WOOLLEN, EVANS
(Building Design, Master Planning)
Woollen, Molzan & Partners, Inc.
(317) 632-7484
47 S. Pennsylvania St. Indianapolis IN 46204

Awards: FAIA; AIA **Notable Works:** St. Andrew Abbey Benedictine Church, Cleveland OH; Cushwa-Leighton Library, St. Mary's College, Notre Dame IN INSTITUTIONAL/EDUCATIONAL/RELIGIOUS 75%, PLANNING 10%, HOUSING 10%

While he acknowledges his debt to the "tenets of the last decade, which are to show structure and to get interesting forms," his particular interest is in what he calls "situational architecture—architecture that makes every effort to be particular to the place where it is built."

His library design for St. Mary's College in Notre Dame IN emerged after long interviews with college staff and students. The closing element of a quadrangle, the library embraces an athletic facility designed by Helmut Jahn to the north. Mindful of what he heard in interviews about the athletic facility—that it had nothing to do with the campus—he borrowed extensively from campus buildings for the library exterior. Its west facade has zig-zag bays that "lead the building into the quadrangle." Gables and part of the steeply slated roof are cut away to create an outdoor deck and tower. The entrance is from the south, on a major pedestrian path connecting residences with other academic buildings. Open stacks are in the core of each of the two floors, each with its own mezzanine. On the second floor, reading areas are tucked around the stacks that extend beyond the mezzanine all the way to the steeply sloping roof. This gives the whole mezzanine the feeling of an oversized attic. Interior finishes—exposed mechanical ducts, beams and concrete columns, metal stair and mezzanine, railings—are in stark and thoroughly concealed contrast to the contextual exterior.

YAMASAKI, MINORU
(Building Design)
Minoru Yamasaki and Associates
(313) 689-3500
350 West Big Beaver Road
Troy Michigan 48084

Born: 1912 **Studied:** New York University **Awards:** Fellow, AIA; Fellow, American Academy of Arts and Sciences; Design Award, *Progressive Architecture*, 1956 **Notable Works:** World Trade Center, New York; Easter Airlines Terminal, Logan International Airport, Boston; World Trade Center, Bangkok, Thailand

His work is a study in contradictions. He has often professed that man is happiest in an environment of soft, delicate, humanely proportioned elements. Yet he typically works on a monumental scale, in rough, unyielding materials. He advocates a place for Oriental serenity in Occidental architecture, yet his best known 'mega-creations' are profoundly imposing, even overwhelming. His 1974 World Trade Center in New York City was briefly the world's tallest occupied building and is still gargantuan by any measure. To distance the Center from the brute verticality of New York's mid-town skyline, he designed a tapering window scheme in which parallel columns separating the windows smoothly curve together as they reach the roof. This subtle closure, especially when viewed from ground level at intermediate distance, is meant to suggest a great gothic 'sky-arch,' and soften the hard angles and uncompromised mass of the twin rectangular towers. It's a startling place to find such notes of grace.

YOUNG, MARTIN RAY, JR.
(Building Design)
50 S. Udall St. (602) 964-3429
Mesa AZ 85204-1099

Born: 1916 **Studied:** Brigham Young University **Awards:** Tempe Chamber of Commerce & Planning Dept. Outstanding Building **Notable Works:** Chapman Chevrolet, Tempe AZ; Globe LDS Church, Globe

Miroru Yamasaki, *World Trade Center*, New York, New York.

AZ. COMMERCIAL 50% RELIGIOUS 20% INDUSTRIAL 15%

He has designed 1600 projects in his 39 years of practice. Of these, 260 have been religious buildings, including more than 100 for his own Mormon church. A strong contextualist and longtime friend of Frank Lloyd Wright, he strives for simplification, often with the interplay of light and shadow. The strong Arizona sunlight encourages him to design with a bright color palette, and he insists on handling the colors and interiors as part of his overall designs, which are usually executed in brick, stucco and stone, which best stands up to the Arizona climate. He avoids exterior paint of any kind. His Chapman Chevrolet building has a 30-foot cantilevered roof, carried by six columns and a center bearing wall, giving the effect of the whole agency being outside. The structure is elevated four feet up a grassy slope, putting its interior on more prominent display to passersby.

YOUNGREN, RALPH
(Building Design)
Metz/Train/Youngren 224 South Michigan Avenue Chicago Il 60604

Born: 1924 **Awards:** FAIA; Reynolds Aluminum Award **Notable Works:** New City YMCA, Chicago; U.S. Air Force Academy Chapel (and master plan), Colorado Springs,Colorado; Eastman Kodak Technical Facility, Rochester, New York

He is a veteran designer who displays a protean ability to jettison preconceptions and craft solutions which derive organically from his task environments. In his seventeen years at Skidmore, Owings and Merrill, he collaborated with Walter Netsch on innumerable institutional commissions, including the master plan for the U.S. Air Force Academy at Colorado Springs, and designs for classroom and laboratory buildings for the mammoth concrete campus of the University of Illinois at Chicago Circle. His recent projects include the New City YMCA, in Chicago's rapidly recovering Near North(west) Side. The complex is part of a larger plan to link middle- and upper-income communities through a series of joint facilities on a 14-acre site. Horizontal bands of red, orange, green and blue glazed bricks top the building's main elevation, emphasizing its planar qualities and creating a sense of festivity and approachability.

ZEIDLER, EBERARD
(Urban Design, Building Design, Exibition Design)
Zeidler, Roberts Arcitects 315 Queen Street West, Toronto Ontario M5V 2X2 Canada

Born:1926 **Studied:** Bauhaus, Weimar, Germany **Awards:** Urban Design Award, 1978; National Design Award, 1962, 1967, 1972; National Honor Award, AIA, 1980 **Notable Works:** Ontario Place, Toronto Canada; Eaton Centre, Toronto; Yerba Buena Gardens, San Francisco

His largest commissions are a seductive blend of experimental Modernism, Disney 'futurism' and epic-scale industrial and maritime design. During his studies at the Bauhaus he felt uneasy with the narrow emotional vocabulary of the International Style. Slowly he learned that "progress could be a circle rather than a straight line." His current work retains the exciting machinist dynamic of early Modernism, and fuses it with a fanciful and adventurous sense of lightness and mirth.

His 1969 Ontario Place in Toronto, the sometime-site of the Canadian National Exhibition, is a sprawling, aquatic "Fun Center." The entire complex—save the expansive geodesic dome which contains a panoramic movie theater and live performance spaces—is suspended on tubular stilts offshore in Lake Ontario. Visitors travel between steel and glass techno-pavilions, copiously fitted with exposed industrial lighting and vertical transport systems, on long cabled walkways. Or they can taxi around the complex in paddle boats, stopping to board and tour a permanently anchored battleship.

ZERG, JERRY
(Construction Administration, Building Design, Interior Architecture, Landscape Archi-

tecture, Renovation, Lighting)
United Design Associates, Inc.
(213) 938-2441
7427 Beverly Boulevard
Los Angeles CA 90036

Born: 1927 **Studied:** University of California at Los Angeles Notable Work: Apartment House, Santa Monica CA COMMERCIAL 25% OFFICE 25% HOUSING 25% RETAIL 25%

He believes that the practice of architecture has become too fragmented. Though not decrying specialization, he feels that an architect should be familiar with all the elements of architecture: interior design, landscape, lighting, etc, and approach building development and design as a single unified discipline. The end-user should be the architect's principle influence. Just as an actress assumes the mask of the person she plays, so should a good architect assume the needs and desires of his client. He says he would "cringe with embarrassment" if his work were identifiable, for that would suggest a particular self-congratulatory style. The cohesion of a given project rises out of serving its functions well. Without regard for function, "beauty is a fleeting attribute."

His award-winning Santa Monica CA apartment house features a readily apparent entrance whose lobby facilities convey a receptive feeling. Contrasting colors are used to highlight different functions: dark colors indicate doors and passageways, and light-colored walls create a distancing effect. Without veering either toward a clinical look or an overly decorative facade the impression conveyed is of quiet dignity.

Building Design

Alabama: *Auburn:* Gwin, William R. **Arkansas:** *Fayetteville:* Jones, E. Fay; Womack, John Calvin *Ft. Smith:* Lane, John **Arizona:** *Mesa:* Young, Martin Ray, Jr. *Phoenix:* Kunz, Ken, *Scottsdale:* Soleri, Paolo *Sedona:* Schweiker, (Robert) Paul *Tucson:* Chann, Earl Kai; Dinsmore, Philip W. **California:** *Berkleey:* Alexander, Robert Evans; DeMars, Vernon Armand; Greene, Herbert *Beverly Hills:* Starkman, Maxwell *Culver City:* Moss, Eric Owen. *Long Beach:* Killingsworth, Edward Abel *Los Angeles:* Ain, Gregory; Aleksich, John; Ellwood, Craig; Erickson, Arthur Charles; Holzbog, Thomas Jerald; Jerde, Jon Adams; Kalban, Jeffrey M.; Keating, Richard; Koenig, Pierre; Lautner, John; Lumsden, Anthony; Mayne, Thom; Moore, Charles Willard; Pereira, William Leonard; Phelps, Barton; Rotondi, Michael; Zerg, Jerry *Manhattan Beach:* Blanton, John A. *Morro Bay:* Maul, James H. *Newport:* Summers, Gene, *Oakland:* Howard, Lucia, Weingarten, David *Palm Desert:* Urrutia, Francisco J. *Palo Alto:* Cody, George, *Pasadena:* Smith, Whitney Roland *Sacramento:* Unger, Dean F. *San Diego:* Ferris, Robert D.; Keniston, Stanley; Meredith, W. Dean; Mock, John R.; Niblack, Richard C.; Reeslund, Geoffrey B. *San Francisco:* Allen, Robert E.; Bull, Henrick; Ciampi, Mario Joseph; Ehrenkrantz, Ezra; Esherick, Joseph; Hood, Bobbie Sue; Mack, Mark; Turnbull, William Jr.; Warnecke, John Carl; Werner, William Arno *San Rafael:* Takashina, Makoto *Santa Barbara:* Kruger, Kenneth C. *Santa Fe:* Miller, J. Arthur *Santa Monica:* Campbell, Douglas; Campbell, Regula; Flood, David Jay; Wolf, Harry Charles *Sea Ranch:* Bowman, Obie G. *Sepulveda:* Railla, Joseph J. *Tiburon:* Callister, Charles Warren,; Soriano, Ralph Simon *Venice:* Ehrlich, Steven; Gehry, Frank O.; Tanaka, Ted Tokio *Victorville:* Bergum, Christian **Canada:** *Edmonton:* Cardinal, Douglas Joseph *Montreal:* Afleck, Raymond Tait; Charney, Marvin; Prus, Victor; Rose, Peter; Vecsei, Eva *Ontario:* Markson, Jerome *Regina:* Wiens, Clifford Donald *Toronto:* Baird, George; Diamond, Abel Joseph; Dubois, Macy; Grossman, Irving; Moriyama, Raymond; Parkin, John Crestwell; Thom, Ronald *Vancouver:* Downs, Barry, *West Ontario:* Myers, Barton **Colorado:** *Aspen:* Reno, August, Gibson, David, *Boulder:* Sauer, Louis, *Colorado Springs:* Brown, Bill, Gilbert, Mowry C., *Denver:* Havekost, Daniel J.; Hoover, George; Muchow, William Charles **Connecticut:** *Bridgeport:* Paniccia, Mario, *Essex:* Arbonies, Glenn W.; Floyd, Chad; Grover, William H.; Harper, Robert L.; Riley, Jefferson B.; Simon, Mark *Greenwich:* Furno, Robert *Hamden:* Roche, Eamonn Kevin, *Hartford:* Kim, Tai Soo, *New Haven:* Greenberg, Allan, Newman, Herbert S., Pelli, Cesar,*Shelton:* Carlson, Van J. **District of Columbia:** Schlesinger, Frank; Cox, Warren Jacob; Hartman, Craig; Jacobsen, Hugh Newell; Lewis, Roger K.; Moore, Arthur Cotton; Neighbors, Glenn Allen **Florida:** *Coral Gables:* Fort-Brescia, Bernardo *Jacksonville:* Morgan, William, *Miami Beach:* Lapidus, Marvin **Georgia:** *Atlanta:* Mount, James; Pope, Janet Campbell; Portman, John Calvin Jr. **Hawaii:** Lawton, Herbert T.; Umemura, Robert K. **Illinois:** *Chicago:* Booth, Lawrence; Brubaker, Charles William; Cohen, Stuart E.; DeStefano, James R.; Goldberg, Bertrand; Gonzalez, Joseph A.; Graham, Bruce John; Himmel, Scott D.; Horn, George; Jahn, Helmut; Johnson, Ralph; Keck, William; Kerbis, Gertrude Lempp; Landon, Peter; Legge, Diane; Lohan, Dirk; Merci, William Paul; Moses, Irving Byron; Nagle, James L.; Nereim, Anders; Netsch, Walter Andrew Jr.; Olsen, Keith Rodney; Phillips, Frederick; Pran, Peter C.; Smith, Adrian; Solfisburg III, Roy J.; Tigerman, Stanley; Vinci, John; Weber, Hanno; Weese, Harry Mohr; Youngren, Ralph *Deerfield:* Carlson, Walter *Glenview:* Morgan, Harry S., *Oak Brook Terrace:* Stephens, Thomas *Riverside:* Potokar, Richard A. M. *South Holland:* Kraai, John W *Wilmette:* Goldsmith, Myron **Indiana:** *Indianapolis:* Hibler, Robert;

Meier, Henry G.; Woollen, Evans **Kansas:** *Topeka:* Karst, Gary G. **Kentucky:** *Crestview Hills:* Fisk, Halsey B. **Louisiana:** *Lafayette:* Branch, Dan P. **Massachusetts:** *Boston:* Ardalan, Nader; Blake, Peter; Forbes, Peter; Goody, Joan; Graham, Gary; Kallmann, Gerhard Michael; Koch, Albert Carl; Lewis, Sir George Stephen; McKinnell, Noel; Menders, Claude Emanuel; Meus, Daniel L. *Cambridge:* Catalano, Eduardo; Cole, Doris; Goyette, Harold L.; Gund, Graham; Kruger, Kenneth; Lyndon, Donlyn; McCue, Gerald Mallon; Stubbins, Hugh Asher Jr.; Thompson, Benjamin *Somerville:* Safdie, Moshe *Wellfleet:* Chermayeff, Serge Ivan **Maryland:** *Cabin John:* Manion, Thomas **Maine:** *Bucksport:* Lewis, Donald M. **Michigan:** *Detroit:* Blessing, Charles Alexander; Kessler, William *Grand Rapids:* Wold, Robert L. *Troy:* Yamasaki, Minoru **Minnesota:** *Minneapolis:* Pfister, Peter John; Rapson, Ralph **Missouri:** *Kansas City:* Keleti, Peter, *Oakland:* Marti, Paul, *Springfield:* Butler, Geoffrey H., *St. Louis:* Helmuth, George Francis; Obata, Gyo; Spector, Pat L.; Stinson, Nolan; Wilson, Donald P. **Mississippi:** *Jackson:* Mockbee, Samuel *Natchez:* Peabody, David **Montana**: *Bozeman:* Kommers, Peter **North Carolina:** *Raleigh:* Harris, Harwell Hamilton *Winston-Salem:* Kirby, J. Aubrey **North Dakota:** *Jamestown:* Dura, Arthur U. **New Hampshire:** *Nashua:* Carter, John A. **New Jersey:** *Moorestown:* Hassinger, Herman *Paramus:* DiGeronimo, Louis; DiGeronimo, Suzanne; *Princeton:* Graves, Michael; Sussna, Robert; Geddes, Robert *Rocky Hill:* Burns, Michael **New Mexico:** *Albuquerque:* Boehning, Joe; Peters, Ronald L.; Predock, Antoine; Prince, Bart *Santa Fe:* Dorman, Richard L. **New York:** *Bridgehampton:* Jaffe, Norman *Cortland:* Seligmann, Werner *Ithaca:* Downing, William S. *Katonah:* Baker, John Milnes *Middletown:* Abt, Wheldon A., *New York City:* Abramovitz, Max; Ambasz, Emilio; Barnes, Edward Larrabee; Barnett, Johnathan; Belle, John; Berke, Deborah; Bunshaft, Gordon; Burgee, John; Cavaglieri, Giorgio; Cecil, Russell C.; Cobb, Henry Nichols; Conklin, William; Cooper, Alexander; Dattner, Richard; DeVido, Alfredo; Eisenman, Peter; Franzen, Ulrich; Freed, James Ingo; Giurgola, Romaldo; Gwathmey, Charles; Hardy, Hugh Gelston; Helfand, Margaret; Helpern, David Paul; Holl, Steven M.; Holub, Martin; Johansen, John; Johnson, Philip Cortelyou; Knowles, Edward Frank; Louie, William C.; Malhotra, Avinash K.; Marson, Bernard A.; May, Arthur; Meier, Richard Alan; Mitchell, Ehrman Burkman Jr.; Nelson, George; Owen, Christopher H.L.; Pasanella, Giovanni; Pederson, William; Perkins, Lawrence Bradford Jr.; Pfeiffer, Norman; Polshek, James Stewart; Robertson, Jacquelin; Rudolph, Paul Marvin; Scutt, Der; Stern, Robert A. M.; Torre, Susana; Tsien, Billie; Weinstein, Richard S.; Williams, Terrance R.; Williams, Tod; Wines, James *Nyack:* Ceraldi, Theodore M., *Ridgewood:* Stiene, Frank J., *Riversdale:* Hejduk, John, Roche, Bonnie **Ohio:** *Cincinnati:* Wolff, Darrell B. *Cleveland:* Bowen, Richard L.,; *Dayton:* Betz, Eugene W. **Oklahoma:** *Oklahoma City:* Baumeister, Terry K. *Rose:* Ryan, William Henry **Oregon:** *Medford:* Skelton, Douglas, *Portland:* Belluschi, Pietro **Pennsylvania:** *Bala Cynwyd:* Bennett, Robert Thomas, *Philadelphia:* Bacon, Edmund Norwood; Baker, F. Cecil; Cywinski, Bernard; Knowles, Brigitte L.; Knowles, John Christopher; Scott Brown, Denise; Wallace, David A. *Pittsburgh:* Celli, Thomas C.; Katselas, Tasso; Whitehead, Paul Allen *Wilkes-Barre:* Bohlin, Peter Q. **Rhode Island:** *Bristol:* Pozzi, Lombard John *Exeter:* Warner, William D. **South Carolina:** *Greenville:* Neal, James A. *Hilton Head:* Pasco, Merrill, Jr. **Tennessee:** *Nashville:* Everton, Gary L.; Hinton, Ken Gardner; Tuck III, Seab A. **Texas:** *Austin:* Black, Sinclair; Landes, Robert P. *Dallas:* Pratt, James Reece *Houston:* Bolton, Preston; Casbarian, John; Edwards, Richard; Fitzwater, James; Lundy, Victor Alfred; Samuels, Danny; Stern, William F.; Tapley, Charles; Timme, Robert, *San Antonio:* Hightower, Irby; Lanford, Michael L.; Lawrence, Billy A.; McGlone, Bobby Michael **Utah:** *Salt*

Lake City: Chong, Richard D. **Virginia:** *Alexandria:* Ritter, James W.

Exhibition Design

Canada: Charney, Marvin **District of Columbia:** *Washington* : Lewis, Roger K. **Massachusetts:** Ardalan, Nader **New York:** Hejduk, John; Holub, Martin; Nelson, George **Tennessee:** Hinton, Ken Gardner **Wisconsin:** Heike, Thomas A

Facility Programming

California: *Palo Alto:* Cody, George *San Diego:* Niblack, Richard C. *San Francisco:* Hood, Bobbie Sue, *Santa Monica:* Flood, David Jay **Colorado:** *Colorado Springs:* Gilbert, Mowry C. **Connecticut:** *Hartford:* Kim, Tai Soo **Illinois:** *Chicago:* Barney, Carol Ross; Solfisburg III, Roy J.; McCurry, Margaret I. *Glenview:* Morgan, Harry S. **Kentucky:** *Crestview Hills:* Fisk, Halsey B. **Massachusetts:** *Boston:* Meus, Daniel L., Cambridge: Goyette, Harold L. **Maine:** *Bucksport:* Lewis, Donald M. **Michigan:** *Grand Rapids:* Wold, Robert L. **Missouri:** *Springfield:* Butler, Geoffrey H. *St. Louis:* Spector, Pat L. **New Hampshire:** *Nashua:* Carter, John A. **New Jersey:** *Princeton:* Sussna, Robert *Rocky Hill:* Burns, Michael **New Mexico:** *Albuquerque:* Boehning, Joe **New York:** *New York:City* : Helpern, David **Pennsylvania:** *Pittsburgh:* Celli, Thomas C. **Tennessee:** *Nashville:* Everton, Gary L; Hinton, Ken Gardner; Tuck III, Seab A. **Texas:** *Austin:* Landes, Robert P. **Utah:** *Salt Lake City:* Chong, Richard D. **Washington:** *Seattle:* Kolb, Keith R. **Wisconsin:** *Brookfield:* Heike, Thomas A.

Historic Preservation

Alabama: *Auburn:* Gwin, William R. **California:** *Los Angeles:* Phelps, Barton, *San Diego:* Ferris, Robert D. **Colorado:** *Aspen:* Reno, August *Denver:* Havekost, Daniel J. **Illinois:** *Chicago:* Barney, Carol Ross; Bauhs, William; Hasbrouck, William R.; Nagle, James L.; Pran, Peter C.; Vinci, John **Louisiana:** *Lafayette:* Branch, Dan P. **Massachusetts:** *Boston:* Lewis, Sir George Stephen; Menders, Claude Emanuel **Michigan:** *Grand Rapids:* Wold, Robert L. **Missouri:** *Natchez:* Peabody, David **New York:** *Ithaca:* Downing, William S. *New York:* Cavaglieri, Giorgio; Conklin, William; Marson, Bernard A.; Williams, Terrance R. **Oregon:** Medford: Skclton, Douglas **Rhode Island:** *Bristol:* Pozzi, Lombard John **Texas:** *San Antonio:* McGlone, Bobby Michael **Virginia:** *Middlebury:* Kulski, Julian E. *Sterling:* Hansen, Alan L. **Wahington:** *Tacoma:* Liddle, Alan

Interior Architecture

Arkansas: *Fayetteville:* Womack, John Calvin *Ft. Smith:* Lane, John **Arizona:** *Phoenix:* Kunz, Ken **California:** *Los Altos:* Bentley, Robert **Los Angeles:** Holzbog, Thomas Jerald; Kalban, Jeffrey M.; Zerg, Jerry *Palo Alto:* Cody, George *San Diego:* Mock, John

R. *San Francisco:* Werner, William Arno *Santa Monica:* Hebald-Heymann, Margo, *Venice:* Tanaka, Ted Tokio **Colorado:** *Aspen:* Reno, August **Connecticut:** *New Haven:* Newman, Herbert S. **District of Columbia:** *Washington:* Lewis, Roger K. **Illinois:** *Chicago:* Bauhs, William; Bonner, Darcy R.; Himmel, Scott D.; Lohan, Dirk; McCurry, Margaret I.; Nereim, Anders; Phillips, Frederick *Glenview:* Morgan, Harry S., *Riverside:* Potokar, Richard **Massachusetts:** *Boston:* Graham, Gary; Menders, Claude Emanuel; Meus, Daniel L., *Cambridge:* Cole, Doris; Gund, Graham; Thompson, Benjamin **Minnesota:** *Minneapolis:* Pfister, Peter John **Missouri:** *Oakland:* Marti, Paul, *St. Louis:* Spector, Pat L.; Wilson, Donald P **North Carolina:** *Winston-Salem:* Kirby, J. Aubrey **New Jersey:** *Paramus:* DiGeronimo, Louis; DiGeronimo, Suzanne *Princeton:* Sussna, Robert *Rocky Hill:* Burns, Michael **New Mexico:** *Santa Fe:* Dorman, Richard L. **New York:** *New York City:* Bromley, R. Scott; Cavaglieri, Giorgio; Dattner, Richard; DeVido, Alfredo; Helfand, Margaret; Holub, Martin; Malhotra, Avinash K.; Owen, Christopher H.L.; Perkins, Lawrence Bradford Jr.; Williams, Terrance R. *Ridgewood:* Stiene, Frank J., **Ohio:** *Cincinnati:* Wolff, Darrell B. **Oklahoma:** *Rose:* Ryan, William Henry **Pennsylvania:** *Philadelphia:* Knowles, Brigitte L., Knowles, John Christopher **Texas:** *Houston:* Stern, William F., *San Antonio:* Hightower, Irby, Lanford, Michael L., Lawrence, Billy A. **Virginia:** *Middlebury:* Kulski, Julian E., Sterling: Hansen, Alan L., *Warrenton:* Tucker, James F. **Wisconsin:** *Brookfield:* Heike, Thomas A., *Lake Geneva:* West, Derald M.

Landscape Architecture

Arizona: *Scottsdale:* Soleri, Paolo **Arkansas:** *Fayetteville:* Womack, John Calvin **California:** *Berkeley:* DeMars, Vernon Armand *Los Angeles:* Zerg, Jerry *Mill Valley:* Carlisle, Pat *Palm Desert:* Gregory, Ronald *San Francisco:* Eckbo, Garrett, Halprin, Lawrence, Campbell, Douglas, Campbell, Regula **Florida:** *Jacksonville:* Morgan, William **Illinois:** *Chicago:* Netsch, Walter Andrew Jr. **Indiana:** *Indianapolis:* Meier, Henry G. **Massachusetts:** *Watertown:* Sasaki, Hideo **New Mexico:** *Santa Fe:* Dorman, Richard L. **Ohio:** *Cincinnati:* Wolff, Darrell B. **Pennsylvania:** *Philadelphia:* McHarg, Ian Lennox *Pittsburgh:* Simonds, John Ormsbee **Virginia:** *Middlebury:* Kulski, Julian E. **Vermont:** *Charlotte:* Kiley, Daniel Urban

Planning

Arizona: *Scottsdale* : Soleri, Paolo **California:** *Los Angeles* : Keating, Richard *Pasadena* : Smith, Whitney Roland *San Francisco:* Warnecke, John Carl **Canada:** *Montreal:* Vecsei, Eva *West Ontario:* Myers, Barton **Connecticut:** *New Haven:* Newman, Herbert S. **Illinois:** *Chicago:* Legge, Diane; Lohan, Dirk; Smith, Adrian; Weese, Harry Mohr **Massachusetts:** *Boston:* Graham, Gary; Gund, Graham **New Jersey:** *Paramus:* DiGeronimo, Louis, DiGeronimo, Suzanne, *Princeton:* Geddes, Robert **New Mexico:** *Albuquerque:* Boehning, Joe, Peters, Ronald L. **New York:** *New York City:* Barnes, Edward Larrabee; Giurgola, Romaldo; Holub, Martin; Mitchell, Ehrman Burkman Jr.; Weinstein, Richard S. **Pennsylvania:** *Philadelphia:* Knowles, John Christopher; Wallace, David A. *Pittsburgh:* Simonds, John Ormsbee **Rhode Island:** *Exeter:* Warner,

William D. **Texas:** *Houston:* Stern, William F. **Washington:** *Seattle*: Thiry, Paul

Urban Design

California: *Berkeley:* Alexander, Robert Evans; DeMars, Vernon Armand *Los Altos:* Bentley, Robert, *Los Angeles:* Lautner, John; Lumsden, Anthony *San Rafael:* Takashina, Makoto *Santa Monica:* Campbell, Douglas; Campbell, Regula **Canada:** Afleck, Raymond Tait; Baird, George; Diamond, Abel Joseph; Zeidler, Eberard **District of Columbia:** *Washington:* Moore, Arthur Cotton **Illinois:** *Chicago:* Cohen, Stuart E.; Weber, Hanno; *Wilmette* : Goldsmith, Myron **Massachusetts:** *Boston:* Koch, Albert Carl **New York:** *New York:* Cooper, Alexander; Friedburg, Marvin Paul; Pasanella, Giovanni; Robertson, Jacquelin; Williams, Terrance R. **Pennsylvania:** *Philadelphia:* Crane, David Alford; Knowles; Brigitte L.; Knowles; John Christopher; McHarg, Ian Lennox; Scott Brown; Denise; Wallace, David A. *Pittsburgh:* Lewis, David **Rhode Island:** *Exeter:* Warner, William D. **Texas:** *Austin:* Black, Sinclair **Washington:** *Seattle:* Kolb, Keith R.